T0369785

You are alone. You are exhausted, bruised and battered. You have no real friends and you are surrounded by enemies. You have no money to pay your bills, and you have scarcely the means to defend yourself. You have no sure way to put your house in order, but you have built this house in a vast wilderness of mountains, rivers, forests, jungle, and desert. This is no country for old men, no country for young republics. In 1781, at the moment of the British surrender at Yorktown, this was the situation of the United States of America. Victory in the Revolutionary War did not bring glory—freedom did not mean safety. One false step and this ambitious experiment in republican government would fail forever. So just how, not even fifty years later, had the United States become the undisputed master of North America and the self-proclaimed guardian of the Western Hemisphere?

The transformation of a string of rebellious colonies along the eastern seaboard into a military superpower is the most remarkable story of modern political history. Yet this rapid ascension was not the manifest destiny of the United States—there was nothing naturally 'great' about the new republic. Time and again, the United States came close to disaster. What if Benjamin Franklin had not brought the French into the Revolutionary War? What if the Federalists had not forced through a constitution that could bind thirteen states into the Union? What if 'Mad' Anthony Wayne had started a war with the British in Ohio in 1794? Or if the British had re-taken New Orleans in 1815?

The Founding Fathers had no safety net. They had no reputation either, for Washington, Adams, Hamilton, and Jefferson played only supporting roles on the global stage. At every turn, they were faced with problems that spelled life or death for the United States. Somehow, the Americans got it right. How did they do it? They asked the right questions about foreign affairs, the military, taxes, and trade. With skill, wisdom, experience, and no little luck, they found the right answers too.

Michael S. Kochin is Professor Extraordinarius in the School of Political Science, Government, and International Relations at Tel Aviv University. **Michael Taylor** is a Visiting Fellow at the British Library Eccles Centre for American Studies, 2019–21.

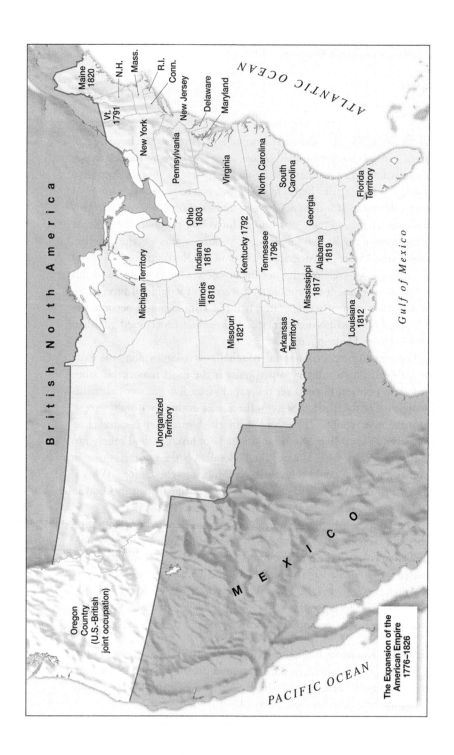

The Expansion of the
American Empire
1776–1826

AN INDEPENDENT EMPIRE

*Diplomacy and War in the
Making of the United States*

Michael S. Kochin and Michael Taylor

University of Michigan Press • *Ann Arbor*

Published in the United States of America by
the University of Michigan Press
Printed and bound by CPI Group (UK) Ltd, Croydon, CR0 4YY

First published January 2020

A CIP catalog record for this book is available from the British Library.

ISBN 978-0-472-07440-2 (hardcover : alk. paper)
ISBN 978-0-472-05440-4 (paper : alk. paper)
ISBN 978-0-472-12648-4 (ebook)

To the memories of
Major Milton S. "Mike" Kochin (USA)
Staff Sergeant Jonas Schleifer (USA)
Lance Corporal Ad Leckey (British Army)
—Allies

Acknowledgments

Michael Kochin's work on this book was supported by a Henry Salvatori fellowship from the Henry Salvatori Center for the Study of Individual Liberty at Claremont McKenna College, and he benefited there from the administrative support of Mark Blitz, Elvia Huerta, and Jennifer Valdez, and the research assistance of Nadeem Farooqi. Material from this project was presented to audiences at Claremont McKenna College, the University of California at San Diego, the Herzl Institute, the Midwest Political Science Association, and the American Political Science Association. For comments on parts and on the whole he would like to thank Anna Kochin, Charles Kesler, Paul Carrese, Levis Kochin, Lauren Davis, Scott Segrest, Rafael Castro, Joseph Bessette, Charles Lofgren, George Thomas, Steve Lenzner, James Nichols, Andrew Bibby, Jeremy Rabkin, David Lorenzo, Angela Doll Dworin, Gerry Mackie, David Wiens, and Ike Sharpless.

Michael Taylor is a Visiting Fellow at the Eccles Centre for American Studies at the British Library. Much of his work on this book was done in the Main Library of the University of Manchester and it was completed while he was Lecturer in Modern British History at Balliol College at the University of Oxford. For comments on drafts of this book he would like to thank Kevin Waite, David Sehat, Allegra Fryxell, Murray Power, and Hubert Taylor.

The maps were produced with great skill and artistic flair by Glen Pawelski of Mapping Specialists, Ltd. in Fitchburg, Wisconsin. Further thanks must be given to our agent, Peter Riva, and to our editors at the University of Michigan Press, Elizabeth Demers and Danielle Coty.

For the mistakes that remain the authors plan to blame each other.

Contents

Digital materials related to this title can be found on the Fulcrum platform via the following citable URL https://doi.org/10.3998/mpub.11334573

Introduction

An Independent Empire

The rebellious war now levied is become more general, and
is manifestly carried on for the purpose of establishing an
independent empire.[1]

—King George III's Address to Parliament, October 27, 1775

On a frozen morning in February 1807, in a Colorado wilderness "bound
in the adamantine chains of winter," Zebulon Pike was informed of "the
report of a gun." Pike was twenty-eight years old, a captain in the United
States Army, and a man devoted to the arts and science of warfare. The
son of a military father, he claimed to have "read every Book which could
be procured in the French & English language on my profession." Pike
was also a celebrated pioneer of the new American West who had led a
"Dam'd set of Rascels" to the headwaters of the Mississippi River in 1805.
On this cold February morning in 1807, when a gunshot broke the hiber
nal silence, Pike was the commanding officer of another daring frontier
expedition. But Captain Pike was in the wrong place.[2]

Eight months previously, he had received his orders from General
James Wilkinson, the Senior Officer of the Army. Pike's destination was
the west of Louisiana, the vast continental territory that the United States
had just acquired from Napoleonic France. Ostensibly, the purpose of the
mission was scientific. "In the course of your tour," wrote Wilkinson, "you
are to remark particularly upon the Geographical structure, the Natural
History, and population of the country through which you may pass." The
American explorers were instructed to take "particular care to collect &

preserve specimens of every thing curious on the mineral or botanical Worlds, which can be preserved & are portable." Wilkinson also relayed an order from the highest heights of the federal government: "It is an object of much Interest with the Executive," he told Pike, "to ascertain the Direction, extent, & navigation of the Arkansaw & Red Rivers." Having overseen the Louisiana Purchase in 1803, President Thomas Jefferson now wanted to know what he had bought.[3]

However, Wilkinson's orders also came with a warning. "The Head Branches of the Arkansaw, and Red Rivers," he advised, were "approximate to the settlements of New Mexico," the Spanish colony that stretched from Juarez in the south to present-day Colorado in the north. Pike was cautioned to "move with great circumspection, to keep clear of any Hunting or reconnoitring parties from that province, & to prevent alarm or offence." The Spanish government in New Mexico was not to be disturbed, for "the affairs of Spain, & the United States appear to be on the point of amicable adjustment." Wilkinson emphasized how President Jefferson wished "to cultivate the Friendship & Harmonious Intercourse, of all the Nations of the Earth, & particularly our near neighbors the Spaniards." In other words, Pike was told not to cross the Spanish border and, if that was impossible, not to get caught.[4]

The Pike Expedition left Fort Bellefontaine on the south bank of the Missouri River in July 1806. Besides fifty-one Osage Indians who had recently been ransomed by the United States, Pike took with him "two lieutenants, one surgeon, one serjeant, two corporals, sixteen privates, and one interpreter." At first, the expedition enjoyed no little success. Pike's men returned the Osages to their homeland and then forced the Pawnees of southern Nebraska to raise the American flag in place of the Spanish. Yet by late October the expedition had split in two: five men and two Osage scouts followed Lieutenant James Wilkinson, the son of the general, back down the Arkansas River, while thirteen enlisted men, the surgeon, and the interpreter plowed on with Pike. From here, wrong turn followed wrong turn. Soon caught between the wilds of winter and "the insolence, cupidity, and barbarity of the savages," Pike and his men resolved to build a stockade "in a small prairie on the west fork" of the Red River. As the palisades rose from the ground, Pike spent his days reading, hunting deer, and "refreshing [his] memory as to the French grammar." Heeding some of his instructions from Wilkinson, Pike also investigated the wild terrain around his base, marveling at the "numerous springs, which issued from the foot of the hill, opposite to our camp, which were so strongly impregnated with mineral qualities as . . . to keep clear of ice."[5]

This serene exploration was not to last. In mid-February, during one of his many sorties, Pike and a companion were spied from the summit of a hill by "a Spanish dragoon and a civilized Indian." Mindful not to give "alarm or offence" to America's neighbors, Pike strove to lose the scouts, to avoid further exposure, but the Spaniard and the Indian would not be deterred. Giving chase through the ice and snow of the cold western winter, they pursued Pike "at full charge, flourishing their lances" and when at last the four met in a ravine, pleasantries were exchanged only "with great precaution." The tension eased, Pike invited the Spaniard and the Indian back to the American stockade, and his unwelcome guests eventually left without incident, but Pike was unnerved. He now feared further attention "from the Spaniards or their emissaries" and so, later that month, when his lookout heard gunfire and reported "the approach of strangers," Pike was not surprised. The strangers were Frenchmen in the service of the Spanish Crown and they claimed to come with an offer of help. The Yuta Indians, they told Pike, were planning to attack the Americans, but the benevolent governor of New Mexico, Joaquin del Real Alencaster, would not stand for such atrocity. Fifty dragoons were being sent to the aid of Pike and his men.[6]

The promised dragoons arrived almost immediately and with them, ominously, were "50 mounted militia of the province, armed in the same manner, viz: Lances, escopates and pistols." Unable to protest, Pike welcomed the Spanish officers inside and they "breakfasted on some deer, meal, goose, and some biscuit." The Americans hoped that if they parleyed, and if the Spanish simply returned to New Mexico, a diplomatic crisis could be avoided, but this hope proved false. "Sir," the Spanish told Pike, "the governor of New Mexico, being informed you had missed your route, ordered me to offer you, in his name, mules, horses, money, or whatever you may stand in need of, to conduct you to the head of the Red River . . ."

"What?" interrupted the American, "Is not this the Red River?"

"No, sir!" came the reply. It was the Rio del Norte.

Pike, the great explorer, was mortified. He had confused the rivers and inadvertently erected his palisades on Spanish soil. "I ordered my flag to be taken down and rolled up," he noted, "feeling how sensibly I had committed myself, in entering their territory." Pike and his men were promptly arrested and marched southward through Santa Fe and Albuquerque, coming at last to Los Coabos in Chihuahua. It was not until July, five months after his apprehension, that Pike was returned to the United States, appropriately on the Red River in Louisiana.[7]

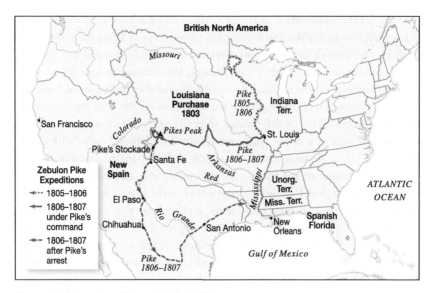

Figure 0.1: Pike's expeditions, 1805–1807

Pike's abortive foray into the West might be considered a curious place to start any history of the United States. Certainly, the Pike Expedition is much less known than the widely lauded Lewis and Clark Expedition, and for good reason. Meriwether Lewis and William Clark charted a course from St. Louis to the Pacific Ocean and back again, laying the path for the westward expansion of the United States, and so their names belong to the American pantheon; Zebulon Pike got lost, captured, and humiliated. His reputation for posterity was secured only at the Battle of York (1813), where he was fatally wounded during the American victory over the British. Yet of these two explorations of the American West, the Pike Expedition better reflects the early imperial history of the United States. In trying to conduct official business in alien, unforgiving environments, Pike was undermanned and underresourced, just as the early federal government struggled to impose order on the enormous American continent. On his travels, Pike was obliged to deal with Native American tribes both friendly and hostile, just as the federal government was forced to treat and fight with the Iroquois, the Western Confederacy, the Creeks, and the Seminoles to the east of the Mississippi River. Pike also struggled to avoid conflict with a rival empire, just as the United States sought to avoid open war with the British, French, and Spanish. The failure of the Pike Expedition remains a salutary reminder of the uncertain prospects of the early republic itself.

Indeed, the transformation of thirteen British colonies into the United States of America, and then into one of the great powers of the world, is the most remarkable story in modern political history. When the seeds of the American Revolution were first sown in the 1760s, the thirteen colonies were but a string of coastal settlements along the Eastern Seaboard, mere pawns in the imperial games of the Old World. That those colonies would even attempt to overthrow the might of the British Empire was for many observers, on both sides of the Atlantic, simply absurd. When reconciliation with Great Britain became impossible and when independence was declared in 1776, the new American nation was nothing more than an ambitious experiment in republican self-government. There was no guarantee of its success, and several good reasons to expect its failure. "We have not Men fit for the Times," wrote John Adams. "We are deficient in Genius, in Education, in Travel, in Fortune—in every Thing. I feel unutterable Anxiety." Nevertheless, despite Adams's pessimism, these "United States of America"—a term first coined by Jefferson in June 1776—quickly became what George III feared, "an independent empire." By 1826, after only five decades of independence, the American Union had become the imperial master of much of North America and the self-proclaimed guardian of the Western Hemisphere.[8]

Diplomacy and war were essential to the creation and the survival of the United States. It was only with foreign assistance that the Revolutionary War was won. Even when independence was secured in 1783 by the Treaty of Paris, the new republic was surrounded by European colonies and hostile forces. To the north, smarting from their recent defeat, were the British in Canada. To the south, governing the Gulf of Mexico, was Spanish Florida. To the west were Native American tribes and Spanish Louisiana, which controlled the vital conduit of the Mississippi and the port of New Orleans. Independence did not bring security. The initial borders of the United States were painfully vulnerable to European and indigenous forces: American troops, wrote James Madison, were "an object of contempt . . . to the inimical Tribes, with which we are surrounded. It is also to be apprehended that we suffer much from the agency of British and Spanish partizans." The presence of these hostile powers meant that the United States—the American empire—could not and did not expand inexorably into a continental vacuum. Territorial growth was not the "manifest destiny" of the nation; in fact, it required careful planning, negotiation with rival empires, and the steady, guided use of military force. It was not a coincidence that each of the four presidents elected between 1800 and 1824 had also been secretary of state.[9]

More prosaically, but no less importantly, the United States needed to make international trade deals. Although possessed of an abundance of natural resources, the American economy, where it went beyond the bountiful but cash-poor agriculture of western settlements, was commercial and mercantile. The clear majority of Americans lived within fifty miles of the eastern coast, and all the leading cities—Boston, New York, Philadelphia, Charleston, and Savannah—were ports whose merchants depended upon international custom. Yet by declaring independence from Great Britain, American merchants were denied favorable terms of trade with the British and their remaining colonies. This was potentially disastrous because, from the first tobacco planted in Virginia to the first ships launched in Massachusetts, the American economy had been designed to supply the British Empire. American diplomats urgently needed to negotiate better access to British markets, to make deals with other European nations, and even to arrange the protection of American shipping from the pirates of the West Indies and North Africa.

Most significant of all, by trying to build a federal government to support and sustain its independence, the United States was obliged to answer three challenges that faced all aspiring masters of the North American continent. First, how best to acquire new lands while defending settlers from hostile Native Americans and other foreign powers? Second, how could political and military control be exerted over distant and extensive territories? Third, what was the most appropriate and affordable system of government that could unite such a diverse nation? These questions had confounded the British and the success and survival of the United States were therefore contingent upon the right choices being made by politicians at home, by diplomats at negotiating tables, and by military men in the field. Missteps and humiliations, like Zebulon Pike's calamitous expedition, were the frequent result of this ad hoc process. However, in the half century following 1776, American politicians, diplomats, and generals found workable answers to their challenges. By doing so, American leaders also confirmed the imperial character of the nation. The United States might have been republican and, in the words of Jefferson, an "empire of liberty," but by conquering territory, by subjugating Native Americans and European settlers, and by developing and then using military force, the United States became the paramount empire in North America, "an independent empire."

CHAPTER 1

The British and the Problems of American Empire

The rulers of Great Britain have, for more than a century past, amused the people with the imagination that they possessed a great empire on the west side of the Atlantic. This empire, however, has hitherto existed in imagination only. It has been not an empire, but the project of an empire; not a gold mine, but the project of a gold mine. . . . It is surely now time that our rulers should either realize this golden dream, in which they have been indulging themselves perhaps, as well as the people; or that they should awake from it themselves, and endeavour to awaken the people.

—Adam Smith, *The Wealth of Nations* (1776)[1]

If the fifteenth century belonged to the Portuguese and the sixteenth to the Spanish, and if the seventeenth century was defined by *la gloire* of the Sun King, Louis XIV, it was in the long eighteenth century that Great Britain emerged as a global force. This rise to power began with the Glorious Revolution of 1688 when the Catholic King James II was deposed and replaced by William of Orange, the Protestant Dutch stadtholder. According to its most revered historian, this was "of all revolutions the least violent" and "the most beneficent," being both the "signal deliverance" of England from "Popery" and absolutism and "the vindication of ancient rights."* Crowned at Westminster Abbey as William III, the new king was a "pensive, severe, and solemn" man who had "never been young." He soon dragged his Brit-

---

*In Ireland, conversely, James II was regarded as a beneficent ruler and the Williamite invasion of the island provoked a bloody and prolonged civil war that served only to entrench the division between Ireland's Protestants and Catholics.

ish subjects into his ongoing continental war with France, the War of the League of Augsburg. With memorable military victories at the Boyne in Ireland and La Hogue off the Normandy coast, and with the concurrent development of stable parliamentary government in London, the British ascent had begun.[2]

Nine years of war against France were ended by the Treaty of Ryswick (1697), but this brought only momentary peace. In 1700, Europe was again thrown into turmoil when the king of Spain, the infirm and "bewitched" Carlos II, died without issue. Addled by generations of inbreeding, the Habsburg line of Philip II had failed and by 1702 the nations of Europe were fighting over who would ascend the Spanish throne. In this, the War of the Spanish Succession, the British were established as a major military power. The Duke of Marlborough, the direct ancestor of Winston Churchill, recorded stunning triumphs over French forces at Ramillies, Oudenarde, Malplaquet, and notably Blenheim, after which he wrote to his wife, Sarah, that "God had blessed Her Majesty's army with as great a victory as has ever been known." Marlborough's royal reward was the construction of the magnificent Blenheim Palace in Oxfordshire and his success produced the terms of the Peace of Utrecht (1713) that made Britain dominant in the Atlantic world. The British were given the *asiento*, the effective monopoly of the lucrative slave trade from Africa to Spanish America, the control of Gibraltar and Minorca in the Mediterranean, and possession of the New World colonies of Newfoundland, Nova Scotia, and St. Kitts.[3]

With the death in 1714 of Queen Anne, the last Stuart monarch, the British throne passed to a middle-aged German prince of the House of Hanover. George I was far from the model king. He was deeply stupid, indolent, and irascible. He could not speak a word of English, and his divorce and imprisonment of his wife had earned him a justified reputation for vengeful cruelty. He was, however, Protestant, and that mattered most. George I was also the first British monarch to have a "prime minister," with Robert Walpole establishing power in the wake of the financial crisis caused by the South Sea Bubble. In the reign of his son, George II, there came the War of the Austrian Succession (1740–48), which saw the king himself lead troops into battle at Dettingen in Germany. Despite British defeat at the Battle of Fontenoy in present-day Belgium in 1745, the Treaty of Aix-la-Chappelle (1748) allowed the British to renew the *asiento* and to regain the Indian city of Madras. George Frideric Handel, who had written *Zadok the Priest* for George II's coronation, celebrated the peace by composing *Music for the Royal Fireworks*. In domestic politics, the reigns of the first two Georges were not without drama. In both 1715 and 1745, the Hanoverian monarchy was challenged by the rebellion of Jacobites who remained loyal to the deposed Catholic line of the House of Stuart. The latter of these risings was led by the Young Pretender, Bonnie Prince Charlie, but a decisive victory for governmental forces at Culloden in the Scottish Highlands meant that Britain's constitutional monarchy survived and grew stable.[4]

The British ascendancy was confirmed by the Seven Years' War (1756–63) begun under the reign of George II, and concluded by the Treaty of Paris, of the accession of his grandson George III. Known in North America as the French and Indian War, this was a global conflict, the first "world war." Its theaters ranged from Quebec to West Africa, from the cockpit of Europe in the Netherlands to the subcontinent of India, and the British left these battlefields as the world's leading political, commercial, and colonial power. National heroes were made of James Wolfe, who died on the Plains of Abraham outside Quebec, and Robert Clive, the commander-in-chief of British India. By the terms of peace, Great Britain won recognition of its Indian enclaves and gained control of French Canada, a host of Caribbean islands, and the two Floridas, East Florida and West Florida, on the Gulf of Mexico. Even more significantly, the French were humiliated. Yet such was Britain's position of strength that many regarded the Treaty of Paris as a diplomatic failure. One truculent observer even wrote that its terms had "drawn the contempt of mankind on our wretched negotiators." This, then, was the British Empire of the 1760s, unmatched in extent and wealth, and a global power without peer.[5]

The growth of the British Empire, however, had come at a cost. To finance the Seven Years' War, the government had borrowed extensively from domestic and Dutch bankers, causing the national debt nearly to double from £72 million in 1755 to almost £130 million in 1764. Moreover, with the addition of French Canada to the American colonies, the ongoing expense of defending this transatlantic empire had increased enormously. The government calculated that it would cost more than £220,000 per year to station ten thousand additional troops in North America, and this deployment was rendered all the more urgent by the outbreak of Pontiac's Rebellion in 1763. Here, the decision of the British general Jeffrey Amherst to stop traditional payments and presents to Indian allies had provoked a confederacy of Native Americans into attacks on British forts and towns throughout the Great Lakes region. All but three forts were destroyed and more than two thousand settlers were slain. Amherst elected to respond in kind: "I am determined to take every measure in my power," he declared,

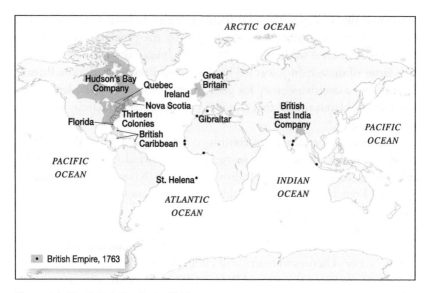

Figure 1.1: The British Empire in 1763

"not only for securing and keeping entire possession of the country, but for punishing those barbarians who have thus perfidiously massacred his Majesty's subjects." The British general even tried to pioneer the egregious art of biological warfare, asking one of his colonels, "Could it not be contrived to send the small pox among the disaffected tribes of Indians?" With Pontiac threatening the security of the American colonies, it was incumbent upon George Grenville, who had replaced the unpopular Earl of Bute as prime minister, to find new means of financing the defense of Britain's western empire.[6]

Taxation and Trade

Before 1765, the American colonies had been tightly bound into the British imperial economy, and so to the British exchequer. British taxation of the Americans was indirect, which meant that taxes were levied not on income, assets, or domestic produce, but on exports and imports; in accordance with Britain's Navigation Laws, American trade was routed through London, from which a watchful eye made sure these taxes were paid. Besides this, American industrial development was discouraged by a ban on competition with British manufacturers: the boon of the Industrial Revolution, fueled by the inventions of Thomas Newcomen, Richard Arkwright, and

James Hargreaves, would be protected at all costs. American exportation to Britain of certain goods, grain, and meat was meanwhile outlawed completely. Not yet the free-trade nation of David Ricardo and Richard Cobden, Great Britain in the 1760s was protectionist and jealous, even of its own colonies. All this chafed the Americans, but British economic policy was tolerated because it was imperfectly enforced and easily circumvented. Smuggling, for instance, was rife along the Eastern Seaboard and shipping illicit rum and molasses from the West Indies was a popular and profitable display of defiance.

When the British Parliament passed the Stamp Act in 1765 to raise money for the defense of the American colonies, it represented something different: it was the first attempt to impose *direct* taxation upon the colonists. Replicating a measure that had raised revenue effortlessly in Great Britain, the Stamp Act stipulated, first, that a wide range of documents had to be printed on paper imported from London and, second, that the documents had to carry a revenue stamp that could be purchased only from colonial officials. Thomas Whateley, the junior minister who had drawn up the Stamp Act, deemed "this Mode of Taxation [to be] the easiest, the most equal and the most certain that can be chosen." The ministers cleared the proposal with the agents of the colonies in London, who raised no objection.[7]

When it reached the colonies, however, Americans protested that this parliamentary direct taxation scheme was unconstitutional because the colonists were not represented—notwithstanding the British counterargument of "virtual representation"—in Parliament. The scenario prompted many well-read Americans to recall the Personal Rule of Charles I and the "ship money" controversy, when coastal areas of England were taxed by the king without legislative consent. The comparison might have been apt, but London still expected the colonists to pay up. After all, the tax had been authorized by Parliament, whose authority had been "supreme" since the Glorious Revolution. Many at Westminster also blamed the Americans for starting the Seven Years' War in the first place, so they believed the colonists should pay for what they had brought upon themselves. Charles Townshend, the MP for Harwich, derided any kind of opposition to the tax. "Will these Americans," he asked, "children planted by our care, nourished up by our indulgence until they are grown to a degree of strength and opulence, and protected by our arms, will they grudge to contribute their mite to relieve us from the heavy weight of the burden which we lie under?" The Americans were to disappoint Townshend, for the breaking news of the tax caused civil unrest throughout the colonies. Archibald Hinshelwood, a Nova Scotia lawyer, wrote to the distiller Joshua Mauger of "a violent spirit of opposition raised on the continent against the execution of the Stamp Act." Effigies of Andrew Oliver, the colonial official responsible for collecting the tax in Boston, were hung by the Sons of Liberty from the city's "Liberty Tree." Attached to Oliver's effigy was a sign stating "He that takes this down is an enemy to his country." The uproar was contagious.[8]

The Stamp Act also provoked the rancor of a more sophisticated constituency. By taxing printed materials such as newspapers and legal documents, it directly affected the journalists and lawyers who were best placed to articulate colonial discontent. One such lawyer was John Adams, a bustling attorney in the provincial town of Braintree, Massachusetts. Recently married to his third cousin Abigail and already dabbling in political theory, Adams marveled in his diary at the fury provoked by the tax. "The Year 1765 has been the most remarkable Year of my Life. That enormous Engine, fabricated by the British parliament, for battering down all the Rights and Liberties of America, I mean the Stamp Act, has raised and spread, thro' the whole Continent, a Spirit that will be recorded to our Honor. In every Colony, from Georgia to New Hampshire inclusively, the Stamp Distributors and Inspectors have been compelled, by the unconquerable Rage of the People, to renounce their offices." Along the seaboard, throughout the colonies, a unifying political consciousness emerged. "The People, even to the lowest Ranks, have become more attentive to their Liberties, more inquisitive about them, and more determined to defend them, than they were ever before," Adams wrote.[9]

The collective response of the colonists was to convene the Stamp Act Congress. Representatives of nine mainland colonies (Massachusetts, Rhode Island, Connecticut, New York, New Jersey, Pennsylvania, Delaware, Maryland, and South Carolina) met in New York City in October 1765. Few details of the debates survive, but after three weeks of deliberation in the City Hall and New York's coffeehouses and taverns, the delegates reached a conclusion that would be repeated so long as the Americans could imagine remaining British subjects: Parliament could regulate the external trade of the colonies, but it could *not* impose direct taxes on Americans colonists who were not directly represented before the king. Put more pithily, the colonists demanded "no taxation without representation." It was a memorable turn of phrase, rooted in the Americans' belief that only local assemblies could legitimately levy taxes in the colonies. Yet one must also consider that few Americans had any real interest in being represented at Westminster. The major, insuperable obstacle was the distance involved, and Massachusetts lawyer James Otis described the idea as "generally much disliked in the colonies, and thought impracticable." Indeed, the objections to representation in Westminster essentially reduced the Americans' argument to "no taxation," at least by Parliament.[10]

Other developments in London encouraged the colonists to place more trust in their colonial assemblies than in Parliament. The treatment of John Wilkes was the major case in point. Wilkes was a scurrilous radical, a notorious scoundrel, and a leading member of Sir Francis Dashwood's debauched Hellfire Club. Famously ugly and once described as "a most shocking dog to look at," Wilkes relied on a razor-sharp wit to make friends, curry favor, and deflect criticism. When told by the Earl of Sandwich, the eponym of the snack, "Sir, I do not know whether you will die of the gallows or the pox," Wilkes replied, "That depends, my Lord, on whether I embrace your lordship's principles or your mistress." He was also an MP and a journalist who employed his weekly publication, the *North Briton*, to lampoon and harangue both Court and Parliament. Yet when in 1763 the *North Briton* disparaged George III and the Treaty of Paris, a line was crossed and there were calls for his expulsion from the House of Commons. When Parliament met to discuss the matter, and when Wilkes's pornographic *Essay on Woman*—a satire on Pope's *Essay on Man*—was read aloud by Sandwich, the hysterical outcry forced Wilkes to flee to Paris. Tried in absentia for obscene and seditious libel, Wilkes was found guilty and declared an outlaw. As news of the Wilkes controversy arrived from the motherland, the American colonists became ever more concerned by Parliament's self-interested and heavy-handed conduct. In this context, the imposition of direct taxation assumed increasingly sinister connotations.[11]

Colonial opposition to the Stamp Act was soon joined by British merchants whose business had been affected by the tax. Led by Barlow Trecothick, a former Bostonian and an MP for London, they formed a powerful, effective lobby. In March 1766, only four months after the Stamp Act came into force, it was repealed by the Whig administration led by the Marquess of Rockingham. The repeal was a triumph for the colonists, proof that organized resistance to British policy could yield momentous results. Parliament, however, had not conceded the *principle* of its authority. Indeed, the repeal of the Stamp Act was accompanied by a new law that reaffirmed Parliament's inviolable right to make laws for the colonies. The Declaratory Act proclaimed that Parliament, being "the lords spiritual and temporal, and commons of Great Britain, hath, and of right ought to have, full power and authority to make laws and statutes of sufficient force and validity to bind the colonies and people of America . . . in all cases whatsoever." Parliament was taking a stand.[12]

The principles of both sides were soon put to the test. In 1767 Charles Townshend, now chancellor of the exchequer in a new government led by William Pitt the Elder, pushed a new series of bills through Parliament. Known as the Townshend Acts, they were crafted as another means of raising money from the colonies. The main Revenue Act was designed to make "a more certain and adequate provision for defraying the charge of the administration of justice, and the support of civil government, in such provinces where it shall be found necessary; and towards further defraying the expenses of defending, protecting, and securing, the said dominions." This would be done by levying taxes on flint, glass, lead, paint, tea, and every variety of paper. There was a practical, understandable aspect to the Townshend Acts. Quite simply, Parliament needed the money. The chancellor, however, was also trying to make a point about Parliamentary authority: "The superiority of the mother country," he declared, "can at no time be better exerted than now." Townshend knew the duties would be unpopular, but he nevertheless expected the Americans to accept them as the kind of external, indirect taxes to which they had supposedly consented.[13]

Again, Townshend misjudged the Americans. In an atmosphere already radicalized by the Stamp Act, colonial objection was reflexive. In his *Letters from a Pennsylvania Farmer*, the Philadelphia lawyer John Dickinson railed that any taxes levied by Parliament on Americans designed purely to raise revenue were unconstitutional. Merchants began to boycott British produce, and colonial courts refused to uphold the rights of the newly appointed customs commissioners. In fact, colonial courts with their colonial juries were happy to try royal officials for enforcing the new laws, and to acquit civilians for attacks on the same officials. London's apoplectic response was to bypass the obstructive colonial judiciary by creating Vice Admiralty courts that could operate without juries. As the relationship deteriorated, the Boston merchant John Hancock wrote to colleagues that Massachusetts, "as well as America in general, is now reduced . . . [to] melancholy and very alarming Circumstances." The problem, he thought, was that "Taxes equally detrimental to the commercial interests of the Parent country and the colonies are imposed upon the People, without their consent." Despite petitions to Court and Parliament, the colonists were suffering the infringement of "a Right naturally inherent in every Man, and expressly recognized by the glorious Revolution as the Birthright of an Englishman."[14] Even an eventual loyalist like the jurist William Smith, who would flee New York and become chief justice of Quebec, saw that "to tax the colonies by act of Parliament, was totally to *disanglify* them."[15]

For the most part, the British defended their policy fiercely. Writing to the *London Chronicle*, the pseudonymous "Anti-Sejanus" propounded "the necessity of enforcing the Stamp-act, with spirit and resolution" and he damned "the waywardness and ingratitude of the Americans." Many others were determined to make an example of the insubordinate colonists. Benjamin Franklin, the Pennsylvanian polymath, was at the time a colonial agent in London and he observed that "Every man in England seems to consider himself as a Piece of Sovereign over America; seems to jostle himself into the throne with the King, and talks of OUR subjects in the Colonies." There were few dissenting voices among British politicians, but the most eloquent belonged to Edmund Burke, the man of letters and Whig statesman. "If [parliamentary] sovereignty and their freedom cannot be reconciled," Burke asked the Commons, "which will [the colonists] take?" He answered, of course, that "They will cast your sovereignty in your face. Nobody will be argued into slavery." As often the case, Burke was prophetic, but he would go unheeded.[16]

All the while, the saga of John Wilkes continued to blacken American perceptions of Parliament. In 1769, Wilkes returned to England and twice won reelection to the Commons; the Commons, however, refused to let him take his seat and Henry Luttrell, Wilkes's defeated opponent in the second election, was declared the winner instead. To Americans holding radical Whig beliefs about popular sovereignty, it was increasingly apparent that Parliament was a self-appointing oligarchy answerable to corrupt interests, not to the electorate. The cry of "Wilkes and Liberty" became a standard of colonial protest, and the Wilkes controversy even triggered the collapse of royal government in South Carolina. In December 1769, the colony's House of Assembly ordered a grant of £1,500 in support of "our Fellow Subjects who by asserting the Just Rights of the People, have or shall become obnoxious to administration, and suffer from the hand of Power." Naturally, they meant Wilkes, but South Carolina's lieutenant-governor, under orders from London, refused to sign off on the grant. Cooperation on all matters between his office, the colony's Council, and the House of Assembly soon ground to a bad-tempered halt.[17]

In Massachusetts, dissent became so fierce that Lord Hillsborough, the colonial secretary at Westminster, instructed Thomas Gage, the British commander-in-chief in North America, to send "such Force as You shall think necessary to Boston." Yet the presence of the redcoats, far from having a pacific influence, served only to heighten the tension in the city. It boiled over on March 5, 1770. That night a British soldier, Hugh White, was on duty outside the Custom House on King Street when Edward Garrick, a local wigmaker's apprentice, walked past and provoked an altercation. When Private White struck Garrick with his musket, a crowd gathered and church bells were rung, bringing hundreds more to King Street. Surrounded by the angry locals, White called for reinforcements and seven troops were sent as relief. The young bookseller Henry Knox tried to defuse the situation, pleading with Thomas Preston, the British officer, "For God's sake, take care of your men! If they fire, your life must be answerable!" Yet when something was thrown at the soldiers, the redcoats replied with a shot. As the "mob" retaliated with fists and cudgels, the British unleashed a volley: six civilians were injured and five were killed. Known in the colonies as the Boston Massacre, and to the British as the "Incident on King Street," the events were memorialized—and embellished—by Paul Revere:

> Unhappy Boston! See thy sons deplore,
> Thy Hallow'd Walks, besmear'd with guiltless Gore:
> While faithless P[resto]n and his savage Bands,
> With murd'rous Rancour stretch their bloody Hands;
> Like fierce Barbarians grinning o'er their Prey,
> Approve the Carnage, and enjoy the Day.

To calm the waters, the aftermath of the "Massacre" was managed carefully. John Adams, driven by his belief in the right to counsel, defended the soldiers before a Boston jury and, though two were convicted of manslaughter, six were acquitted. The longer-term impact of the Boston Massacre was more profound, for Adams later wrote that, in the violence of the redcoats on the evening of March 5, 1770, the "foundation of American independence was laid."

The Boston Massacre, however, was not the only momentous event of that early spring day. Across the Atlantic, Lord Frederick North, a portly and vacillating Tory, was now prime minister, the seventh to serve George III since 1762. Only a few hours before Private White struck Edward Garrick, North had presented a motion in the House of Commons calling for the partial repeal of the Townshend Acts. Within a month, many of the objectionable duties had been lifted, but one would remain: the tax on tea.[18]

Tea and the Intolerable Acts

For three years from 1770 there was a false peace between the American colonies and the Parliament at Westminster. Even when the government schooner *Gaspee* ran aground in Rhode Island and was burned by a mob of tax protestors, the threat of conflagration was contained. The

Tea Act of 1773, however, revived and aggravated the latent problems of trade and taxation. On the surface, the Act was designed to let the financially troubled East India Company dump its surplus tea, tax free, on the American colonies. The Company, the leviathan of the British imperial economy, would benefit by not paying export duties to London; the Americans, or so Westminster presumed, would benefit by importing cheaper tea. Yet such tea would still have the Townshend duty levied on it, and so the Act was perceived as an underhanded means of foisting further taxation on the Americans. When news of the Tea Act reached the colonies, resistance was organized immediately; and that resistance culminated, as every schoolchild used to know, on December 16, 1773, when a gang of Patriots—some of them disguised as Mohawk Indians—stalked aboard the *Dartmouth* in Boston harbor and dumped 342 chests of East Indian tea into the water. It was a stunning act of political vandalism: the cargo was worth close to £10,000, just short of $4 million in today's money, and John Adams likened the Tea Party to Caesar crossing the Rubicon. "The Dye is cast," he wrote in his diary. "The People have passed the River and cut away the Bridge. . . . This is the grandest Event which has ever yet happened Since the Controversy with Britain opened!"[19]

Reports of the Tea Party reached London in January 1774 and, initially, were met with incredulity. George III, who maintained a fervent desire to keep the Americans under control, could not believe that "the instigation of bad men hath again drawn the people of Boston to take such unjustifiable steps." When more detailed reports of colonial subversion were received, that incredulity turned to outrage; by March, the House of Lords was discussing measures "for enforcing a due obedience to the laws of this Kingdom throughout all His Majesty's Dominions." The British government's eventual response was a series of laws designed to punish the Bostonians for their impudence. In London, they were called the Coercive Acts; in the colonies, they were termed "Intolerable." The first of them, the Boston Port Act, closed the city's harbor until restitution for the destroyed tea was made to the British Treasury and the East India Company. The Act also condemned the "dangerous commotions and insurrections [which had] been fomented and raised in the town." The Massachusetts Government Act was even more contentious, remodeling the government of the colony so that power was concentrated in the hands of the London-appointed governor, Thomas Gage. The Administration of Justice Act became law on the same day. It meant that royal officials could be tried *outside* of Massachusetts, far from the potentially vindictive judgment of Boston juries. George Washington, stirred from his agrarian calling at Mount Vernon, called it the "Murder Act" because it seemed that British officials could now commit any manner of atrocity and escape punishment. The fourth Intolerable Act was an amendment to the Quartering Act of 1765. Applicable to all the colonies, it allowed royal governors to provide housing for British soldiers by seizing buildings, should the colonial assemblies fail to provide accommodation themselves.[20]

A fifth law of 1774 was equally "Intolerable," for if the four canonical Acts underscored the incompetence of British imperial governance, the Quebec Act showed how the British failed, and could hardly help but fail in light of their wider responsibilities in North America, to satisfy the expansionist ambitions of George III's American subjects. Although the Act's provisions applied only to the Province of Quebec, which had been newly created from the ceded territory of French Canada, they were of immense concern to the American colonists to the south. For one thing, the Quebec Act gave the French Canadiens freedom to worship as Catholics. It also removed reference to the Protestant faith from their oath of allegiance and restored the Catholic Church's right to impose tithes in Canada: for the first time since 1689, then, the British Crown had recognized Catholic authority in its territories. For some Protestants in the American colonies, this represented the dereliction of George III's sacred duty, as sworn to in his Coronation Oath, to "maintain the Protestant Religion." One Patriot reportedly declared that "The King had broke [sic] his Coronation Oath by establishing the Roman Catholic Religion at Quebec and that he could not in Conscience serve his Majesty . . . [and] that he would not on any occasion or for any consideration supply the King's troops then at Boston with any kind of relief or necessaries." Even worse, Quebec would be ruled by a Crown-appointed governor. That governor would be assisted by a legislative council, but he would appoint that council himself and there was no provision for an elected assembly of colonists. The Quebec Act therefore seemed to establish the kind of arbitrary government against which free-born Britons—and free-born British American colonists—had been fighting since the reign of Charles I. As a further affront to American sensibilities, English common law would be applied only selectively: in many affairs, the Canadiens would be subject to French civil law.[21]

From London's perspective, the Quebec Act made sense. The province had seventy-five thousand French colonists and only three thousand British settlers, including American newcomers from the south. By allowing the operation of certain elements of French law and by preventing the subjugation of the French by a British minority, the Act sought to mollify the "conquered" majority. The Quebec Act also appeased the Native Americans whom the British now governed: George III had replaced Onontio, their term for the governor of New France, as their protector. In such ways, the Quebec Act *was* successful, securing the civil and religious rights of the French Canadiens under a tolerable form of government while protecting Native Americans from the enmity and greed of the whites.[22] The three thousand British settlers, however, were incensed, and their sentiment was shared by their American brethren. Unchecked, arbitrary government seemed to have become London's policy for all America.

Worse still was the redefinition of Quebec's borders. American settlers might have fled political, religious, and economic oppression in Europe, but they were also drawn to the New World by the promise of their own land, their own farm, their own plantation. As populations swelled along the eastern coastline, settlers moved inland in pursuit of fresh, uncultivated soil, and this desire to move west, to push back the frontier, quickly became essential to the American psyche. One of the triggers of the Seven Years' War, the 1754 killing of the French officer Joseph Coulon de Jumonville, stemmed from this impulse: George Washington's troops met the French only because the Ohio Company had paid for the defense of "virgin" land. Two years after Jumonville was killed, the New York official Peter Wraxall noted that "an unaccountable thirst for large Tracts of Land . . . hath prevailed over the inhabitants of this and the neighboring provinces with a singular rage." London, however, impeded expansion at almost every turn. When French Canada was ceded to the British in 1763, the Americans had expected that western lands would be opened for cultivation, but that year's Royal Proclamation forbade white settlement to the west of the Appalachians. Extensive lands were reserved instead for His Majesty's Indian subjects, and some colonists found themselves on the "wrong" side of the line. Eleven years later, much of this land was turned over to Quebec, which, far from the settled parts of old French Canada, now extended southward and westward to incorporate parts of present-day Illinois, Indiana, Michigan, Ohio, Wisconsin, and Minnesota. London, it seemed, would stop at nothing to frustrate the ambitions of the Americans.[23]

Combined with oppressive taxation and the Intolerable Acts, the Quebec Act convinced many that Parliament wished to degrade the colonies into subservience. Answering the call for united resistance, twelve of the thirteen colonies sent delegates to Philadelphia, where the First Continental Congress was convened in September 1774. Sitting for less than eight weeks in Carpenters' Hall, the Congress agreed to two measures: first, a boycott of all British goods from December 1, 1774, which crippled British exports to the colonies; second, a petition to George III for the repeal of the Intolerable Acts. Claiming that all American "distresses, dangers, fears, and jealousies" flowed from the "destructive system of Colony Administration adopted since the conclusion of the last war," Congress begged the king's "clemency for protection." The petition reached London, but it was ignored. "It came down among a great Heap of letters," reported Benjamin Franklin, ". . . and I do not find, that it has had any further notice taken of it." The colonists' pleas were disregarded. Within months, the crisis would descend into war.[24]

From Crisis to War

The British had failed to establish equitable systems of colonial commerce and taxation. They had failed to reform colonial government adequately; in fact, the Admiralty courts and customs boards had encouraged dissension, not fraternity. The British had also failed to satisfy the expansionist ambitions of their colonists. In short, the British failed to govern their American empire. Such failures filled a powder keg and the match was lit as night turned into day on April 19, 1775.

Acting on intelligence that a cache of Patriot arms had been stored in the Massachusetts village of Concord, seven hundred British regulars, commanded by Lieutenant-Colonel Francis Smith, crossed the Charles Estuary and began marching toward their quarry in Middlesex County. When the British came to the village of Lexington, the Patriot militia—informed of the British mission by the midnight ride of Paul Revere—made a show of defiance. Shots were fired and, outnumbered almost ten to one, the colonists fell back. The British marched on and soon arrived, the sun now risen, at their destination of Concord. The redcoats split up and began searching for the munitions, which the colonists had long since moved. At the town's North Bridge, about a hundred royal troops came upon four hundred Patriot militiamen. What followed is celebrated famously in Ralph Waldo Emerson's *Concord Hymn*:

> By the rude bridge that arched the flood,
> Their flag to April's breeze unfurled,
> Here once the embattled farmers stood,
> And fired the shot heard around the world.

Gradually, the British retreated from Concord and then withdrew to Charlestown, harried all the way by militia from the surrounding countryside. On hearing the news from Lexington and Concord, the colony's

Provincial Congress organized the "Massachusetts Line" of regular troops. Forces from across New England soon gathered to besiege the British base of Boston.[25]

Indeed, Patriots and redcoats began to clash throughout the northern colonies. In May 1775, the New York fort of Ticonderoga was seized— "in the name of the Great Jehovah and the Continental Congress"—from an undermanned British garrison by Ethan Allen's Green Mountain Boys. The largest defensive complex in the northern colonies, Ticonderoga occupied a key position on the "Great Warpath" between New York and Montreal, and its loss, compounded by the seizure of its heavy artillery, was a telling strategic blow to the British. In June, the newly formed Continental Army commenced its first major expedition, the invasion of Canada. Seeking to deprive the British of a major military base and to encourage the Canadiens to join the Revolution, two American armies were led by the Irish-born Richard Montgomery and the Connecticut merchant Benedict Arnold. Having set out from Ticonderoga, Montgomery quickly took Montreal, almost capturing the British general Guy Carleton, but when he joined with Arnold they were repelled by the British—led by Carleton— from the fortified town of Quebec. A diplomatic delegation including Benjamin Franklin then failed to persuade all but a few Canadiens to rebel. The Americans might have had the sympathies of the French peasantry and many of the ordinary English settlers -- two regiments of young men would eventually leave in the summer of '76 with the American retreat -- but the Canadien gentry reasoned that the Quebec Act had given them all they could expect from an English-speaking government. Moreover, the Americans, having failed to dislodge the British from the fortress of Quebec, could not offer the Canadiens an outlet to the wider world. Early American success, whether military or diplomatic, was far from certain.[26]

As 1775 drew on, reconciliation with the motherland became ever less likely. The British were besieged in Boston and when, on June 17, they attempted to clear Patriot encampments on the Charlestown peninsula, open battle was waged again. The first two British assaults, bloody and brutal both, were turned back; the third, when the Patriots ran out of ammunition, was not. Much of the fighting occurred on Breed's Hill, but the battle was named for the nearby Bunker Hill, which overlooked the Mystic River. It was nonetheless a Pyrrhic victory for the British. Henry Clinton, who later became British commander-in-chief, wrote that "a few more such victories would have shortly put an end to British dominion in America." Even worse was the dawning reality that the rebels had raised a disciplined military force. An anonymous "officer of rank" wrote home that

"We have . . . learned one melancholy truth, which is, that the Americans, if they were equally well commanded, are full as good soldiers as ours." By the summer of 1775, then, American independence was no longer a spurious fantasy and many Britons began to accept that self-government was the sincere, realistic ambition of the rebels. Permanent separation was not necessarily the determined goal across the colonies, but when George III refused to receive Richard Penn and Arthur Lee, the envoys who carried Congress's last-ditch Olive Branch Petition, most Americans were decided in their choice. As the king then told Parliament in October 1775, "The rebellious war now levied is become more general, and is manifestly carried on for the purpose of establishing an independent empire."[27]

Tom Paine

Thomas Paine was the Norfolk-born son of a corset-maker. A thin man with a sharp nose and a red face, Paine had been a privateer and a schoolteacher in London before he settled in 1768 in Lewes, a Sussex town with a rich history of protesting royal authority. He was an unreliable, possibly incompetent, employee: in 1774, Paine was dismissed as an exciseman because of repeated, unexplained absences from work. Laden with debts incurred during an unsuccessful venture as a tobacconist, he sold his belongings and, following a chance encounter with Benjamin Franklin, emigrated to the American colonies. Arriving in Philadelphia on the London packet, Paine took an immediate interest in the colonial crisis and when, in February 1775, he became editor of the *Pennsylvania Magazine*, he began his career as the leading propagandist of the American Revolution. Trebling the sales of the magazine within five months, Paine depicted American resistance to British policy in righteous, millennial terms. "We live not in the world of angels," he counselled. "The reign of Satan is not ended." In late 1775, as the Americans trod the path toward independence, Paine began to write *Common Sense*, a pamphlet that became the manifesto of the Revolution.[28]

Published in January 1776, when the British were in Boston and the Continental Army was occupying Montreal, *Common Sense* was a searing indictment of British maladministration and a clarion call for immediate independence. It was also one of the most influential documents in the history of American foreign policy. "For a long time," as historian Felix Gilbert noted in the 1960s, "every [American] utterance in foreign policy starts from Paine's words and echoes his thought." Paine's vision was clear and audacious. Although resident in the New World for little more than

Figure 1.2: *Thomas Paine* (1793) by George Romney. Library of Congress.

a year, he had already foreseen the expansion of the independent colonies across the American continent. "Continental," indeed, was a word Paine used often. He meant it literally, referring to Quebec, the Ohio Valley, the Trans-Appalachian West, and beyond. Paine's continental empire would expand northward at the expense of British Canada, westward at the expense of Native Americans, and southward at the expense of the Spanish. The last vestiges of French interests would suffer too. Supremacy was the destiny of the continental American empire, just as the scale of the continent made independence inevitable: "There is something very absurd," reasoned Paine, "in supposing a continent to be perpetually governed by an island," for "in no instance hath nature made the satellite larger than its primary planet."[29]

Paine's continental empire would be republican, organized by fundamental laws and popular charter, and defined by popular sovereignty. There would be a strong central government that would *support* and not repress the people's rights to religious freedom and property. It would also mobilize the resources of the continent in the cause of self-defense. "No country on the globe," wrote Paine, "is so happily situated, or so internally capable of raising a fleet as America. . . . We need go abroad for nothing." Paine prescribed to the new republic only limited interaction with the overthrown motherland, which belonged to a different world: "England to Europe, America to herself." Nor was there any prospect of reconciliation, since "England consults the good of *this* country no farther than it answers *her* own purpose." Cutting the imperial cord would protect Americans from wars they would never wage of their own accord, so independence meant happy divorce from the balance-of-power chicanery that had defined European politics since 1648's Peace of Westphalia. American international relations would be purely commercial. The chains of the Navigation Acts would be broken, restrictive British policies would be abandoned, and the American empire would be a "free port" for global commerce. This may strike modern readers as the first major articulation of American isolationism; for Paine, it was simply "common sense."[30]

More than half-a-million copies of *Common Sense* were printed or copied during the Revolution. That was one for every five Americans. Proportionally, it remains the most widely read American publication of all time, and perhaps the most important: "Without the pen of the author of *Common Sense*," John Adams reportedly observed, "the sword of Washington would have been raised in vain." *Common Sense* was far from the only artifact of Paine's genius. *The American Crisis*, a series of pamphlets begun in late 1776, was read aloud to American soldiers before the Battle of Trenton to stiffen their resolve: "The harder the conflict," wrote Paine, "the more glorious the triumph." Of his later works, The *Rights of Man* (1791), written in defense of the French Revolution, remains a classic case for democratic equality, while *The Age of Reason* (1794) was a high point of Enlightenment deism. Paine's work was so highly regarded in France that he was elected to the National Convention despite not speaking French. While a later fall from grace meant that the Americans had to rescue Paine from the guillotine, his reputation was soon restored: Napoleon is thought to have told Paine that "A statue of gold should be erected to [you] in every city in the world."[31]

Independence as Foreign Policy

As Paine imagined a foreign policy for an independent America, the war for freedom raged. In early 1776, the major theater was still New England and specifically Boston, from which the Continental Army was seeking to drive the British. Here, the Americans reaped further reward from the victory at Ticonderoga, for besides the fort's strategic value the British had also lost its cannon. Now, thanks to the ingenuity of Henry Knox—the erstwhile peacemaker of King Street—the cannon were moved to Boston. In one of the great logistical feats of American history, Knox used oxen, sleds, and manpower to haul more than sixty tons of weaponry across three hundred miles of forests and swamps, all in the dead of winter. This "noble train of artillery" arrived at Boston in January 1776 and its cargo enabled the construction of fortified gun emplacements to the south of the city on Dorchester Heights. By March, unable to lift the siege, the British were forced to evacuate: on St Patrick's Day, almost ten thousand redcoats shipped out and the British left Boston, never to return. This was the last major military action before the Continental Congress resolved on July 2, 1776—*not* on July 4, as often believed—that "these United Colonies are, and, of right, ought to be, Free and Independent States . . . , absolved from all allegiance to the British crown." Finalizing and approving the declaration of reasons for American independence took another two days.[32]

With more than half the grievances enumerated in the July 4 document addressing the interference of the British government, the Revolution was defined as a political movement in defense of American autonomy. Revolution was both the rejection of the assumed supremacy of Parliament and the beginning of a quest for a more perfect union of the American colonies than was offered by the British Empire. The Declaration was also an act of foreign policy. In the later months of 1775, the Continental Congress had authorized the formation of the Committee of Secret Correspondence. Its "sole purpose" was "corresponding with our friends in Great Britain, Ireland, and the rest of the world," and the committee's earliest business involved sounding out Britain's enemies about assisting the Revolution. Declaring independence was essential to this diplomatic intrigue since, as it was later written, "the probability of obtaining foreign aid would be much increased by holding out the dismemberment of the British to rivals of that nation, as an inducement to engage in that contest." Only by declaring independence could the Americans reap the bitter harvest sown by British power and arrogance throughout Europe, for only through independence could the Americans become lawful combatants and potential "allies." Only by declaring independence could the Americans convince the nation most likely to help, the French, that reconciliation with Great Britain would not happen. There was a compelling, if circular, logic to all this: independence was essential to forming foreign alliances, and foreign alliances were essential to securing independence.[33]

CHAPTER 2

Foreign Alliance and the Revolutionary War

Our union is perfect. Our internal resources are great, and, if necessary, foreign assistance is undoubtedly attainable.[1]

—*A Declaration of the Causes and Necessity of Taking Up Arms,* July 1775

In the summer of 1776, when the American colonies declared their independence to "a candid world," the Founding Fathers were faced with endless possibilities in foreign affairs. The United States was now free to choose its political and military allies as well as its trading partners, but American statesmen knew that making the wrong choices could have disastrous consequences. With the Continental Army undermanned and undersupplied, with the United States surrounded by hostile forces, and with Great Britain enforcing a blockade on American ports, pursuing the "right" foreign policies was essential to the survival of the new republic. Anticipating this occasion, Congress had ordered the drafting of a "model treaty" to set out the principles of American diplomacy. Five men were appointed to the drafting committee: John Adams, John Dickinson, Benjamin Franklin, the Virginian merchant-planter Benjamin Harrison, and the English-born financier Robert Morris. Adams, regarded as the Congress's expert on foreign affairs, emerged as the principal author of the Model Treaty, which was accepted by Congress in September 1776. As if copied from Paine, the Treaty made no mention of balance-of-power politics or military alliance; instead, it focused entirely on commerce. Under its terms, signatories would agree to free trade in free ports, freedom of trade with neutral nations during wartime, and a defined list of contraband. Although visionary, it was the first policy planning by the United States in diplomacy and foreign policy.

More than trade deals, however, the summer of 1776 found the United States in dire need of immediate military support. In August, William Howe defeated George Washington at the Battle of Long Island, forcing the Americans back to Brooklyn Heights and then to Manhattan. There followed an impromptu peace conference on Staten Island, where Howe met with Adams, Franklin, and Edward Rutledge of South Carolina, but nothing came of it. The Americans would not negotiate before their independence was recognized by Britain, and Howe neither could nor would grant that recognition. So "they met, they talked, they parted," and "nothing remained but to fight it out." Despite their use of the first military submarine, the *Turtle*, Washington's men were then pushed farther to the north of Manhattan, suffering further defeat in September at Harlem Heights. In early December, with the British commanding Manhattan and the harbor, Washington's army withdrew across the Delaware River into Pennsylvania. The campaign for New York was a rout. By the winter of 1776–77, the British were in control of the largest American port and this put them in an enviable strategic position. With the Royal Navy supreme on the Atlantic, British control of the Hudson River Valley could stop Patriot reinforcements from New England reaching Washington's army; in turn, the British could prevent the delivery of supplies from the Mid-Atlantic colonies to the isolated New Englanders. "These are the times," wrote Tom Paine, "that try men's souls."[2]

In these, the early years of the Revolutionary War, the American situation was perilous. Foreign aid was needed desperately, but the two most likely Samaritans were the French and the Spanish, whom the Americans, due to their British history, had long regarded as natural enemies. Even with the cord to London cut, the Protestant, republican Americans still feared and hated the Catholic absolutism of these European monarchies. As John Adams wrote in his diary, "I am not for soliciting any political connection, or military assistance, or indeed naval, from France. I wish for nothing but commerce, a mere marine treaty with them." Yet such was the American desperation that almost as soon as Congress had approved the Model Treaty, envoys were sent to France, to the royal palace of Versailles. It was no small stroke of luck that the French were already willing to help.[3]

Choiseul and Beaumarchais

The political history of eighteenth-century France is the history of French ministers of state as much as the Bourbon kings they served. Etienne François, Duc de Choiseul, was one of those ministers. Born in Lorraine in 1719, the young Choiseul distinguished himself in military service during the War of the Austrian Succession before gaining the favor of Madame de Pompadour, the mistress of Louis XV. Choiseul's patroness secured his appointment as French ambassador to Rome and then Vienna before, in 1758, he became the king's chief and foreign minister. In this dual role, Choiseul oversaw French involvement in the Seven Years' War, leading a coalition of the Holy Roman Empire, Russia, Spain, Sweden, and the Mughals of India against the British-led alliance of Prussia, Portugal, the Iroquois, and several German states. Concluded in 1763 by the Treaty of Paris, the terms of British victory might have been "the best peace possible" for France, but they meant the end of French paramountcy in Europe.[4]

Senior ministers were forced from office in shame. French public finances were left in ruins. The French army and navy suffered devastating blows to their reputations. The monarchy was embarrassed, and a new statue in Paris of Louis XV became the target of public derision. Choiseul, however, retained his position and immediately embarked on a long-term plan to restore French prestige. He tried to reform and rebuild the French forces; he directed the conquest of Corsica; and, to strengthen the Bourbon-Habsburg alliance, he arranged the marriage of the Dauphin to an Austrian princess, Marie-Antoinette. By the time of his eventual dismissal in 1770, Choiseul had also established a lasting principle of French foreign policy: revenge (*revanche*) over the British. "We must employ the genius and all the power of the nation," he told Louis XV, "against the English." In the unfolding American crisis, the French spied their opportunity. French support, however, was neither automatic nor explicit. At first it came slowly, in secret, and it was directed by a major figure of the French Enlightenment, Pierre-Augustin Caron de Beaumarchais.[5]

Beaumarchais was a musician, an inventor, and a financier. He was a noted dramatist and the author of *The Barber of Seville* and *The Marriage of Figaro*, egalitarian plays that were adapted into operas by Gioacchino Rossini and Wolfgang Amadeus Mozart. He was also a spy, a diplomat, and a gunrunner, in which roles the Frenchman became integral to American history. In 1775, Beaumarchais was in London, negotiating the return from exile of the Chevalier d'Éon. A member of the French spy ring the Secret

Figure 2.2: *Portrait of Pierre-August Caron de Beaumarchais* (n.d.) by Jean-Baptiste-Francois Bosio. Elisha Whittelsey Collection, Elisha Whittelsey Fund, 1949; Metropolitan Museum of Art, New York.

du Roi, d'Éon had blackmailed the Court of Louis XV and, although he was paid off, he had been banished to London. One of the more colorful characters of diplomatic history, d'Éon was androgynous and a transvestite, and speculation over his true gender fueled a cottage industry of illegal wagers and insurance policies: the Court of King's Bench was forced to rule on the matter, and it held that d'Éon was in fact a woman. While embroiled in this madness, and keeping company with the radicals who surrounded John Wilkes, Beaumarchais was approached by Arthur Lee, the colonial agent for Massachusetts. Throughout the summer of 1775, Lee worked assiduously on Beaumarchais, who became convinced that even if the French did not intervene openly, they could still further the American rebellion by means of secret loans and supplies. Enamored of the Patriot cause, Beaumarchais returned to Versailles and lobbied for "unofficial"

French aid that might, in the event of an American declaration of independence, precede a formal alliance. There was little danger in this plan, he argued, since "supplies don't talk."[6]

Beaumarchais also followed the line that revenge over the British was both desirable and necessary for the French. Echoing Choiseul, he told the new king, Louis XVI, that it was "the English . . . which it concerns you to humiliate and to weaken." There was resistance to this plan, notably from Anne Robert Jacques Turgot, the distinguished economist and minister of finance who prophesied that involvement in an American war would bankrupt the French Crown. However, the new foreign minister, Charles Gravier, the Comte de Vergennes, was more sanguine about French prospects and by June 1776 royal approval had been granted to a program of clandestine aid. To this end, and by happy coincidence on July 4, 1776, Beaumarchais established a shell corporation called Roderigue Hortalez & Company. Funded by the French and Spanish monarchies, Hortalez & Co. would funnel supplies to the Americans through the Dutch Caribbean island of St. Eustatius. The importance of this matériel should not be underplayed. There were bombs, mortars, and tents; clothing for an entire army; and muskets, cannon, and gunpowder that the Americans could not make for themselves. In fact, Beaumarchais supplied almost all the matériel used by the Patriots at the pivotal battle of the Revolutionary War, Saratoga.[7]

Saratoga

In the early years of the war, British strategy had been simple: isolate the radicals in New England from the rest of the continent, and the colonists in the Mid-Atlantic and the South could either be defeated or would fall back into line. Accordingly, Howe's capture of New York in late 1776 was crucial. The next step was planned by Lord George Germain, a former professional soldier who had been disgraced in battle in Germany in 1759 as "the Coward of Minden," but who was now the secretary of state for the colonies. From London, Germain planned that Howe should march up the Hudson River from New York and that another British army, under General John Burgoyne, should march southward from Quebec. The two armies would meet at Albany, having stationed garrisons along their routes. This line of defence and the consequent control of the Hudson Valley would cut off New England, allowing Howe to focus on the rebel capital at Philadelphia. Nothing was wrong with the plan; the problem lay in the execution.

On his march southward, Burgoyne at first advanced rapidly. The British general might have been a shameless careerist and self-promoter, but he was an innovative military theorist and a capable commander. Reinforced by Indian allies and loyalists who had fled to Quebec, Burgoyne took Crown Point, a fort on the narrows of Lake Champlain, before recapturing Fort Ticonderoga. The news was greeted in England with euphoria: "I have beat them!," exclaimed George III to his queen. "Beat all the Americans!" By this stage, Howe had not yet left New York City. When he heard of Burgoyne's success at Ticonderoga, and knowing that his colleague outnumbered the American forces under Philip Schuyler, Howe assumed that Burgoyne would make unimpeded progress toward Albany. He therefore chose *not* to march northward to meet Burgoyne and, instead, he embarked for Philadelphia from Staten Island. The going for Burgoyne, though, soon became slow and treacherous, the terrain more difficult. Worse still, a stretched line to the rear and Schuyler's scorched-earth policy meant that provisions were running low. Then, in July, Burgoyne suffered an embarrassing setback in his efforts to rally the locals to the British cause.[8]

As he approached Fort Edward on the Hudson, Burgoyne sent forth a scouting party of Wyandot Indians. Among the people they came upon was Jane McCrea, the fiancée of a loyalist soldier who was stationed at Ticonderoga. As the legend goes, two of the Indians were escorting McCrea to the British base when they fell out with each other and, in the skirmish that followed, slew and scalped McCrea. Burgoyne was outraged, but he could not punish the Wyandots: if he did, he would lose *all* the Native Americans supporting his campaign. As word spread of McCrea's killing and Burgoyne's equivocation, the condemnation of the British general was universal. When Burgoyne later complained to Horatio Gates—the American general who replaced Schuyler—about the Americans' treatment of British prisoners, Gates's widely printed riposte claimed the high ground for the Patriots:

That the savages of America should in their warfare mangle and scalp the unhappy prisoners who fall into their hands is neither new nor extraordinary; but that the famous Lieutenant General Burgoyne, in whom the fine gentleman is united with the soldier and the scholar, should hire the savages of America to scalp Europeans . . . is more than will be believed in England.[9]

The death of Jane McCrea was a monumental victory for the propagandists of the American Revolution. If the British treated the wives of their own soldiers with such brutality, how much more brutally might they treat the rebels?

Burgoyne's prospects soon darkened further. In August, a detachment of his army commanded by the German mercenary Friedrich Baum was defeated at Bennington by a force of New England militiamen and the Green Mountain Boys. Provoked into fighting by British courtship of local Indians, the American force was led by John Stark and Seth Warner. In one of the more splendid (or infamous) examples of patriotic bluster, Stark rallied his men with the cry, "Yonder are the Hessians. They were bought for seven pounds and ten pence a man. Are you worth more?" He then challenged his men to "prove it" before declaring, "Tonight the American flag floats from yonder hill or Molly Stark sleeps a widow!" Stark's rhetoric was redeemed only by a decisive victory: at this one battle, Burgoyne lost a thousand troops, the support of his Native American allies, and precious provisions.

By the start of September 1777, Burgoyne's army had been reduced by defeat, defection, and disease. He then learned of the failure of an auxiliary mission under Barry St. Leger to remove the American garrison from Fort Stanwix and, worse, that Howe had left for Philadelphia instead of marching north from New York. Finally reaching Fort Edward, Burgoyne dithered over the choice of marching on to Albany or retreating to Quebec. He chose the former, telling his troops that "Britons never retreat." Yet Burgoyne's advance was anticipated by Gates, who had taken up a strong position on the road to Albany. Everything now tilted in the Americans' favor. They possessed superior knowledge of the area; they had the support of the local people; and, what is more, they were much better supplied, courtesy of Beaumarchais.[10]

Over the coming weeks, Burgoyne's men suffered a series of debilitating defeats in and around Saratoga, surviving into October only because of the arrival of Baron Riedesel's German mercenaries. Loath to admit weakness, Burgoyne eventually asked for help from New York, where Henry Clinton—in Howe's absence—now commanded the British forces. Clinton moved north, but he failed to save Burgoyne, for news of British victories at Forts Clinton and Montgomery did not reach Gates soon enough to distract him from his prey at Saratoga. By mid-October, following conclusive defeat at the Battle of Bemis Heights, Burgoyne was surrounded. He agreed to terms with the Americans in what he called a "convention" as opposed to what it was, a capitulation. The news of Burgoyne's downfall was not well received in London. George III "fell into agonies," while in the House of Commons "such a gloom appeared on the countenance of every member, as might be supposed to have settled on the face of every Roman senator, when the defeat of Cannae was announced."[11]

For two reasons, Saratoga was a turning point in both the Revolutionary War and the history of the American empire. First, the defeat of the British allowed the Continental Army to confront and subjugate the Iroquois who had fought with the redcoats and who, even after Saratoga, continued to raid American settlements in the Hudson River Valley. Implored to act by Congress, Washington issued orders "to chastise and intimidate the hostile nations . . . and to relieve our frontiers from the depredations to which they would otherwise be exposed." War would be carried "into the heart of the county of the six nations—to cut off their settlements, destroy their next year's crops, and do them every other mischief which time and circumstance will permit." Led by John Sullivan and James Clinton in the summer of 1779, the American campaign sought to "extirpate [the Iroquois] from the Country." During its July 4th celebrations Sullivan's army even toasted "death to all American savages." The only major encounter of the campaign came in August 1779 at Newtown, a comprehensive American victory after which the Iroquois fled into the backcountry. This was not cowardice. The tactic of retreating then returning had worked for decades against the French, but it would fail against Sullivan and Clinton, who razed more than forty Indian towns. The Iroquois had already given Washington the name of Conotocaurious ("Destroyer of Towns"), but the Sullivan Campaign ensured the name would stick. While Iroquois warriors continued to launch raids from their refugee encampments around the British-held Fort Niagara, American domination of Iroquoia thus was made permanent and so, as one soldier wrote home, Sullivan's army was "sowing the seeds of Empire."[12]

Second, and far better known, Saratoga was the trigger for open and official French support of American independence, beyond the clandestine supplies coordinated by Beaumarchais and a trickle of volunteers including, most famously, the young Marquis de Lafayette. In December 1777, news of Gates's victory reached the French court at Versailles, where Benjamin Franklin had long been agitating for open French support. Franklin's joy at Saratoga was tempered by reports that the British had taken Philadelphia, but Louis XVI was now confident that French military intervention would guarantee British defeat. Two days later, on December 6, he consented to formal negotiations with Franklin. By February 1778, two Franco-American treaties had been signed.

The French Alliance

The first of these, the Treaty of Amity and Commerce, followed the Model Treaty almost verbatim. The second, the Treaty of Alliance, was Franklin's crowning diplomatic glory. The French renounced their ambition of a continental North American empire and committed to realizing American independence by providing indefinite military support; the Americans were bound not to make peace with the British without French consent, and to protect French Caribbean colonies from British predations. The Alliance was inherently lopsided, promising little direct advantage to the French, but it made sense in the context of *revanche*: Versailles was simply hell-bent on hurting the British. Later diplomatic correspondence made that clear: in 1787, instructions sent to the French chargé d'affaires at Philadelphia confirmed that "France had never pretended to make America a useful ally. . . . She had no other end in view than to deprive Great Britain of that vast continent." French foreign minister Vergennes had little interest in American independence for its own sake, or in the territorial expansion of the United States.[13]

Yet Vergennes also had an eye on the long-term balance of power. He believed that French interests would not be well served if the United States grew into a powerful independent nation, so he thought it better for France if the Americans were treaty-bound to Versailles. Writing to Louis XVI, Vergennes advised that "there is a numerous party in America which is attempting to fix as a basis of the political system of the new States that no engagement be contracted with the European powers." In American independence and in American isolation, Vergennes foresaw the source of great vexation for the French:

> Necessity alone has prevented its being established; but as soon as that [necessity] ceases to exist, the insurgents, who will have asserted their independence without our help, will think they do not need it in order to maintain their independence. Then we shall be without any bond with them, exposed to their avidity and perhaps to their resentment.

French consent to an American alliance was therefore the deliberate entanglement of the United States in European affairs. Shared enmity toward the British and Louis XVI's enlightened altruism might have been *among* French motives, but Bourbon foreign policy remained driven by revenge and this kind of balance-of-power politicking.[14]

For the United States, such a binding alliance had never been the object of foreign policy. In fact, many politically aware Americans wished to reject entirely the traditional machinations and alliances of the European system. In the context of the Revolutionary War, however, the enemy of Great Britain was the friend of the United States and, in the winter of 1777–78, notwithstanding Saratoga, the Americans needed friends. Following the Battle of Brandywine, the British had taken Philadelphia, where officers gamed in casinos and where "Howe's strolling players" performed *Henry IV, Part I* to the delight of the redcoats. Eighteen miles to the northwest, George Washington's army camped for the winter at Valley Forge, where exposure, malnutrition, and smallpox killed 2,500 American troops. Gouverneur Morris, who became a spokesman for the army, recorded that "The skeleton of an army presents itself to our eyes in a naked, starving condition, out of health, out of spirits." The French offer of help was therefore accepted and celebrated, and the absolutism of the new American ally was either forgotten or ignored. The soldier Henry Brockholst Livingston exulted that "America is at last saved by almost a Miracle." Thomas McKean, the chief justice of Pennsylvania, proclaimed that Louis XVI was "the most wise, most just, & magnanimous Prince not only in the World at present but to be found in history." The Massachusetts preacher John Murray even forgave the French their Catholicism, depicting them as the goodly neighbors who helped the distressed Americans while the "Protestant powers . . . like the priest and Levite shunned our cries."[15]

The Americans were so emboldened by the French Alliance that, in the summer of 1778, British overtures toward peace were dismissed abruptly. Despite Washington's tribulations at Valley Forge, the British were still reeling from Saratoga; they were also increasingly nervous about the potential impact of French intervention. Lord North therefore dispatched a commission, led by the young Earl of Carlisle, to inform the Americans of parliamentary contrition over the Tea Act and to propose a settlement based on American self-government within the British Empire. Over summer and fall, Carlisle, his commissioners, and two secret agents embarked on a campaign of flattery, bribery, and appeals to public opinion through the *Hartford Courant*. Congress, however, reacted bluntly: only the withdrawal of British forces and the recognition of American independence would suffice. The American people were scarcely more hospitable to the commissioners, with a chastened Carlisle writing to his wife that "the common people hate us in their hearts." There would be no conciliation until the Americans were either independent or subjugated.[16]

Despite this renewed American confidence, the French Alliance did not bring immediate success. In July 1778, the French engagement of the Royal Navy near Ushant in the English Channel was indecisive. Although the battle drove the British into an internecine squabble in naval courts martial, the fallout in France was arguably worse. When the French admiral the Comte d'Estaing then sailed for the United States with twelve ships of the line, four frigates, and infantry reinforcements, he could not help the Americans to victory at the Battle of Rhode Island; the Allies' failure to remove the British from Newport in August 1778 actually equated to a strategic defeat. The Franco-Spanish armada, which gathered in the English Channel in the summer of 1779, was likewise ineffective. The ambition was to invade Great Britain through Portsmouth, a major port on the south coast of England. If successful, the invasion could have forced the government at London to abandon the American colonies and to concentrate on the defence of mainland Britain. Endemic illness on the French ships and the British weather put paid to those plans. Even when the French launched the *Expédition Particulière* ("Special Expedition"), with its first wave when the Comte de Rochambeau landed at Newport in July 1780 with six thousand infantrymen, French influence was negligible: due to the British blockade of the Brittany port of Brest, the Expédition's second wave could not leave France, so Rochambeau's men lay inactive for a year. "The flattering prospect which seemed to be opening to our view," wrote George Washington, ". . . is vanishing like the Morning Dew." Indeed, until 1781 the financial assistance of the Bourbon monarchy and French merchants had merely sustained the Revolution, the rebels incurring debts to French creditors that would take decades to repay. Yet from July that year, when Rochambeau's expedition finally headed south, French intervention became decisive.[17]

The French were not the only foreigners whose help turned the tide. There was Tadeusz Kościuszko, the Polish military engineer who strengthened American bases from New York to Virginia and who erected the fortifications at Bemis Heights that helped Horatio Gates to victory at Saratoga. "The great tacticians of the campaign were hills and forests," wrote Gates to Benjamin Rush, "which a young Polish engineer was skillful enough to select for my encampment." There was Kościuszko's compatriot Casimir Pulaski and the Hungarian nobleman Michael Kovats de Fabriczy, soldiers who were swayed to the American cause by Franklin and who are now regarded as the "fathers of the American cavalry." There was also the self-styled "Baron" Friedrich von Steuben, the Prussian who drilled the Continental Army into shape over the winter at Valley Forge. Hundreds of professional Swedish soldiers, desirous of pay and combat, meanwhile enlisted in both the French and American armies. The contributions of two other European nations were of even greater importance.[18]

The Spanish

The Bourbon royal family had ruled France since Henri IV famously declared that Paris was well worth a Mass, converted to Catholicism, and ascended the throne in the late sixteenth century. The Bourbons also ruled Spain, albeit through a different branch of the family, since the early eighteenth century. The natural consequence of this kinship was an easy alliance that was formalized by three "Family Compacts" in 1733, 1743, and 1761. By the Treaty of Aranjuez of April 1779, the Third Family Compact of 1761 was renewed and the Spanish were brought into the American War. Here, the French promised to help Spain regain the territories that had been lost to Britain over the preceding century; in return, the Spanish agreed to assist the French in the ongoing war *without* contracting an alliance with the Americans. In June 1779, Spain therefore declared war on the British with the aim of recovering the Iberian promontory of Gibraltar, the two Floridas (East and West), the Bahamas, and Britain's largest sugar island, Jamaica. The Spanish had little interest in American independence. Even if the king at Madrid, Carlos III, might have believed that Spain's American colonies "would be less threatened by a divided Anglo-Saxon presence in North America," his ministers were less optimistic. With some degree of prescience, they feared the prospect of American expansion into Spanish territory and the example that successful revolution would set to Spanish America. For these reasons, the Spanish refused to recognize the independence of the United States until *after* the war or to grant the Americans substantial direct aid.[19]

Even so, Spanish intervention was telling. In the fall of 1779, the Spanish governor of New Orleans, Bernardo de Gálvez, launched a series of attacks on British settlements along the coast of the Gulf of Mexico. Within months he seized Manchac, Natchez, and Baton Rouge, expelling British settlers from the Mississippi Delta. When the British subsequently tried to pressure Spain into withdrawing from the war, it led to military catastrophe in Central America. At the behest of John Dalling, the governor of Jamaica, and in line with Britain's long-held ambitions in the region, George Germain sent an expedition into Spanish-controlled lands around Lake Nicaragua. Hoping to win support from British settlers on the Mosquito Coast, Indians who had long fought the Spanish, and even disgruntled Spanish colonists, Germain and Dalling aimed to wrest the

Panamanian isthmus from the Spanish. The expedition met with calamitous failure. Despite the heroics of a young Horatio Nelson and the future conspirator Edward Despard, the mission was hamstrung by yellow fever and malaria, by its failure to win over the locals, and by its use of inaccurate maps. Germain later reflected that "no public Benefit has been derived from the Loss of so many brave men," and the few gains that were made were soon reversed by Spanish counteroffensives. The Central American campaign, designed to open another front against the Spanish and to give leverage to British negotiators in Madrid, in fact served as an ironic distraction from Britain's own efforts in North America. With British positions undermanned, Gálvez continued his eastward march, capturing the key port of Mobile in March 1780. A year later, following a lengthy siege, the British surrendered Pensacola and the rest of West Florida. The United States might not have benefited directly from Spanish belligerence, but the British had been weakened significantly.[20]

The Dutch

If the Spanish intervention against Great Britain was important, the role of the Dutch in the Revolutionary War was vital. Since the late seventeenth century, the foreign policy of the United Provinces of the Netherlands—as the Dutch state was called—had been aligned with British interests. This was not just because of shared financial interests, such as the sizeable Dutch holdings in the British national debt, or even because the reign of William III had bound the two nations' governments, but also because a defensive alliance of the 1670s had stipulated that, should England be attacked, the Dutch had to come to England's aid with a force of six thousand men and a fleet of twenty ships. Another marine treaty of the 1670s further allowed the Dutch to trade with any nation fighting the British (and vice versa) but, one hundred years later, this proved problematic since, in the context of the Revolutionary War, it meant that Dutch merchants were free to trade with American Patriots without restriction on the goods they could supply. By mid-1776, the British had noted that Dutch gunpowder mills were operating at full capacity, producing for the rebels what they could not make for themselves.

Existing agreements with Britain also allowed the Dutch Caribbean island of St. Eustatius to act as an entrepôt for trade between Europe and the Americans. Although tiny, no more than eight square miles, St. Eustatius was one of the most important trading posts in the Western Hemisphere, its seafronts lined by warehouses. From the earliest days of the

Revolution, the island had been a thorn in the British side. In January 1776, the American loyalist Philip Callbeck reported that "at most of the Ports east of Boston, [there] are daily arrivals from the West Indies, but most from St Eustatia; every one brings more or less Gunpowder." It was also the island through which Hortalez & Co. routed its business. Not without reason, the British described St. Eustatius as "inhabited by Rebellious Americans and their agents, disaffected British factions who from base, and lucrative motives, were the great support of the American Rebellion." Yet because of the Treaty of Westminster, the trade from St. Eustatius was legal and the British could do nothing to rebuke the Dutch.[21]

In September 1780, when the cruiser HMS *Vestal* intercepted the *Mercury* off the coast of Newfoundland, the British found their pretext to intervene. On board the *Mercury* was Henry Laurens, a merchant and rice planter from South Carolina who was also the American minister to the Netherlands. Among his papers, Laurens carried the usual paraphernalia of the diplomat: his passport, letters of recommendation, and instructions from Congress. Yet Laurens also possessed a draft of a treaty drawn up by fellow American diplomat William Lee and Jean de Neufville, an Amsterdam banker of dubious reputation but undeniable zeal for the American cause. Having met in Frankfurt, Lee and Neufville had reconvened in Aachen, where they composed the outline of a treaty that committed the Dutch to the cause of American independence. This was in no sense a binding document. It was a treaty between the United States and Amsterdam, a city without diplomatic status, and it was drafted by a Dutchman without diplomatic authority. Even so, Laurens knew the danger it posed. When the British apprehended the *Mercury* he threw his papers overboard, but having failed to weight them correctly they resurfaced and were seized. Laurens was arrested, imprisoned in the Tower of London, and the British had their smoking gun. The unofficial treaty was construed by British ministers as a violation of the 1678 Anglo-Dutch agreement and so, in December 1780, Britain declared war on the United Provinces.

Almost the first action of this Fourth Anglo-Dutch war was the voyage of Admiral George Rodney to St. Eustatius. An experienced seaman, Rodney was the stereotypical swashbuckler of the age, an inveterate gambler who was languishing in a French debtors' prison at the outbreak of the war. Released through the largesse of a benefactor, he returned to naval command and became the British hero of the "Moonlight Battle" of Cape St. Vincent (1780). His new orders were to capture St. Eustatius, which had become the first foreign territory to salute an independent American ship, and to stop the "illicit" trade that proceeded therefrom. Rodney succeeded with aplomb. The few Dutchmen on St. Eustatius offered no resistance and on February 3, 1781 the island surrendered unconditionally. Indirectly, this was the costliest victory in the history of British warfare. Rodney and his sailors spent the next three months plundering the warehouses and sundry riches of St. Eustatius. Rodney then used some of his fighting ships to guard the precious cargo that was sent back to Britain. Distracted in this quest to secure "prize money"—and so to redeem his massive gaming debts in London—Rodney failed to intercept a French fleet making its way to Chesapeake Bay, the inlet that separates Virginia and Maryland. Met instead by an inferior British fleet led by Thomas Graves, the French admiral the Comte de Grasse won a pivotal victory at the Battle of the Capes. Thus was the French navy able to surround the peninsula of Yorktown, where a British army under Lord Charles Cornwallis had been trapped by the allied forces of Washington and Rochambeau.[22]

Yorktown and Victory

After Saratoga, Britain could not isolate New England. When George Washington then avoided conclusive defeat in the Mid-Atlantic, and when William Howe abandoned Philadelphia in 1778, British attention turned to the southern colonies. Here, the British had hoped to exploit latent loyalism among the southerners, their vulnerability to discontent among their slaves, and the tension between coastal elites and hill-country settlers in Virginia and the Carolinas. These endeavors were not unproductive. The ports of Savannah and Charleston were captured, Cornwallis defeated Horatio Gates at the Battle of Camden, and Thomas Jefferson's government of Virginia was driven out of Richmond. But the redcoats failed to hold the Carolina countryside, and loyalist militias were defeated and massacred at King's Mountain in October 1780. By the fall of 1781, Cornwallis had been ordered to move north and to found a base from which to await reinforcement by sea. He chose Yorktown, on the western shore of Chesapeake Bay, and there he waited. Yet because Rodney had tarried at St. Eustatius and because Graves could not defeat de Grasse, Cornwallis was soon surrounded by the French navy and the allied army led by Washington and Rochambeau. The only mobile British force on the continent was trapped and, following a three-week siege, Cornwallis surrendered. As the British marched out of Yorktown they "paid the Americans, seemingly, but little attention as they passed them, but they eyed the French with considerable malice depicted in their countenances." The British military band played "The World Turned Upside Down." It was a pointed, apt choice of tune.[23]

With the loss of Cornwallis's army, British hopes of reconquering America were quashed. As reports of Yorktown filtered through London, enthusiasm for the war dissipated and despair prevailed. George Germain reported that Lord North was beside himself, taking the news "as he would have taken a ball on his breast. . . . 'Oh God!'" cried the Prime Minister, "'It is all over!'" In February 1782 a House of Commons resolution to end hostilities against the Americans passed without opposition, and the Commons moved for the adoption of measures "most conducive to the restoration of harmony between Great Britain and the revolted colonies, so essential to the prosperity of both." Moreover, the Commons would henceforth "consider as enemies to His Majesty and this country, all those who shall endeavor to frustrate His Majesty's paternal care for the ease and happiness of his people, by advising, or by any means attempting, the further prosecution of offensive war on the continent of North America, for the purpose of reducing the revolted colonies to obedience by force." Though the British fought on against the French and Spanish, and though Rodney remade himself into a national hero by defeating de Grasse at the Battle of the Saints (1782), Britain's American war was over. Lord North's resignation, which had been tendered on an annual basis during the preceding decade, was at last forced upon George III when the prime minister lost a motion of no confidence in the Commons. The Marquess of Rockingham, who had led the repeal of the Stamp Act sixteen years earlier, formed a new administration with the express intention of making peace and recognizing American independence.[24]

In 1781, John Adams was convinced that all the powers of Europe were hostile to the United States. He fretted to Benjamin Franklin that "Great Britain has been moving earth and hell to obtain allies against us. . . . Great Britain has borrowed all the superfluous wealth of Europe, in Italy, Germany, Holland, Switzerland, and some in France, to murder us." Adams exaggerated. Such support for the British was merely financial and it was often sourced from individuals, not governments. The American Revolutionary War was in fact the first conflict in more than a century in which Great Britain could not muster a major coalition of European allies. In fighting their rebellious American colonists, the British were also obliged to fight the French and the Spanish, the resources of the Dutch and certain Italian bankers, and volunteers from Sweden, Prussia, and Poland. Feared and hated for its preeminence since the 1760s, Great Britain was almost completely isolated. The British might have enjoyed the support of Native Americans, American loyalists, and the minor German princes who sent their subjects as mercenaries, but that was it. At times, Lord North struggled to procure the support of even the British people, many of whom despised fighting against fellow freeborn Protestants.[25]

In contrast, the Americans had struck international deals, cultivated sympathy across Europe, and made treaties that contributed decisively to the outcome of the war. In time, Adams realized that diplomatic circumstances had been essential to American success. He credited the Dutch in particular. Writing in 1823 to François Adriaan van der Kemp, a radical Dutch politician who had emigrated to America in the late 1780s, Adams conceded that "neither France nor England nor the friends of France or England in America would ever acknowledge the Dutch contribution." He nonetheless insisted that the Dutch "separation from England, [the] Union with France and Spain, and their Treaty with us was the event which ultimately turned the scale of the American Revolutionary war." The international relations of the United States, combined with British failures and the tenacity of the Continental Army, had indeed won the war for American independence. Yet, after 1781, the United States had to win the peace.

CHAPTER 3

Peace and the Treaty of Paris

We are now Friends with England and with all Mankind. May we
never see another War! There never was a good war, or a bad peace.[1]
——Benjamin Franklin, September 11, 1783

After Yorktown, the British cut their losses. Although Henry Clinton still
had sixteen thousand troops in New York, ministers in London feared that
pursuing a lost cause against the Americans would expose the British West
Indies to the rapacious French and the Spanish. Humiliated and desperate,
mocked and despised by their former colonists, the British were ready to
sue for peace. This meant negotiating with the representatives of Congress, the American government that had been formalized in 1781 by the
nation's first constitution, the Articles of Confederation.

The Articles were a long time coming. As early as the summer of 1776,
Congress had appointed a thirteen-man committee, led by John Dickinson,
to draft a constitution for the new republic. There had been more than a year
of back-and-forth between committee and Congress, of debate and revision,
before the proposed constitution was approved in November 1777 and sent to
the individual states for ratification. Formally titled the Articles of Confederation and Perpetual Union, it was ratified almost immediately by the southern
powerhouse of Virginia. By April 1778 nine more states had followed suit, but
New Jersey, Delaware, and Maryland dragged their heels until the southern
states agreed to limit their claims on land in the American West. It was not
until March 1781, the spring before Yorktown and almost five years after the
drafting committee first met, that the Articles came into force.

Comprising fifty or so delegates and exercising few novel powers, Congress under the Articles was the first national government of the United

States. Among its better-known presidents were Richard Henry Lee, the Virginian whose motion of 1776 led to the Declaration of Independence, and John Hancock, the Boston merchant whose florid script made his name a byword for "signature." The main function of the Congress, as New York's Alexander Hamilton put it, was "to manage our foreign concerns." To this end, Congress was the executive and the secretary of foreign affairs was its clerk, the day-to-day overseer of diplomatic relations with foreign powers. This was not an extensive apparatus of government: in 1781, the secretary of foreign affairs, Robert Livingston of New York, had only two assistants.[2]

All the same, Congress was empowered to direct the military, commercial, and diplomatic affairs of the nation. By 1782, it was moving toward peace with the British. These advances began in earnest when Benjamin Franklin told the Scottish diplomat Richard Oswald, a one-eyed slave trader, that four concessions were essential to any pacific treaty. The first was British recognition of American independence. Second, the border between Canada and the States was to be drawn according to what it was before the 1774 Quebec Act. Third, all redcoats were to leave American soil and, finally, the Americans were to be granted fishing rights off the coast of Newfoundland.

Arranging peace between the United States and Great Britain was not, however, a merely bilateral process, for the diplomatic and military alliances that had swung the war in the Americans' favor also complicated its resolution. The 1778 Franco-American Alliance, for example, meant the United States could not make a separate peace with Great Britain: terms could be agreed only with French consent. Indeed, when the Americans and the British subsequently discussed preliminary terms of peace without involving Versailles, the Comte de Vergennes was enraged. "I am at a loss," he wrote to Franklin, "to explain your conduct and that of your colleagues on this occasion. You have concluded your preliminary articles without any communication between us, although the instructions from Congress prescribe that nothing shall be done without the participation of the King." The 1779 Treaty of Aranjuez between France and Spain meanwhile compelled the French to fight until Spain had recovered Gibraltar. The British garrison of "the Rock" had been under siege since June 1779, but on that outcrop of Iberian limestone the band of plucky redcoats endured. A double bind therefore prevented the arrangement of peace. Until the Spanish took Gibraltar, the French, although close to bankruptcy and desperate to end the war, had pledged to continue fighting; and if the French could not make peace, then neither, by the terms of the Franco-American alliance, could the Americans. As the eminent diplomatic historian Samuel Bemis has written, "The French alliance, that indispensable instrument of American diplomacy, that life-saving alliance, which procured American independence, [was] itself an example of the way in which even the most useful of alliances entangled the nation in purely European questions." Great Britain, moreover, had to make individual treaties with the United States, France, Spain, and the Dutch, all of whom could demand specific and even conflicting concessions.[3]

This labyrinth of diplomatic obligations was further complicated by repeated changes of government in Great Britain. When the exhausted Lord North resigned in March 1782 and when the Marquess of Rockingham formed a new administration, hopes were high for a speedy, amicable settlement. Just as during their first ministry, when the Stamp Act was repealed, the Rockingham Whigs were sympathetic to the American cause; the Americans in turn were ready and willing to negotiate. Rockingham, however, fell victim to an influenza epidemic and died after only three months in office. He was replaced by William Petty, the Earl of Shelburne, and this was not received well in the United States. "The Death of the Marquess of Rockingham, [and] the Advancement of the Earl of Shelburne," wrote George Washington, ". . . have given us very different Impressions from those we at first received." This caution was due to the new prime minister's designs on maintaining British sovereignty in America. An Irish-born philosopher and free trader, Shelburne nurtured hope that the royal Personal Union that bound Britain to Ireland and Hanover could be extended to the United States. The Irish example was thought especially appealing since legislative independence had just been granted to "Grattan's Parliament" in Dublin. The prime minister, though, would be denied in his ambitions, for the Americans insisted on the complete severance of political ties. "My Lord Shelburne," wrote John Adams, ". . . refuses to do what all the World sees to be necessary. . . . We should insist on an Acknowledgement of our Independence as a Preliminary Condition to entering into any Treaty or Conference." Negotiations were at an impasse.[4]

It took the arrival at Gibraltar of the British admiral Richard Howe to break the chains. Howe was the older brother of the general, William, and with the French and Spanish blockade scattered by a storm, he sailed unimpeded into Gibraltar's harbor in September 1782, delivering much-needed supplies and sixteen hundred reinforcements to the beleaguered British garrison. Although the Siege of Gibraltar technically continued until the spring of 1783, Howe's mission had broken the Spanish resolve. In December 1782, a letter from Madrid was sent to the Spanish ambassador at Paris, the Count of Aranda. Inquiry was made as to "what considerable advantage Spain could expect from [a] treaty, if, for any reason, [the Spanish] made the sacrifice" of releasing France from its obligations. In other words, the Spanish now realized that capturing Gibraltar was beyond them, so they wanted out of the war. Aranda showed the letter to Vergennes, who was delighted at the prospect of peace and wrote to his agent in London, who in turn sounded out the British. Word came back to Paris and the question was put to the Spanish ambassador: Would Madrid abandon its demand for Gibraltar if the British conceded Minorca and the Floridas instead? Aranda consented without even consulting Madrid, and the diplomatic ties that had prolonged the war were dissolved. Peace was now possible.[5]

The Terms of Peace

The Treaty of Paris was signed on September 3, 1783, after seventeen months of back-channel chatter and formal negotiation. The Americans had been represented by four commissioners. John Adams had spent much of the Revolutionary War in Europe, first at Paris and then in the Netherlands, trying but failing to curry favor with the diplomatic elite of the Old World. Indeed, it was at Vergennes's behest that three other commissioners were appointed so the French would not have to deal with the irascible Adams alone. One of them was John Jay, the New York lawyer who had recently been sent as American minister to Spain. Jay's time at Madrid had been defined by frustration, the Spanish having refused to accept his credentials or to recognize the United States: "This Court," he wrote in November 1781, "continues to observe the most profound Silence respecting our Propositions. I cannot as yet obtain any answer of any kind to any of my applications." During the laborious negotiations in Paris, Jay's was an often irritated, dissenting voice. The third commissioner was Henry Laurens, whose arrest on the high seas had triggered the Anglo-Dutch conflict. Released from the Tower of London so "that Earl Cornwallis should in exchange be absolved from his parole," Laurens dealt mainly with secondary issues and enjoyed cordial relations with Richard Oswald, a former business partner who had even paid Laurens's bail. The fourth American commissioner was the most important diplomatic figure of the whole Revolution.[6]

Figure 3.1. *Benjamin Franklin* (1778) by Joseph Duplessis. The Friedsam Collection, Metropolitan Museum of Art, New York.

Benjamin Franklin

In the 1770s and 1780s, Benjamin Franklin was the most celebrated American in Europe. His political savoir-faire was admired in the corridors of power at Versailles and his intellect was fêted in the salons of Paris. He was also hailed as the hero of the American struggle. "It is universally believed," noted the jealous John Adams, "that his electric wand has accomplished all this revolution." Franklin was one of the most accomplished Americans of his and any era, a man whose achievements are as many as they are astounding. As a scientist—or what contemporaries termed a "natural philosopher"—he conceptualized the electric charge, formulated a revolutionary one-fluid theory of electricity, and demonstrated the electrical nature of lightning by means of the famous kite experiment. As a theorist of population, Franklin had a profound impact on the demographer Thomas Malthus and the economist Adam Smith. He also advanced theories in meteorology, oceanography, thermodynamics, and the wave theory of light. As an inventor, Franklin's contributions included bifocal spectacles, lightning rods, and an eponymous stove also known as the "Pennsylvania fireplace." He gave these inventions "freely and generously," noting that "as we enjoy great advantages from the inventions of others, we should be glad of an opportunity to serve others by any invention of ours." In public life, meanwhile, Franklin was a pre-Revolutionary colonial agent in London, the first postmaster general of the United States, the American minister to France and Sweden, and later a delegate to the Constitutional Convention. He was also the only man to sign the four major documents of early American history: the Declaration of Independence; the 1778 French Alliance; the Treaty of Paris; and the United States Constitution.[7]

Without Franklin's presence at Versailles, ongoing French support for the United States would have been less forthcoming. Vergennes had almost exclusive control over the French war effort and he frequently despaired of American conduct. For example, when the Marquis de Lafayette returned from the United States in 1782, he found the foreign minister exasperated: "I am not marvelously pleased with the country that you have just left," raged Vergennes. "I find it barely active and very demanding." He was further irritated by the obstructive, and occasionally delusional, behavior of John Adams, who "mean[t] well for his country, [was] always an honest man, often a wise one, but sometimes and in some things, absolutely out of his senses." Thus, it was often Franklin alone who kept the United States in Vergennes's good graces, and Adams observed begrudgingly that Franklin had "the most affectionate and insinuating Way of charming the Woman or the Man that he fixes on." Thomas Jefferson, who succeeded Franklin at Paris, reflected that he "possessed the confidence of [the French] government in the highest degree, insomuch that it may truly be said, that they were more under his influence, than he under theirs." There are few better examples of the personal dimension of diplomacy.[8]

During his time at Versailles, Franklin became a master of intrigue and manipulation. He understood that duplicity was an integral aspect of diplomacy, and that it was no reason to think less of man. "If I was sure," he wrote, "that my Valet de place was a Spy, as probably he is, I think I should not discharge him for that, if in other respects I lik'd him." Accepting that he was surrounded by potential enemies, Franklin strove to marry his interpersonal bonhomie with considered discretion, but he also mastered that subtle branch of espionage of knowing how and when to reveal information to adversaries. Reasoning that "it is impossible to discover in every case the Falsity of pretended Friends who would know our Affairs . . . and more so to prevent being watch'd by Spies," Franklin resolved "to be concern'd in no Affairs that I should blush to have made Publick, and to do nothing but what Spies may see & welcome." Such studied transparency was manifest during the peace negotiations, when Franklin played many of his cards face up. He leaked information to both the French and the English, playing on their respective fears, keeping them suspicious of each other as well as of the Americans. Even Adams, who disliked Franklin intensely, admitted that he "has been able and useful, both by his sagacity and reputation, in the whole negotiation."[9]

The terms of the Treaty of Paris confirmed several outright victories for the United States. As desired almost universally by American leaders, peace was restored and amicable relations were established, at least on paper, with Great Britain. Both nations were disposed by Divine Providence "to forget all past misunderstandings and differences . . . and to establish such a beneficial and satisfactory intercourse, between the two countries upon the ground of reciprocal advantages and mutual convenience as may promote and secure to both perpetual peace and harmony." Crucially, the Treaty also acknowledged the American states as "free, sovereign, and independent," with the British Crown renouncing all claims "to the Government, property, and territorial rights of the same." The "independent empire" of which the King had warned Parliament was now recognized as such by Great Britain.[10]

In establishing the boundaries of this American empire, the British ceded land to the north, west, and south of their former colonies. In the north, the land between the lakes of the Province of Quebec and the Ohio River became part of the vast Trans-Appalachian West that was ceded to the new republic. The Shelburne government was hopeful that American settlement of this territory would create lucrative business for British merchants while simultaneously relieving London of its laborious administration and expensive defense. In the South, the treaty defined the border as the thirty-first parallel, which today serves to divide Florida and Alabama. At sea, islands within twenty leagues of the coast except those belonging to Nova Scotia were to be considered American. In short, Britain gave up her claims to everything south of present-day Canada, everything east of the Mississippi, and everything north of the Floridas. The Indians, transferred after years of struggle to the republican sovereignty of their settler enemies, were not consulted or even considered by their British allies. "England had Sold the Indians to the Congress," snarled one Indian leader, but the eastern United States as we know it was beginning to take shape.[11]

The Americans were also given the right to fish in the Gulf of Saint Lawrence and on the Grand Banks off Newfoundland, something that had

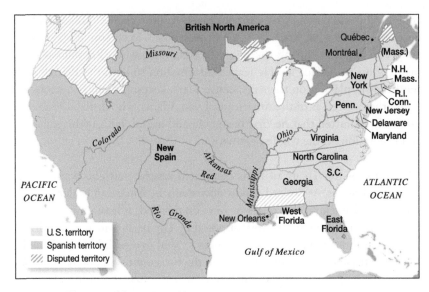

Figure 3.2. The United States in 1783

been indispensably important to New Englanders. Elbridge Gerry, whose later electoral trickery bequeathed Americans with the term "gerrymandering," even threatened the secession of Massachusetts if these rights were not secured. John Adams was consequently and "unalterably determined" to gain this point from the British. "We have been constantly fighting," he wrote, "in Canada, Cape Breton, and Nova Scotia for the defense of the fishery, and have expanded beyond all proportion more than you. If then the right [to fish] cannot be denied, why then should it not be acknowledged?" When in December 1782 the fisheries were at last conceded, Adams was elated. "Thanks be to God," he wrote to Gerry, "that our Tom Cod are Safe, in Spite of the Malice and Enemies, the Finesse of Allies, and the Mistakes of Congress. The Fisheries were attacked through my Sides, but they have not been wounded."[12]

Elsewhere in the Treaty, the British were obliged to evacuate all military posts on American land and to restore runaway slaves to their American masters. During the war, royal officers had promised freedom to any slave who fought for the king; thousands had been swayed by the promise, but now they—and all "property"—were to be returned to their American owners. It seemed to many Europeans that Shelburne's government had been profligate, that the Americans had wrought a peace to their exclusive benefit. Vergennes, indeed, was astonished by the generosity of the Treaty. "You will notice," he wrote to his under-secretary, Gérard de Rayneval, "that the English buy peace rather than make it. Their concessions, in fact as much to the boundaries as to the fisheries . . . , exceed all that I should have thought possible." Rayneval in turn gloated that Britain had been "plucked like a chicken." An angry British public agreed. Although one of the British negotiators, Henry Strachey, described the peace as "the best that could have been made," the Treaty was widely disparaged at home for betraying the loyalists and the Indians. The diplomat and spymaster William Eden, who had served on the Carlisle Peace Commission of 1778, wrote of "the reproach and obloquy of the Peace which must rise every day." He noted in his journal that "a great variety of people" thought the Peace "as infamous as I do, . . . dishonorable and ruinous." Little wonder, then, that Benjamin West's painting of the signing of the Treaty was unfinished: Oswald and Strachey refused to sit for a portrait of their defeat.[13]

Concessions and reactions such as these have led one historian to describe the Treaty of Paris as "the greatest victory in the annals of American diplomacy," but in truth there were several major problems with it. Most importantly, it was not a commercial treaty: *nothing* was said of American trade with Great Britain and its remaining empire for, having recognized the independence of the United States, the British simply did not care about encouraging British-American commerce. British economic policies had long been designed to benefit only British subjects, only British colonies, and only British shipping, which was regarded as the nursery of the Royal Navy. The Treaty of Paris confirmed the independence of the United States, so the new republic would be excluded from British trading compacts and treated like any other foreign nation. Though William Pitt the Younger championed the American Intercourse Bill, a measure that would have given American merchants access to the West Indies, the bill was buried when a new government, the Fox-North coalition of Charles James Fox and Lord North, took power in April 1783. From this point, British policy aimed to banish the United States from the imperial economy. Even if future orders in council (the British equivalent of executive orders) encouraged the importation of American raw materials such as cotton and tobacco, and even if John Adams begged for redress as the American minister at the Court of St. James, London would not budge. Trade restrictions were maintained because they were popular: "The [British] nation," reported Jefferson, "is against any change of measures."[14]

Although it was not clear at the time, the Treaty of Paris also failed to properly define the borders of the United States, in part because the nego-

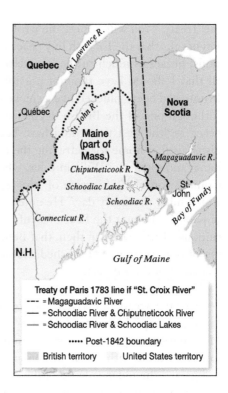

Figure 3.3. Enlarged map of the
Northeast border

tiators relied upon the Mitchell Map of 1755, which the best geographic
knowledge of the time already knew to be inaccurate and obsolete.

In the northeast, for instance, the Treaty purported to demarcate mainland Nova Scotia from Maine, which at the time was part of Massachusetts:
this border began "From the north west Angle of Nova Scotia, Viz that
Angle which is form'd by a Line drawn due north, from the Source of St.
Croix River to the Highlands, along the said Highlands which divide those
Rivers that empty themselves into the River St Laurence, from those which
fall into the Atlantic Ocean, to the northwesternmost Head of Connecticut River." Apart from the St. Lawrence and the Atlantic, none of these
place-names had clear meaning on the ground. Which river was the "St.
Croix" was uncertain: Was it the stream that bore the Algonquin name
of Magaguadavic (which would yield a line more favorable to the United
States), the Schoodiac and its longest source the Chiputneticook, or the
Schoodiac followed by the string of Schoodiac Lakes to the west (which
would yield a line more favorable to the British)? Moreover, neither party
would readily agree on whether the "Highlands" meant the demarcation

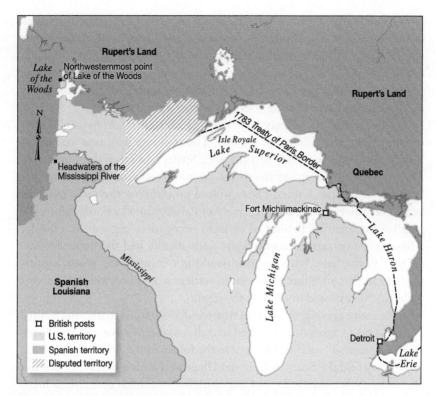

Figure 3.4. Enlarged map of the North-West border

between the St. Lawrence and Atlantic watersheds or the first notable hills north of the "St. Croix" River. There was further dispute over which of the many streams draining into the Connecticut River should count as "the northwesternmost head" while the upper reaches of the streams draining into Passamaquoddy Bay had not been mapped and would not even be surveyed until the 1790s. Disputes over territory and logging rights would rumble on for decades.[15]

The border in the northwest was nonsensical. The Treaty held that it should run "through Lake Superior Northward of the Isles Royal & Phelipeaux to the Long Lake; Thence through the middle of said Long Lake and the Water Communication between it & the Lake of the Woods, to the said Lake of the Woods; Thence through the said Lake to the most Northwestern Point thereof, and from thence on a due West Course to the river Mississippi." One deficiency here was that "the Isle Phelipeaux" did not exist, while the Long Lake would never successfully be identified.

A more fundamental error still was that the Lake of the Woods—which straddles present-day Minnesota, Manitoba, and Ontario—is to the north, not the east, of the Mississippi. If such a border could have been drawn, it would have given the British access to the northern branches of the Mississippi. In reality British access to the Mississippi, supposedly guaranteed by the Treaty, was barred by the confused terms of the Treaty itself.

In the South, the Treaty of Paris had created an American border running along the thirty-first parallel. The problem here was that Great Britain, in a separate treaty of 1783 with Spain, had given the Floridas to Madrid without specifying the extent of the concession. This meant that both Spain and the United States wound up claiming the same patch of land. The Americans, as per the Treaty of Paris, claimed a border along the parallel; the Spanish, by dint of de facto occupation, argued for a border a hundred miles farther north. Spain undoubtedly had the better historical title to the land, but Congress would not concede the point, expecting instead that an influx of American settlers would overwhelm whatever authority Spain could impose on the region.

Even more gravely, the various treaties of 1783 failed to give the United States access to Spanish-controlled stretches of the Mississippi. This "Mississippi Question" was fundamental to the future of the American West for, as John Jay told the Spanish diplomat Diego de Gardoqui, "the Americans, almost to a man, believed that God Almighty had made that river a highway for the people of the upper country to go to sea by." This situation was aggravated by the ongoing dispute over Florida, because of which the Spanish took drastic action. First, the port at New Orleans and the lower Mississippi were closed to American ships, thereby stifling the trade of western American settlers. Spanish officials then demanded that Americans living in the southern settlements of Vicksburg and Natchez should swear an oath of allegiance to Madrid. The Spanish also claimed dominion over parts of Georgia, the westernmost reaches of Virginia (now Kentucky), and parts of the South-Western Territory (now Tennessee). Most dangerous of all, the Spanish made allies of the Creeks and other Native Americans. The *Knoxville Gazette* later reported that Madrid's emissaries had "opened the stores of the king of Spain, in West Florida, to the Creeks and Cherokees" and that the Spanish were "advising and stimulating them to go to war with the frontier inhabitants of the United States." The Treaty of Paris thus bequeathed problems with Spain that went unresolved, some for almost forty years.[16]

Figure 3.5. Enlarged map of the Southern border

Debts and Dead Letters

If the boundary clauses of the Treaty of Paris were problematic, others were dead letters that proved impossible to enforce. One article stipulated that "creditors on either side shall meet with no lawful impediment to the recovery of the full value in sterling money of all bona fide debts heretofore contracted." Yet during the war, debts held by individual Americans had often been assumed by the newly formed states, who then stiffed British creditors by closing debt cases in the courts, or by disallowing interest accumulated since 1775, or by simply refusing to pay up. Congress was powerless to intervene: it could only *recommend* a course of action to the states, and the states either ignored or resisted those recommendations. In

Virginia, where planters owed more than £2 million to British merchants, unpaid debts were justified as "compensation" for slaves that were "stolen" during the war.

State legislatures were also supposed to "provide for the restitution of all estates, rights, and properties, which have been confiscated belonging to real British subjects." Those "real British subjects," of course, were the loyalists, and many American citizens reacted to this provision with utter disbelief. Of the ordained restoration of loyalist property, Henry Laurens asked rhetorically, "With what face can any Man say either by himself or his [Counsel] to Congress, 'I am a Loyalist, I used my utmost endeavors to get you all hanged and to confiscate your estates and beggar your wives and children. Pray make a provision for me or let me enjoy my Estate?'" With such contemptuous sentiment shared widely, Congress was again powerless to compel the fair treatment of loyalists by the states. New York's legislature even passed a Trespass Act, enabling citizens to bring claims for loss of property against anyone who had been "within the power of the enemy" during the war. The loyalists were forbidden by the same Act from citing "any military order or command whatever of the enemy" in their defense.[17]

British observers were not surprised by this American turmoil. Andrew Kippis, a Presbyterian minister and pamphleteer in London, perceived that it was never "in the power of the American Commissioners to proceed farther than they did." Kippis also understood that it was not "in the power of Congress to do more than *earnestly to recommend* to compassion and favor." Each state, he explained, "is sovereign and supreme in itself, with regard to legislative and judicial authority; and, therefore, cannot be controlled in the exercise of its jurisdiction over its own subjects." In other words, Kippis had recognized—and it was dawning on many Americans—that the Articles of Confederation had created a weak, ineffective national government.[18]

Yet American refusals to honor debts and to treat loyalists fairly were not just demonstrations of defiance. They were also acts of hubris that gave the British an excuse not to evacuate their military posts in the American Northwest. East of the Mississippi and north of the Ohio, the British persisted in supplying and arming their former Native American allies. Thus enabled, the Indians continued to resist American settlers in defense of their freedom, their lands, and their way of life. Over the next decade, British interference in support of these Indians became the defining security challenge of the early republic.

Peace without Power

By 1783, the United States had won its Revolutionary War and secured its independence. Yet if American diplomats had done much to win the war and arrange the peace, it was clear that several clauses of the Treaty of Paris were defective and that others were useless because the Congress could not enforce them. Arguably worse was that, when the redcoats were vanquished, American attention reverted to local issues and the Union was soon debilitated by parochialism. American leaders quickly realized that all of this—the failure to protect loyalists and to honor debts; the inability to expel the British from the Northwest; the failure to secure terms of trade; and the disintegration of national unity—stemmed from the same cause: the inadequacy of Congress under the Articles. Consequently, there were no postwar years of plenty. The 1780s became almost a missing decade in American history, a "Critical Period" defined by diplomatic weakness, commercial embarrassment, threats of disunion, and geopolitical insecurity. In short, the new republic was already failing to answer the questions of American government that had confounded Great Britain and caused the Revolution. It was only by addressing the root cause of these problems, by reforming the Union itself, that the United States could hope to address the crises threatening the survival of the republic.

CHAPTER 4

Foreign Policy and the United States Constitution

The principal purposes to be answered by union are these—the common defense of the members—the preservation of the public peace as well against internal convulsions as external attacks—the superintendence of our intercourse, political and commercial, with foreign countries.[1]

—"Publius" [Alexander Hamilton], *Federalist* 23

The new federal government was skeletal. The powers of Congress under the Articles of Confederation were limited. Even so, *some* of the United States' early foreign-policy achievements were substantial. A series of treaties were signed with Native Americans at Fort Stanwix, Fort McIntosh, and Hopewell, the last of which promised optimistically that "The hatchet shall be buried forever." Relations with those nations were further improved when the Proclamation of 1783 forbade states from taking Indian lands without the consent of the federal government.* The Land Ordinance of 1785 then set up a profitable, practical system for settling the Trans-Appalachian West, while the Northwest Ordinance of 1787 organized the northern part of that territory and banned slavery therein. Congress also made the nation's first postwar treaty, with Prussia, the German state ruled by the enlightened despot Frederick the Great. Besides recognizing American independence and the inevitable commit-

---

*The Yazoo Fraud, however, was a scandal that erupted in the 1790s. Here, Georgia legislators had been bribed to sell the land of what is now Mississippi at well below market rate. When it came to dealing fairly with Indian territory, there was quite some distance between governmental ideals and reality.

ment to "amity," the Treaty provided for mutually beneficial rights in commerce, navigation, and land ownership. It even established a novelty in foreign relations by guaranteeing humane custody to each party's prisoners of war.

That, however, was the extent of American diplomatic success in the years after the Treaty of Paris. Indeed, the foreign policy and security situation of the United States remained perilous. The first major failing of the Union came early when there was an embarrassing delay in the ratification of the Treaty. The terms of peace were received by Congress when it was based at Nassau Hall in New Jersey, but sufficient delegates were not in attendance; Congress thus lacked the quorum required under the Articles, and it had no procedural power to recall its members. The treaty lay on the table for months. Neither could Congress make provisions for permanent garrisons in the West, much to the chagrin of George Washington, who complained that "Congress have come to no determination *yet* respecting the Peace Establishment, nor am I able to say when they will. . . . There is not a sufficient representation to discuss *Great* National points." Although the Treaty of Paris was ratified at last at Annapolis, Maryland, in January 1784, it was an ominous sign. The Articles had created a government woefully inadequate to the needs of the American empire.[2]

Indeed, American foreign policy in the 1780s was in critical respects marked by humiliation. In terms of fostering commerce, making and enforcing treaties, developing federal military forces, expanding westward, and establishing international credit, the United States fell repeatedly short of expectations. In 1787, Charles Cotesworth Pinckney, the South Carolinian who later stood twice for the presidency, published his "Observations" on the national failings of the United States. "There is no one," he wrote, "who doubts there is something particularly alarming in the present conjuncture." Pinckney railed that the American government was "despised" and that American laws were both "robbed of their respective terrors" and the "subject of ridicule." More pointedly, Pinckney wrote that American "foreign politics are as much developed, as our domestic economy." Foreign allies were "slackened in their affection," and the nation's own citizens were "loosened from their obedience." Like many citizens of the 1780s, Pinckney diagnosed the cause of these national ailments as "the weakness and impropriety of [our] government." In previous decades, this weakness of government had undermined Great Britain's North American empire; it now threatened to overwhelm the republican heirs of the continent.[3]

Commerce and Diplomacy

The gravest American weakness was probably commercial isolation, for in the 1780s the United States struggled badly to make trade deals with the great powers of Europe. The sorest case in point was Great Britain, toward which American industry and commerce had long been geared. Even when the Eden Treaty of 1786 opened British trade to the French, restrictions on American commerce remained in place, a development that was particularly galling because the treaty's author, William Eden, had been a vocal detractor of Pitt's American Intercourse Bill of 1783. With their traditional market discriminating against them, American producers and merchants were forced to look elsewhere for custom. Some statesmen, including James Madison, believed that American trade could be reoriented toward France, but after the war the French returned to their mercantilist, zero-sum principles and refused to open even their Caribbean ports to American shipping. In fact, French trade with the United States fell sharply between 1782 and 1789: as John Jay noted, the French had been "interested in separating us from Great Britain, but it is not in their interest that we should become a great and formidable people."[4]

European powers were further disinclined to cut trade deals with the United States because of the weakness of Congress. In an influential pamphlet of 1783, the Earl of Sheffield explained that the "unsettled" nature of the American government dissuaded the British from making any kind of commercial arrangement. "No treaty can be made with the American states," he wrote, "that can be binding on the whole." Sheffield argued that Britons "might as reasonably dread the effects of combinations among the German as among the American States, and deprecate the resolves of the Diet, as those of Congress." Sheffield and many others agreed that Anglo-American commercial treaties were impossible because the effective power to enforce such treaties lay with the individual American states and *not* with the federal Congress. John Adams reported the British view that "there is not as yet any national government," and such opinions were commonplace in the Old World.[5] Writing for the *Leiden Gazette*, Thomas Jefferson described how Europeans regarded America as "a scene . . . of riot and anarchy," a republic "on the verge of falling again into the lap of Great Britain." American citizens were thought by Europeans, Jefferson claimed, to be "groaning under heavy taxes" and "flying for refuge to the frozen regions which still remain subject to Great Britain," while American political bodies, despite supposedly "possessing no power or influence," were "tyrannizing over their constituents." For Alexander Hamilton, the "imbecility of [the American] government" inhibited foreign powers from treating American diplomats with even courtesy. "Our ambassadors abroad," he declared, "are the mere pageants of mimic sovereignty."[6]

Americans endorsed these European opinions by echoing them. For one thing, it was agreed that Congress had failed to enforce existing international agreements. "Are there engagements," asked Hamilton, "to the performance of which we are held by every tie respectable among men? These are the subjects of constant and unblushing violation." James Madison likewise bemoaned "those violations of the law of nations & of Treaties which if not prevented must involve us in the calamities of foreign wars." The "files of Congress," he declared, "contain complaints already from almost every nation with which treaties have been formed." The executive had not, for example, ensured the protection of American loyalists and their property, nor had it compelled the states to honor bona fide debts to British creditors. Complaints were not confined to the British, either, for the Chevalier de Luzerne, the French minister to the United States, complained of how Pennsylvania had not passed laws to protect French subjects and their property. For Charles Pinckney, these failings were unavoidable: Congress simply did not "possess the power of taking such measures as will ensure an attention to [treaties]." George Washington, in an undelivered draft of his first inaugural address, would reflect on the same point: "Congress, constituted in most respects as a diplomatic body, [had] possessed no power of carrying into execution a simple Ordinance, however strongly dictated by prudence, policy, or justice."[7]

The unwanted bequest of constitutional inadequacy, exacerbated by the want of trade deals, was commercial embarrassment. In 1787, Alexander Hamilton remarked that American commerce was "at the lowest point of declension," a point on which John Jay elaborated in his *Address to the People of the State of New York*. "Although our increasing agriculture and industry extend and multiply our productions," wrote Jay, ". . . they constantly diminish in value; and although we permit all nations to fill our country with their merchandises, . . . their best markets are shut against us. Is there an English, or a French, or a Spanish island or port in the West Indies, to which an American vessel can carry a cargo . . . for sale? Not one." Other nations were "taking advantage of [the Union's] imbecility and daily multiplying commercial restraints upon us. Our fur trade is gone to Canada." Given these dire circumstances, John Adams suggested to Thomas Jefferson that economic warfare might be the best response. "If we cannot obtain reciprocal liberality," wrote Adams from London, "we must adopt reciprocal prohibitions, exclusions, monopolies and imposts." Yet even Adams understood, as did the British, that retaliation was beyond the United States "until Congress shall be made Supreme in foreign Commerce."[8]

Taxes and Security

The inability to make and enforce treaties was far from the only American weakness. The Articles of Confederation had also created a federal system without fiscal power or financial stability. Roger Sherman was a Connecticut lawyer who, per Thomas Jefferson, "never said a foolish thing in his life"; speaking in Philadelphia in May 1787, he explained that Congress had been crippled by its Revolutionary exertions. The executive might have "carried us through the whole war . . . , performing all the functions of a good government by making a beneficial peace," but there was now "the great difficulty" of paying "the public debt incurred during that war." The nonpayment of those debts had become a rallying cry for political change and, for some, a matter of national disgrace. "Do we owe debts to foreigners and to our own citizens contracted in a time of imminent peril for the preservation of our political existence?" asked Hamilton. The answer was "Yes," and such debts "remain[ed] without any proper or satisfactory provision for their discharge." In turn, Congress had little credit, which placed the future of the republic in danger: "Is [not] public credit," asked Hamilton, "an indispensable resource in time of public danger? We seem to have abandoned its cause as desperate and irretrievable." Hamilton argued that the only effective means of raising revenue and creating credit was a federal fiscal policy. "One national government," he wrote, "would be able, at much less expense, to extend the duties on imports, beyond comparison, further than would be practicable to the States separately, or to any partial confederacies."[9]

In 1775, the Americans had gone to war for the legislative independence of their local assemblies, an independence that encompassed the exclusive right to levy local taxes, so they created a Congress that did not have the power to impose taxes at the federal level. And so, if Congress had no means of paying its bills beside unpopular and, in peacetime, mostly ineffective requisitions, it could not develop the military forces needed to defend the Union. On American shipping, John Jay delivered an eloquent lament. "Our shipyards," he wrote, "have almost ceased to disturb the repose of the neighborhood by the noise of the axe and hammer and, while foreign flags fly triumphantly above our highest houses, the American Stars seldom do more than shed a few feeble rays about the humble masts of our sloops and coasting schooners. The greater part of our hardy seamen are plowing the ocean in foreign pay, and not a few of our ingenious ship-wrights are now building vessels on alien shores." Such embarrassment was a major concern for the United States, whose naval prowess lagged well behind the British, the French, the Spanish, and even the jihadist Islamic Barbary States of northern Africa: "The Algerines [Algerians]," Jay noted, "exclude us from the Mediterranean, and adjacent countries; and we are neither able to purchase, nor to command the free use of those seas."[10]

In planning for a powerful navy, American statesmen were taken with the exemplar of Britain's Royal Navy. Its supremacy, reasserted by the end of the Revolutionary War, was often attributed to the British Navigation Laws, under which foreign vessels trading with Britain were taxed, raising income that was spent on naval development. British merchant vessels, guaranteed business by the same laws, all the while acted as a "nursery" for the Royal Navy's sailors. For John Adams, the United States needed to replicate this British model. "We are sure of one thing," he wrote, "that a navigation Act is in our Power, as well as theirs, and that ours will be more hurtful to them than to us. In short, it is scarcely possible to calculate, to what . . . Height of naval Power a navigation Act, will raise the United States in a very few Years." Once again, however, it was clear that consolidated navigation laws regulating the commerce of the entire Union could be implemented only by a strong federal government.[11]

The West

The weakness of Congress was even more obvious in the American West. Here, in defiance of the Treaty of Paris, Great Britain had retained military posts from which the redcoats fed, clothed, and armed Native Americans hostile to the encroachment of American settlers. "Have we valuable territories and important posts in the possession of a foreign power," asked Hamilton, "which, by express stipulations, ought long since to have been surrendered?" Such posts were "still retained, to the prejudice of our interests, not less than of our rights." The United States, however, was unable to expel the British: "We have neither troops, nor treaty, nor government."[12]

The West also played host to the defining failure of American diplomacy in the 1780s. The Treaty of Paris had stipulated that the United States— along with Great Britain—should enjoy free and "perpetual" navigation of the Mississippi River, the vital conduit that allowed western American settlers to move their produce to sea. The Mississippi and its port of New Orleans, however, were controlled by the Spanish and, because of the ongoing dispute over the Floridas, the Spanish had closed them to American vessels. For George Washington, continued American failure to access the Mississippi threatened to induce western settlers—of whom there were more than fifty thousand in Kentucky alone—to forsake their allegiance to the United States. "No well-informed Mind need be told," he wrote, "that the flanks and rear of the United territory are possessed by other powers, and formidable ones too. . . . For what ties should we have upon those people; and how entirely unconnected should we be with them if the Spaniards on their right, or Great Britain on their left, instead of throwing stumbling blocks in their way as they now do should invite their trade and seek alliances with them?" Under the Articles of Confederation the United States lacked the military force or diplomatic heft to neutralize threats from the Spanish in New Orleans and the British in their forts. The West was where the republic could either triumph or die.[13]

In 1786, John Jay, now the secretary of foreign affairs, therefore began negotiations with the Spanish minister Diego de Gardoqui over American navigation of the Mississippi. Jay tried to strike a deal where the United States would in fact *forgo* navigation rights on the river for twenty-five, even thirty years. In return, the Spanish would mediate between the Americans and the British over the military posts, pledging that the United States would get "justice, by force of arms if it otherwise cannot be promptly secured," and all Spanish ports outside the Caribbean would be opened to American shipping. When word spread of these terms, the northern states—whose interests lay in transatlantic commerce—were delighted. However, southern states, including those who maintained territorial claims in the Mississippi basin, were apoplectic. "Our Gazettes," wrote Richard Henry Lee, "continue to be filled with publications against the Spanish treaty." Fellow Virginian James Monroe wrote scathingly of how "Mr. Jay was desirous of occluding the Mississippi," and South Carolina's Charles Pinckney declared it "most extraordinary that . . . because we have not at present a government sufficiently energetic to assert a national right, it would be honorable to relinquish it."[14]

Many assumed that Jay had been forced to sacrifice access to the Mississippi by the machinations of northeastern merchants and thus would sectional division emerge over foreign policy. Indeed, the Jay controversy even encouraged talk that western settlers might swear loyalty to New Orleans. Writing to Henry Lee in July 1786, George Washington emphasized the need to "keep the settlement of Kentucky in a state of quietness." There were in those parts "ambitious & turbulent spirits" and Washington was fearful that "the present difficulties in their intercourse with the Atlantic States [had] turned their eyes to New Orleans." If their "hope of traffick" with the Spanish port was "cut off by treaty," he predicted they would become "riotous & ungovernable." In the end, Congress made it known they would not ratify any treaty that came from Jay's negotiations. Neither "the Mississippi Question" nor the issue of transatlantic trade with Spain was resolved, and the problems endured. Jay's fruitless negotiations were a painfully clear reminder of American diplomatic weakness and of the dysfunction between Congress and its diverse constituents.[15]

The State of the Union

The quarrel over Jay's negotiations, endemic weakness in the West, the penury of the federal government, and the absence of commercial treaties soon brought the American union to the precipice. John Jay wrote to the people of New York that "almost every national object of every kind, is at this day unprovided for." For Alexander Hamilton, the United States had "reached almost the last stage of national humiliation. There is scarcely anything that can wound the pride or degrade the character of an independent nation which we do not experience." Moreover, the relationship between the government and the states was often nonexistent: when Pennsylvania's leaders debated the merits of abolishing the Bank of North America without first informing Congress, the Philadelphia lawyer Jonathan Dickerson Sergeant declared that "We are not bound by any terms made by Congress—Congress are our creatures." Edmund Randolph of Virginia agreed on the relative powers of the states and the national government. "No judge," he declared, "will say that the confederation is paramount to a State constitution." But what else could be expected when the second Article of Confederation stated that "each state retains its sovereignty, freedom, and independence"? James Madison was all too close to the truth when he decried the Articles as "nothing more than a treaty of amity and commerce and of alliance, between so many independent and Sovereign States."[16]

As each of the Union's problems was rationalized as a problem of national government, there developed consensus that Congress was inadequate to the needs of the nation. In his *Letter from Phocion*, Hamilton wrote that recent history had "exhibited us in the light of a people, destitute of government, on whose engagements of cause no dependence can be placed." Randolph was likewise "persuaded that the confederation was destitute of every energy which a constitution of the United States ought to possess." Congress was especially incompetent to direct the foreign and security policies of the nation. As John Jay wrote, "They may make war, but are not empowered to raise men or money to carry it on. They may make peace, but without power to see the terms of it observed. They may form alliances, but without ability to comply with the stipulations on their part. They may enter into treaties of commerce, but without power to enforce them at home or abroad. They may borrow money, but without having the means of repayment. They may partly regulate commerce, but without power to try or punish [men] for misdemeanors." Jay's exposition reaffirmed what he had written to Jefferson in 1786: "To be respectable abroad it is necessary to be so at Home, and that will not be the Case until our public Faith acquires more Confidence, and our Government more Strength." Hamilton, speaking in 1787, issued a similar warning that "No Government could give us tranquility & happiness at home, which did not possess sufficient stability and strength to make us respectable."[17]

Even those who would eventually oppose the Constitution of 1787 agreed that such national problems could not be solved without constitutional reform. The "Federal Farmer" argued that "our federal system is defective." Melancton Smith, a New York merchant and antislavery campaigner, recognized that "the defects of the Old Confederation needed as little proof as the necessity of a union." William Grayson of Virginia likewise admitted the deficiency of the Articles, writing to Monroe that "the present Confederation is utterly inefficient, and that if it remains much longer in its present State of imbecility we shall be one of the most contemptible Nations on the face of the Earth." George Mason, who famously would refuse to sign his name to the Constitution, "candidly acknowledge[d] the inefficacy of the Confederation."[18]

By 1787 there was widespread demand that American statesmen should improve or replace the Articles of Confederation. Benjamin "Candidus" Austin of Massachusetts wrote that "the PEOPLE of the several States are convinced of the necessity of adopting some Federal Commercial Plan." Mercy Otis Warren, the political confidante and historian of the Revolution, demanded the investiture of all "adequate powers in Congress, for all national purposes." As Delaware's Gunning Bedford put it, the American people had instructed their representatives: "Go, and give additional powers to the confederation—give to it the imposts, regulation of trade, power to collect the taxes, and the means to discharge our foreign and domestic debts."[19]

The Constitution of 1787

In response to the national crisis of government, the Philadelphia Convention—also known as the Federal or Constitutional Convention—

opened formal sessions on May 25, 1787. Presided over by George Washington, the original mission of the Convention was the revision and improvement of the Articles of Confederation. Certain delegates, though, Hamilton and Madison among them, argued from the outset for the creation of an entirely new constitution, a blueprint for which (the "Virginia Plan") had been drafted by Madison. Designing a strong and effective federal union that would not tend toward despotism was a task of immense difficulty. Pierce Butler, a soldier and planter from South Carolina, observed that the United States were "a great Extent of Territory to be under One free Government," with "the manners and modes of thinking of the Inhabitants differing nearly as much as in different Nations of Europe." Devising a constitution to govern such varied interests and to secure "tranquility at Home, and respect from abroad" would be "great points gain'd."[20]

Supporters of a new constitution focused on the foreign and security challenges faced by the United States. "We have seen," wrote Madison, "the necessity of the Union as our bulwark against foreign danger, as the conservator of peace among ourselves, as the guardian of our commerce, . . . as the only substitute for those military establishments which have subverted the liberties of the Old World." To convince the skeptics, Madison argued that a new union would be an improvement, not an innovation. "The powers relating to war and peace armies and fleets, treaties and finance, with the other more considerable powers," he assured them, "are all vested in the existing Congress by the articles of Confederation. The proposed change does not enlarge those powers; it only substitutes a more effectual mode of administering them." Only "the regulation of commerce" would be "a new power," but even this was as "an addition which few oppose, and from which no apprehensions are entertained."[21]

Such improvements were couched in the language of "energy." "Energy in the Executive," it was declared, "is a leading character in the definition of good government. It is essential to the protection of the community against foreign attacks." The new constitution would offer a "frame . . . of a NATIONAL GOVERNMENT adequate to the EXIGENCIES OF GOVERNMENT, and OF THE UNION." Even opponents of a new constitution concurred. George Clinton, the governor of New York, wrote to Hamilton that "the object of both of us is a firm, energetic government." The pseudonymous "Medium" wrote that all could see "that an Energetic Federal Government is essential to our happiness and existence as a nation."[22]

In terms of specific provisions, the Constitution of 1787 made the federal government the exclusive vehicle of foreign policy and the coordinator and director of the Union's security. At the federal level, authority was divided again between the office of an elected executive (the president) and the bicameral United States Congress, wherein power was further split between the Senate and the House of Representatives. The creation of this lawmaking body was a vital improvement upon Congress under the Articles. The former Congress had replaced the British monarchy as an executive power, but it had no legislative authority: under the Articles, the power to make laws and to raise taxes had remained with the states, hence the impotence of Congress itself. Command of the armed forces was then removed from Congress and vested in the president. Unified command would prevent the hesitant confusion which throughout the eighteenth century had infested the civilian boards that controlled the Dutch military. At the Constitutional Convention, Pierce Butler argued strongly for such unity, contending that "a single magistrate" was best placed to represent the many different interests of the nation. "If one man should be appointed," said Butler, "he would be responsible to the whole, and would be impartial to its interests. If three or more should be taken from as many districts, there would be a constant struggle for local advantages. . . . A unity of the Executive would be necessary in order to promote [efficiency]. . . . A plurality of Persons would never do." The president would also shape foreign policy, with American ambassadors reporting directly to him. Other delegates were more suspicious of such a concentration of powers. The presidency was designed with George Washington in mind, but many feared the United States would not produce worthy successors to the Virginian. Where the Americans looked for Cincinnatus (the Roman leader who had retired humbly to his farm), they might find Sulla (the bloodthirsty tyrant who had plunged Rome into civil war). "Where is there a breed of such Dictators," asked Patrick Henry in the Virginia ratifying convention. "Shall we find a set of American Presidents of such a breed? Will the American President come and lay prostrate at the feet of Congress his laurels? I fear there are few men who can be trusted on that head."[23]

Much of Congress's authority over foreign policy was vested in the Senate. As a direct response to southern anger over Jay's Spanish negotiations, a two-thirds majority of senators would be required to ratify treaties. This was a distinct departure from the British system, where treaties were an act of the Crown. It was also a safeguard against corrupt treaties being ratified by corruptible individuals. Even more important, the authority to declare war was defined as a congressional and *not* as an executive power. The stability of the Senate, where members were elected for longer, fixed terms of office, was a further bulwark against volatility and manipulation.

While the federal army would be commanded by the president, it would be created and regulated by Congress, which was given sole power to raise federal forces to protect the nation. The navy would be strictly federal, with the states now forbidden to issue letters of marque, the documents that made lawful privateers out of pirates. The states, however, retained their militias, subject to congressional regulation and presidential calls to service. Authority over judicial matters in foreign affairs was vested in federal courts, which were bound to maintain "the peace of the confederacy." The administration of Indian affairs was also transferred—on parchment— from the states to the federal government, but this would not be completed in practice until the mid-twentieth century.

Ratification

Drafting the Constitution of 1787 was not the same as implementing it. For that to happen, nine of the Union's thirteen states had to ratify the document. This process was devolved to conventions in each state, and in many cases the fight over ratification was heated and acute. In New York, the adopted state of Alexander Hamilton (born on the Caribbean island of Nevis), opposition to the Constitution was fierce. New Yorkers had subjugated the Iroquois; they had imposed profitable tariffs on the trade of New Jersey and Connecticut as it passed through their ports; and many of them were content with the status quo under their governor, George Clinton. Hamilton took up the task of persuading his fellow New Yorkers—and all who might read him—of the need for ratification. Hamilton thus became the driving force behind *The Federalist Papers*, a series of articles and essays that argued in favor of the Constitution. He is thought by modern scholars to have written fifty-one of the eighty-five papers; James Madison, the chief architect of the Constitution, authored twenty-six; and five were contributed by John Jay, whose diplomatic experience made him an authority on foreign affairs and national security.[†] All three wrote under the pseudonym "Publius," an homage to the Roman statesman who in 509 BC had helped to overthrow the last king of Rome and to establish the Roman Republic. Published between October 1787 and August 1788 in New York's *Independent Journal* and the *New York Packet*, the *Federalist Papers* would become the authoritative exposition of the United States Constitution. "Publius" held out the promise of a strong, energetic federal government that could realize the ambitions of American foreign policy: continental expansion, the

---

†The three remaining *Federalist Papers* were cowritten by Hamilton and Madison.

expulsion of the British from the Northwest, and European commercial treaties would all become possible. As a mark of the *Papers'* importance, supporters of the 1787 Constitution started calling themselves "Federalists"; supporters of the existing union under the Articles were labeled by the Federalists as "Anti-Federalists."[24]

One major Federalist argument was the need for unity in the face of sundry national threats. "The Union," wrote Madison in *Federalist* 45, is "essential to the security of the people of America against foreign danger; [it is] essential to their security against contentions and wars among the different States." The dangerous flip side of national unity was "disunionism," which could lead easily to "separate confederacies" forming among the states. There was enough in the recent history of the United States to give purchase to this argument. Rhode Island, for example, had boycotted the Constitutional Convention and was imposing taxes on all *American* traffic that crossed its borders. Maryland and Virginia had bickered over control of the Potomac River, resolving their differences only at the Mount Vernon Conference of 1785. Most seriously, in Shays' Rebellion, four thousand men in Massachusetts had revolted against heavy-handed fiscal policies and perceived corruption.[25] "The late turbulent scenes in Massts.," wrote Madison, "have done inexpressible injury to the republican character in that part of the Un. States." There was even the occasional murmur that Anti-Federalist southerners, still furious at Jay's Spanish talks, would rather secede than commit to the Constitution. Writing to Jefferson's secretary William Short, the magnificently named John Hector St. John de Crèvecoeur calumniated "the partisance [*sic*] of your nefarious & highly Criminal P[atrick] Henry, to form a Confederation of the Southern States."[26]

"Disunionism" also invoked the specter of European powers, which were jealous of American potential and anxious to smother the newborn republic, intervening in domestic disputes. "Alliances will immediately be formed," warned Hamilton, "with different rival & hostile nations of Europe who will foment disturbances among ourselves, and make us parties to all their own quarrels." He warned again that "a firm Union of this country . . . will probably be an increasing object of jealousy to more than one nation of Europe; and . . . enterprises to subvert it will sometimes originate in the intrigues of foreign powers." It was even possible that Britain would send ambassadors to individual states and so make divisive commercial treaties with the states instead of the Union. On that point, the New York jurist William Smith told John Jay that it was not "improbable, after they have established as many Consuls as they think will answer their ends, [that] those gentlemen . . . will be found coming gently forward, with separate proposals to the States or districts where they may respectively reside, for the establishment of a commercial intercourse independent of Federal systems." Sensing his opponents' rhetorical vulnerability, "Publius" stoked fears of civil wars with each side backed by a different European power. "The foreign nation with whom the Southern confederacy might be at war," cautioned Jay, "would be the one with whom the Northern confederacy would be the most desirous of preserving peace and friendship." The Federalists concluded that unity was essential to the security of the Union: "America united," wrote Madison in *Federalist* 41, "with a handful of troops, or without a single soldier, exhibits a more forbidding posture to foreign ambition than America disunited, with a hundred thousand veterans ready for combat." Such unity, they argued, was possible only under the new Constitution.[27]

Yet more than a specific vision of the United States and American foreign policy, the Federalists argued for the *immediate* ratification of the Constitution. They held that a longer process of constitutional reform would imperil the republic. "Every prudent and honest man of whatever party," stated *Federalist* 8, ". . . will not hesitate to part with trivial objections to a Constitution, the rejection of which would in all probability put a final period to the Union." William Pierce, a Georgian delegate to the Constitutional Convention, agreed that "unless we can settle down into some permanent system very shortly, our political schemes will be nothing more than chimeras and disorders." In *Federalist* 85, Madison elaborated on "the jeopardy of successive experiments, in the chimerical pursuit of a perfect plan." In the forty-fourth number, he equated the question of "whether or not a government commensurate to the exigencies of the Union shall be established" to that of "whether the Union itself shall be preserved." Any kind of delay, any "conditional amendments, or a second general Convention . . . [would be] too serious to be hazarded." Ironing out the details would only waste time, since "the general GENIUS of a government is all that can be substantially relied upon for permanent effects." The priority was founding an energetic, effective federal government, *not* perfecting the minutiae by which it was organized. The Federalists thus presented the decision over ratification as a decision over American survival. There was no middle ground: the choice was between "life and death, blessing and cursing," and the Federalists urged the states to "choose life that both thou and thy seed may live." Exploiting the agreement that national challenges were insuperable under the Articles, the Federalists sought to strong-arm the states into ratification.[28]

Though the Federalists branded opposition to the 1787 Constitution as "disunionism," their opponents did not contest the need for a binding union. In fact, the vast majority of them advocated the institution of a stronger federal government that could address the republic's international dilemmas. The Anti-Federalist "Candidus" acknowledged that "Every man must be sensible that a federal system is of the utmost importance to our national prosperity." Anti-Federalists mostly agreed that a renewed federal government was essential to the foreign standing of the United States. The "Federal Farmer" wanted the federal government's powers to "extend exclusively to all foreign concerns, causes arising on the seas to commerce, imports, armies, navies, Indian affairs, peace and war." Such powers "respecting external objects," he wrote, ". . . can be lodged nowhere else, with any propriety, but in this government."[29]

What provoked the sharpest Anti-Federalist dissent was the Federalist demand for *immediate* ratification. For the "Federal Farmer," the pace of ratification mattered not: "Whether we adopt a change, three or nine months hence, can make but little odds." In this sense, Anti-Federalists were not wrong. It is indeed hard to believe, if a second convention was required or if ratification took time, that such delay would have fatally undermined the United States. The Anti-Federalists were also apt to denounce Federalist rhetoric as sensationalist. A New York critic of "Publius" avowed that "All the powers of rhetoric, and arts of description, are employed to paint the condition of this country in the most hideous and frightful colors." Patrick Henry claimed that many of the problems enumerated by the Federalists, such as "no peace—a general cry and alarm in the country—commerce, riches, and wealth vanished," were "new to [him]." Another Anti-Federalist, "Centinel," railed against the "specter that has been raised to terrify and alarm the people out of the exercise of their judgment." He ridiculed "the dread of our splitting into separate confederacies or republic[s], that might become rival powers and consequently liable to mutual wars," arguing that such a "hobgoblin appears to have sprung from the deranged brain of Publius."[30]

Nonetheless, the Constitution of 1787 was ratified and implemented at breakneck speed to the accompaniment of the Federalist drumbeat. Confronted by serious foreign policy and security threats, neither the Federalists nor the required quorum of nine states was prepared to wait. Delaware became the first state to ratify on December 7, 1787, five days before Pennsylvania. The next week, New Jersey followed suit. Georgia became the fourth American state on January 2, 1788 and Connecticut the fifth a week later. With each state that ratified the Constitution, the Anti-Federalists grew weaker: they might have objected to immediate ratification, but they

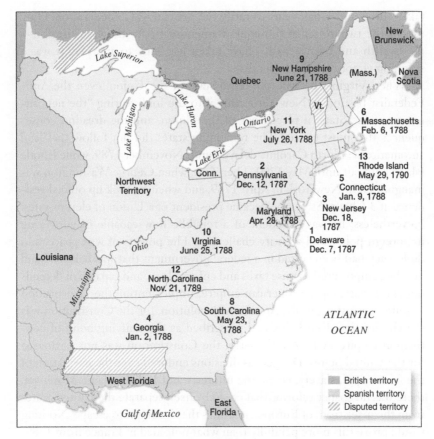

Figure 4.1. The ratification of the 1787 Constitution

were still pro-*Union* and, as the Union re-formed around the 1787 Constitution, it became increasingly difficult to be pro-Union *and* antiratification.

When Massachusetts, the military powerhouse of the Union, ratified in February 1788, the balance swung firmly in favor of the Federalists. Needing federal resolution of territorial disputes with Virginia, two months later Maryland became the seventh American state. The next month, craving federal protection from Spanish-backed Creeks and Cherokees (as well as its own slaves), South Carolina became the eighth. New Hampshire was the critical ninth state. Suffering from its predatory neighbors and facing the prospect of losing towns to the unrecognized but independent republic of Vermont, New Hampshire voted for ratification in June 1788: the United States Constitution was now valid, only 278 days after its proposal in Philadelphia. To put this in context, it had taken three-and-a-half years to ratify the Articles of Confederation. Only two of the twenty-seven subsequent amendments to the Constitution—the twelfth and twenty-sixth—have taken less time to approve. It was a stunning victory for the Federalists.

When Virginia became the tenth state of the Union, even the Anti-Federalist bastion of New York came into the fold, fearing "the new situation of the State, if placed out of the Union, and the dreadful consequences that must ensue." The remaining states did not follow that lead automatically: North Carolina delayed until November 1789, while Rhode Island held out until May 1790. Therefore, when George Washington was inaugurated in New York in April 1789, and when he took up official residence at 3 Cherry Street, he became president of a Union of eleven states. Nevertheless, he was president of a republic now capable of answering its foreign policy and security challenges. The powers of war, peace, and diplomacy had been vested in a federal government that was balanced and durable, empowered to raise taxes and enforce laws, and capable of defending and expanding the American empire. Implementing the Constitution was also the last act of the American Revolution, for the Constitution was the charter that Tom Paine had prescribed as the unifying bond of continental empire in 1776. Of course, the Constitution was not a panacea for the United States: Dangerous divisions endured over the navigation of the Mississippi, slavery, economic interests and Indian affairs. Moreover, there was no "paper reform" that could by itself separate the United States from the maelstrom of European politics that it sought to escape. Nothing would prove this more painfully than what unfolded in France from 1789.

CHAPTER 5

The United States and the French Revolution, 1789–1794

[The French Revolution] was more complete . . . than that of America, and of consequence [it] was attended with greater convulsions . . . because the Americans, satisfied with the code of civil and criminal legislation which they had derived from England, having no corrupt system of finance to reform, no feudal tyrannies, no hereditary distinctions, no privileges of rich and powerful corporations, no system of religious intolerance to destroy, had only to direct their attention to the establishment of new powers to be substituted in the place of those exercised over them by the British.

—Marquis de Condorcet, *The Progress of the Human Mind* (1794)[1]

In the last of the *Federalist Papers*, Alexander Hamilton had written that "a nation without a national government . . . is an awful spectacle." A national government was at last provided for the American nation when the United States Constitution came into force in March 1789. The gradual establishment and expansion of that government would, in time, allow the United States to deal with the dangers it faced. Those dangers were not insignificant. To the north lay British Canada, a constant reminder of the American colonial past. It was also a base from which British military operations could yet be launched. In defiance of the Treaty of Paris, the British were also ensconced in the Northwest, arming and feeding Native Americans who were implacably hostile to the United States. To the south and the southwest, the Spanish held the Floridas and Louisiana and controlled the Mississippi. The Nootka Sound Crisis of 1789, when the British and Spanish clashed in a bay of what is now Vancouver Island, served as further

75

notice that North America was not the exclusive domain of the United States. The British were meanwhile the dominant force in Atlantic commerce, and they still refused to sign trade deals with their former colonists. These problems of commerce and security were the essential business of American statesmen and diplomats in the 1790s. Addressing these problems was made all the more difficult by the greatest political shock of modern history.[2]

The French Revolution

The narrative of the French Revolution is lengthy and complex, but its importance to the history of the United States justifies this digression.[3] If French involvement in the American Revolutionary War was essential to American independence, it was an equally important cause of the French Revolution. When Vergennes and Louis XVI first conspired to abet the American rebels, when they funneled funds through Beaumarchais, the French state was already in serious financial trouble. The cost of fighting the Seven Years' War and an antiquated fiscal system had combined to mire the Bourbon monarchy in debt. Turgot, the minister of finance, had argued strenuously against French intervention on grounds of expense, but he was ignored and so became the Cassandra of the French Revolution. The cost of supplying the Americans was extraordinary. Even before the alliance of 1778, some five million livres had been smuggled to the rebels. When the Expédition Particulière was launched under Rochambeau, when ships and armies were sent across the Atlantic, costs spiraled further: in 1781, the French exchequer was forced to stop domestic payments. The cost of the war was then felt more keenly when, at the Battle of the Saints off Dominica, millions of livres were lost to the seabed. By 1783, the debts of the French crown totaled more than 520 million livres.

Jacques Necker, a Genevan Protestant, had been appointed director general of the crown's finances in 1777. To balance the books of his profligate master, he had implemented reforms of the *taille* land tax and the *vingtième* (one-twentieth) income tax. Yet Necker's policies won him powerful enemies, and he was forced from office in 1781. The timing could not have been worse. In the following years, terrible winters and ruined harvests meant that revenue raised from the land—the traditional source of French fiscal power—fell dramatically, while successive years of hardship contributed to the simmering discontent of the French people. In 1787, Necker's successor, the Vicomte de Calonne, tried to instigate another program of financial reform, but the Parlement of Paris—the body that usually ratified the king's edicts into law—refused to cooperate. Calonne then tried to push a universal land tax through the Assembly of Notables, but he too was dismissed from his position. Over the next two years, the pattern repeated: attempts to reform, to raise taxes, and to procure loans met with failure; debts incurred at high rates of interest went unpaid; and by early 1789 the French monarchy, the defining political institution of Europe, was effectively bankrupt.

On January 24, 1789, Louis XVI looked to his last resort. He summoned the Estates-General that was the nearest French equivalent to the British Parliament. The Estates-General assembly that represented the estates of the French polity: the clergy (the first), the nobility (the second), and the commons (the third). On May 5, with the Third Estate's representation doubled as a means of popular appeasement, the Estates met for the first time since 1614. Yet instead of focusing on the Crown's urgent fiscal problems, the delegates spent weeks debating the procedure for voting: Would each Estate have one vote, in which case the clergy and nobility could outvote the commons? Or would each delegate have one vote, in which case the commons could outvote the clergy and nobility? The funereal pace of proceedings quickened only in June, when the Commons broke with the other two and declared itself to be the National Assembly. Louis XVI was incensed. Having tried but failed to restore the Estates as they were, the King closed the Salle des Etats where the Assembly was meeting. The Assembly responded by convening nearby in a real—that is, royal—tennis court.* Here, on June 20, 1789, the Tennis Court Oath was sworn, by which the Assembly vowed "to God and the *Patrie* never to be separated until we have formed a solid and equitable Constitution, as our constituents have asked us to." Though growing numbers of clergymen and noblemen would back the Assembly, and though messages of support poured in from the country, troops in the pay of the Crown were gathering ominously around Paris.[4]

Three days later, Louis XVI addressed the Assembly in the church of his namesake saint and ordered the deputies to disperse: "I command you, Messieurs, to adjourn directly." The noblemen and clergymen obeyed, but the representatives of the people refused. When the king and his entourage departed, the assemblymen were again ordered to break up, but no ground was given. Instead, the Comte de Mirabeau delivered his famous rejoinder, "Go tell those who have sent you that we are here by the will of the people and that we will not be dispersed except at the point of bayonets." All the

---

*Real tennis is the original, indoor racquet sport from which lawn tennis developed.

while, troops were continuing to arrive in Paris and when, on July 9, the Assembly requested their removal, the king refused: battle lines had been drawn. The trigger was pulled two days later when the reappointed Necker, now a symbol to reformers of good faith within the royal ministry, was dismissed for the second time. On July 12, the radical journalist Camille Desmoulins mounted a table outside the Café du Foy near the Palais-Royal, announcing Necker's dismissal to a smattering of dissidents. He issued an impassioned call to action: "To arms, to arms, and let us all take a green cockade [a knot of ribbons worn on hats], the color of hope!" The next day, heeding Desmoulins and fearing attack from the troops under royal command, the Assembly formed its own militia, the National Guard.[5]

There now began a race for arms and ammunition across Paris. On the morning of July 14, the rebellious militia went first to the Hôtel des Invalides, the military hospital where tens of thousands of muskets had been stored. They took the muskets, but the gunpowder—about thirty thousand pounds of it—had been moved to the Bastille, the medieval fortress that now served as a royal prison and the preeminent symbol of Bourbon power over Paris. From midmorning, a crowd swelled outside the prison, demanding the surrender of its garrison. Fighting broke out, the crowd became a mob, the courtyard was stormed, and shots were fired. By late afternoon, the Bastille's governor, Bernard-Réné de Launay, offered terms of surrender; they were rejected, but the governor capitulated anyway. As the *vanqueurs* rushed the prison and celebrated their triumph, Launay was pummeled by the rebellious crowd. "Enough," he cried. "Let me die!" The mob debated tying the governor to a horse and dragging him over the cobbled streets of Paris, but they settled on knives, bayonets, and pistols. The Bastille had held only seven prisoners: four forgers, two lunatics, and an aristocratic deviant (*not* the Marquis de Sade, who had been moved out some weeks earlier). This was not, therefore, a major military victory, but capturing this royal prison would come to possess overwhelming symbolism. July 14, now celebrated as Bastille Day, is justly remembered as the pivotal date of the Revolution.[6]

The Storming of the Bastille set in train a series of momentous events across the summer of 1789. The Marquis de Lafayette, the veteran of the American Revolutionary War, was appointed commander of the National Guard; Necker was recalled once more, and he removed royal troops from the capital; Desmoulins called for the establishment of a republic, and he began to justify violence in pursuit of it; outside Paris the peasantry began to revolt against the baronial system that had oppressed them for centuries. The first of the Assembly's August Decrees abolished feudalism, and the essential document of the Revolution, the Declaration of the Rights of Man and of the Citizen, was adopted on August 26. "Ignorance, forgetfulness or contempt of the rights of man" were damned as "the only causes of public misfortunes and the corruption of Governments," and those same rights were proclaimed as "natural, unalienable, and sacred." The language was unmistakable.[7]

The political objective of most revolutionaries was not yet the abolition of the monarchy, but the establishment of a constitutional monarchy retaining Louis XVI as the head of a weak executive branch. However, urged on by the queen, the king would not submit to every demand of the Assembly, resisting stoutly but futilely against the subjugation of the French Catholic Church to the legislature. He therefore conspired with foreign monarchies, notably with the queen's Austrian family, to undo the Revolution. Forced from Versailles, the French royal family was by June 1791 prepared to flee France altogether, designing to meet with royalist exiles and Austrian forces on the Alpine border. The planned escape failed dramatically. The king and all who traveled with him were captured close to Varennes, a town some 140 miles east of Paris, and they were returned to the Tuileries Palace in Paris. Despite all this, the French retained their desire for a constitutional monarchy: in July, the Assembly declared the king to be inviolable and Louis XVI was reinstated; in September, the Constitution of 1791 was accepted by the king.

American Reaction

At first, the French Revolution was perceived in the United States as a flattering imitation of its American precedent, as the realization of American principles. An American, after all, had helped to refine and define the French revolutionary fervor: Thomas Jefferson, the American minister in Paris, had helped to draft the Declaration of the Rights of Man. The Marquis de Lafayette even sent the key to the Bastille, "that fortress of despotism," to George Washington, writing that it was "a tribute Which I owe as A Son to My Adoptive father, as an aid de Camp to My General, as a Missionary of liberty to its patriarch." The conveyance of the key was entrusted to Tom Paine, who marveled that "the principles of America [had] opened the Bastille." Most American observers therefore professed sympathy for the French republican aspirations, which, they hoped, would continue to be peaceful.[8]

This is not to say that France had risen above American suspicion. Jefferson, who left Paris in September 1789, remained extremely wary of

French imperial ambitions in the New World. He warned William Short, the American charge d'affaires whom he left behind in Paris, of a French "project of again engaging . . . in a colony upon our continent" and he noted that the Comte de Moustier, the recent French minister to America, had "directed his views to some of the country on the Mississippi, and obtained and communicated a good deal of matter on the subject to his court." Jefferson claimed that Moustier had plans for the economic entanglement of the Spaniards in the Mississippi Delta, that he had seen "the immediate advantage of selling some yards of French cloths and silks to the inhabitants of New Orleans." Jefferson was nonetheless hopeful that French imperialist ambitions in North America were on the wane: "The National Assembly," he reasoned, "has constitutionally excluded conquest from the objects of their government."[9]

Yet while the attention of American statesmen was drawn to France, the French Revolution was not yet the defining issue in American politics. What mattered more, at least until 1792, was the development of the federal government. Given the precarious diplomatic situation of the United States, it was fitting for the new government's first department to be that of Foreign Affairs. Led by John Jay, who had been secretary for foreign affairs under the Congress, it was soon renamed the Department of State; Jefferson became its first secretary. State was followed by the Department of War. Henry Knox, the bookseller who had driven the "noble train of artillery" from Fort Ticonderoga to Boston, had been secretary of war under the Congress and he continued in this role under Washington. The task before Knox was enormous: he had to transform the seven hundred remaining Continental soldiers, stationed in frontier garrisons, into a formidable federal army. September 1789 then saw the passage of the Judiciary Act, which established the federal court system, and the creation of the Department of the Treasury, which would be led by Alexander Hamilton.[10]

As secretary of the treasury, Hamilton became one of the most influential American statesmen never to serve as president and one of the most important men of his era of any nation. Indeed, a French diplomat would later remark that "if I were forced to decide among [Napoleon, Charles James Fox, and Hamilton], I would give without hesitation the first place to Hamilton." His influence derives from the fiscal policies that he advocated, policies that supported the whole machinery of the American federal government, policies that were articulated in three critical documents submitted to Congress: The *First Report on Public Credit* (January 1790), the *Second Report on Credit* (December 1790), and the *Report on the Subject of Manufactures* (December 1791). Altogether, the Hamiltonian system had seven main goals. The first three focused on debt and here Hamilton desired the United States to honor international debts, to redeem governmental debts to domestic creditors, and to assume state debts into the national debt. The next concerned a fiscal system that could finance the federal government. Two more focused on banking (to charter a national bank) and monetary policy (to establish a national mint) and, lastly, Hamilton wanted to reduce American dependence on imports by encouraging domestic manufacturing.

Hamilton thus created the blueprint for the early American economy. Without executing his plans, the United States could not have built its government, paid its bills, or obtained international credit. The Hamiltonian vision also had serious implications for American foreign policy, not least because the crux of the plan was taxation. With the direct taxation of American citizens politically painful, and export duties outlawed by the Constitution, the federal government instead relied on revenue generated by tariffs. Hamilton and his supporters, who assumed the name of "Federalists," therefore sought amicable relations with Great Britain, the commercial leviathan of the Atlantic whose trade could best fill the national coffers. Opponents of Hamilton's system coalesced around Jefferson and James Madison. These men and their followers called themselves "Republicans," claiming that there was little difference between Hamiltonian economics and the corrupt British system that had provoked the Revolution.[11]

The Whiskey Rebellion and Post Office

Hamilton's policies even threatened another war over taxation. In March 1791, to reduce the national debt, a so-called whiskey tax—propounded as a tax on luxury and "sin"—was laid upon distilled spirits. In the Trans-Appalachian West, transporting grain by land or by river was onerous and expensive. Distilling grain into whiskey was therefore practical, profitable, and immensely popular; in more distant regions where cash was scarce, whiskey even served as currency. There was also a salutary purpose to the spirit, for adding whiskey to unsanitized water made the latter both palatable and, as modern science has proved, safer. Thus, when the federal government introduced the excise on whiskey, many westerners damned it as a detestable "internal" tax imposed upon them by an aloof federal government that had done little to secure American access to the Mississippi or to protect westerners from British-armed Native Americans. The whiskey tax was for many western Americans a call to arms.[12]

Resistance mounted in the western regions of the Appalachian states. In

Kentucky and the western part of North Carolina, nobody could be found to impose the tax, but the violence was worst in southwestern Pennsylvania. An assembly of the discontented was convened in Pittsburgh in September 1791 and petitions were duly dispatched to the Pennsylvania Assembly and the House of Representatives. By May 1792, the tax was reduced by a penny per gallon, but violent protest had broken out long before. Tax collectors were being assaulted, tarred and feathered, and, by the time that a second whiskey-tax convention had been called in August 1792, the radical Mingo Creek Association was erecting liberty poles, directing local militias, and evicting the federal excise collector for western Pennsylvania, John Neville, from his premises in Pittsburgh. The pseudonymous "Tom the Tinker" distributed threatening notes to those who dared to enforce or pay the tax. By late 1793, effigies of tax collectors were burning throughout the Trans-Appalachian West. As a modern president of the United States quipped, "The nation which had fought a revolution against taxation without representation discovered that some of its citizens were not much happier about taxation *with* representation."[13]

In summer 1794, resistance became rebellion. William Rawle, the district attorney for Pennsylvania, had issued writs to noncompliant distillers; in mid-July, John Neville and Federal Marshal David Lenox were delivering those writs when they were fired upon at the farm of Oliver Miller. Neville, a brevet brigadier general during the Revolutionary War, retreated to his home at Bower Hill, which was surrounded the next day by Mingo Creek militiamen. They demanded that Lenox, whom they mistakenly believed to be inside, should surrender himself. A standoff ensued, but a nervous hand shot from the house, killing Miller. The militiamen fell back, regrouped, and came again the next day, but this time with six hundred men commanded by Major James McFarlane. Neville too had called for reinforcements and, at the ensuing Battle of Bower Hill, eleven United States soldiers fought the Mingo Creek men, killing McFarlane and at least one other as Neville's property was burned to the ground. McFarlane's "murder" only served to energize resistance to the whiskey tax; seven thousand protestors soon gathered east of Pittsburgh at Braddock's Field.

Talk abounded of secession from the Union, of arson and looting, but the mediation of Hugh Henry Brackenridge limited the mob to marching through Pittsburgh. Albert Gallatin, a Genevan émigré, who had briefly served as US Senator until unseated because he had not been long enough a citizen, urged further reconciliation upon the crowds but within weeks George Washington ordered the rebels to disperse and called out the militia of the neighboring states. When negotiation failed completely,

Washington himself—intent on demonstrating the authority of the federal government—rode forth at the head of thirteen thousand federalized militiamen.† Though opponents of the administration derided Washington's force as the "Watermelon Army," the very approach of the federal force caused the Rebellion to collapse. The tax on whiskey remained in place until 1801, enduring as a lightning rod for political dissent. It was out of such differences on fiscal and federal policy, not yet in attitudes toward foreign relations, that the First Party System evolved. Opponents of Hamilton's policies, headed by Jefferson and Madison, called themselves "Republicans," to claim that their opponents were deferential to Hamilton's and perhaps Washington's monarchical ambitions. Hamilton and his supporters then called themselves "Federalists," to indicate that their Republican opponents threatened the new Constitution and the Union it had remodeled.

Another major but often overlooked development of the period was the establishment of the United States Post Office. Its transportation of heavily subsidized newspapers and political intelligence was an integral means not only of binding the disparate states into an American nation but of creating an informed republic that might, in the best spirit of republicanism, keep the federal government honest and accountable. Describing "the good sense of the people" as "the best army," Jefferson had written in 1787 to fellow Virginian Edward Carrington, responding to Shays' Rebellion, that "the way to prevent these irregular interpositions of the people is to give them full information of their affairs thro' the channel of the public papers, and to contrive that those papers should penetrate the whole mass of the people." An informed populace, Jefferson continued, was vital to the United States: "The basis of our government being the opinion of the people, the very first object should be to keep that [opinion] right; and were it left to me to decide whether we should have a government without newspapers, or newspapers without a government, I should not hesitate a moment to prefer the latter."[14]

Such were the perceived benefits of the press that, in his Fifth Annual Message to Congress in 1793, Washington recommended that newspapers should be freed from all postal charges. Conflating such charges with a dreaded three-letter word, the president urged "a repeal of the *tax* on the transportation of public prints." For Washington, there was nothing

---

†This is one of only two occasions on which the president has also been commander-in-chief in the field, the second coming in 1862 when Lincoln led an expedition against the rebel stronghold of Norfolk, Virginia. A prohibition on the president taking the field in person had been proposed in the Constitutional Convention, but it was ultimately rejected.

so beneficial to the federal government "as the affections of the people, guided by an enlightened policy," but policy could not be understood by the people without "a faithful representation of public proceedings, diffused without restraint throughout the United States." The previous year, the House of Representatives had confirmed its own commitment to the Post Office. "The operation of the law establishing the post office, as it relates to the transmission of newspapers," the House resolved, "will merit our particular inquiry and attention, the circulation of political intelligence through these vehicles being justly reckoned among the surest means of preventing the degeneracy of a free government, as well as of recommending every salutary public measure to the confidence and cooperation of all virtuous citizens." The Constitution had provided for an effective federal government; the Hamiltonian system now financed that government; and the work of the Post Office would allow that government to be scrutinized by a virtuous citizenry spread over half a continent. The American republic was now in operation; across the Atlantic, a new republic, with its own republican empire, was being founded.[15]

Revolution Revisited

In April 1792, accusing the Habsburgs of harboring aristocratic French refugees, the National Assembly declared war on the Austrian Empire. "The Battle Hymn of the Army of the Rhine," better known as "La Marseillaise," was composed in the same week that French forces invaded the Austrian Netherlands (present-day Belgium). The song is more memorable than the invasion, which was a farce: French soldiers buckled at the first sight of the Austrian positions and fled, and one French general was killed by his own troops. Such was the calamity that, when the Austro-Prussian Coalition launched its retaliatory invasion of France in July, the Assembly declared that the fatherland was in danger ("La patrie en Danger"). That month also witnessed the issue of the Brunswick Manifesto. A month earlier, an armed mob had stormed the Tuileries and berated Louis XVI as "Monsieur Veto." In response, the duke of the German state of Brunswick, a leader of the Coalition and the brother-in-law of George III, declared that the Coalition would restore the French monarchy to full authority and punish anyone found to have harmed the Bourbon family. The revolutionaries in Paris took the Brunswick Manifesto as proof that Louis XVI was conspiring with foreign powers. They were not wrong: the king had approved the Manifesto by means of a secret correspondence. In August, then, the Tuileries were stormed again and Louis XVI and his family were arrested and taken into custody. In September, the tide of the war began to turn. Despite losing many of their most experienced officers to voluntary exile and ideological purges, the French won their greatest military victory so far, repelling Prussian and Austrian armies at Valmy in northeastern France. Two days later, on September 22, the newly constituted and newly emboldened National Convention abolished the French monarchy and proclaimed the French Republic.

The trial of Louis Capet, as the former king was now called, began in December 1792 and lasted until the third week of January 1793. Although Tom Paine, who had contrived to be elected deputy despite knowing no French, argued for Louis's exile to the United States, where he might undergo ideological rehabilitation, the sentence of death was passed and the guillotine was erected on what is now the Place de la Concorde. On the cold morning of January 21, Louis spoke from the scaffolding to a crowd of twenty thousand people. He proclaimed his innocence and prayed that "the blood you are about to shed may never be required of France." Louis was spared none of the guillotine's indignity. His hair was cut roughly, a drumroll drowned out his final words, and when the blade fell his severed head was lifted from the basket and brandished by the executioner. News of the regicide shocked Americans, no matter their politics: after all, Louis XVI had taken France to war for American independence.[16]

Developments in France were characterized increasingly by judicial violence and this, more than France's war, became the divisive factor in American party politics. Oftentimes, the carnage in France was discounted by many Republicans, or at least forgiven as an evil necessity: "My own affections," wrote Jefferson, "have been deeply wounded by some of the martyrs to this cause, but rather than it should have failed, I would have seen half the earth desolated." In contrast, Alexander Hamilton and the Federalists reacted to the mayhem with horror. Hamilton later urged all Americans to reject Jacobinism entirely, so that foreign powers would not perceive his countrymen as "a people whose best passions have been misled and whose best qualities have been perverted from their true aim by headlong fanatical and designing leaders." The Jacobins, he charged, were leading the French "to the perpetration of acts from which humanity shrinks—to the commission of outrages over which the eye of reason weeps—to the profession and practice of principles which tend to shake the foundation of morality—to dissolve the social bonds—to disturb the peace of mankind."[17]

The peace of mankind was further disturbed in February 1793 when the French declared war upon Great Britain and the Dutch. The War of the First Coalition, the first of the French Revolutionary Wars, was now in full swing and it became the topic du jour in the United States. John Marshall recounted that "a great majority of the American people deemed it criminal to remain unconcerned spectators of [the] conflict between their ancient enemy and republican France." George Washington, now in his second term as president, recognized that "the posture of affairs in Europe" placed his government in "a delicate situation." He expressed to Hamilton his "anxious desire to keep this Country in Peace" and his personal need for "circumspect conduct." Republican opinion, however, was markedly pro-French. An interested "CITIZEN" wrote to Washington that "a very large majority of the citizens of the United States are warmly interested in the success of the French Revolution." Marshall later noted that "disregarding totally the circumstances which led to the rupture . . . and disregarding equally the fact that actual hostilities were first commenced by France, the war was confidently and generally pronounced a war of aggression on the part of Great Britain." The British were alleged to have made war "with the sole purpose of imposing a monarchical government on the French." Federalists who offered dissenting opinions were "held up as objects of public detestation; and were calumniated as the tools of Britain, and the satellites of despotism."[18]

In spite of their goodwill toward the French Republic, American leaders strove *not* to ally themselves with the French or to enter the war. It remained "indispensably necessary to prevent the nation from inconsiderably precipitating itself into calamities," since war would be disastrous for the federal fiscal system: only so long as the United States was neutral could it trade with both France and Great Britain. To quiet any argument for intervention, George Washington issued a proclamation of neutrality in May 1793. Observing that "a state of war exists between Austria, Prussia, Sardinia, Great Britain, and the Netherlands on the one part, and France on the other," Washington proclaimed "the duty and interest of the United States . . . [to] adopt a conduct friendly and impartial toward the [warring] powers." Washington further warned "our citizens to avoid all acts which may in any manner tend to [go against] this position." Alexander Hamilton, writing as "Pacificus," reinforced the importance of peaceful neutrality, contending that "foreign influence is truly the GRECIAN HORSE to a republic." Americans, he argued, could "not be too careful to exclude its entrance. Nor ought we to imagine, that it can only make its appearance in the gross form of direct bribery. It is then most dangerous, when it comes under the patronage of our passions, under the auspices of national prejudice and partiality." The American commitment to neutrality, however, would soon be sorely tested.[19]

Figure 5.1. *Edmond Charles Genet* (1784) by Adolf Wertmuller. Bequest of Nancy Fuller Genet, Albany Institute, New York.

Citizen Genet

In the spring of 1793, American opinions on foreign policy usually fell into one of three camps. Federalists prized commercial relations with Great Britain; Republicans sympathized with the French revolutionaries but did not want to activate the military alliance of 1778; and Washington, a host in himself, sought to maintain American neutrality. Into this morass came the Frenchman Edmond-Charles Genet. Initially a translator within the French foreign ministry, Genet was a career diplomat whose first major appointment was chargé d'affaires to the French legation at St. Petersburg. His fervor for the Revolution at home, though, translated into contempt for the Tsarist court of Catherine the Great, who soon declared him persona non grata. Genet's career was rescued by the ascent in Paris of his political patrons, the Girondins, a faction that preached foreign war as a means of furthering the Revolution at home. They soon appointed Genet as French minister to the United States, and he arrived at Charleston in April 1793.

Genet's "official" objectives were to obtain credit to finance the war against Britain and to secure the repayment of debts incurred during the American Revolution. He was also instructed to improve diplomatic relations between the countries: "The letters [that Genet] brought to the executive of the United States, and his instructions, which he occasionally communicated, were, in a high degree, flattering to the nation, and decently respectful to the government." In reality, Genet's plans were more extensive, more intriguing, for he "was also furnished with private instructions, which . . . indicate[d] that, if the American executive should not be found sufficiently compliant with the views of France, the resolution had been taken to employ with the people of the United States the same policy which was so successfully used with those of Europe." This meant that Genet, who activated a secret military commission during his trip, had been ordered to compromise American neutrality, to cultivate the United States as a military ally, and to resurrect French dreams of a North American empire.[20]

The minor part of these plans involved war at sea. Genet had been ordered to seduce American sailors to serve as privateers in the French cause, something with which the governor of South Carolina, William Moultrie, was happy to help. Four ships were commissioned on behalf of the French: the *Républicaine*, the *Anti-George*, the *Sans-Culotte*, and the *Citizen Genet*. On land, Genet's machinations were more ambitious: he aimed to carve out a French puppet republic from the American West and to instigate revolution in Spanish-held, formerly French, Louisiana. Ousting the Dons from the Mississippi was already a popular program among settlers in the American West, and so Genet sent his agent, André Michaux, to assess the nebulous plans of the soldier George Rogers Clark. A noted botanist, Michaux used his scientific credentials as cover for the mission. Thomas Jefferson was even asked to write a letter of recommendation that Michaux might present to Isaac Shelby, the governor of Kentucky. Compelled by an enduring interest in the expansion of the American empire, Jefferson obliged: if the French could disturb the Spanish grip on the Mississippi, he was ready to help. Yet Jefferson also had to maintain a public commitment to American neutrality, so at the same time he warned that any Americans assisting Genet in his maneuvers against Spain would "assuredly be hung if they commenced hostilities against a nation at peace with the United States." Being a neutral imperialist was not straightforward.[21]

Genet and his masters could also have exploited discontent in British Canada. The French-speaking Canadiens were growing restless and, with their interest piqued by the ongoing revolution in France, they were supposedly reconsidering allegiance to Great Britain. The *Vermont Gazette* reported in March 1793 that "republican principles [were] prevalent in that province." In Canada, "revolution societies [were] formed and [held] frequent meetings, and the decrease of monarchical folly and vassalage [had] become conspicuous in the complexion of their public papers." News of the French Revolution was "eagerly sought" and "the Rights of Man [were] investigated with avidity." The *Gazette* predicted only ruin for the remainder of Britain's North American empire: "It appears highly probable," it declared, "that the extensive province of Canada will, at an early period, add one to the number of independent free republics to grace the western hemisphere."[22]

The Frenchman who called himself "Citizen" Genet was received with profuse enthusiasm by the American public. Having landed at Charleston, he was lauded during his festive progress to Philadelphia, his very presence encouraging the growth of Democratic-Republican Societies, organizations that railed against the perceived "fatal imitation here of the corrupt policy of trans-Atlantic monarchy and aristocracy." Yet as the enthusiasm for these Societies grew more boisterous, and as suspicions about Genet's mission grew stronger, there developed among many fierce hostility toward both the Frenchman and the Societies. George Washington, writing to his former aide-de-camp Burgess Ball, was moved to condemn the Societies as hotbeds of Francophile treason. Members of the Societies were damned as "Incendiaries of public peace & order" and the president lambasted their "attempts to spread their nefarious doctrines, with a view to poison & discontent the minds of the people against the government." There was nothing more "absurd—more arrogant—or more pernicious to the peace of Society" than for these organizations to meet "under the shade of Night in a conclave," and then to disseminate claims that federal laws were "pregnant of mischief, & that all who vote contrary to their dogmas are actuated by selfish motives, or under foreign influence; nay, are pronounced traitors to their Country." For Washington, the Democratic-Republican Societies were even the fount of the Whiskey Rebellion: "The Insurrection in the Western counties of this State," he claimed, was "the first *ripe fruit* of the Democratic Societies." Blame for the turmoil was laid squarely at the door of Genet, who was accused of instituting the Societies "for the express purpose of dissention, and to draw a line between the people & the government, after he found the Officers of the latter would not yield to the hostile measures in which he wanted to embroil this Country." When Washington's condemnation was published in milder terms in his 1794 message to Congress, the Societies quickly disappeared into obscurity.[23]

Genet's star waned quickly. By August 1793, only three months after his arrival in Philadelphia, his meddling had become intolerable to Washington and his cabinet. The recent experience of the Dutch Republic had provided Americans with a salutary lesson about the consequences of infiltration by French agents. Moreover, Genet's intrigues threatened to compromise the United States' dearly held neutrality toward Europe. Fearing that further toleration of the French ambassador might provoke war with either Britain or Spain, Washington demanded that the Convention recall its agent. Jefferson, despite his sympathy for the French, agreed in full. He wrote to James Madison that "We have decided unanimously to require the recall of Genet. He will sink the republican interest if they do not abandon him." The Jacobin Montagnard faction, which had overthrown Genet's Girondins, consented to recall the French emissary. They sent his successor, Jean Fauchet, to the United States with the remit of arresting Genet and returning him to Paris for trial, but Washington, fully aware that such a return would conclude at the guillotine, took pity and granted asylum to Genet. The Frenchman stayed in the United States, marrying the daughter of George Clinton, and he died a gentleman farmer in the Hudson Valley.[24]

The United States escaped potential disaster with the Genet Affair, but its consequences were substantial. On March 24, 1794, Washington warned anyone who aspired to take up Genet's commissions—with respect to Spanish Louisiana—of the dire fate that would befall them. The president proclaimed that he had "received information that certain persons, in violation of the laws, have presumed, under color of a foreign authority, to enlist citizens of the United States and others within the State of Kentucky." The purpose of this conspiracy was to invade and plunder "the territories of a nation at peace with the said United States." Washington counseled anyone "not authorized by the laws, against enlisting any citizen or citizens of the United States, or levying troops, or assembling any persons within the United States for the purposes aforesaid, or proceeding in any manner to the execution thereof, as they will answer for the same at their peril." The proclamation was followed by the Neutrality Act, which stipulated that "If any person shall within the territory of the United States begin or set on foot or provide or prepare the means for any military expedition or enterprise . . . against the territory or dominions of any foreign prince or state of whom the United States was at peace, that person would be guilty of a misdemeanor."

During this period of constant international conflict, the effects of which threatened to drag the United States into Europe's wars, American statesmen sought not only to maintain neutrality but also to create a strong national government that could resist foreign intrigue. By implementing the Constitution and building this government, the republic had addressed a problem that had crippled the United States in the 1780s: the inability to make and enforce treaties. The United States was now a respectable diplomatic partner and, in the mid-1790s, its diplomats and its generals went to work.[25]

CHAPTER 6

Three Treaties

If we can avoid war for ten or twelve years more, we shall then have
acquired a maturity which will make it no more than a common
calamity and will authorize us on our national discussions to take
a higher and more imposing tone. . . . Should we be able to escape
the storm which at this juncture agitates Europe, our disputes
with Great Britain terminated, we may hope to postpone war to a
distant period.

—Alexander Hamilton, July 1795[1]

While American statesmen resisted French intrigue, they were confronted
with another series of international problems. Two of them involved Great
Britain, and the first was commercial. As we have seen, the Treaty of Paris
had contained no provisions for encouraging trade between the United
States and Great Britain, and British opinion remained steadfastly in favor
of discriminating against American merchants. In 1787, Matthew Montagu, the MP for the rotten Cornwall borough of Bossiney, defended the
government's decision to negotiate a trade deal with the French but *not*
with the Americans: "In the present state of prejudice and animosity on
the part of America," Montagu told Parliament, and "from late hostility
and unexpired rancor, it was not so easy for Ministers to negotiate [with] a
nation so alienated from its mother country." More importantly, Montagu
believed that an American treaty was unnecessary, since the structure of
the Americans' economy would eventually bring them to heel. The "silent
operation of time," he explained, would bring the colonists back to the
British market, which "could best supply her wants, and give the most valuable equivalent for her produce." When that happened, the British manufacturers who had "long experience in working for the American consump-

tion" and who had "such a momentum in the employment of their capital to that purpose" would "bear down all opposition." Commercial primacy and existent patterns of trade would perpetuate British supremacy, so there was no incentive for London to concede anything to the Americans.[2]

Restricted access to British domestic and colonial markets was cause for serious American concern. As Montagu pointed out, the economy of the United States had been geared since the colonial period to supply Great Britain with tobacco, cotton, fish, furs, and lumber. Without a trade deal, and subject to the same British tariffs as all foreign nations, Americans were marginalized in their primary market. When the British would not relax their restrictions, some Americans called for retaliation, to be implemented through the first substantive legislation of the new federal government, the 1789 Tariff Act. Steered through Congress by James Madison, the Act aimed "for the support of government, for the discharge of the debts of the United States, and the encouragement and protection of manufactures." Accordingly, "duties [would] be laid on goods, wares, and merchandise." The tariff would be universal, applicable to all imports into the United States, but during the debate on the bill Madison argued for higher, discriminatory duties on British goods. This, he hoped, would encourage Great Britain to open at least its Caribbean ports to American merchants. It was an ill-conceived plan: discrimination might have reduced British exports to the United States, but it would not weaken Britain generally. Madison's proposals were also resisted by Alexander Hamilton, who needed as much taxable trade as possible to bolster the federal fiscal system with the revenues therefrom.

Commercial isolation was compounded by tension on the high seas. At first, the outbreak of the French Revolutionary Wars had boosted American trade with Europe. Flying the flag of a neutral nation, American ships were protected by international law from the warring navies and became a vital source of supplies to *both* sides. The British, however, eager to starve their enemy, wanted to stop the French trading with the Americans. They also had an eye on the long term balance of power, and so the Royal Navy would not permit the unfettered development of the American commercial marine. The British therefore began seizing goods bound for France from American ships, citing as authority the arcane maritime law of the old Kingdom of Aragon, the Consolato de Mare, which rendered enemy goods on neutral ships as fair prey or "lawful prize." This British rapacity stood in painful conflict with developing international principles that "free ships" made "free goods," and that enemy goods on neutral ships should be immune from seizure since they were "covered" by a neutral flag.

Tension at sea was aggravated in June 1793 when an Order in Council expanded the British definition of contraband. Now, the Royal Navy was authorized "to stop and detain all [American] vessels loaded altogether in part with corn, flour, or meal, bound to any port in France, or any port occupied by the armies of France." In November, another order in council extended the British blockade to the French West Indies, thereby subjecting American ships in the Caribbean to the same depredations. Again, the Americans threatened retaliation, and Representative Jonathan Drayton of New Jersey proposed sequestering British debts as compensation for the marine seizures. Yet, in early 1794, Americans had neither friendly commercial relations with Britain nor the means of defending their ships at sea.

The Indians, the British, and the Northwest

Even more serious was the situation in the American Northwest. The Treaty of Paris had stipulated that the British should evacuate their military posts in the region, but the redcoats, clinging to the excuse that the United States would not honor prewar debts or protect loyalists, had not budged. There was also a strategic rationale behind this British obstinacy, for by maintaining their posts they could not only keep watch on a rival empire but also sustain Native American alliances that could be reactivated in the event of another war with the United States. Some British commanders even felt a duty of care to indigenous allies who had been betrayed by the diplomats at Paris. The Earl of Carlisle, who had led that ill-fated peace commission of 1778, regarded the Treaty of Paris as nothing better than the repudiation of Britain's Native American allies. "Twenty-five nations of Indians," he told the House of Lords, had been "made over to the United States." This had happened without "the smallest apparent advantage resulting to Great Britain" and, worse, without "that solitary stipulation which our honor should have made us insist upon, and have demanded with unshaken firmness: a place of refuge for those miserable persons before alluded to, some port, some haven, for those shattered barks to have been laid up in quiet."[3]

Other Britons conceived of a "special relationship" with the Indians and therefore resented direct American communication with their former allies. The British commander at Fort Ottawa, Allan Maclean, conceded the Americans' right to cultivate diplomatic relations around the globe: "The Americans being now Independent States," he wrote to Detroit, "will say they have a right to send Ambassadors or Emissaries to whom they please, without our consent—no doubt they may to all nations that we know of." Yet in the case of the Indians, Maclean was "of a different opinion, it being clearly an exception to the Rule." The Indians, he believed, were natural British allies, bound to the Crown. They got "from the King's Stores the bread they are to eat tomorrow, and from his magazines the clothing that covers their nakedness." The Indians were, in short, "not only our allies, but they are a part of our Family; and the Americans might as well . . . attempt to seduce our children & servants from their duty and allegiance, as to convene and assemble all the Indian Nations." Of the Native American leaders in the north, none was more readily associated with this British "Family" than the Mohawk chieftain Joseph Brant.[4]

Joseph Brant

His birth is shrouded in mystery, and the exact time and place remain a matter of debate, but somewhere along the Cuyahoga River in the spring of 1743 Thayendanegea was born into the Wolf Clan of the Mohawk. When his father fell victim to an epidemic, his mother took the family from the Ohio Country to New York, where the young boy was baptized as "Joseph." By the early 1750s, Joseph's mother had remarried to a Mohawk Sachem named Brant. The Brants soon became involved with the British through William Johnson, the superintendent for northern Indian affairs. Known to the Mohawks as "A Man Who Undertakes Great Things," Johnson was a friend of Brant's stepfather and the conjugal partner of Brant's older sister, Molly. A precocious, intelligent teenager, Joseph Brant began his English education during the last years of the French and Indian War, moving to Lebanon, Connecticut, to learn from the Reverend Eleazar Wheelock at Moor's Indian Charity School.* A Congregational minister who had been a prominent figure in the First Great Awakening, Wheelock often despaired of teaching Native Americans, whom he thought were "as unpolished & uncultivated within as without." Brant, however, was a capable scholar and in Wheelock's words "a considerate, modest, and manly spirited youth." Having learned several languages and converted to Anglicanism, Brant's education was cut short in 1763 by Pontiac's Rebellion, but his progress was not to be curtailed: as the British commander at Fort Niagara later observed, Brant possessed "a very great share of Ambition to become a man of the first consequence."[5]

By 1775, Brant had become secretary to the new British superintendent

---

*The school went on to great things. In 1769 it moved to New Hampshire and in December of that year it was rechartered as Dartmouth College.

Figure 6.1.
Thayendanegea (Joseph Brant) (1785) by Gilbert Stuart. The British Museum, London.

of indian affairs, Guy Johnson, who was the nephew of William. Empowered as a spokesman of the Mohawk, he traveled with Johnson to London to negotiate the military support of the Iroquois, meeting with George III and the writer James Boswell among others. Upon his return to North America, Brant featured in several memorable wartime episodes. He fought at the Battle of Long Island in 1776; he joined Colonel Barry St. Leger on his expedition in 1777; and between 1778 and 1780 he led a campaign of fire and terror against American settlers in southern New York and western Pennsylvania. All the while, he campaigned for Native American allegiance to the British Crown. Even when London seemed to abandon the northwestern Indians in the Treaty of Paris, Brant persevered with the British. In 1785, he traveled to London once more to petition George III for protection from the United States and, during the Northwest Indian War, he sought military assistance from Lord Dorchester at Quebec. Even so, Brant also came to act as a peacemaker between the American empire and the Native Americans: involved in early negotiations that led to the Treaty of Fort Stanwix, Brant declared to Congress in 1797 that he would "never again take up the tomahawk against the United States." An adept and practical politician who recognized the Native Americans' ever-worsening position, Brant even courted the French. His Mohawk name, Thayendane-gea, aptly means "he who places two bets."[6]

Brant's later years were defined by the struggle to maintain Native American sovereignty in the face of rampant American imperialism. While the Indians considered themselves sovereign on a par with George III and the French, such pretensions were humored by the United States only when necessary and dismissed whenever convenient. Just as the American empire threatened the Native Americans, they were threats in turn to the American empire, enemies who endangered the integrity and security of the Union and against whom open war could and had to be waged. As early as 1756, Benjamin Franklin had predicted the necessity of such war, writing "I do not believe we shall ever have a firm Peace with the Indians till we have well drubb'd them." In their pursuit of equitable treatment, the Native Americans found sympathizers in George Washington, Henry Knox, and Timothy Pickering, but Washington always knew that his powers in this realm were narrowly constrained: the ordinary Americans to whom he was accountable under God might sometimes have heard their better angels, but more often they hungered after Indian lands. No wonder that Brant's last words went unheeded: "Have pity upon the poor Indians; . . . endeavor to do them all the good you can."[7]

By keeping their Northwest posts, by smuggling arms to the Native Americans, and by the operation of Canada's Indian Department, the British deliberately hindered the expansion of the United States. In what amounted to a serious insult, they also offered to mediate negotiations between the United States and the Indians on *United States* land. The redcoats then refused to allow American commissioners to meet with the Indian Council at Detroit on what was, according to the Treaty of Paris, sovereign American soil. When Gouverneur Morris was sent to London in 1790 to persuade the British to honor the peace terms, he encountered nothing but obfuscation. Unwilling to uphold the terms of 1783, the British instead offered to negotiate anew. Morris spat back at Pitt the Younger, "You wish to make a new treaty instead of complying with the old one," and the prime minister conceded that such was "in some sort" his plan. By May 1792, Alexander Hamilton was so riled by British obstruction that, despite having stoutly resisted commercial warfare, he was ready for "actual" war. London was told that continued possession of the military posts would be intolerable to the Americans: "Any plan, which comprehended anything like a cession of territory or right or the allowance of any other power to interfere in the disputes with the Indians, would be considered by this government as absolutely impracticable and inadmissible." British officials, though, were committed to their Northwest conspiracy.[8]

One such official was the Crown superintendent of Indian affairs, Sir John Johnson, the son of Sir William and a loyalist who was the subject of a bill of attainder in New York. Another was Guy Carleton, Baron Dorchester, the last British commander-in-chief of the Revolutionary War and the governor-general of Canada. In the latter role, Dorchester had inflamed tension between Britain and the United States by ordering the construction of a new British fort on the banks of the Miami River in present-day Ohio, and by denouncing the expansionary politics of the American empire. In what Dorchester thought was a confidential letter to the Western Confederacy, but which was intercepted and leaked to the Americans, he declared that "From the manner in which the people of the States push on, and act and talk on this side, and from what I learn of their conduct towards the sea, I shall not be surprised if we are at war with them in the course of the present year: and if we are, a line must then be drawn by the warriors." Even in February 1794, then, eleven years after the Treaty of Paris, the British in North America had no intention of honoring its terms. Whatever London intended, their men on the spot appeared ready for the resumption of open war with the United States. The Americans, though, were already fighting.[9]

The Northwest Indian War and the Treaty of Greenville

The American empire was informed by the Roman concept of *imperium*, which meant command over both land and people; and while Washington and Knox might have aspired to do right by the Native Americans, the needs and aspirations of the American republic required the domination of the Indians and the acquisition of their lands. Indeed, for the Americans, sovereignty over Indian lands was a necessity and, where compromise on the ownership of that land was impossible, conquest was imperative. From 1785, the United States therefore fought the Northwest Indian War against a confederation of tribes supported by the British. Also known as the Ohio War and Little Turtle's War, the conflict escalated in 1790 as the federal government strove, once and for all, to assert its empire over the Northwest Territory.

The first major campaign was launched in autumn 1790 when Washington and Knox ordered General Josiah Harmar to journey into the lands of the Miami and the Shawnee. Harmar was to exact retribution for Indian assaults on American settlers and to raze the principal Miami settlement of

Kekionga. He did not succeed: the Harmar Campaign resulted in crushing defeat for the United States. First, at the Battle of Heller's Corner, a reconnaissance mission led by John Hardin and James Fontaine was deceived, led into swampland, and routed by Native Americans commanded by the Miami chief Little Turtle. The next day, October 20, Philip Hartshorn was ambushed by an Indian force some eight miles outside Kekionga. With morale diminishing rapidly, Hardin advanced on Kekionga with 350 men. Outnumbered almost three-to-one, he sent an urgent request to Harmar for reinforcements, but General Harmar, who allegedly was drunk, refused and arranged his troops into a defensive formation around his *own* camp. This left Hardin in an impossible position. When the Indians attacked, all he could do was resist and after three hours he fell back after the loss of 150 men. The steam that rose from the American scalps is said to have reminded the Indians of hot squash in the cool autumnal air, so the encounter is known as the Battle of the Pumpkin Fields. With winter approaching, Harmar concluded he could no longer attack and he retreated in disgrace. On receiving the dispatches from the field, Washington was crestfallen. "My mind," he wrote, "is prepared for the worst; that is, expense without honor and profit." Harmar's defeat also acted as a catalyst for further Indian aggression. In January 1791, the Big Bottom Massacre saw eleven American settlers killed by Menape and Wyandot Indians in the southeast of present-day Ohio; the next week, the Siege of Dunlap's Station saw thirty Americans attacked by five hundred warriors of the Western Confederacy.[10]

Washington reacted to Harmar's calamities and the Indian insurgency by ordering Major General Arthur St. Clair, the governor of the Northwest Territory, to assemble another force for another campaign. It did not begin auspiciously. It took months for St. Clair to recruit the necessary troops, and before the campaign had even started about a quarter of his force had deserted. By the autumn of 1791, St. Clair was ready at last. Once more, the American objective was to destroy the Miami village of Kekionga. By early November, however, several hundred more soldiers had deserted and St. Clair, hobbled by gout and incapable of imposing discipline, had only 920 troops—and two hundred ancillary followers—at his disposal. On the night of November 3, his bedraggled party made camp at the present-day location of Fort Recovery, Ohio. At dawn, as St. Clair's troops ate breakfast, Little Turtle and Blue Jacket led a thousand Native Americans from the surrounding woods. Over the next few hours and during the flight from battle, the United States Army suffered one of the worst defeats in its history and the worst United States defeat in the course of two centuries of

Indian wars. Of the 920 soldiers, 632 were killed and 264 were wounded. Only 24 were unharmed. Nearly all the 200 camp followers were killed too. On his return to Philadelphia, St. Clair requested a court-martial that he might be exonerated; the courtesy was refused and he was forced to resign. The House of Representatives then took St. Clair's Defeat as the subject of its first special committee investigation. The fallout was such that Washington summoned for conference the secretaries of all governmental departments: St. Clair's humiliation thus "inspired" the first meeting of the United States cabinet. When the same news was received in London, the British were elated. Still ensconced in their posts, still furnishing arms to the Indians, Pitt the Younger's government began to contemplate an Indian "buffer state" between the United States and Canada.

Yet St. Clair's Defeat was also a turning point in the Northwest Indian War and the history of the United States Army. In March 1792, Congress voted for the establishment of more regiments, for longer enlistments, and for better pay for soldiers. "Mad" Anthony Wayne, a former congressman from Georgia, was made Senior Officer of the Army and ordered by Washington to create a regular military force that could at last pacify the Northwest. Recruited and trained in Pittsburgh, and combining infantry, cavalry, and artillery, Wayne's force was named the Legion of the United States. "The Americans must certainly be a restless People," observed one Detroit trader, "for no sooner is one army destroyed than another springs up in its place."[11]

Wayne's Legion soon reversed the course of the Indian War. Establishing Fort Recovery at the precise location of St. Clair's Defeat and building fortifications throughout the Northwest Territory, the Legion's campaigns culminated in August 1794 at the Battle of Fallen Timbers. Here, a force of 2,000 United States soldiers conclusively defeated the Native Americans and a company of Canadian militiamen.

In the prelude to the battle, Wayne's Legion marched northward; Blue Jacket's Indians took a defensive position along the Maumee River, where scores of trees had been uprooted by recent storms, hence "Fallen Timbers." The battle itself was anticlimactic. Wayne's infantry launched a bayonet charge and his cavalry outflanked the Native Americans, who were routed. The defeated Indians fled to Fort Miamis, which by April 1794 had been rebuilt and reoccupied by the redcoats. This was significant, even momentous, because in June of that year, Henry Knox—still secretary of war —had authorized an American military assault on the fort. "If . . . in the course of your operations," Knox had written to Wayne, "it should become necessary to dislodge the party at the rapids of Miami, you are

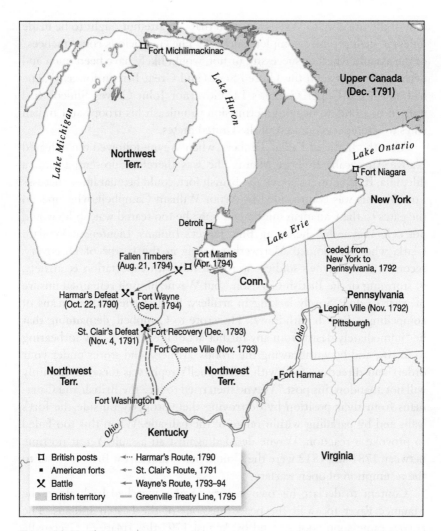

Figure 6.2. Northwest Indian wars

hereby authorized in the name of the President of the United States to do it." These orders to Wayne are an often-forgotten episode in the history of the United States. They also represent a remarkable volte face. As late as March 31, Knox had ordered Wayne to abstain "from every step or measure which could be . . . construed into any aggression on your part against England or Spain." Yet in his orders of June 7, explicitly countermanding the previous orders, Washington, through Knox, had authorized a military assault on this new British fort. Washington and Knox knew the potential cost of the mission, so Wayne was told that "no attempt ought to be made unless it shall promise complete success." The "pernicious consequences" of the assault, whether successful or not, would likely have been open and declared war between the United States and Great Britain for, as Wayne had advanced, Upper Canada's Lt. Governor John Graves Simcoe had written to London, begging permission to unleash his troops and Indian allies to attempt reconquest of the United States.[12]

After the Battle of Fallen Timbers, when Wayne followed the defeated Native Americans to Fort Miamis, he was therefore presented with a dilemma. If he chose to attack the British fort, could he guarantee success? Fort Miamis was commanded by Major William Campbell, who opened the gates to the Canadian militiamen only: he too feared war, so he would not defy Wayne by sheltering Blue Jacket's Indians. Lieutenant William Clark, who later joined Meriwether Lewis in the Corps of Discovery, recorded that Wayne's soldiers were "all full with expectation & anxiety, of storming of the British Garrison," but Wayne himself remained unsure of what to do.[13] Sorely lacking in artillery, he first tried other means of compelling a British withdrawal. He wrote to Campbell, demanding that he "immediately desist from any further act of hostility . . . , by forbearing to fortify, and by withdrawing the troops, artillery, and stores under your orders and direction, forthwith." Campbell's reply was terse: "I certainly will not abandon this post." Wayne then tried to lure the British and Canadians from their position by destroying their property outside the fort's walls and by parading within range of the palisade. When this too failed to provoke a reaction, Wayne decided against an assault. Yet at no time between 1781 and 1812 were the United States and Great Britain closer to the resumption of open warfare.[14]

Content to declare his own victory, Wayne marched back along the Maumee River to await the peace missions of the beaten Indians. The envoys came soon enough, and by August 1795 the Treaty of Greenville had been agreed to. Signed by the Wyandots, the Delawares, the Shawnees, the Ottawas, the Chippewas, the Potawatomis, the Miamis, the Eel River Tribe, the Weas, the Kickapoos, and the Kaskaskias, the Treaty substantially diminished the danger of the Western Confederacy to the northwestern United States. Trade was opened with the tribes, who were permitted "to hunt . . . without hindrance or molestation, so long as they demean themselves peaceably, and offer no injury to the people of the United States." The federal government meanwhile disavowed any American citizen who presumed to settle upon Indian lands, the extent of which— and therefore of American territory—was defined at length. But most important, in return for $20,000 and an annual stipend of $9,500 (paid in kind with "useful goods"), the tribes relinquished to the United States the title to all the land beyond a line that ran, in present-day terms, south from Cleveland to the Portage Lakes, along the Tuscarawas River to Bolivar, and then southwest to Fort Loramie. The line then ran gently northwest to Fort Recovery before turning abruptly southwest toward Carrollton, Kentucky. The Greenville Treaty Line, as it became known, became the effective border between the United States and the Western Confederacy. This would not be the end of hostilities in the American Northwest—far from it—but the Treaty brought an unprecedented degree of security to the region and, most significant of all, it undercut British plans for future intrigue and subversion.

The Jay Treaty

The postwar tension between Great Britain and the United States had been complicated by the French Revolutionary Wars. Yet while the outbreak of the War of the First Coalition brought the nations into conflict at sea, Britain could ill-afford military action on the American continent. The defeat of the Native Americans at Fallen Timbers meant that the Western Confederacy had failed despite British support, while the escalation of the war in Europe meant that Britain was desperate to prevent the Americans from honoring their still-extant alliance with France. The Pitt administration, as Gouverneur Morris told John Quincy Adams, was now "well disposed" to the United States: "They have made their arrangements upon a plan that comprehends the neutrality of the United States, and are anxious that it should be preserved." Reconciliatory sentiment prevailed at Philadelphia, too. The Federalists, who controlled the cabinet and the Senate, were anxious to strike a deal not with France but with Britain, a deal that might foster the commerce needed by the Hamiltonian system.[15]

John Jay, now the chief justice of the Supreme Court, was sent to London to make this treaty. Technically instructed by the secretary of state, Edmund Randolph, but reliant upon talking points drafted by Hamilton and answering directly to Washington, Jay's position was compromised from the start. To gain concessions from Great Britain, he could have threatened American participation in the League of Armed Neutrality, the Russian-led alliance of northern European states that strove to uphold the immunity of neutral shipping. Yet British spies had learned that American flirtation with the League was far from serious; the British also knew from their diplomatic network in Europe that the League did not even want

American membership. Jay's only leverage came from Wayne's recent victory in the Northwest and British anxiety to maintain American neutrality. He could not, therefore, press the British on several key issues, such as the impressment of American sailors into the Royal Navy. Even so, a treaty was signed on November 19, 1794, by Jay and Lord Grenville, the British foreign minister, and its terms resolved several issues festering between the nations. Most significantly, Britain engaged to withdraw all "Troops and Garrisons from all Posts and Places within the Boundary Lines assigned by the Treaty of Paris to the United States." Commissions would be established to settle the northwestern and northeastern borders with British Canada, while the entire border would be renegotiated if the Mississippi was found not to extend into British territory. Further commissions would resolve claims for unpaid British debts and plunder on the high seas. Finally, American rights in British trade and vice versa were fixed, abolishing defunct "colonial" privileges and opening British ports in Europe and the East Indies to American vessels. Even the British West Indies was opened to American commerce, but only so narrowly that the Senate struck out the provision during ratification.

Upon its receipt in the United States, the Treaty became a source of violent partisan controversy, not least because it failed to outlaw the impressment of American sailors. Moreover, Jay had accepted significant limits to American participation in the West Indian trade. The British were also allowed to seize French goods from American ships, and there was nothing about compensation for slaves who had been freed by the British during the Revolutionary War: possessed of antislavery sympathies, Jay was never likely to press that point. For these reasons, many Americans interpreted the Treaty as a form of genuflection to the British, a betrayal of fellow republicans in France, and a repudiation of the principle of "free ships, free goods." Public meetings in Boston, New York, Philadelphia, Baltimore, Richmond, Charleston, and Savannah voted to condemn the Treaty. The Republican Party, which opposed the Treaty, swelled its numbers accordingly. Jay understood what this meant for his reputation: "I could walk from Charleston to Boston," he is supposed to have mused, "by the light of my own burning effigies."[16]

The Jay Treaty thus became a decisive factor in the development of American partisan politics. "Pro-British" Federalists demanded its ratification, with Alexander Hamilton and Rufus King apologizing for the Treaty under the pseudonym of "Camillus." In the first of their essays, "The Defense," they argued that Jay had covered "in a reasonable manner the points in controversy between the United States and Great Britain." No "improper concessions" had been made, nor were any "restrictions which are incompatible with their honor" laid upon the Americans. Compared to the "other commercial treaties" of the United States, Jay's effort was "entitled to a preference"; in fact, the Americans had obtained "concessions of advantages . . . which no other nation has obtained from the same power." Most pointedly, Hamilton suggested that "the too probable result of a refusal to ratify [the Jay Treaty] is war" and so "violations of our rights" would go "unredressed and unadjusted."[17]

Conversely, the Republicans derided Jay's work, which they labeled the "Grenville" Treaty and explained it as the product of addled Anglomania. Writing to the Italian physician and gunrunner Philip Mazzei, Jefferson balked at the symbiotic relationship between Federalism and pro-British policy. "The aspect of our politics," he wrote, "has wonderfully changed since you left us. In place of that noble love of liberty and republican government which carried us through the war, an Anglican, monarchical, and aristocratical party has sprung up." Their "avowed object," wrote Jefferson, "was to draw over us the substance as they have already done the forms of the British government." Within this "Anglican" party Jefferson identified most of American political society. "Against us," he listed "the Executive, the Judiciary, two out of three branches of the legislature, all of the officers of the government, all who want to be officers, all timid men who prefer the calm of despotism to the boisterous sea of liberty, British merchants and Americans trading on British capital, speculators and holders in the banks and public funds." These merchants and speculators had conspired "for the purposes of corruption and fear" to involve the American people in "the rotten as well as the sound parts of the British model." Jefferson warned Mazzei that he would suffer "a fever were I to name to you the apostates who have gone over to these heresies, men who were Samsons in the field and Solomons in the council, but who have had their heads shorn by the harlot England."[18]

Such was the partisan rancor that the Treaty was ratified by the Senate without a vote to spare: the necessary two-thirds majority, twenty to ten, reflected the parties' share of seats precisely. Yet when Washington received the Treaty from the Senate, news from London threatened to undo everything. In a stunning display of bad faith, the British had now authorized the seizure of *all* foodstuffs bound for Europe from the United States. Only the Randolph Affair persuaded the president to ignore British duplicity and to sign the Treaty. It transpired that the secretary of state, Edmund Randolph, had been in private correspondence with Joseph Fauchet, the French minister to the United States, and Fauchet's dispatches had been captured by the British and turned over to the Americans. In his letters, Randolph had depicted the American cabinet as extremely hostile to French interests and to republicanism in general, alleging that "under pretext of giving energy to the government, it was intended to introduce absolute power and to mislead the President in paths which would conduct him to unpopularity." The passage that damned Randolph the most, at least in the eyes of John Quincy Adams, the son of the vice president, was this: "Thus the consciences of the pretended patriots of America have already their prices." Randolph was in disgrace. As secretary of state, whether from principled or pecuniary motives, he had opposed the Jay Treaty. He had even asked Washington to delay approving the Treaty. Almost in protest at Randolph's betrayal, the president now signed it into law. Randolph was humiliated in front of the cabinet and dismissed. In a forlorn attempt to clear his name, he published *A Vindication of Mr. Randolph's Resignation*.[19]

Even *after* the Jay Treaty became law it remained the subject of dispute. The prescribed commissions on borders and debts had to be financed by the Republican-controlled House of Representatives, so House Republicans held up proceedings while they tried to undermine public confidence in the Treaty, the defining symbol of Federalist foreign policy. Washington and Federalists such as the Congressman Fisher Ames, though, built support assiduously. In one memorable speech in the House, Ames rose despite serious illness to plead that rejection of the treaty—that is, rejection of Britain's offer to surrender its military posts—meant war against the Indians without the means of peace. "Until the posts are restored" to American possession, Ames declared, "the treasury and the frontiers must bleed. . . . By rejecting the posts, we light the savage fires—we bind the victims. . . . The voice of humanity issues from the shade of their wilderness. It exclaims that, while one hand is held up to reject this treaty, the other grasps a tomahawk."[20] In the end, Ames succeeded and the necessary grants were made by April 1796.

The Jay Treaty fomented American partisan division more than any other event of the 1790s. As "Camillus" reflected, "There was no measure in which the government could engage so little likely to be viewed according to its intrinsic merits." Support and opposition to the Hamiltonian system of federal finance had been the first polarizing factor; reaction to the French Revolution and Citizen Genet might well have been the second; but the Jay Treaty and the associated debates about American foreign policy had much vaster effect in mobilizing the wider political public around the elite partisan factions. Thus was the division between Republicanism and Federalism simplified as the division between support for the French Republic and support for Great Britain.[21]

Pinckney's Treaty

Jay's Treaty was not the only major foreign agreement of the mid-1790s. The Americans' continued exclusion from the lower Mississippi, from the port of New Orleans, and disputes over the southern border meant that the United States—unwilling to make war over these issues—needed a treaty with Spain. Spanish willingness to compromise was the direct consequence of the Jay Treaty. With the British and Americans now "at peace," the Spanish feared that a formal Anglo-American alliance might materialize and then succeed in forcing Spain from North America altogether. The Spanish prime minister, Manuel de Godoy, to whom effective government of the Spanish state and its empire had been conferred by the placid and unengaged Carlos IV, was especially perturbed by this phantom threat. He therefore declared his willingness to talk, and Thomas Pinckney, the South Carolinian serving as the American minister in London, was dispatched to Spain to negotiate.

Also known as the Treaty of San Lorenzo, the site of the El Escorial Palace some thirty miles northwest of Madrid, the terms of "Pinckney's Treaty" were extraordinarily generous to the United States. American shipping was granted free navigation of the Mississippi; American merchants were granted duty-free use of the port of New Orleans; the Spanish agreed to withdraw their support from the Indian tribes who had inhabited disputed territory; and the southern border was formalized as the thirty-first parallel. Signed in October 1795, the treaty was ratified by the Senate by March 1796, by Spain the next month, and proclaimed in August. The one-sided nature of its terms and the alacrity with which Godoy acceded to Pinckney's demands might suggest this was not a major diplomatic milestone; an important treaty, it might be argued, could not have been agreed to so rapidly. Yet in terms of the imperial history of the United States, Pinckney's Treaty was arguably as important as Jay's. Access to the Mississippi and New Orleans meant that westward expansion became commercially viable. George Washington had suggested that the construction of canals running eastward to the Ohio River could provide sufficient transportation, but most Americans believed that the future of the West depended on access to the Gulf of Mexico via "the Spanish river," The Mississippi. As for the other terms of the Treaty, Spanish guarantees not to provoke Indian attacks made westward expansion much safer, while agreement on the border between Georgia and Florida began to consolidate the Union. By means of three treaties of the mid-1790s, first with Native Americans, second with Great Britain, and third with Spain, the United States had secured its territory and developed workable commercial relations with two European powers. The treaties were not perfect, nor would they remedy all the ailments of the republic, but the great problems of North American empire were gradually being solved.

James Wilkinson

Benedict Arnold is renowned as the great traitor of American history, the man who defected to the British and who planned to surrender West Point. The life and deeds of James Wilkinson were no less villainous. Born into a wealthy Maryland family that was bankrupted during his formative years, Wilkinson entered the military and rose through the ranks of the army. Having served during the Siege of Boston and having helped to place the guns on Dorchester Heights, he became an aide to Horatio Gates, the hero of Saratoga. It even fell to Wilkinson to report the news of Saratoga to Congress at Philadelphia: in a remarkable display of egotism, Wilkinson kept Congress waiting while he sorted out personal affairs, then exaggerated his contribution so much that he received an ill-deserved brevet as brigadier general. By 1778, Gates was so fed up with Wilkinson that he forced his resignation. The following year Congress appointed Wilkinson clothier-general of the Army, but, failing in that position, he resigned again in 1781. This, however, was not the end of Wilkinson's military career. He returned to lead American forces in the Northwest Indian War and, reinvigorated, he conspired to replace Anthony Wayne as commander of the Legion of the United States. Upon Wayne's death in 1796, Wilkinson was appointed the Senior Officer of the Army, a position he held until July 1798 and then again from 1800 until 1812.

Wilkinson secured his infamy in the American West. Following his second resignation from the army, he had moved in 1784 to Kentucky. Three years later, he traveled to New Orleans, the governing seat of Spanish Louisiana. There he met the Spanish governor, Esteban Rodriguez Miró, and, in return for allowing Kentucky merchants tariff-free access to the Mississippi, Wilkinson agreed to promote Spanish interests in the Trans-Appalachian West. Remarkably, he promised to agitate for the secession of Kentucky and Tennessee from the American Union. By the terms of this "Spanish Conspiracy," Wilkinson swore loyalty to Carlos IV and undertook to transmit intelligence on the western activities of the United States; in return, as "Agent Thirteen" of the Spanish secret service, he would be rewarded handsomely. Betrayal was long suspected, but in his lifetime Wilkinson—who encoded his correspondence using rows of numbers grouped in fours—eluded discovery.

Figure 6.3. *James Wilkinson* (1797) by Charles Willson Peale. Independence National Historical Park, Pennsylvania.

On several occasions he came close to exposure. In the mid-1790s, Miró's successor, Francisco de Carondelet, contacted Wilkinson through another American double agent, Thomas Power. This second act of the Kentucky Conspiracy was almost brought to light when three thousand of Wilkinson's silver dollars were scattered across the state by five Spanish boatmen who had murdered his messenger. When the Spaniards were apprehended and it became clear they spoke no English, the magistrate sent for an interpreter. Were it not that the summoned interpreter was Thomas Power, the masquerade would have been laid bare, but Wilkinson survived. Among other crimes, he communicated details of the Lewis and Clark Expedition to New Orleans and urged the Spanish to dispatch armed patrols to intercept the American explorers; they followed his advice, but could not find Lewis and Clark. Wilkinson was then appointed the first governor of the Louisiana Territory that was organized out of the Louisiana Purchase. From this high office, Wilkinson forewarned his paymasters that the United States intended to make further incursions into Spanish territory, thereby frustrating the Pike Expedition that he had himself commissioned.

Yet as the intrigue and subterfuge continued, so too did Wilkinson's rise. Having avoided indictment by a grand jury and conviction by a military tribunal for further, unproven betrayals, he returned to military command during the War of 1812, successfully capturing Mobile in West Florida in 1813 but suffering conclusive defeat at Montreal in 1814. His last appointment was as the American embassy to Mexico during the Mexican War of Independence: Wilkinson died in the role in 1825, awaiting the Mexican government's approval of a request for a Texan land grant. It was not until decades after his death that Wilkinson's treason was proved by the discovery of his correspondence with Miró. Elegantly labeled "an artist in treason" by one of his most recent biographers, Wilkinson's standing among historians is best summarized by Theodore Roosevelt, who condemned him with the words "In all our history, there is no more despicable character."[22]

Farewell

By 1796, the United States had resolved many of the issues outstanding from the Revolutionary War and had opened the gateway to the West. This was achieved during the presidency of George Washington, who had strived to commit neither himself to a party nor the United States to any foreign power, alliance, or war. Such detached neutrality, such isolation from the European system, was the defining characteristic of Washington's ideas about foreign relations, ideas that were best articulated in his Farewell Address. This was not a speech, but an open letter to the American people, first printed in September 1796 in the *American Daily Advertiser* and circulated throughout the United States. By publishing the Address in this way, Washington employed the same machinery of political intelligence that had developed during his presidency: just as newspapers were distributed to create an informed public that could safeguard the republic from tyranny, the Farewell Address sought to create a public to which future presidents would be held accountable on foreign policy.

Washington paid glowing tribute to the accomplishments of American diplomats, reminding the American people that "they have been witnesses to the formation of two treaties, that with Great Britain, and that with Spain, which secure to them everything they could desire, in respect to our foreign relations, towards confirming their prosperity." Even so, the president emphasized the hazardous international situation that confronted the United States in 1796: the French were prosecuting a global ideological war and they retained their imperial ambitions in North America; although

Jay's Treaty had improved Anglo-American relations, Great Britain held Canada, much of the Caribbean, and command of the Atlantic; and, despite Pinckney's Treaty, Spain remained the dominant power in the lower Mississippi. More famously, Washington delivered the classic articulation of American exceptionalism. One paragraph became a blueprint for American foreign policy for more than a century:

> The great rule of conduct for us in regard to foreign nations is in extending our commercial relations, to have with them as little political connection as possible. So far as we have already formed engagements, let them be fulfilled with perfect good faith. Here let us stop. Europe has a set of primary interests which to us have none; or a very remote relation. Hence she must be engaged in frequent controversies, the causes of which are essentially foreign to our concerns. Hence, therefore, it must be unwise in us to implicate ourselves by artificial ties in the ordinary vicissitudes of her politics, or the ordinary combinations and collisions of her friendships or enmities.

Why, asked Washington, should the United States "interweav[e] our destiny with that of any part of Europe, [or] entangle our peace and prosperity in the toils of European ambition, rivalship, interest, humor or caprice?" He reasoned that such a policy would jeopardize the current "detached and distant situation" that allowed the United States "to pursue a different course." Hence it was "the true policy" of the nation "to steer clear of permanent alliances." Washington also reaffirmed his belief that, in the context of the French Revolutionary Wars, the United States "had a right to take, and was bound in duty and interest to take, a neutral position." This was indeed the policy that the United States, from its independence, had pursued. Yet during the administration of Washington's successor, John Adams, who acceded to the presidency in January 1797, American neutrality would be pushed to its limits.[23]

CHAPTER 7

Saint Domingue and the Quasi-War, 1797–1800

Might I be permitted to hazard an opinion it wou'd be the Atlantic only can save us, & that no consideration will be sufficiently powerful to check the extremities to which the temper of this government [of France] will carry it, but an apprehension that we may be thrown into the arms of Britain.

—John Marshall, October 1797[1]

As the United States waged its Indian War, and then as it made treaties with Britain and Spain, the French Revolution rolled on. In September 1792, the monarchy had been abolished and the French Republic proclaimed. In January 1793, Citizen Louis Capet, the former king, had been executed for treason. That April, the nine-man Committee of Public Safety was established and, led by Maximilien Robespierre, it quickly assumed control of the French government. In a summer of violence, the Girondins were expelled from the National Convention and Charlotte Corday murdered the radical journalist Jean-Paul Marat in his bathtub. "With this one dead," Corday told an interrogator, "the others, perhaps, will be afraid." Many indeed became afraid. Beginning in September 1793, the Reign of Terror combined the judicial persecution of the "enemies of the Revolution" with the mob violence of the *sans-culottes*, so known because they wore ankle-length trousers instead of the silk *culottes*, the knee-breeches of the wealthy. French politics descended into carnage. The Law of Suspects gave the Committee the power to arrest and to execute its enemies; anticlerical laws made priesthood in communion with Rome punishable by death; and "terror" became synonymous with the "virtue" of the Revolution. "If the basis of popular government in peacetime is virtue," declared Robespierre, "the basis of popular government during a revolution is both virtue and terror. . . . Terror is nothing more than speedy, severe, and inflexible justice." In October, Marie Antoinette followed her husband to the guillotine. Accused of treason, embezzlement, and incest with her son, the former queen was given one day to prepare her defense. "Terror is the order of the day," reported Gouverneur Morris, the American minister in Paris. "The Queen was executed the day before yesterday. Insulted during her trial and reviled in her last moments, she behaved with dignity throughout." The massacres continued until July 1794, when Robespierre and his allies on the Committee were ousted then executed during the coup known as the Thermidorian Reaction. This marked the end of the Terror, a yearlong purge that had seen more than forty thousand Frenchmen murdered.[2]

All the while, the French had sought to export the ideology of the Revolution and to maintain control over their extensive colonies. These, however, were conflicting policies. The first article of the Declaration of the Rights of Man stipulated that "Men are born and remain free and equal in [their] rights" and this was incompatible with a French colonial empire that was acquired by an absolutist monarchy and still defined by hierarchy and slavery. Consequently, white colonial planters (the *grands blancs*) began to demand greater representation in the Estates-General and successive Revolutionary governments. Lower classes of colonial whites and free people of color (*petits blancs* and *gens de couleur*) likewise insisted on greater freedoms. In a scenario that few had imagined, the egalitarian sentiments of the Revolution were even imbibed by the slaves of the French Empire. On Caribbean islands such as Guadeloupe and Martinique, there ensued social unrest, slave rebellions, and economic collapse, but the effects of the Revolution were felt most keenly in Saint Domingue. Forming the western half of the island of Hispaniola (the eastern half was Spanish-controlled Santo Domingo), Saint Domingue was the jewel of the French Empire, a sugar colony so fertile and so profitable that all others, even Great Britain's Jamaica, paled in comparison. A British expert on the island later observed that "whoever has read the history of St Domingo . . . has been impressed with an idea of its richness, of its varied scenery, and of its fertile condition."[3]

The first steps in Saint Domingue's revolution were taken in the fall of 1790 when Vincent Ogé, a wealthy man of mixed race, returned to the island from Revolutionary Paris. Funded by British abolitionists and armed by sympathetic Americans, Ogé demanded that the French governor of Saint Domingue should enforce a recent decree of the National Assembly that gave "without distinction, to all free citizens, the right of admission to all offices and functions." Ogé responded to the denial of his request with an attack on the colonial stronghold of Cap Français. Upon its failure he fled to Santo Domingo. When the Spanish handed Ogé back to the French, he and his men were subjected to months of trial and torture after which they were beaten, broken, bound to wheels, and beheaded. Their martyrdom, though, served as a symbol of resistance to white rule and in August 1791, at the signal of the voodoo priest Dutty Boukman, a major slave revolt broke out in the island's northern province. Within a year, the rebellious slaves had gained control of a third of the island. The insurrection was ferocious, in the revolt and its repression four thousand whites and fifteen thousand black slaves were massacred, and tales of atrocity lived long in the memories of slaveholders across the Caribbean. An ally of the British West Indians later wrote that "more monstrous crimes never disgraced human nature. . . . Ingratitude, robbery, [and] murder" had created in Saint Domingue "a scene of atrocity more horrible than any perpetrated in France under the terrific tyrant of Robespierre."[4]

By 1792, the National Assembly was so desperate to regain control of Saint Domingue that it granted political rights to all free inhabitants of the island, irrespective of color. To restore peace, commissioners were then sent to Saint Domingue, accompanied by six thousand troops and a new governor-general. Arriving in September 1792, Leger-Félicité Sonthonax and Etienne Polverel set about rallying islanders of all colors to the standard of the French Republic, but their campaign of reconciliation was hamstrung by developments in Europe. First, news of Louis XVI's arrest and execution horrified white, royalist planters. Of the ideological confusion and bloody havoc that followed, the *Aurora General Advertiser* reported that "Each port [in Saint Domingue] is wishing to destroy the other; some in favor of the king, others of the [Republic], the mulattoes, the free negroes, the slaves, etc. What will be the consequence, God only knows." The planters were now as likely to appeal to the British monarchy as to republican Paris for protection from the rebellious slaves. They understood that London would not want France to regain control of Saint Domingue, nor for the slave rebellion to set an example for their own West Indian colonies. Second, the French declaration of war upon Great Britain—and Spain— turned Saint Domingue into a theater of the European conflict. The British now entertained the prospect that, with Spanish support, the French could be expelled from Saint Domingue and the colony transferred into their power: When order and slavery were safely restored, the wealth of the island would then flow into the British exchequer. An expert on the West Indies urged the prime minister, William Pitt the Younger, that "the deplorable situation of the French West Indies seems loudly to crave the protection of Great Britain," and his advice was heeded: Pitt and his foreign minister Dundas dispatched an expeditionary force. Landing in September 1793 at Jérémie on the southwestern cape of the island, the British troops' cries of "Long live King George!" were taken up even by the white French colonists. Battle then raged for control of Saint Domingue with the British, the French, the Spanish, the planters, and the rebellious slaves involved in ever-shifting alliances and vicious conflict. It was the British who gained the upper hand, and by June 1794 they had captured the colonial capital of Port-au-Prince. British command of the island appeared to be secure.[5]

The French commissioners had meanwhile persisted with their schemes of reconciliation. In August 1793, desperate to win the loyalty of the slaves, Sonthonax proclaimed the freedom of those in the north; two months later, Polverel abolished slavery in the south. Since a free Saint Domingue was better for France than none at all, the National Convention confirmed in February 1794 that slavery was "abolished in all the colonies." It declared that "all men, without distinction of color, domiciled in the colonies, are French citizens, and enjoy all the rights assured under the Constitution." For the war in Saint Domingue, the decree proved telling. In early 1794, the black military leader Toussaint L'Ouverture had been fighting along-side the Spanish, despite suspecting them of conspiring with the British to restore slavery in Saint Domingue. Yet when Toussaint learned of the Convention's emancipation decree, he abandoned the Spanish and his four thousand men joined forces with the French. By early 1796, he had retaken Saint Domingue's northern and western provinces in the name of the French Republic.[6]

A French squadron under the command of Victor Hugues had in the meantime arrived in the southeastern Caribbean to expel British invaders from the French colony of Guadeloupe. When Hugues arrived in October 1794, alarm bells went off in London: Great Britain's colonies in the eastern Caribbean were now vulnerable to the audacious Hugues. Then, in September 1795, the Spanish and the French made peace at the Treaty of Basel, swinging the balance of power on Saint Domingue decisively against the British. Indeed, by the early months of 1797 the British situation had become hazardous. Toussaint was leading the dominant military force on the island; both the French *and* the Spanish were hostile to the redcoats; and the cost of the campaign in manpower—at least forty thousand were lost to fighting and illness—was unsustainable. Needing to redeploy their naval forces elsewhere, the British were already beginning their gradual withdrawal from Saint Domingue. Now, in a demonstration of how vulnerable the United States remained to the whims of the European empires, Great Britain's accelerated abandonment of Saint Domingue plunged the new republic into a naval and diplomatic crisis.

Saint Domingue and the United States

Throughout the 1780s, American merchants had conducted an extensive and lucrative trade with the islands of the Caribbean. Buying flour, meat, fish, and lumber in exchange for sugar, coffee, and molasses, the European colonists of the Caribbean accounted for almost one-third of the United States' international commerce. Saint Domingue was a market of special importance: because of its size and wealth, it was by 1790 the Americans' second-largest export market after Great Britain. In the wake of the island's revolution, northern Federalists, many of whom harbored antislavery sentiments, were keen to foster commercial relations with the rebellious slaves. Southern Republicans were less enthusiastic. South Carolina, for example, had a social structure worryingly similar to that of Saint Domingue, and so American slaveholders, like the British, feared the example of a successful black revolution. Even so, Americans continued to trade as neutrals with Saint Domingue and the wider region.[7]

By the mid-1790s, circumstances conspired to render American ships engaged in this trade as "fair prize" for French privateers. First, the Jay Treaty was interpreted by the French Directory as a violation of 1778's Franco-American Alliance. The French foreign minister, Charles Delacroix, warned James Monroe, the American minister in Paris, that the French would rather have "an open enemy [in the United States] than a perfidious friend." Second, as we have seen, the French had sent armies to the Caribbean to quell colonial slave rebellions. When those islands could not supply necessary provisions to the French troops, American ships—laden with goods—were boarded and looted. Third, and perhaps most important, as the British accepted that Saint Domingue was a lost cause and as the Royal Navy redeployed, the harbors and coves of Hispaniola became safe havens for French privateers. When circumstances in Europe led the Spanish and Dutch to abandon the British and ally with the French, their Caribbean islands also became hospitable to the French corsairs. Worse still, as the British retreated from their schemes of Caribbean expansion, the French could harass American shipping without fear of encountering British warships.[8]

As the French attacks on American vessels increased in both frequency and severity, Timothy Pickering, the Federalist secretary of state, sought an explanation from the French minister, Pierre Adet. "The flag of the

Republic," replied Adet, "will treat the flag of neutrals in the same manner as they shall suffer it to be treated by the English." Pickering protested that France was bound by the 1778 treaty to respect American neutrality, but he was told by the French minister that "The United States, by virtue of their treaty of commerce with France, stand on different ground." The French Republic, insisted Pickering, was obliged by law to respect American shipping, even if its cargo was bound for Great Britain. "The American Government," he told Adet, "conscious of the purity of its intentions, of its impartial observance of the laws of neutrality, and of its inviolable regard to treaties, cannot, for a moment, admit, that it has forfeited the right to claim a reciprocal observance of stipulations on the part of the French Republic, whose friendship, moreover, it has ever cultivated with perfect sincerity." The French ignored Pickering; the depredations continued. Indeed, a series of declarations virtually confirmed this piracy as an avowed French policy. On February 1, 1797, Victor Hugues issued a decree from Guadeloupe stating that, with "the Government and commerce of the United States hav[ing] strangely abused the forbearance of the republic of France," any vessel caught trading with any French island in revolt against the French Republic—and nearly all the French islands in the Caribbean were in revolt—would be subject to capture. Hugues reasoned that it was "against every principle to treat a horde of insurgents, destitute of country, without government, and without a flag, with the same respect as civilized nations preserve towards each other during a war." The Directory in Paris would not overrule Hugues. In fact, it declared that any American vessels containing anything bound for Great Britain were good prize, while its edict of March 1797 authorized the seizure of any American vessel that did not have a *rôle d'équipage* (a list of crew and passengers). By the spring of 1797, American shipping was prey to remorseless French piracy. The French Republic would not respect the American flag, so American commerce required effect armed protection.[9]

John Adams and the Pursuit of Peace

Determining the American response was the task of John Adams. The Federalist from Massachusetts had served as the American minister to France, the Netherlands, and Great Britain, and then as vice president to George Washington. In the presidential election of 1796, Adams had won a narrow victory over Thomas Jefferson in the electoral college (seventy-one votes to sixty-eight) and he assumed office in March 1797. From the outset of his presidency, Adams knew the American situation was fraught with danger, but in keeping with the foreign policy of his predecessor he was determined to avoid war with France, so long as he could avoid sacrificing American dignity. "My entrance into office is marked by a misunderstanding with France," wrote the president, "which I shall endeavor to reconcile." Adams would not, however, rule out war in the last resort. Having convened a special session of Congress in May 1797 to discuss the growing crisis with France, Adams declared that "while we are endeavoring to adjust all our differences with France by amicable negotiation, the progress of the war in Europe, the depredations on our commerce, the personal injuries to our citizens, and the general complexion of affairs render it my indispensable duty to recommend to your consideration effectual measures of defense." Since French aggression had been confined to sea, and since he was obliged to respect the American abhorrence of standing armies, Adams focused on the development of the federal navy, which had been founded in 1794. "The naval establishment," he stated, "must occur to every man who considers the injuries committed on our commerce, the insults offered to our citizens, and the description of vessels by which these abuses have been practiced."[10]

More than a simply pragmatic solution to the current security problems of the nation, Adams construed the navy as "the natural defense of the United States." The geography of the United States made a strong navy necessary. "Our seacoasts," the president explained, "from their great extent, are more easily annoyed and more easily defended by a naval force than any others." The United States was also replete with the skills and material required for the construction of a federal fleet. "With all the materials our country abounds," Adams stated; "in skill our naval architects and navigators are equal to any, and commanders and seamen will not be wanting." Moreover, the recent history of the nation had proved that naval defense was essential to American security. Looking back to the Revolutionary War, Adams argued that "a moderate naval force," such as the Union could now afford, would have stopped the British from moving their armies with such ease. Revisiting some of the major themes of American political discourse in the 1780s, and building on Washington's Farewell Address, Adams insisted that the United States would not appear as "humiliated under a colonial spirit of fear and [a] sense of inferiority, fitted to be the miserable instruments of foreign influence, and regardless of national honor, character, and interest." The president therefore decried French attempts to foment an insurrectionary spirit in the United States. French policy was evincing "a disposition to separate the people of the United States from the government, to persuade them that they have different affections, principles, and interests from those of their fellow citizens whom they themselves have chosen to manage their common concerns, and thus to produce divisions fatal to our peace." For Adams, "such attempts ought to be repelled with a decision which shall convince France and the world that we are not a degraded people."[11]

That "decision" was not a declaration of war, which Adams did not solicit from Congress. The president also declined to license privateering against French shipping. Rather, he sent a diplomatic mission to France to resolve things peaceably. The mission would be led by Charles Cotesworth Pinckney, who had just spent five months as the American minister at Paris. Joining Pinckney were John Marshall, the Virginian who had previously *declined* to serve as minister to France, and Elbridge Gerry of Massachusetts. They were charged with making peace, the ideal being an agreement with France comparable to the Jay Treaty with Britain. By October 1797, the commissioners had arrived in France and had begun to seek meetings with representatives of the Directory, the foreign affairs of which were managed by Talleyrand.

Talleyrand

Men rarely define the arts they practice, but if Niccolò Machiavelli is synonymous with amoral political machination then so is Charles Maurice de Talleyrand with cynical, cunning diplomacy. Born into the Parisian aristocracy, Talleyrand had been deprived of his primogenital rights by a clubfoot. Unfit to pursue a career in the army and scorned by his parents at a time when physical deformity was thought to suggest moral iniquity, he was deemed unworthy to lead a proudly military family. Instead, Talleyrand entered the clergy, first coming to prominence as the agent-general who represented the interests of the Church to the Bourbon monarchy. By 1789 he had been made a bishop in Bourgogne and he was elected as a clerical member of the recalled Estates-General. Over the next eight years, few men would experience more of the turbulence of the French Revolution. Having helped to draft the Declaration of the Rights of Man and to nationalize the lands of the Catholic Church in France, Talleyrand was excommunicated by Pope Pius VI before becoming a diplomatic agent of the National Assembly. Twice he went to Great Britain and twice he urged peace between the British and the French Republic. On neither occasion was Talleyrand received favorably. Gouverneur Morris reported to George Washington that the British considered Talleyrand, a defrocked Catholic priest *and* a republican, as "offensive to Persons who pique themselves on

Figure 7.1. *Talleyrand* (1808) by Francois Gerard. Metropolitan Museum of Art, New York.

Decency of Manners and Deportment." In the fall of 1792, Talleyrand traveled to London once more, this time charged with justifying to the British the Storming of the Tuileries and the deposition of Louis XVI. It might have seemed a fool's errand, but Talleyrand was desperate to leave Paris: twelve hundred prisoners of the Revolution had just been murdered in the September Massacres and Talleyrand was unsure of his standing. The night that he spent pacing the corridors of the Ministry of Justice, waiting for his passport, was perhaps the longest of his life. Talleyrand's fears were in fact well founded: while in England he was placed on the Convention's list of proscribed emigrés. He sought asylum in London until September 1794, at which point—during the height of British paranoia about infiltration by the French—he was expelled.[12]

For his next sanctuary Talleyrand chose the United States, where he worked in finance and stayed as the house guest of Senator Aaron Burr of New York. By 1796, the Convention had been replaced by the five-man Directory and Talleyrand's friends in the new French government won guarantees of his safety. Within a year he had not only returned to France but had even, thanks to the sponsorship of Madame de Staël and Paul Barras, secured the ministry for foreign affairs. It was a hugely contentious appointment. Lazare Carnot, a member of the Directory and the father of the pioneer in thermodynamics, told Barras: "That cunning little priest of yours will sell us all down the river." Barras, however, won through and as the French foreign minister, Talleyrand left his mark on the world. He served almost continuously until 1807, when he resigned from Napoleon's government, and then served again under the restored Bourbon monarchy. As France's leading diplomat and negotiator, Talleyrand was integral to many of the epochal events of the late eighteenth and early nineteenth centuries including the Treaty of Amiens, which brokered peace with the British in 1802, and the Congress of Vienna of 1815, which sought to stabilize postwar Europe. He also proved a formidable foe of the United States: the restoration of French control in Saint Domingue and the annexation of Louisiana and the Floridas were cornerstones of his program for the French Empire in the Americas, a vision that clashed with the Americans' own imperial ambitions. The first confrontation with Talleyrand, though, came in 1797, when Adams's commissioners sought him out for an audience.[13]

The "XYZ" Affair

Only a few days after arriving in Paris, the Americans met with Talleyrand. It was a brief meeting during which the French minister accepted—or seemed to accept—the commissioners' credentials. No more was done, for Talleyrand was simply testing the water, gauging the character of each American. Soon afterward, the commissioners learned that the French minister wanted an explanation for Adams's bellicose speech to Congress, a speech that had predisposed several members of the Directory *not* to treat with the United States. It seemed the reaction of the commissioners would determine whether the Directory entered formal negotiations; the commissioners, though, refused to apologize for the president. The tit-for-tat continued when the Americans asked to begin formal talks. The French response came through back channels, first through the English merchant Nicholas Hubbard ("W," as he is known to history), who told Pinckney that Baron Jean-Conrad Hottinguer ("X") wished to meet him. "X" subsequently demanded a bribe: if the Americans wished even to *see* Talleyrand again, the French minister was to be paid handsomely for the privilege and the French government was to receive a substantial loan. The demand was rejected. Over the next few weeks, both Pierre Bellamy ("Y") and Lucien Hauteval ("Z") came forward to reiterate the message: a princely sum was required for negotiations to commence. The commissioners had been willing to buy peace, but they refused point blank this demand for a bribe merely to talk about it. "No," asserted Pinckney. "No, not a sixpence." Still, the message from the French ministry was relayed continually, now through American intermediaries such as Tom Paine, that "a great deal of money" was required for negotiation. For French satellites such as Genoa or Geneva, paying this kind of "tribute" was common practice. The United States was being treated just like any other French vassal.[14]

The French also knew enough about American politics to exploit the partisan division between the "pro-French" Republicans and "pro-British" Federalists. Indeed, everyone involved in what would be called the "XYZ" Affair realized that, if the American envoys refused to pay the bribe, their failure to deal with the French would be misconstrued at home as the work of "Anglomaniacs." In his dispatches from Paris, John Marshall wrote of how "Y" often "returned to the danger of our situation," of how "Y" warned that exposing French demands for money would *not* unite Americans "in their resistance to those demands." Rather, "the diplomatic skill of France" and "the French party in America" would "throw the blame which will attend the rupture of the negotiations on the Federalists as you term yourselves, [and] on the British party." The commissioners' dispatches reached John Adams at Washington on March 4, 1798. When Congress demanded to inspect the correspondence, Adams at first refused. When the president eventually relented, he had the documents redacted, replacing the names of the French officials with the soon-to-be-infamous pseudonyms of "W," "X," "Y," and "Z."[15]

As news of the commissioners' ordeal became common knowledge, the Federalists rallied. Support grew for rapprochement with Britain, and for war with France. Nelson's victory over the French at the Battle of the Nile in August 1798 was celebrated in Philadelphia with communal singing of "God Save the King." As usual, Hamilton employed the press to influence public opinion and in a series of essays called "The Stand" he damned the French Directory as "FIVE TYRANTS of France [who] after binding in chains their own countrymen . . . have . . . decreed war against all nations not in league with themselves." Rumors of a French invasion took hold and Congress even provided funds for a larger army: "Millions for defense," went a popular slogan, "not one cent for tribute!" Robert Goodloe Harper, a Federalist from South Carolina, told Congress that Victor Hugues was prepared "to make a blow upon Southern country." Even the sagacious Henry Knox was caught up in the militaristic fervor. He warned of "ten thousand blacks" from the French Caribbean invading "the defenseless parts of South Carolina or Virginia."[16]

At Adams's behest, Congress called the country to arms. The American army would be led by George Washington, who accepted the command so long as he could remain at Mount Vernon until needed in the field. "We must have your Name," Adams wrote to Washington, for "there will be more efficacy in it, than in many an army." Washington imposed on Adams his choice of subordinates, including Hamilton as second-in-command and inspector-general. The president soon realized, however, that the risk of French invasion was minimal: "There is no more prospect," Adams told James McHenry, who had become secretary of war in 1796, "of seeing a French army here, than there is in Heaven." Hamilton, meanwhile, merely wanted to collaborate with a British fleet and to lead an American army southward. He dreamed of conquering Louisiana and the Floridas from France's ally, Spain, or, farther south, of revolutionizing Spanish America at the side of the British-supported Venezuelan exile Francisco de Miranda. Along the way, Hamilton fantasized that this army would reduce Virginia Republicans to obedience.[17]

Tireless as ever, Hamilton wrote, schemed, organized, and daydreamed. Yet in the country at large, support for military action against the French was far from universal. In fact, criticism of the government was so widespread that Federalists in Congress, who had won back control of the House in 1796, passed four laws in June and July that allowed the executive to repress dissent and to punish its enemies. Known collectively as the

Alien and Sedition Acts, these laws dominated political discourse in the summer of 1798. The Naturalization Act lengthened the time period that an immigrant had to spend in the United States before becoming a citizen. Although presented as a means of stopping foreign agents from infiltrating American politics, the Act was really designed to prevent immigrants, who tended to support the Republicans, from voting against the Federalists. The Alien Friends Act allowed President Adams to deport without trial any foreigner who was suspected of "treasonable or secret" plans or deemed "dangerous to the peace and safety" of the United States. The Alien Enemies Act then enabled Adams to arrest, detain, or deport any citizen of any nation with which the United States was at war. Finally, and most infamously, the Sedition Act authorized fines and imprisonment against those who would "write, print, utter, or publish . . . any false, scandalous and malicious writing" against the Federalist administration. In an ironic twist of fate, it became law on the anniversary of the storming of the Bastille.

More than twenty Republican newspaper editors were arrested for protesting Adams's actions and the Sedition Act itself. The most notorious victim was Matthew Lyon, the congressman from Vermont and the editor of *The Scourge of Aristocracy and Repository of Important Political Truth*. Lyon was already a firm Federalist enemy on account of decrying the president's alleged "unbounded thirst for ridiculous pomp, foolish adulation, and selfish avarice"; yet with the new laws in their arsenal, the Federalists now contrived to republish one of Lyon's letters in the *Vermont Journal*. He was promptly arrested and sentenced to four months in prison, where he became a Republican cause célèbre. While incarcerated, Lyon was reelected to the House with an *increased* majority. For Thomas Jefferson, the militarism provoked by the French crisis and the repressive nature of the Alien and Sedition Acts threatened to return the United States to the clutches of tyranny. He hoped, however, that maturity and tolerance would yet win the day. "A little patience," he wrote, "and we shall see the reign of witches pass over, their spells dissolve, and the people, recovering their true sight, restore their government to its true principles."[18]

The Quasi-War

As domestic American politics erupted into vicious disputes, the United States began naval actions against the French Republic. On July 9, 1798 Congress authorized the naval engagement of the French but it did *not* declare war, hence the name of "the Quasi-War." The collisions of the conflict occurred off the southern coast of the United States and in the

Caribbean, where the United States Navy pursued and harried French privateers. Strategically, this was not an easy war to win, or even to fight. Although the United States Navy could deploy twenty-five vessels and the French had few frigates in the Caribbean, the Americans had no bases from which to secure provisions or make repairs. Nonetheless, the Quasi-War was a resounding success for the United States. The Americans lost only one ship, the *Retaliation*, to the French and even then it was recaptured within seven months. The most sensational triumphs were those of the U.S.S. *Constellation*, one of the first six frigates to have been commissioned in 1794. In February 1799 off Nevis, under the command of Captain Thomas Truxtun, it fought and captured the French frigate *L'Insurgente*, a thirty-six-gun ship and the fastest in the French navy. Known as the "Yankee Racehorse" for its own speed, the *Constellation* also inflicted serious damage on the French frigate *La Vengeance*. Appropriately, given the cause of the war, American merchant vessels played their part in defeating the French, with Albert Gallatin telling Congress that "the armed private vessels had been of much greater service in preserving our vessels from plunder, than our navy." Perhaps the most expressive index of American success was the reduction in marine insurance rates. From peacetime rates of 5 to 7 percent, they had skyrocketed as American shipping was preyed upon by the French. In April 1797, it was reported that major underwriters "will not take a risk to the West Indies and back under 33½ to 40 percent against all risks." Yet by early 1800, even before the Quasi-War was concluded, rates had fallen back to about 10 percent.[19]

Indeed, such was the comfort with which the U.S. Navy patrolled its waters that the greatest wartime threat to the United States arguably came from a Pennsylvanian auctioneer named John Fries. To finance the development of the navy, the Federalist Congress, undeterred by the violent reaction to the "whiskey excise," had levied another direct tax upon the citizens of the Union. Applied to dwelling-houses, land, and slaves, the measure aimed to raise $2,000,000, and Pennsylvania, one of the larger and wealthier states, was ordered to contribute about one-eighth of the sum. Although there were few slaves in Pennsylvania, the other assessments— and the intrusive nature of their collection—caused serious discontent. In February 1799, Fries started organizing protests, and by March bands of protestors led by Fries himself had begun to harass tax assessors. As taxmen were harangued across Pennsylvania, arrest warrants were issued for those who refused to pay. The more extreme Federalists agitated for severe repression of the protest and the draconian punishment of its ringleaders. *Porcupine's Gazette*, the newspaper edited by the British immigrant William

126 · AN INDEPENDENT EMPIRE

Cobbett, demanded that "the principals of the insurrection must be eradicated, or anarchy must ensue." The militia were soon directed to arrest the protestors, three of whom—including Fries—were convicted of treason and sentenced to hang. John Adams, however, eager to restore domestic tranquility, commuted the death sentences and eventually granted amnesty to Fries's "rebels."[20]

Peace and "Revolution"

Almost as soon as the Quasi-War began, so too did the quest for peace. In a rare mistake, Talleyrand had goaded the United States into naval conflict by seeking personal enrichment and aggrandizement, thus antagonizing the American commissioners and their government. Talleyrand did not want this war. Peace with the United States was vital to his program for the restoration of the French Empire in the Americas: the French could not reconquer and hold Saint Domingue, or reclaim and retain Louisiana from the Spanish, if they were also fighting the Americans. Talleyrand therefore urged the Directory to pursue an armistice; by August 1798, he was begging for negotiations. These were not hollow overtures. Some of the French legislation that had been so obnoxious to American shipping was annulled that July, while an embargo on American vessels was lifted shortly afterward. Many Americans desired peace too. George Logan, a pacifist Quaker from Pennsylvania, traveled to France of his own volition to negotiate a truce between the nations. He did so without authority, acting only as a private citizen. When Logan returned from France bearing Talleyrand's good wishes, the Federalists were sufficiently outraged to pass the eponymous Logan Act, which made it a federal crime for private citizens to interfere in governmental disputes with foreign nations. The greatest obstacle to peace between the nations was removed by the Coup de 18 Brumaire on November 9, 1799. Here, the Directory, which had maintained collective antipathy toward the United States, was overthrown by the Corsican general Napoleon Bonaparte, who established himself as First Consul of the Republic. Talleyrand, who had helped to instigate the coup, returned to the foreign ministry and repealed the remaining decrees that authorized the seizure of American ships. In a further gesture of goodwill, Napoleon ordered ten days of mourning in France for George Washington, who had died in December 1799.

By April 1800, peace negotiations had been opened, the United States having sent another three-man commission to France. This time it consisted of William Vans Murray of Maryland, the American minister to the

Netherlands; Oliver Ellsworth, the chief justice of the Supreme Court; and William Richardson Davie, the former governor of North Carolina. Despite a protracted negotiating process that took almost six months, the Convention of 1800 was agreed on October 1. It was signed two days later, with much ceremony, at Mortefontaine to the north of Paris. The Convention terminated the Franco-American Alliance of 1778, ensuring that the United States was no longer obliged to make war on Great Britain simply because France was doing the same. By its other terms, the Convention stipulated that there "shall be a firm, inviolable, and universal peace" between the United States and France, that each was to grant the other "most favoured nation" status in trade, that the French would enjoy fishing rights in the North Atlantic, and that privateers would take out insurance against potential damage due to unlawful captures.

The Convention of 1800 was not received with universal acclaim in the United States, not least among Francophobe Federalists. The first time around, it was rejected by the Senate, partly because it did not make the French pay indemnities for the ships they had captured, and partly because it gave France special "neutral" privileges. Even Ellsworth's friend Oliver Wolcott, the former governor of Connecticut, was perturbed by the terms: "You will read the treaty with astonishment. . . . I can account for it only on the supposition that the vigor of Mr. Ellsworth's mind has been enfeebled by sickness." Yet when the Senate voted again, enough Federalists agreed with Hamilton that to reject the treaty "would . . . utterly ruin the Federal party and endanger our internal tranquillity." When the article on indemnities was expunged and the treaty's operation limited to eight years, the Convention of 1800 was ratified.[21]

Nevertheless, preventing the Quasi-War from escalating into full-on warfare and then making a painless peace were, for John Adams, two of the crowning achievements of his presidency. "I desire no other inscription over my gravestone," he wrote, "than 'Here lies John Adams, who took upon himself the responsibility for peace with France in the year 1800.'" In keeping the peace, Adams believed he would "leave the state with its coffers full, and the fair prospects of a peace with all the world smiling in its face, its commerce flourishing, its navy glorious, its agriculture uncommonly productive, and lucrative." Adams's peace, however, would not save his presidency. In late 1800, the Federalists were plunged into internecine squabbling, with Alexander Hamilton deliberately turning on the president in response to the congressional disbandment of his armies and Adams's dismissal of Timothy Pickering and James McHenry from the cabinet. In the election held between October and December, Adams was defeated conclusively by Thomas Jefferson and his running mate, Aaron Burr, with the Republican candidates winning 61 percent of the popular vote. Thanks to the quirks of the early electoral college, in which votes for president were not distinguished from votes for vice president, Burr and Jefferson tied. It required thirty-six ballots in the House of Representatives to separate them, and Jefferson was at last elected as president on February 17, 1801. The guard was changed, but the Republicans of the 1800s would face many of the same problems as the Federalists of the 1790s. In securing the expansion of the American empire, Republican foreign policies were no less single-minded than those pursued by Washington and Adams.[22]

John Marshall

In one of the eulogies delivered upon his death in 1835, the Virginian jurist and statesman John Marshall was described as "six feet high, straight and rather slender, [and] of dark complexion." He possessed "eyes dark to blackness, strong and penetrating, beaming with intelligence and good nature," and "raven-black hair of unusual thickness and strength." Marshall's appearance conveyed the impression of a serious, intelligent, and forceful man, and the impression did not misrepresent his character. As a young man, Marshall had served in the Continental Army, rising to the rank of captain and enduring the brutal deprivations of the winter at Valley Forge. After the war, he trained as a lawyer and made his first major contribution to national politics by supporting ratification of the 1787 federal Constitution in Virginia. Although he resumed private legal practice, Marshall remained active in politics, coming to identify with the Federalist Party. In 1795, he declined the position of United States attorney general, but returned to the national stage when appointed to the "XYZ" peace commission. There followed a series of offers, rejections, appointments, and elections before Marshall eventually became Adams's secretary of state, at which post he oversaw the negotiation of the Convention of 1800. Yet it was Marshall's next office that defined both his career and much of the legal history of the United States: chief justice of the U.S. Supreme Court.[23]

Marshall was one of the appointees selected by Adams to prevent the incoming Jefferson from filling empty judicial seats. His tenure, though, was far from a stopgap: at the helm of the Supreme Court for thirty-four years, Marshall remains the longest-serving chief justice. Among the cases referred to Marshall's Court, two became landmarks of United States jurisprudence. The first was *Marbury v. Madison* (1803), where the seemingly insignificant refusal of James Madison, as secretary of state, to deliver documents of commission to Judge William Marbury led to a ruling that secured

Figure 7.2. *John Marshall* (1833) by Asher Duran after Henry Inman. Metropolitan Museum of Art, New York.

the practice of judicial review under the 1787 Constitution. As Marshall put the matter: "It is emphatically the province and duty of the Judicial Department to say what the law is. Those who apply the rule to particular cases must, of necessity, expound and interpret that rule. If two laws conflict with each other, the Courts must decide on the operation of each."[24]

The second of Marshall's great cases was *McCulloch v. Maryland* (1819). Here, in order to impede the operation of the Second Bank of the United States, the state of Maryland had been taxing all paper money that was not issued by a bank chartered within its borders. The case hinged on whether

Congress had the power to pass laws for which the Constitution had not provided explicitly. Marshall's interpretation of the "Necessary and Proper Clause" held the following:

> The sound construction of the Constitution must allow to the national legislature that discretion with respect to the means by which the powers it confers are to be carried into execution which will enable that body to perform the high duties assigned to it in the manner most beneficial to the people. Let the end be legitimate, let it be within the scope of the Constitution, and all means which are appropriate, which are plainly adapted to that end, which are not prohibited, but consistent with the letter and spirit of the Constitution, are constitutional.

It also followed from the Court's decision that the states of the Union did not have the constitutional power to interfere with the operation of federal laws.

In later years, Marshall's Court delivered a trilogy of judgments that framed the relationship of the United States with Native American tribes. In *Johnson v. M'Intosh* (1823), *Cherokee Nation v. Georgia* (1831), and *Worcester v. Georgia* (1832), the Marshall Court held that the federal government was supreme in disputes between the states and tribes; that the tribes were "domestic dependent nation[s]" as opposed to foreign nations; and that tribal sovereignty was protected from the states by the federal government. The last of these opinions provoked the famous, though probably apocryphal reaction from Andrew Jackson that "John Marshall has made his decision; now let him enforce it!"[25]

The early United States had survived almost constant security crises by constructing federal institutions that were sufficiently powerful and durable to meet those challenges. In this way, John Marshall and his Court proved as vital to the eventual success of the United States as Washington's military leadership, Franklin's diplomacy, and Hamilton's fiscal policies. Even if successive administrations were antagonized by Marshall's Court, its rulings on the extent of federal power, in time, improved the ability of the federal government to protect the Union and the national interest. Moreover, the checks and balances for which the United States Constitution is so lauded were not effective until Marshall's Court had established its power to overrule the legislature and the executive on constitutional questions. Thanks to Marshall, the judiciary became a strong third branch of an increasingly stable system of federal government.

CHAPTER 8

The Purchase and the Pirates, 1800–1805

To the deadly climate of St Domingo, and to the coarse and obstinate resistance made by its black inhabitants are we indebted for the obstacles which delayed the colonization of Louisiana, till the auspicious moment, when a rupture between England and France gave a new turn to the projects of the latter, and destroyed at once all her schemes as to the favorite object of her ambition.

—Alexander Hamilton, July 1803[1]

By the spring of 1801, new men with new ideas governed the great Atlantic powers. In the United States, Thomas Jefferson had succeeded John Adams as president, while the Republicans had won majorities in both chambers of Congress. This "Revolution of 1800," as Jefferson later reflected, "was as real a revolution in the principles of our government as that of 1776 was in its form." The secretary of state, the Union's chief diplomat, was now James Madison. The architect of the Constitution and a former congressman, Madison was also a foundational figure of the Republican Party. Albert Gallatin, a Swiss-born émigré and one of the few Republicans who fully understood the Hamiltonian fiscal system, had been made secretary of the treasury. Across the Atlantic, Great Britain was now the United Kingdom: the Act of Union of 1800 had come into force in January 1801, merging the Irish parliament in Dublin with that at Westminster. William Pitt the Younger, prime minister since 1784, resigned in March 1801 in protest at George III's opposition to Catholic Emancipation, and his replacement was the reluctant Henry Addington. In France, the Revolution was over. The bloodless Coup de 18 Brumaire had overthrown the Directory and established the Consulate with three executive officers of the French Republic. The Third Consul was Charles-Francois Lebrun; the Second Consul was Jean Jacques Régis de Cambacérès; and the First Consul, of course, and effective dictator, was Napoleon Bonaparte. The game, however, had not changed with the players. The British and French still vied for global supremacy, and the Americans—in the words of Jefferson's inaugural address—maintained their commitment to "peace, commerce, and honest friendship with all nations." Having freed itself from the French Alliance, Jefferson declared the Union now sought "entangling alliances with none."[2]

One player had not changed: Talleyrand, the foreign minister of the French Consulate, who had set in motion a grand plan to restore France's American empire. The twin pillars of Talleyrand's vision were Louisiana, stretching from the Gulf of Mexico into present-day Canada, and Saint Domingue. Although Talleyrand was not the first French minister to seek the reclamation of Louisiana, since both Vergennes and Moustier had similar designs, his plans were the most extensive. He envisioned the territory's settlement: French colonists would control the Mississippi, check the westward expansion of the United States, dominate the North American continent, and provide a lucrative export market for manufacturers in France. Sugar from Saint Domingue would meanwhile raise customs revenue for the French exchequer. The restoration of this empire would be complex, laborious, and immensely difficult. For a start, Louisiana had been Spanish since 1763 and Saint Domingue had been in revolt since 1791. Talleyrand also understood that he could not build an empire while fighting both the Americans and the British. Peace with the United States was achieved through the Convention of Mortefontaine of 1800, but peace with the British took longer: negotiations began only when the bellicose Pitt was replaced by Addington. Preliminary terms were signed in September 1801, the Treaty of Amiens in March 1802.

By this time, the French acquisition of Louisiana had already been accomplished. It was unexpectedly easy, too, for the Spanish simply gave it back. By the late 1790s, Spain had become the "sick man" among the European empires. In the Second Treaty of San Ildefenso (1796) with France, the Spanish king Charles IV—best known, perhaps, for his patronage of Francisco Goya—had been obliged to declare war on the British, who in retaliation seized the Caribbean colony of Trinidad and the Balearic island of Minorca. Worse still, continual warfare had plunged Spain into financial distress: the British blockaded the Spanish ports of the Iberian Peninsula; convoys from the New World were attacked by the Royal Navy; and the national debt was soon eight times higher than in 1793. Thus exhausted, Spain's New World empire obtained, to quote Henry Adams, "the influence of a whale over her captors." Talleyrand was not slow to pounce. As early as the summer of 1798, he urged Spain to relinquish Louisiana. Such a move, Talleyrand urged, would benefit both France *and* Spain, while harming the United States, whom neither wished to see grow further. "Let the Court of Madrid cede these districts to France," he purred, "and from that moment the power of America is bounded by the limit which may suit the interests and the tranquility of France and Spain to assign her. The French Republic, mistress of these two provinces, will be a wall of brass forever impenetrable to the combined efforts of England and America. The Court of Madrid," he insisted, had "nothing to fear from France." The French maintained this pressure on the Spanish and, by the fall of 1800, an agreement was reached: Louis Alexandre Berthier, representing the French Republic, and Mariano Luis de Urquijo, representing Charles IV, concluded the *Third* Treaty of San Ildefonso. The Spanish ceded all of Louisiana to the French, who in return created the paper Kingdom of Etruria in Tuscany for the Duke of Parma, a cousin of the Spanish king and the husband of his daughter, the Infanta. The French also promised *not* to transfer Louisiana to any party other than Spain. Signed in secrecy only two days after France's Convention of Mortefontaine with the United States, the Treaty meant that the first piece of Talleyrand's puzzle had fallen into place: Louisiana once again was French. The restoration of French power in Saint Domingue, however, would prove more difficult.[3]

Losing Saint Domingue

In 1793, planning to seize the island from the French, the British had invaded Saint Domingue. Yellow fever and military defeats led to the failure of the campaign, enforcing a gradual withdrawal, but a smaller British military presence was maintained on the island until 1798. Encamped at Port-au-Prince on the western coast, the British were commanded by Thomas Maitland, a practical, competent general who often acted on his own initiative instead of waiting for instruction from London. In April 1798, recognizing the weakness of his position, Maitland signed his first treaty with Toussaint L'Ouverture, the black general who led Saint Domingue's former slaves. Maitland agreed to withdraw from the west of the island; in exchange, French royalists were granted amnesty from Toussaint's forces, who still fought in the name of the French Revolution. Later that summer, admitting the futility of the British campaign, Maitland struck another deal with Toussaint: if the British could evacuate safely, they would never return to Saint Domingue, nor would the Royal Navy interrupt trade with the island. In a quid pro quo, Toussaint promised not to interfere with Britain's slave colony of Jamaica. Terms were agreed on August 31, 1798. With the British gone for good, Saint Domingue now belonged to the former slaves.

Without a common enemy, however, challengers to Toussaint emerged. One was Gabriel d'Hédouville, sent by the Directory to govern Saint Domingue and to undermine Toussaint, whom the French regarded as a threat to their direct control of the island. Forced to flee as tension rose, Hédouville transferred his command to André Rigaud, a free "mulatto" who had helped to consolidate slave freedom in the southwest of Saint Domingue and to repel the British invasion. Rigaud respected Toussaint's leadership in the north but he would not bow to it, not least because he believed in a racial hierarchy that placed mulattos above the former black slaves. The resultant discord led to the War of Knives between these champions of the Haitian Revolution. In fighting between June 1799 and March 1800, Toussaint was victorious, his forces often commanded in the field by Jean-Jacques Dessalines. The decisive blow was struck when Toussaint's men invaded Rigaud's southern territory and defeated the future Haitian president Alexandre Pétion at the port of Jacmel. With his adversaries vanquished, Toussaint instituted autocratic rule in Saint Domingue. In December 1800, in defiance of instructions from Napoleon, who was by now supreme in France, Toussaint invaded Santo Domingo, freeing the Spanish slaves and establishing dominion over the whole island of Hispaniola. The next July, Toussaint even promulgated a new constitution for Saint Domingue: while nominally "attached to the French republic," the "colony" was in fact armed and autonomous, and Toussaint was to be its governor-general for life.

The French then dispatched a thirty-thousand-strong army of reconquest that was commanded by Charles Leclerc, the husband of Bonaparte's sister, Pauline. Among its other leaders were Pétion and Rigaud, the exiled enemies of Toussaint. At first in league with the remaining whites and Pétion's mulattos, Leclerc's troops made significant inroads. Two of Toussaint's most trusted lieutenants, Dessalines and Henri Christophe, became so convinced of defeat that they abandoned their leader and declared allegiance to the French. Toussaint was then invited to parley with Leclerc but, rather than consider his terms, the French arrested him: as a prisoner of war, the Haitian general was remanded to Fort-de-Roux in the Alps. From "the depths of this prison," at "the frontiers of the republic . . . in an awful cell," Toussaint would invoke "the justice and the magnanimity of the first consul" to hear his pleas for freedom, but within a year he would die of exposure and pneumonia.[4]

That summer of 1802 was the high point of the French campaign in Saint Domingue. In the end, Leclerc struggled and failed because he faced an insuperable difficulty: he had been ordered to reenslave men, women, and children who would rather fight to the death than be returned to bondage. Ever since the first insurrection of 1791, freedom and civil equality had been the sine qua non of black support for the French Republic. Indeed, the third clause of Toussaint's Constitution of 1801 had stated: "There cannot exist slaves [in Saint Domingue], servitude is therein forever abolished. All men are born, live, and die free and French." Yet the liberation achieved by Toussaint sat poorly with reformulated French policy toward the colonies: free blacks, it was reasoned, could not be controlled, nor, as they shifted from producing sugar for market to producing food for themselves and their families, would they produce enough sugar or demand enough French goods to sate the exchequer. Napoleon therefore issued a decree in May 1802 that ordered the maintenance of slavery in colonies where it had not yet been abolished. Believing that the defeat of rebellious slaves on Guadeloupe was a fait accompli, the restoration of slavery was commanded there too. Denis Decres, the minister of the marine and the colonies, then sent a similar order to Leclerc at Saint Domingue. Slavery would not be reinstated immediately, for Decres believed that "vigilance, order, [and] a discipline at once rural and military must take the place of the positive and pronounced slavery . . . for some time yet." Eventually, however, the right moment would come to return the black islanders "to their original condition, from which it has been so disastrous to have drawn them." This intended restoration of slavery was not only a repudiation of Revolutionary principles, but the betrayal of the blacks who had fought with the French against the British.[5]

For the French campaign in Saint Domingue, this betrayal proved fatal. Rumors of the prospective restoration of slavery now united the island's armed factions *against* the French. Dessalines, Pétion, and Christophe switched allegiances (again) and attacked Leclerc's forces. Within months, twenty-four thousand French troops were dead, the victims of warfare, yellow fever, and malaria; a further eight thousand were hospitalized. In dire need of provisions, Leclerc began to assail American shipping, thereby angering the only merchants who could supply his army. Leclerc succumbed himself in November 1802 and was replaced by the Vicomte de Rochambeau, the son of the hero of the American Revolutionary War. Rochambeau fully supported Napoleon's plan to restore slavery, describing to the First Consul the need to "declare the negroes slaves, and destroy at least 30,000 negroes and negresses—the latter being more cruel than men," conceding that "These measures are frightful, but necessary." On Rochambeau's watch, the conflict on Saint Domingue degenerated further into a series of vengeful atrocities. After one battle, Rochambeau buried five hundred alive; Dessalines responded by hanging five hundred Frenchmen. Every such act weakened the French, who soon fought only for survival. It would take the devastation of Rochambeau's forces at Vertières in November 1803 for the French army to collapse entirely, but Napoleon had given up long before. With the resumption of war against the British on the horizon, France no longer had the time, resources, or maritime security to support Talleyrand's vision for a western empire. Faced with a choice between continental Europe on the one hand and Saint Domingue and Louisiana on the other, Napoleon decided to rid France of its American burdens. On January 1, 1804, Dessaline proclaimed the independent Haitian Republic on Hispaniola.[6]

The Louisiana Purchase

Napoleon had not been alone in desiring the restoration of slavery in Saint Domingue. Thomas Jefferson, fearful of the example that a free black republic might set, had supported Bonaparte's ambition and, as president, he embargoed Saint Domingue, cut off American aid to the rebels, and refused to recognize Haitian independence. Jefferson did not, however, pursue a pro-French foreign policy. For all his sympathy for the French Revolution and its ideology, he would not reorient American foreign policy to favor the French Republic or the Napoleonic Consulate. Nowhere was this more evident than in Jefferson's attitude toward the American West. As early as 1785, he had suspected French ambitions in North America, drawing the attention of John Jay to the planned Pacific expedition of Jean-François de Galaup, the Comte de la Pérouse. The official objectives of the mission were to surpass the British voyages undertaken by James Cook, to collect examples of exotic flora and fauna, and to chart unknown coasts and waters. Jefferson, then the American minister in Paris, admitted that La Pérouse's vessels carried "men of eminence in different branches of science." Yet he had also come across certain details "in conversations and some other circumstances" that seemed to indicate "some other design." Perhaps the French had designs on "colonies on the western cost of America, or perhaps only to establish one or more factories there for the fur trade." Whatever the case, Jefferson did not believe the French had been "perfectly weaned from the desire of possessing continental colonies in America." Nor did he think French ambitions were limited to the remote reaches of the continent. "If they would desire a colony on the Western side of America, I should not be . . . satisfied that they would refuse one which should offer itself on the Eastern side." In turn, French diplomats understood that Jefferson was not an unshakable ally. "Jefferson is an American," wrote the French minister Pierre Adet, "and as such cannot sincerely be our friend. An American is the enemy of all the peoples of Europe."[7]

It was therefore entirely consistent for Jefferson, as president, to insist that the United States and *not* France should possess New Orleans and thereby control the Mississippi. Jefferson might have supported the French campaign in Saint Domingue, and the French might have been natural allies of the Americans, for Jefferson admitted that "of all nations of any consideration France is the one which hitherto has offered the fewest points on which we could have any conflict of right, and the most points of any communion of interest." Yet when the president learned of the retrocession of Louisiana, he became desperate to prevent the consolidation of French power in the American West. "The cession of Louisiana and the Floridas by Spain to France," he wrote to the American Minister in Paris, Robert Livingston, "works most sorely on the [United States]." There could be no compromise here. There was "on the globe one single spot the possessor of which is our natural and habitual enemy," and that spot was New Orleans.[8]

As Jefferson explained to Livingston, New Orleans was the port "through which the produce of about three-eighths of our territory must pass to market, and from its fertility it will ere long yield more than half of our whole produce and contain more than half of our inhabitants." While the feeble and impotent Spanish could have held New Orleans for decades without troubling the United States, French possession of the city posed immense danger:

> The impetuosity of her temper, the energy and restlessness of her character, placed in a point of eternal friction with us, and our character, which though quiet, and loving peace and the pursuit of wealth, is high-minded, despising wealth in competition with insult or injury, enterprising and energetic as any nation on earth, these circumstances render it impossible that France and the United States can contrive being friends when they meet in so irritable a position.

Even worse than French possession of New Orleans was the diplomatic arrangement into which it would force the United States. "The day that France takes possession of New Orleans," Jefferson predicted, "seals the union of two countries, who, in conjunction, can maintain exclusive possession of the ocean." If the Americans had to remove the French from New Orleans, Jefferson knew they would be forced to "marry ourselves to the British fleet and nation," thus compromising their cherished principles of neutrality and isolation. In such ways, just as *access* to the Mississippi and New Orleans had been vital to the development of the American West, *control* of the river and its outlet now became essential to the expansion and the integrity of the Union.[9]

The Americans were not the only ones with eyes on Louisiana. During the Peace of Amiens, Rufus King, the American minister in London, reported on a conversation with Henry Addington, the British prime minister. Addington had suggested to King that "if the war [with France resumes], it would perhaps be one of their first steps to occupy New Orleans." King interrupted Addington: although he agreed that the United States "could not see with indifference that Country in the hands of France," he insisted that "it was equally true that it would be contrary to [American] views and with much concern that we should see it in the possession of England." Apprised that the Americans were content to see Louisiana remain Spanish, Addington assured King that British occupation would be only a temporary, strategic measure. "England would not accept the Country ere all agreed to give it to her; that were she to occupy it, it would not be to keep it, but to prevent another Power from obtaining it." Addington even admitted "that this end would be best effected by its belonging to the United States." The Prime Minister would therefore be glad if the Americans could take Louisiana; if not, Addington advised that "we ought to prevent its going into the hands of France." King rejected the advance. British control of Louisiana, even temporary control, was just as offensive to the United States as a revived French Empire on the North American continent.[10]

To the end of excluding European powers from the Mississippi, Jefferson ordered Robert Livingston to purchase New Orleans and the Floridas from the French. In the early stages of negotiation, little progress was made: Livingston was deaf, irritable, and he could barely understand French. Moreover, the French were holding out for good news from Saint Domingue. Yet when the island was lost, Louisiana became useless to Napoleon, who ordered Talleyrand to arrange its transfer to the United States. On April 11, when Livingston sat down to negotiate over New Orleans and the Floridas, the French proposed something remarkable: "What," asked Talleyrand, "will you give for the whole?" James Monroe joined Livingston to offer support—and to claim the lion's share of the credit—and bargaining began over the price of Louisiana, which was not, of course, what the American envoys had been instructed to buy. Within three weeks, the French had been haggled down from $15 million to $11,125,000, which worked out to less than three cents per acre. From the French perspective, the Louisiana Purchase was an act of Napoleonic dictatorship, the sacrifice of territory for cash, much of which would be used to meet American claims against the French dating back to the Quasi-War. Napoleon had also ignored the counsel of his closest advisors. Talleyrand still nurtured hopes for a western empire based on Louisiana; moreover, he hoped that, if Napoleon retained Louisiana, he might then relinquish his claim to Malta and so avoid further war with the British. Not for the last time, the schemes of the French foreign minister were thwarted by the impetuosity of his master.[11]

From the American perspective, the Louisiana Purchase was one of the great historical examples of opportunism. Exceeding their instructions, Livingston and Monroe had doubled the size of the United States and improved the security of their nation's western border. Jefferson was ecstatic. Writing to the radical English intellectual Joseph Priestley, the president described the Purchase in the most glowing terms: "I confess I look to this duplication of area for the extending of a government so free and economical as ours, as a great achievement to the mass of happiness which is to ensue." Some Americans even construed the Purchase as a victory for the French. Just as Addington had been willing to occupy Louisiana and then transfer it to the United States to prevent its acquisition by France, Napoleon wished that Louisiana should never become British. "It will be useful to the whole world," he declared, "if I am able to prevent [the British] dominating America as they now dominate Asia." George Cabot, the senator from Massachusetts, recognized as much when writing to Rufus King in July 1803. "The cession of Louisiana," he wrote, "is an excellent thing for France. It is like selling us a ship after she is surrounded by a British fleet. It puts into safekeeping what she could not keep [for] herself." Moreover, France was "rid of an incumbrance that wounded her pride, [she] receives money, and regains the friendship of [the American] populace."[12]

All the same, the Purchase was not hailed universally as an American triumph, or as a lawful transaction. For one thing, France had promised Spain not to transfer Louisiana to a third party. For another, even if some advocates of states' rights would concede extensive powers to the federal government in order to obtain Pensacola, Mobile, and New Orleans, many others condemned the annexation of Louisiana. Federalists meanwhile feared that Republican-dominated slave states would be carved out of the Purchase land. Settlers in the southwest were further concerned, unsure of how far Louisiana extended, how it would be governed, or how their rights would be balanced against those of the French and Spanish colonists who were now "American." Abraham Ellery of the Mississippi Territory described how many were "anxious . . . to know, in what manner our new acquisition is to be divided & what form of government it will receive; how far W. Florida is comprised in the purchase, or whether the Western Bank [of the Mississippi] will be bartered for it."[13]

As Ellery suggested, the Purchase had failed to define the borders between Louisiana and the Spanish-held Floridas. When Louisiana was transferred to the United States on December 20, 1803, the French simply handed over, without examination or definition, whatever they had been given by the Spanish. There was a notorious exchange between Livingston and Talleyrand on this point:

> LIVINGSTON: "What are the eastern bounds of Louisiana?"
> TALLEYRAND: "I do not know, you must take it as we received it."
> LIVINGSTON: "But what did you mean to take?"
> TALLEYRAND: "I do not know."
> LIVINGSTON: "Then you mean we shall construe it our own way?"
> TALLEYRAND: "I can give you no direction. You have made a noble bargain for yourselves and I suppose you will make the most of it."

As after 1783's Treaty of Paris, the borders of the United States might have been enlarged and redefined, but they were not defined accurately. Moreover, West Florida—including Baton Rouge, Mobile, and vital stretches of the Mississippi's east bank— remained in Spanish hands.[14]

The Purchase had an infamous coda. As the United States sought to define, to organize, and to settle its newly acquired land, Louisiana played host to one of the most notorious plots in American history, the Burr Conspiracy. The land involved in the Purchase was split in two: the southern part, including New Orleans and Baton Rouge, from the Mississippi delta to the thirty-third parallel, was organized as the Orleans Territory. The lands beyond became the Louisiana Territory, and James Wilkinson, the traitorous soldier, was named in 1805 as its first governor. His appointment had been secured by Aaron Burr, the former vice president who in 1804

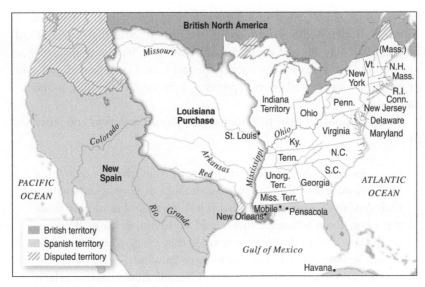

Figure 8.1. The Louisiana Purchase

had killed Alexander Hamilton in a duel. Burr then entangled Wilkinson in his eponymous, alleged conspiracy to establish an independent republic in the American West. Scheming with the Spanish and the British, who were told that "the inhabitants of Louisiana . . . prefer having the protection and assistance of Great Britain," Burr designed to seize vast swaths of land and to encourage the secession of the western states of the Union. Upon the "discovery" of the conspiracy, Burr was charged with treason and tried at Richmond, Virginia, but not convicted. John Marshall, presiding over the trial, ruled that promoting secession was not in itself treasonous: "There must be an actual assembling of men for the treasonable purpose." Moreover, there was no credible evidence of treason, not least because Wilkinson had doctored his own papers to incriminate Burr and exculpate himself. The farrago proved that while the Purchase might have improved the security of the American frontier with respect to rival empires, the Union was still vulnerable to "enemies domestic."[15]

The Barbary Wars

Besides the acquisition of Louisiana, the presidency of Thomas Jefferson also saw the United States fight a war, on land and at sea, against the Barbary States. These North African realms were the autonomous Ottoman city-states of Tripoli, Algiers, and Tunis and the independent Sultanate of Morocco. In the Mediterranean and the eastern Atlantic, their corsairs had long assailed the ships of enemies *and* neutrals under the pretext of war against infidels. In reality, the Barbary pirates seized, imprisoned, and sold or ransomed sailors and other captives as a means of obtaining influence and cash.

As the Tripolitan envoy to Britain had explained to Adams and Jefferson in 1786:

> It was founded on the law of their great Profet: that it was written in the Koran, that all Nations who should not have acknowledged their Authority were sinners: that it was their right & duty to make war upon them wherever they could be found, & to make slaves of all they could take as prisoners; & that every Musselman who should be slain in battle was sure to go to Paradise That it was a Law, that the first who boarded an Enemy's Vessell should have one slave, more than his share with the rest, which operated as an Incentive to the Most desperate Valour & Enterprize. That it was the practice of their Corsairs to bear down upon a ship; for each sailor to take a Dagger in each hand & another in his Mouth & leap on board, which so terrified their Enemies, that very few ever stood against them. That he verily believed the Devil assisted his Country-men, for they were almost allway's successfull—[16]

Because of the strength of their navies and their wealth, the French and British could resist this interference or simply bribe the pirates not to attack. The Americans, however, by declaring their independence, had forgone British protection of Yankee merchant ships, and so the unwanted attention of the Barbary fleet was a curse from the earliest years of independence. The brigantine *Betsey*, for example, was captured by Morocco in 1784 and the schooners *Dauphin* and *Maria* were seized by Algiers in 1785. Although a diplomatic resolution was reached with Morocco, the sailors of the *Dauphin* and the *Maria* remained prisoners of Algiers for more than a decade while the United States erected a government that could afford the ransom. It was not until 1795 that the 115 American prisoners were released at a cost of more than $1 million, not far off one-sixth of the federal budget for the year. An additional agreement with Algiers committed the United States to pay an annual fee of $1 million for the safe passage of American shipping. That decision satisfied the Federalist desire for the protection of Atlantic shipping, but it disgusted Republicans who balked both at paying "tribute" and at the priority given to East Coast commercial interests over western settlement. A 1796 treaty with Tripoli was no less controversial for its apologetic statement, in its English version, that "the Government of the United States of America is not, in any sense, founded on the Christian religion."

Despite these treaties, corsairs from Morocco and the Barbary States continued to harass American shipping when their rulers saw fit, or when those rulers' lost control over their own ports and sailors. Just as debilitating as the French attacks that caused the Quasi-War, this Barbary threat became a major spur toward the establishment of the Department of the Navy and the commissioning of new frigates in the 1790s. Indeed, just before Jefferson assumed office in 1801, Congress appropriated funds for the provision of six new frigates that would "protect [American] commerce and chastise [Barbary] insolence—by sinking, burning or destroying their ships and vessels wherever you shall find them." It was a timely development, for upon Jefferson's inauguration in 1801 the pasha—or, as the Americans called him, the "Bashaw"—of Tripoli, Yusuf Karamanli, demanded tribute of $225,000 from the new administration. When Jefferson refused to pay, the pasha repudiated his 1796 treaty and declared war by cutting down the flagstaff in front of the American consulate in Tripoli. Congress, whose exclusive authority to declare war was not contested by Jefferson, did not respond in kind; rather, the president was authorized to retaliate against Tripolitan shipping, "to cause to be done all such other acts of precaution or hostility as the state of war will justify." As with the Quasi-War, war was not declared by Congress, but was waged nonetheless.[17]

Joined briefly by the kingdoms of Sweden and Sicily, both of which had suffered at the hands of the corsairs, the First Barbary War was fought mostly on the Mediterranean. Once the frigates and schooners of the navy had been deployed, the superiority of the American forces was incontestable. Notable victories were won by the USS *Enterprise* over the *Tripoli* and then at the Second Battle of Tripoli Harbor. In an earlier expedition, the USS *Philadelphia* had been captured by the Tripolitans when it ran aground. The helpless American sailors surrendered and were taken captive, while the Bashaw's men began to refurbish the ship to use against the American fleet blockading Tripoli Harbor. In February 1804, a band of United States Marines, led by Stephen Decatur, deceived the Barbary guards on the *Philadelphia* by sailing a captured Tripolitan ketch alongside it, boarding the American ship, and sinking it, thereby depriving Tripoli of

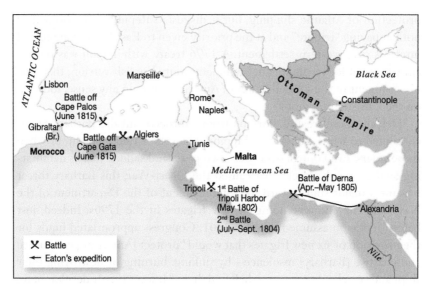

Figure 8.2. North Africa and the Barbary Wars

its most formidable weapon against further American assaults. The British admiral Horatio Nelson described the America action as "the most bold and daring act of the age."

The decisive blow, however, would not be struck until May 1805, when William Eaton, the former consul in Tunis and a veteran of Anthony Wayne's Legion of the United States, led a mercenary army stiffened with Marines to victory at the Battle of Derna. Eaton took in tow with him Hamet, an exiled brother of Yusuf Bashaw and a claimant to the rule of Tripoli. The American commander designed to capture Derna, a strategically important port in the province of Cyrenaica. From there he planned to rally the populace to Hamet, march on Tripoli, overthrow Yusuf and install his puppet, and at last impose a treaty that would shut Tunis to the pirates forever. Eaton's band marched for fifty days across almost four hundred miles of Saharan desert. Upon arrival at Derna, they received naval support from Commodore Samuel Barron, who had the USS *Nautilus*, *Argus*, and *Hornet* at his disposal. Although burdened with managing threats of mutiny and hostility between the Christian and Muslims among their troops, Eaton and his second-in-command, Marine lieutenant Presley O'Bannon, directed the campaign adroitly. On April 27, 1805, Derna was attacked on land from two sides, from the sea by cannon, and within ninety minutes the city had fallen. The American flag was raised, for the first time, over a battlefield to the east of the Atlantic. A momentous occasion in the history of the American military, it is commemorated by the second line of the Marines' Hymn: "to the shores of Tripoli."[18]

By the time of the victory at Derna, the Barbary War had lasted four years. Bashaw Yusuf was wearied, his resources were almost exhausted, and while the Tripolitan people did not rally to Hamet, the Bashaw nonetheless negotiated peace with the American "consul to Barbary," Washington's former private secretary Tobias Lear. Prisoners of war were returned to their respective nations, with the Americans paying an additional "ransom" of $60,000 because they had more prisoners to receive than to release. The American squadron then paraded in front of Tunis's harbor, and through sheer intimidation, secured a treaty with her ruler. Protection from Tripolitanian and Tunisian corsairs was now promised to American sailors, and insurance rates fell accordingly, but safe passage on the high seas was far from certain. Algiers would continue to menace American shipping until the United States defeated the Dey in the Second Barbary War (1815). In the intervening years, it was *British* hostility at sea that became the outstanding foreign policy issue to which Jefferson and the Republicans addressed themselves.

CHAPTER 9

Embargo

On the impressment of our seamen, our remonstrances have
never been intermitted. A hope existed at one moment, of an
arrangement which might have been submitted to, but it soon
passed away, and the practice, though relaxed at times in the distant
seas, has been constantly pursued in those in our neighborhood.[1]

—Thomas Jefferson, January 1806

In the years following the Louisiana Purchase, the principal foreign-policy
challenges of the United States continued to revolve around the French
and the British, who from 1803 led opposing coalitions in the latest war to
engulf Europe. France was now a self-proclaimed empire, having replaced
a series of failed republican governments with a despotic monarchy. Napoleon was styled "Emperor of the French" in May 1804 and his coronation,
a remarkable exhibition of pomp and grandeur, was held in December that
year: in Notre-Dame, "L'Empereur" crowned himself while Pope Pius VII
watched the ceremony as a pliant spectator. Supreme in France, Bonaparte
was supreme across Europe too. In 1805 he mounted the successful invasion of Italy, and in December of that year he achieved his greatest military triumph at the Battle of Austerlitz. A crushing defeat of a much-larger
force of Russians and Austrians, Austerlitz effectively brought about the
dissolution of the Holy Roman Empire, in place of which Napoleon instituted the puppet state of the Confederation of the Rhine. "Roll up that
map of Europe," sighed Pitt the Younger, "it will not be wanted these ten
years." Yet in spite of this Napoleonic mastery of the continent, the British
had maintained their naval supremacy, which was confirmed in October
1805 when Nelson and Cuthbert Collingwood defeated a Franco-Spanish
fleet at Trafalgar off the southwestern coast of Spain.

As the Europeans fought on land and at sea, the Americans strove to maintain diplomatic neutrality, to nurture trade with both the French and the British, and to avoid war at all costs. "Peace is our passion," wrote President Jefferson. "We prefer trying *every* other principle, right, and safety, before we would veer to war." Maintaining this position of detached and amicable neutrality meant convincing London that the United States could align with France, and convincing Paris that the United States could align with Britain: James Madison, for instance, thought it best for the American minister to France to leave Napoleon and Talleyrand "under apprehensions of an eventual connexion" between the United States and the United Kingdom. Yet if a definite choice between the British leviathan and the French behemoth became unavoidable, the British were considered the lesser evil. Not only was British trade vital to the Hamiltonian fiscal system that Jefferson and Gallatin, the secretary of the treasury, had inherited and maintained, but Napoleon's imperialist despotism had persuaded the supposedly Francophile Republicans to shelve their admiration for the French. Writing to the Scottish agriculturist John Sinclair, Jefferson reflected that "the events which have taken place in France have lessened in the American mind the motives which it felt in that revolution." The British were the last, best hope against Napoleonic domination: "We see," continued Jefferson, ". . . the position in which Great Britain is placed, and should be sincerely afflicted were any disaster to deprive mankind of the benefit of such a bulwark against the torrent which has for some time been bearing down."[2]

Yet as the fighting in Europe continued, expanding in 1807 to Iberia by means of the Peninsular War, the British would disregard such goodwill and push the American commitment to peace to the limit. Despite the terms of the Jay Treaty, the British continued to interfere with Native Americans in the Northwest. Although the London bank of Barings had financed the Louisiana Purchase, His Majesty's Government refused to recognize the legality of the transfer. In 1808, the British then made an alliance with the Spanish, who still possessed the Floridas and with whom the Americans had not yet agreed on a southern border. Most grating of all, when the British fleet again found itself undermanned at the recommencement of hostilities in 1803, Great Britain undertook with renewed vigor the practice that threatened to precipitate war almost by itself: the impressment of American sailors into the Royal Navy.

Impressment

Despite its glory and renown, service in the Royal Navy was far from popular. The pay was pitiful, conditions in wartime were horrendous, and discipline was draconian. The warrant officer William Richardson even suggested that, while his fellow Britons talked "of negro slavery and the whip," they would find a more deserving object of sympathy in the "poor sailor arrived [home] after a long voyage." With few volunteers subjecting themselves to such misery, the British manned their ships by means of the time-honored and long-despised practice of impressment, whereby authorized lieutenants and their "press-gangs" abducted able-bodied men from British harbors and merchant vessels into the Royal Navy. In this context, British sailors who were desperate to avoid the press-gang often sought employment aboard ships of neutral nations such as the United States. At the turn of the nineteenth century, half of all sailors on American merchant vessels were British subjects. Here, they enjoyed better pay, greater safety, and theoretical protection from impressment. Service aboard neutral ships, however, offered only limited protection in practice: while the United States recognized the Royal Navy's right to impress British subjects from American ships that were moored in British ports, the Royal Navy insisted on searching American ships on the high seas too. Acquired citizenship of a neutral nation provided little security, either, for the legal process of naturalization went unrecognized by the British. The Royal Navy further claimed the service of anyone, no matter his nationality, who had *ever* enlisted on a British ship, or who had married a British woman, or who had settled in British territory. Moreover, while British ministers disavowed claims to the service of native-born Americans who had no ostensible British connection, the press-gang was less discriminating; its net was cast far and wide. In February 1808, James Madison informed Congress that "four thousand [and] twenty-eight American seamen had been impressed into British service since the commencement of war, and nine hundred thirty-six had been discharged, leaving in that service three thousand two hundred and ninety-two." The fate that befell such Americans was often grisly. Resolutions later passed by American sailors who had been impressed and then imprisoned by the British described their experience as worse than the "Algerine bondage" that had provoked the Barbary Wars. Even more deplorable than personal suffering was the violation of principle: by impressing American citizens, the Royal Navy was denying the neutrality of American shipping and the sovereignty of the United States itself.[3]

Diplomatic attempts to resolve the impressment crisis had failed repeatedly. In 1794, John Jay had broached the issue when negotiating "his" treaty. An article providing for the mutual release of impressed sailors was included in a draft, but *not* in the final treaty. The general eradication of impressment was not discussed at all. When war between the French and the British resumed in 1803, and when the Royal Navy returned to its policy of forcible recruitment, impressment became a grievance of national importance. Writing to James Monroe, who was serving as the American minister in London, Madison delivered a scathing assessment of British policy on the high seas. How could the British, he asked, depict the virtual imprisonment of American sailors on British ships as "voluntary service," while simultaneously seizing Britons on American ships who were genuine volunteers? The result was a British policy of deceit, ignorance, and sophistry:

> When the voluntary consent of the individual favors her pretensions, [the United Kingdom] pleads the validity of that consent. When the voluntary consent of the individual stands in the way of her pretensions, it goes for nothing! When marriage or residence can be pleaded in her favor, she avails herself of the plea! When marriage and residence, and even naturalization are against her, no respect whatever is paid to either!

Madison fumed that the United Kingdom took "by force her own Subjects voluntarily serving in our Vessels" but kept "by force American citizens involuntarily serving in hers." The situation, he concluded, was intolerable. "More flagrant inconsistencies cannot be imagined."[4]

There came another opportunity to address the issue in 1806, when Monroe and William Pinkney met for negotiation with Lord Holland and Lord Auckland, representatives of the Ministry of All the Talents. Talks began in August and the Americans sought guarantees of the neutral trading rights of American merchants and the end of impressment. The latter point was essential: Jefferson instructed Monroe that, should he "sign a treaty not providing satisfactorily against the impressment of our seamen," the whole treaty would be repudiated. The British, though, refused to compromise, deeming impressment essential to their naval struggle against Napoleon. The Monroe-Pinkney Treaty, as it became known, was drafted in December 1806 and received by Jefferson in March 1807. Disgusted by the absence of concessions on impressment, the president kept his word and refused to send the treaty to the Senate. The American negotiators, Jefferson bemoaned, had "concluded to sign such as could be obtained," but what they had obtained was insufficient. Why Monroe and Pinkney considered the treaty worthy of Jefferson's attention remains puzzling. The clashes over impressment continued.[5]

The Continental System and the *Chesapeake*

Besides the humiliation inflicted by the press-gang, the United States was an indirect victim of the economic warfare waged between the United Kingdom and the French Empire. In May 1806, the Royal Navy had declared the blockade of all European ports under French control, aiming to starve the French and their allies of international trade and to redirect continental exports through the ports of Britain's allies. In response, Napoleon constructed his Continental System. First, in November 1806, he issued the Berlin Decree, which forbade his allies and client states from trading with the British. The United Kingdom retaliated with orders in council stipulating that trade with France and France's allies—even by neutral nations—would be permitted only through British ports, and thus be subject to British taxes. British prime minister Spencer Perceval explained this policy by invoking "the short principle . . . that trade in British produce and manufactures, and trade either from a British port or with a British destination, is to be protected as much as possible." Perceval explained that France and French allies "will have no trade, or they must be content to accept it through us." The only trade, "cheap and untaxed," that Britain would allow to its enemies would be "either direct from us, in our own produce and manufactures, or from our allies, whose increased prosperity will be an advantage to us." Perceval conceded that his decisions made for "a formidable and tremendous state of the world," but he defended the British response as proportional to "the new severity with which Buonaparte's decrees of exclusion against our own trade were called into action." It was a classic, explicit statement of economic protectionism, the defense of a policy designed to benefit the British and deprive the French. The United States, as a neutral nation trading with both sides, was caught between a rock and a hard place, as each power sought to diminish the Americans' trade with the other.[6]

As impressment continued and as trade with Europe was interrupted, American calls for retaliation grew louder. The Royal Navy soon gave the United States greater cause for belligerence. On June 22, 1807, HMS *Leopard*, a fourth-rate warship, engaged the USS *Chesapeake* off the coast of Norfolk, Virginia. Under the command of Commodore James Barron—the brother of Samuel, naval commander at the Battle of Derna—the *Chesapeake* was caught unawares by the *Leopard*. The British were under orders to search the *Chesapeake* for deserters, so they hailed the American ship and Lieutenant John Meade was sent aboard. Barron, of course, refused to let Meade search the American ship, so the British sailor returned to the *Leopard*, from which its commanding officer, Salusbury Pryce Humphreys, ordered the *Chesapeake* to submit. Again, Barron refused, whereupon the *Leopard* fired a shot across his bows. The British then unleashed a volley of broadsides and the Americans, unprepared for combat, managed only one shot in return. The *Chesapeake* was humiliated, Barron struck his colors, and the Americans surrendered, having suffered three fatalities and eighteen casualties. The British boarded the *Chesapeake* again, this time in arms, seized four deserters, and then sailed off, leaving the officers and crew of the *Chesapeake* to stew in the shame of their unmanning. Only one of the deserters seized was in fact a British subject.

American reaction to the *Chesapeake* affair was apoplectic. Madison wrote to Monroe, who was still in England, that "this enormity is not a subject for discussion." The secretary of state raged that the British had breached every principle and protocol, since "the immunity of a [neutral] National ship of war from every species and purpose of search, on the high seas, has never been contested by any nation." Madison also damned the affair as an act of absolute hypocrisy, since "Great Britain would be second to none in resenting such a violation of her rights and such an insult on her Flag." The British, Madison continued, could empathize with the Americans, or at least comprehend their outrage, if they imagined a situation where "instead of the customary demand of our mariners serving compulsively . . . on board her ships of war, opportunities had been seized for resourcing them in like manner, whenever the superiority of force or the chance of surprise might be possessed by our ships of war." Many Americans expected that war would be the unavoidable consequence of the affair. Gallatin, the secretary of the treasury, wrote to his brother-in-law that "war was a necessary result" and that his "faculties have been exclusively applied to the preparations necessary to meet the times." Even if Gallatin feared the fiscal consequence of war, he accepted that defending national honor was more important than preserving federal finances:

> We will be poorer both as a nation and as a government, our debt and taxes will increase, and our progress in every respect will be interrupted; but all those evils are not only not to be put in competition with the independence and honor of the nation, they are moreover temporary, and a very few years will obliterate their effects. Nor do I know whether the awakening of nobler feelings and hab-

its than avarice and luxury might not be necessary to prevent our degenerating, like the Hollanders, into a nation of mere calculators.

Gallatin knew that American neutrality was not respected by the great powers of Europe. The public clamored for retribution and so Jefferson, like Gallatin, knew that, if he chose war with the British, war would be popular: "Never since the Battle of Lexington," he noted, "have I seen this country in such a state of exasperation as at present."[7]

In spite of their unceasing aggression at sea, the British were nonetheless anxious to avoid opening an American front to their war with the French. The right to search and to remove individuals from "national vessels" such as the *Chesapeake* had therefore been disclaimed, but in that same proclamation the British had reasserted their right to search neutral (and therefore American) merchant vessels for what they called "deserters," which, when interpreted by the lieutenant of the press-gang, could mean "anyone." Furthermore, the Americans had no guarantee that the offensive orders in council, ostensibly wartime measures, would be rescinded if peace was made. Worse still, Napoleon had reinforced his Continental System with the Milan Decree, ordaining that *all* vessels bound for British ports, even those flying a neutral flag, would be considered British and therefore lawful prey. As a neutral nation trying to trade with both belligerents, the United States was now vulnerable to British taxes and commercial restrictions—which had proved intolerable in the colonial period—*and* to wanton French depredations of the kind that had caused the Quasi-War in 1798. Loud voices demanded retaliation.

Embargo

Despite these affronts to American sovereignty, Jefferson knew that the United States was unready for war with a major European power, especially at sea. He therefore ignored the clamor to fight. Instead, the president elected to place economic pressure on the British and the French by excluding them from American trade. There was some sense in this. In wartime, the United States had become a major supplier to both the French and the British; by denying American supplies to both nations, Jefferson hoped to inflict enough economic damage that Americans demands on shipping and impressment would be heeded. The Non-Importation Act of 1806 had tested this policy by banning the importation of British paper, silk, leather, wool, spikes, hats, playing cards, and beer, goods that Americans could produce for themselves. The Act was enforced when Monroe and Pinkney failed to deliver concessions on impressment, but it was ineffective. John Randolph, then a congressman from Virginia and an extreme Republican enemy of the president, described it as "a milk-and-water bill, a dose of chicken-broth to be taken nine months hence."[8]

In the summer of 1807, Representative John Page, a friend of the president, called for "an immediate embargo . . . in order to retrieve our lost honor & to bring the mad King to his senses." Page was not alone in his thinking, and Jefferson was soon convinced that economic warfare was the appropriate response to the new British orders in council and Napoleon's Milan Decree. Some within his cabinet disagreed. Gallatin, for instance, argued that an embargo would not change European behavior, and he described the hope that it would "induce England to treat us better . . . [as] entirely groundless." Gallatin also suggested that "government prohibitions do always more mischief than had been calculated." In a classic articulation of small-government theory, he then told the president that it was "not without much hesitation that a statesman should hazard to regulate the concerns of individuals as if he could do better than themselves." Jefferson, though, was committed to the embargo, which he described as a "candid and liberal experiment" in "peaceable coercion."[9]

Upon the Embargo Bill's introduction to Congress in December, the president defended the policy as the only practical alternative to an ill-advised war. Jefferson emphasized "the great and increasing dangers with which our vessels, our seamen, and merchandise are threatened on the high seas and elsewhere." Reminding Congress of the "great importance to keep in safety these essential resources," he recommended the "inhibition of the departure of our vessels from the ports of the United States." The bill sailed through, passing the Senate by twenty-two votes to six and the House by eighty-two votes to forty-four. On December 22, only four days after the bill was brought to the floor, Jefferson signed the Embargo Act into law. Now, any and all exports from the United States were illegal. American vessels could dock in foreign ports only with the explicit permission of the president. Economic war against Britain and France had been declared.[10]

Yet while the embargo was designed to give the Americans economic leverage over Europe, it in fact strangled the economic development of the Union. In New England, the hub of the nation's oceanic trade, the embargo was extremely unpopular. Northern Federalists, who believed the embargo was salt being rubbed into the wound of the Louisiana Purchase, attacked Jefferson as "Tom Two-faces," a president who ruled the nation "with mountain salt, horned frogs, [and] prairie dogs." The *Gazette* of Portland, Maine, decried the embargo as an abuse of power "unknown in any other age or nation—a power unknown and contrary to our laws and constitution." The embargo itself was depicted in Federalist cartoons as "Ograbme" a snapping turtle that assaulted all those who would dare trade with the British. Besides the political and philosophical, New Englanders also had good practical reason for their anger: in Massachusetts, exports in the first embargo year of 1808 were only 25 percent of those in 1807; for the rest of New England, just 21 percent.[11]

In the Mid-Atlantic states, too, the effects of the embargo were devastating and deplored. John Lambert, a British painter and an editor of Washington Irving's *Essays*, visited New York during the embargo and depicted the city's port as the scene of desolation. His account is a vivid depiction of economic hardship and a noteworthy catalog of the number and range of industries that were adversely affected:

> How shall I describe the melancholy dejection that was painted upon the countenance of the people, who seemed to have taken leave of all their former gaiety and cheerfulness? The coffee-house slip, the wharfs and quays along South-street, presented no longer the bustle and activity that had prevailed there five months before. The port, indeed, was full of shipping; but they were dismantled and laid up. Their decks were cleared, their hatches fastened down, and scarcely a sailor was to be found on board. Not a box, bale, cask, barrel, or package, was to be seen upon the wharfs. Many of the counting-houses were shut up, or advertised to be let, and the few solitary merchants, clerks, porters and laborers, that were to be seen, were walking about with their hands in their pockets. Instead of sixty or a hundred carts that used to stand in the street for hire, scarcely a dozen appeared, and they were unemployed; a few coasting sloops, and schooners, which were clearing out for some of the ports in the United States, were all that remained of that immense business which was carried on a few months before. The coffee-house was almost empty; or, if there happened to be a few people in it, it was merely to pass away the time which hung heavy on their hands. . . . In fact, everything presented a melancholy appearance. The streets near the water-side were almost deserted, the grass had begun to grow upon the wharfs, and the minds of the people were tortured by the vague and idle rumors that were set afloat upon the arrival of every letter. . . . In short, the scene was so gloomy and forlorn, that had it been the month of September instead of April, I should verily

have thought that a fever was raging in the place, so desolating were the effects of the embargo.

Lambert concluded that Jefferson's embargo was an economic plague. In only five months it "had deprived the first commercial city in the States of all its life, bustle, and activity; caused above one hundred and twenty bankruptcies; and completely annihilated its foreign commerce!"[12]

The embargo crippled more than private enterprise, for it also deprived the federal fiscal system of the customs revenue on which it depended. The likelihood of this effect had been flagged in 1805 by Samuel Smith, a Baltimore merchant and a senator from Maryland.* Bemoaning the "mortifying" fact that the United States could not "in an effectual manner resist the insults and injuries of Great Britain," Smith had written that the United States had "no revenue but [that which] arises from importation." The federal government, Smith explained, was required to raise eight million dollars each year "for the extinguishment of the public debt and the interest thereon," not to mention the costs of operating the "internal government, the army and navy." How, asked Smith, "if we by non-importation cut off that great source of revenue, . . . are we to meet the payment?" Smith was prescient indeed.[13]

The only major aspect of American commerce not ruined by the embargo was the carrying trade, but this was scant consolation when compared to the general losses inflicted upon the economy. John Wayles Eppes, a congressman from Virginia, would concede that "national honor cannot be estimated in dollars and cents," but he damned the embargo nonetheless. "The Carrying Trade," he stated, ". . . yields a revenue of eight hundred and fifty thousand dollars." The embargo, he went on, would protect those "eight hundred and fifty thousand dollars," but would "put at hazard a net revenue of five million, four hundred and thirty-two thousand dollars." In such a policy, Eppes perceived only madness: "A Nation, deliberately forming a commercial regulation, by which it risks millions to protect thousands, manifests more zeal than wisdom." Coming from a Virginia Republican, *not* a New England Federalist or an East Coast merchant, this criticism was surprising. It was all the more unexpected since Eppes was Jefferson's son-in-law.[14]

As the embargo proved ever less popular, its enforcement proved ever more difficult. In New England, upholding the embargo was the responsi-

---

*In a stunning turnaround, Smith then introduced the Embargo Bill to the Senate in 1807.

bility of the customs collectors, but they—like the stamp-tax commissioners of the 1760s—were prone to follow local opinion, not federal instruction. Breakers of the embargo also knew they would be tried, as was their Sixth Amendment right, by a jury of local people that would likely sympathize with their case. The government's inability to enforce the embargo concerned Gallatin. Despite his initial objections, he described the embargo as "the boldest which ever was attempted in a popular government," but confessed to Madison that he "had not anticipated the violations bordering on insurrection which have taken place in so many quarters." He conceded the people's right "to change the administration by elections if they are dissatisfied with the measures adopted," but worried that the "disobedience & resistance which have been encouraged [were sapping] the very foundation of our institutions." *That* was intolerable, and so Gallatin would "rather . . . encounter war itself than to display our impotence to enforce our laws." Most critically, the embargo failed to cripple the British economy as planned. John Quincy Adams, who had lost his Massachusetts seat in the Senate for supporting the embargo, reflected that its impact was minimal when compared to the great cost of the war against Napoleon: "The embargo affects [British] interests no doubt," he noted, "but nations sacrifice men by the hundred thousands and treasure by the hundred millions in War, for nothing, or worse than nothing." In the context of such profligacy, what impact could the American embargo really do?[15]

The embargo was abandoned before Jefferson left office. The American economy was suffering unduly, and so too were federal finances. On March 1, 1809, Congress passed the Non-Intercourse Act, which permitted the exportation of American goods to foreign nations other than France and the United Kingdom. Three days later, James Madison, having beaten James Monroe for the Republican nomination and then routed the Federalist candidate, Charles Cotesworth Pinckney, was inaugurated as the fourth president of the United States.

The Non-Intercourse Act was soon replaced by Macon's Bill Number Two, named for its sponsor, North Carolina Representative Nathaniel Macon. Signed into law in May 1810, this new legislation organized an auction between the United Kingdom and France. Under its provisions, the United States would trade freely with both nations for a period of three months; if either of the European powers stopped attacks on American shipping during this period, that nation would be granted unrestricted trade with the United States, while the other would be subjected to another embargo. In November 1810, Madison declared that the French had ceased their depredations against American vessels. In reality, the French had not, and Napoleon had no intention of doing so; Madison was simply trying to trick the British into granting concessions to the United States. The British, however, called Madison's bluff and made no concessions. In fact, Perceval's government issued further orders in council to constrict Anglo-American trade. In February 1811, therefore, the provisions of Macon's Bill were executed and American ports were closed once more to British ships. The problems of transatlantic commerce, not to mention impressment, continued to fester. Diplomacy had provided few answers; economic sanctions had failed. Open war between the British and the United States now loomed.

Albert Gallatin

Albert Gallatin is the personification of the American experiment. Born in the free city-state of Geneva in 1761, he was a devoted republican who devoured Jean-Jacques Rousseau and Voltaire as a teenager, an advocate of small government who mastered the arts of the federal system, and an explorer and scholar of the American continent. Having arrived in the United States in the summer of 1780, Gallatin quickly took up arms in defense of his adoptive nation, commanding a garrison in Maine during his first American winter. He taught French at Harvard before settling in southwestern Pennsylvania. Having attended the state's constitutional convention in 1789, Gallatin had won election to the Senate by 1793. His service was short-lived. On the day that Gallatin took his seat, Pennsylvania's Federalists protested that he had not been an American citizen for the constitutionally requisite nine years and that his election was invalid. With the Federalists holding a majority in the Senate, a report recommending Gallatin's expulsion was upheld and he was forced to return to Pennsylvania. It was an eventful exile from Congress: the Whiskey Rebellion was in full swing, and though Gallatin had encouraged protest, he also advocated moderation. Having played a key role in defusing the potential crisis, and retaining the admiration of his constituents, he was elected to the House of Representatives in 1795. With the House's seven-year citizenship requirement now satisfied, Gallatin served three terms until 1801.

Upon Jefferson's election to the presidency, Gallatin was appointed secretary of the treasury, an office he held throughout Jefferson's administration and into Madison's second term. The appointment was a perfect fit: Gallatin had mastered the complexity of Hamilton's fiscal system and, having served on the House Standing Committee on Finance, had gained

Figure 9.1. *Albert Gallatin* (c. 1803) by Gilbert Stuart. Metropolitan Museum of Art, New York.

a reputation for financial brilliance. A notable and steadfast advocate of federal retrenchment, Gallatin's economic philosophy was distilled into an 1800 report, *Views of the Public Debt, Receipts and Expenditure of the United States*. At the Treasury Department, Gallatin turned this philosophy into policy: despite financing the Louisiana Purchase and suffering the effects of Jefferson's embargo, the public debt was by 1809 reduced by $14 million. "I am not wrong in the belief," he observed, that the Union's "public funds are more secure than those of all the European powers." For the success and the stability of the United States, Gallatin's stewardship was vital. The direction of American foreign policy, after all, was worthless without the means to support it.

Gallatin resigned from the Treasury Department in February 1814 and, following spells as a peace commissioner (see chapter 10), the negotiator of the Convention of 1818, and American minister to both France and subsequently the United Kingdom, his later years were devoted to intellectual pursuits. In 1831, he helped to found New York University as a place of learning for those without means: "It appeared to me impossible," Gallatin wrote to his friend Jean Badollet, "to preserve our democratic institutions and the right of universal suffrage unless we could raise the standard of *general* education and the mind of the laboring classes nearer to the level of those born under more favorable circumstances." He then became a founding member of the American Ethnological Society. Indeed, Gallatin has been dubbed "the father of American ethnology" and his major publications in this field include *A Table of Indian Languages of the United States* (1826) and *Synopsis of the Indian Tribes of North America* (1836).[16]

CHAPTER 10

The War of 1812

Call out the ample resources of the county, give them a judicious
direction, prosecute the war with the utmost vigor, strike wherever
we can reach the enemy. . . . We are told that England is a proud
and lofty nation, which disdaining to wait for danger, meets it
half-way. Haughty as she is, we once triumphed over her, and, if we
do not listen to the counsels of timidity and despair, we shall again
prevail . . . in one common struggle, fighting for FREE TRADE
and SEAMEN'S RIGHTS.[1]

—Henry Clay, January 1813

In the years after the embargo there lingered a simmering tension between
the United States and the British, and a series of collisions threatened to
catalyze this tension into open, declared war. In 1809, the Irish-born spy
John Henry had corresponded with the governor-general of Canada, Sir
James Craig, claiming that he had recruited northern Federalists into a
conspiracy to seize New England for the British. Yet as Craig grew tired of
Henry's meddling and refused to "reward" him sufficiently, the spy turned
double agent and offered his correspondence with Craig to the United
States. Madison was sufficiently enraged by the alleged intrigue that he
paid $50,000 to obtain Henry's letters, but they provided little evidence of
disloyalty beyond what could be gleaned from Massachusetts newspapers.
In May 1811, the *Little Belt* Affair reversed the roles of the *Chesapeake-
Leopard* debacle. This time, the sloop-of-war HMS *Little Belt* was pursued,
engaged, and badly damaged off the coast of North Carolina by the USS
President, whose officers had somehow mistaken the British vessel for the
much larger HMS *Guerrière*. There was also rumbling discontent in the
West, into which American settlers were pouring, and where the British—

despite abandoning their forts—had maintained relations with the Native Americans. In late 1807 and 1808, in the wake of the *Chesapeake* Affair, Governor-General Craig sent messages to tribes in the Indiana Territory, calling for their assistance in the event of war with the United States. William Henry Harrison, the governor of the Territory, regarded the activity of local Indians as an accurate barometer of British intentions in North America.

The leader of this revived Indian resistance was the Shawnee chieftain Tecumseh, whom Harrison described as "one of those uncommon geniuses." Along with his brother Tenskwatawa, who was known as "the Prophet," Tecumseh preached the formation of a Pan-Indian alliance in the expectation of British military support. Tecumseh was an inveterate enemy of the American empire, and the possibility that other Indians might compromise with the United States only sharpened his zeal: when in 1809 Harrison made a treaty at Fort Wayne to open more than three million acres of Indian land to settlement by white Americans, Tecumseh was provoked to rally support for his ideal of a unified Indian nation. A subsequent meeting of Harrison and Tecumseh at Grouseland almost saw the two men come to blows, but violence was avoided and Tecumseh avowed a desire for peace. The Indian leader, however, continued to build his alliance, and while he was on a proselytizing mission, recruiting allies among the "Five Civilized Tribes" of the South, Harrison seized his chance.* At the head of a thousand men, the future president marched on Tecumseh's base at Prophetstown and defeated an Indian force led by Tenskwatawa.

Taking its name from a nearby river, the Battle of Tippecanoe did not wreck Tecumseh's confederacy, but it acquired national significance because Americans laid the blame squarely for it at the door of the British. The Tennessee general Andrew Jackson argued that the Indians had been "excited by secret British agents." William Grainger Blount, a congressman from the same state, urged the military to "purge the camps of the Indians of every Englishman to be found." These accusations, although inflammatory, were not baseless, for since the *Chesapeake* crisis in 1807 the British had been furnishing Tecumseh's Indians with money and weaponry, not to mention hopes of a military alliance.[2] The United Kingdom's continued interference in the West thus fostered an indignant nationalism that resented these enduring colonial pretensions. Many of the leading "war hawks," the coterie of congressmen who called for reprisal, were from

---

*This contemporary term referred to the five tribes of the Cherokee, Chickasaw, Choctaw, Creek, and Seminole.

the western states whose security was most threatened by Britain's Indian allies: Henry Clay, the Speaker of the House, and Richard Mentor Johnson were Kentuckian; Felix Grundy was from Tennessee.[3]

Even so, the major cause of tension between the United States and the British remained the infringement of American rights at sea. John Quincy Adams, serving as the American minister to Russia, wrote to William Eustis, the secretary of war, that "the practice of impressment is the only ineradicable wound which, if persisted in [by the British], can terminate not otherwise than by war." Adams urged the declaration of war "explicitly and distinctly upon that single point, and never afterwards [to] make peace without a specific article expressly renouncing forever the principles of impressing from any American vessel." Yet Adams also sounded a note of caution, fearing that the United States was still not strong enough to defeat the British. It would be better, he wrote, "to wait [upon] the effect of our increasing strength and of our adversary's more mature decay, before we undertake to abolish [impressment] by war." Adams was not alone in fearing that Americans were unready for wide-scale conflict. Lieutenant Isaac Roach of the Second U.S. Artillery believed that federal policies had rendered the United States an immature military force. "After a peace of thirty years, and entirely engrossed in trade," he wrote, "every means had been neglected to prepare for war." Roach's assessment of the American fighting potential was scathing. "Our treasury [is] poor, our arsenals empty, fortifications in ruin, our Navy neglected, Military Science unknown, our Army nominally 6000 men, the country divided in opinion." Such pessimism was shared by Daniel Sheffey, a Virginia Federalist. "I am fully sensible to the indignities offered to us," he wrote, "and the repeated violations of our rights as a neutral nation." A just war, however, was not enough for Sheffey; it had to be successful too. The United States required "a national hope that war will remedy the evil which we experience, and that it will not bring with it others much more to be dreaded than that under which we labor." Victories against the Indians in the West, against the French in the Quasi-War, and against the Barbary States had not instilled confidence of success against the British.[4]

Others counseled that any declaration of war had to consider the European context, for the United States could not risk provoking the British *and* the French. Writing to Madison in May 1812, Jefferson warned of a "triangular war," which "must be the idea of the Anglomen and malcontents, in other words the Federalists, and quids."[†] And such a war, against both

---

[†] By "quids" Jefferson meant dissident Republicans such as John Randolph who decried Jefferson's and Madison's administrations as corrupt betrayals of strict constitutional principles.

European powers, would satisfy neither Federalist nor Quid: "It would only change the topic of abuse with the former, and not cure the mental disease of the latter." Jefferson had enforced the embargo as a desperate alternative to military conflict, and the former president still feared the Union being thrown into turbulence by prolonged warfare. The loyalty of Anglophiles in New England, he worried, could be lost forever, since war would "take away the only chance of conciliating . . . our eastern capitalists and seamen." Were such merchant sailors kept in port by war, they would "swell the [number of the] discontents." Perhaps ironically, given the embargo, Jefferson also feared the economic consequence of war. It would "[shut] every port to our prizes" and "shut every market to our agricultural productions." Worst of all, it would place the United States in a questionable diplomatic position, exhibiting "a solecism worthy of Don Quixote only, that of a choice to fight two enemies at a time, rather than to take them by succession." These considerations were crucial. The United States had won its independence because Britain had been forced to fight not only the colonists but the French, the Spanish, and the Dutch, too. The Americans could not afford to endanger that independence now by penning themselves into a similarly isolated corner.[5]

Readiness for war also hinged on the assumption that Napoleon would continue to dominate Europe. The president and the "war hawks" hoped the British would be distracted, perhaps fatally, by Bonaparte's continental triumphs. "It was a fair calculation," Madison later claimed, that "Napoleon, whether successful or not against Russia, would find full employment for [Russia] and her associates, Great Britain included." The Americans expected "that it would be required of Great Britain by all the Powers with whom she was leagued, that she should not divert any part of her resources from the common defense to a war with the United States." In such a situation, "Great Britain would have been constrained by her own situation and the demands of her Allies, to listen to our reasonable terms of reconciliation." Instead, Madison was disappointed: Napoleon wrecked his Grand Army in Russia, failing to defeat the tsar's forces decisively at Borodino, before retreating when the Fire of Moscow denied him shelter in that city. The Allies subsequently launched a counterattack in Europe and recorded a stunning victory in October 1813 at Leipzig, where more than half a million men fought in what was the largest pitched battle in European history to that date. The British-led Allies then embarked on a campaign that took them to Paris but this, Madison

---

The term denoted all who considered themselves a "tertium quid," a "third thing" between Jefferson's administration and its Federalist opponents.

asserted in self-defense, was "the great military revolution in Europe, the most improbable of contingencies."[6]

By that time, ongoing issues at sea had long overridden contingent factors. Henry Clay had declared that he could not "subscribe to British slavery upon the water, that we may escape French subjugation upon land." William Jones, the Pennsylvanian who later served as secretary of the navy, wrote that "if Britain can only be kept afloat by the maintenance of her nefarious pretensions, and the consequent prostration of dearest rights and interest, then *let her sink*." At root, the Americans felt they had to force the British to recognize the United States as a sovereign, equal state. In pursuit of those ends, war with Britain was declared on June 18, 1812. The frayed peace with the British at last was over.[7]

London responded to the declaration of war by proposing an armistice. The new government at Westminster was led by Robert Jenkinson, the Earl of Liverpool. He had assumed office when Spencer Perceval, the only British prime minister to suffer this fate, was assassinated by John Bellingham, a merchant seeking revenge for his bankruptcy and imprisonment in Russia. The United States rejected Liverpool's offer, which made no mention of impressment and which would only suspend—not rescind— the orders in council that authorized attacks on American ships. As James Monroe explained, the Americans were bent on resolving every outstanding issue, not simply on gaining minor concessions. "In going to war," he explained, "all matters of controversy ought to be settled. Impressment is one of the first importance & ought not to be neglected. If we give it up now we sanction the practice. We wish our friendship with that country to be permanent; it is not wished to patch a quarrel to begin in a year or two, but to have a lasting peace with it. To secure this, it will be necessary to settle firstly every difference."[8]

While Caleb Strong, the Federalist governor of Massachusetts, lamented fighting "against the nation from which we are descended," bellicose patriotism flourished throughout much of the Union. Prowar speeches were published by the proadministration *National Intelligencer* and reprinted across the United States in Republican newspapers. Madison even conceived of war as a means of reasserting independence. British violations at sea were the "ineradicable wounds" of which Adams had written, and, as the president explained to Congress on November 4, 1812 after an initial series of American failures in the Canadian theater, "to have shrunk, under such circumstances, from manly resistance would have been a degradation blasting our best and proudest hopes." To *not* declare war would have been a betrayal of the Founding Fathers and "the magnificent legacy which we hold in trust for future generations." It would, moreover, have been the confession of servitude at sea, an acknowledgment that "on the element which forms three-fourths of the globe we inhabit, where all independent nations have equal and common rights, the American people were not an independent people, but colonists and vassals."

Those who did not rejoice and mourn with the Republican majority were made to suffer. In Baltimore, the offices of the *Federal Republican* were destroyed in a riot provoked by antiwar articles. The Federalist *American Patriot* of Savannah, Georgia, and the *Herald* of Norristown, Pennsylvania, were likewise driven out of business. The French, as enemies of Great Britain, once more became friends of the Americans. *Nile's Weekly Register* took it as "granted that the French government is a tyranny, and that Bonaparte is ambitious," but the newspaper still asked "what has he done to merit the exclusive reprehension of [the] friends of humanity?" The French emperor's "tyranny" was now thought "far more tolerable than [the tyranny] of Great Britain, over conquered countries, or even over Ireland." The United States now fought to resist that same British tyrant.[9]

The Atlantic Theater

The War of 1812 was conducted in four main theaters. The first was along the Eastern Seaboard and on the Atlantic itself. Perhaps surprisingly, given British oceanic supremacy, the United States Navy at first gained the upper hand. In August 1812, two months after war was declared, and some four hundred miles off the coast of Nova Scotia, the USS *Constitution* destroyed HMS *Guerrière*, the British frigate for which the *Little Belt* had once been mistaken. After an intense battle at close quarters, a boarding party from the *Constitution*, commanded by Isaac Hull, inquired after the surrender of the *Guerrière*. Tradition claims that the British captain, James Richard Dacres, offered this sardonic reply: "Well, Sir, I don't know. Our mizzen mast is gone, our fore and main masts are gone—I think on the whole you might say we have struck our flag!" The *Guerrière* was too badly damaged to be towed to Boston as a prize ship, but the defeat and scuttling of a British warship and the capture of more than two hundred prisoners of war provided the Americans with a major boost in morale. Two months later, the USS *United States* won another famous victory when it captured HMS *Macedonian* south of the Azores off West Africa. Commanded by Stephen Decatur of Tripoli fame, the *United States* inflicted severe damage on the British frigate: three hours of fighting caused two weeks' worth of repairs, after which the *Macedonian* suffered the dubious honor of being the first

British warship taken as prize into an American harbor. Such victories elevated American naval prestige beyond recognition.[10]

American triumphs were not the exclusive domain of national ships, for American privateers took their toll on British vessels, even in the waters of the British Isles. These operations were given impetus by the August 1814 "Proclamation" of the Baltimore sailor Thomas Boyle, who called on fellow privateers to harass British vessels using "all the ports, harbors, bays, creeks, rivers, inlets, outlets, islands, and sea-coast of the United Kingdom." Many heeded the call. The British *Annual Register* lamented the "most mortifying reflection" that "it was not safe for a vessel to sail without convoy from one part of the English or Irish Channel to another." Premiums on journeys across the Irish Sea, in most cases no more than fifty miles, trebled to an unprecedented 13 percent of the value insured. At one point, the terror of American privateers was such that Lloyd's of London, the famous marine insurers, would not take on business at even extraordinary rates. John Wilson Croker, the secretary of the Admiralty, declared that no British vessel was safe to leave port without escort by a man-of-war. In total, 825 British ships were lost to American privateers.[11]

In time, the overwhelming might of the Royal Navy allowed the British to recover dominance at sea. More than fourteen hundred American merchant ships were seized by the Royal Navy or by British privateers, while the British blockade of the eastern coastline reduced American exports, worth $130 million before the embargo, to just $14 million by 1815. With the British forcing the Americans back into port, they launched several major operations along the Eastern Seaboard. In the Northeast, in Maine, the British commander Thomas Masterman Hardy—to whom Lord Nelson spoke his last words, "Kiss me, Hardy," at Trafalgar—captured Moose Island, now Eastport, without firing a shot. Sir John Coape Sherbrooke meanwhile led three thousand redcoats down from Canada on the Penobscot Expedition. A four-week-long raid on American settlements and harbors, the expedition saw the destruction of eighteen American ships, including the USS *Adams*, which the Americans were forced to scuttle after the Battle of Hampden. The eastern half of Maine would be occupied until the end of the war, the British making their base in the town of Castine and even reestablishing the loyalist colony of New Ireland.

The more significant eastern battles occurred in the Chesapeake region. In retaliation for the American destruction of York and Port Dover in Canada, the British aimed to sack Washington. Against the counsel of James Monroe, who was now secretary of state, American defenses were concentrated not at the capital but at Baltimore, and so the redcoats made almost unimpeded progress toward the "Federal City." An assemblage of

Maryland militiamen was routed at Bladensburg and, on August 24, 1814, a British army led by Major General Robert Ross entered the American capital. Madison and his cabinet, who had expected the militiamen to prevail, fled to the village of Brookeville. General Ross recorded that "so unexpected was our entry and capture of Washington; and so confident was Madison of the defeat of our troops, that he had prepared a supper for the expected conquerors." When the British entered the Executive Mansion, "they found a table laid with forty covers." The banquet prepared for the American leadership "was voraciously devoured by *John Bull*; and the health of the Prince Regent and success to his Majesty's arms by sea and land was drunk in the best wines." The British then set light to selected government buildings. The Executive Mansion in which they had just eaten was burned, as were the Capitol and the Treasury. The fires spread rapidly throughout Washington and local resident Mary Hunter recalled how there "never [was] a drawing room so brilliantly lighted as the whole city was that night." Few inhabitants of Washington "thought of going to bed—they spent the night gazing on the fires and lamenting the disgrace of the city." Only a thunderstorm on the following day saved Washington from utter destruction. In time, the federal institutions were rebuilt and the burnt brick of the Executive Mansion was painted over in white.[12]

Razing Washington was not, however, the goal of the British campaign, and the army marched on toward Baltimore, a major port and a vital base for American privateers. Here, the British met with sterner resistance: Major General Ross was killed by an American sniper; militiamen repelled the British advance at the Battle of North Point; and the Royal Navy, supposed to provide covering fire for British land forces, was unable to destroy Fort McHenry, the sentinel post that guarded the city's harbor. When the British failed at Baltimore and retreated, a storm flag flown over Fort McHenry was replaced with a larger ensign that was visible even by the light of mortar fire. Francis Scott Key, a lawyer from Georgetown, had been negotiating the release of American prisoners aboard HMS *Tonnant* when he saw the flag from the deck of the ship. An amateur poet, Key was inspired to memorialize the battle in a poem, "The Defense of Fort McHenry." It was later set to the tune of an old British song, "To Anacreon in Heaven," and Key's words are now sung as "The Star-Spangled Banner."

Canada

For James Madison, the American invasion of Canada was the critical operation of the whole war. It was the only way to attack British territory directly and the only way to cut off the Canadian trade with New York and

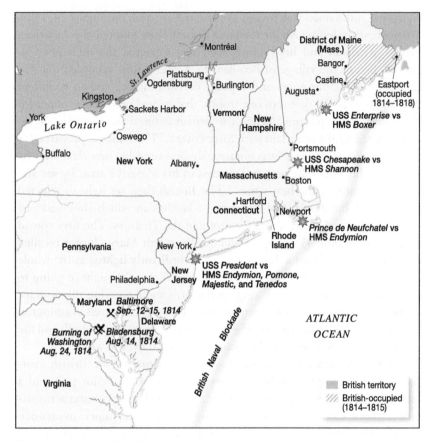

Figure 10.1. War of 1812: The Atlantic theater

New England. As Madison later told Monroe, whom the president considered putting in charge of one attempted invasion, Canada was the main "channel for evading and crippling our commercial laws." The conquest of Canada was also considered the best bargaining chip imaginable, the best means by which concessions on commerce and impressment could be wrested from the British. Writing in December 1813, Henry Clay affirmed that "the object of the war [was] the redress of injuries, and Canada [was] the object by which that redress was to be obtained." The first invasion was mounted by William Hull on July 12, 1812 and American hopes were high. Jefferson had described the conquest of Canada as a mere "matter of marching" and Hull himself issued a proclamation to British settlers, demanding their surrender lest "the horrors and calamities of war . . .

stalk before [them]." The invasion was less successful than imagined. The British commander, Isaac Brock, deciding on bold measures, mounted a counterattack against Detroit, where Hull surrendered without a fight and relinquished American control over much of the Michigan Territory. Brock was rewarded with a knighthood and the epithet "The Savior of Upper Canada." In August, Hull ordered the abandonment of Fort Dearborn (now Chicago), but the evacuees were massacred by Indians allied to the British, and the fort was burned to the ground.[13]

Hull's defeat meant that a second American invasion, a four-pronged assault that had been planned for the fall of 1812, would fail utterly. Hull was to attack Amherstburg through Detroit, but instead he surrendered Detroit and retreated. Henry Dearborn was to attack Montreal, but he tarried at Albany. A third force was supposed to cross the St. Lawrence and capture Kingston, but did not. Only Stephen van Rensselaer, a New York Federalist with no previous combat experience, was able to advance but, when he did, he suffered disaster. Urged "with all possible dispatch" to establish an American foothold in Canada before winter fell, van Rensselaer met Isaac Brock's British forces at Queenston, Ontario, in October 1812. Despite outnumbering the redcoats almost three to one, and despite killing Brock (whose dying words were allegedly "Push on, brave York Volunteers!") the Americans were undone by British discipline and superior artillery. The first major American victory of the Canadian campaign came only in April 1813 when Zebulon Pike, the explorer of the Louisiana Territory, captured the harbor town of York (now Toronto). Even this victory was soon tempered by the expulsion of American forces from the Niagara frontier and then by decisive defeat in October 1813 at the Battle of the Chateauguay, a reverse that put paid to another American plan to seize Montreal.[14]

The Northwest

Connected to the Canadian campaign was the conflict in the American Northwest, where the initial balance of forces did not favor the United States. Beyond a boundary running south from Lake Erie and then west from present-day Ohio, Native American tribes had maintained a strong, even dominant presence. It was here, in the area west of Sandusky, that Tecumseh and the Prophet had cultivated relations with the British and formed their Pan-Indian Alliance. And while the Battle of Tippecanoe might have stunted Tecumseh's confederacy, the Native Americans remained a potent force. The American imperative in the region was sim-

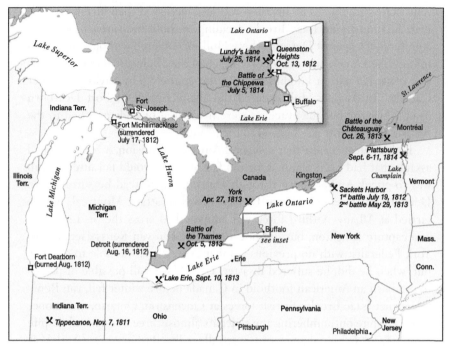

Figure 10.2: War of 1812: The Canadian theater

ple: unless they could take control of Lake Erie—and given the difficulty of communication by land, this was vital—the alliance of British redcoats and Native Americans could maintain control of Detroit and the whole Great Lakes region.

The fall of 1813 witnessed several momentous American victories. In September, the naval commander Oliver Hazard Perry led nine American vessels to triumph over the Royal Navy at the Battle of Lake Erie. Capturing two ships of the line, two schooners, a brig, and a sloop, Perry's victory gave the United States essential control of Lake Erie for the rest of the war. Perry also gave American history one of its greatest one-liners, writing to William Henry Harrison that "We have met the enemy and they are ours." The importance of the Battle of Lake Erie must not be underestimated: in losing control of the lake, the British lost their reason to hold on to occupied Detroit, which Major General Henry Procter soon afterward abandoned. In turn, this allowed Harrison, who had assumed control of the American army in the Northwest, to launch another invasion of Canada in pursuit of Procter's soldiers and their Indian allies. Faring much better than his predecessors, Harrison came upon his quarry on October 5, 1813, at Moraviantown on the River Thames. The ensuing battle was an American walkover. Of four thousand United States troops, many of whom were Kentucky volunteers, only a few dozen were wounded or killed, while almost six hundred British soldiers were captured. Procter was court-martialed, found guilty of "deficiency in energy and judgment," and suspended without pay for six months. More importantly, Tecumseh was slain. The exact details of his demise are unknown, but one account holds that "one of the Big Knives raised a gun loaded with ball and several buckshot and aimed at the left side of the chief's chest and fired." An American soldier then claimed to have skinned Tecumseh's body and "brot two pieces of his yellow hide home with me to my Mother & Sweet Harts." Whatever the truth, the Indians had lost their leader and talisman, and with the scattering of the Western Confederacy the British campaign in the Northwest met its end. The defeat of the Royal Navy on the Lakes, the abandonment of Detroit, and the rout on the Thames combined into humiliation.[15]

Attention now reverted to Canada, but subsequent campaigns along the Niagara and St. Lawrence Rivers did little to change the balance of power on land, while a naval conflict over Lake Ontario ended in stalemate. The next pivotal moment came at Plattsburgh, New York, in September 1814. Earlier that year, in April, Napoleon had been defeated, forced to abdicate, and exiled to the Mediterranean island of Elba. Fifteen thousand British soldiers had thus been freed to reinforce their straggling comrades in North America. Under the command of Sir George Prévost, who had replaced James Craig in Canada, these forces were directed to invade the United States and to eliminate the American naval presence on the Great Lakes. Prévost was advised to attack the naval base at Sackets Harbor, which had already suffered two assaults, but he settled instead on Lake Champlain, which straddled Quebec and the states of New York and Vermont.‡ Not wanting to rile the Vermonters, who had shown little enthusiasm for the war, Prévost marched southward along the western, New York shore of the lake, a route that required seizure of the lakeside settlement of Plattsburgh. Prévost therefore sent for the naval squadron commanded by George Downie and an amphibious assault was planned. Yet when Downie arrived on HMS *Confiance*, Prévost was late to support him; and when the naval battle was lost, he retreated in haste. The consequent victory of the American commanders Thomas Macdonough and Alexander Macomb

---

‡Vermont had become the fourteenth state of the Union in 1791, but like its New England neighbors, the state preferred quiet and trade with British-controlled Quebec to a more active part in "Mr. Madison's War."

was a threefold triumph. First, it gave the United States control of Lake Champlain; second, it brought an end to British incursions from Canada; and third, it denied leverage to the British in concurrent negotiations for peace. As for Prévost, when papers critical of his conduct were published in London, he requested a court-martial that he might clear his name. He died ten days before it was due to take place.

The triumph at Lake Champlain did not, however, mean that another American invasion of Canada would be more likely to succeed. The Americans might have won the war of attrition, but the war in the North remained at a stalemate. In hope of reviving the campaign, Lord Liverpool asked the Duke of Wellington, the hero of the Peninsular War in Spain, to sail to North America to take command of the British forces, but Wellington perceived the deadlock as permanent and advised peace. The "Iron Duke" even described the British campaign as so poorly directed that British negotiators would be unable to extract much from the United States. "I think you have no right, from the state of war," he wrote, "to demand any concession of territory from America. . . . You have not been able to carry [the war] into the enemy's territory, notwithstanding your . . . undoubted military superiority, and have not even cleared your own territory . . . . You can get no territory: indeed, the state of your military operations . . . does not entitle you to demand any." Wellington got his wish to stay in Europe, and his reluctance to cross the Atlantic was soon vindicated by events. In 1815, Napoleon returned from his exile in Elba and the Hundred Days of his restored rule were ended on June 18 by Wellington's victory at Waterloo.[16]

The South

In the first major flashpoint of the Southern theater, the Creeks were broken by Andrew Jackson at the Battle of Horseshoe Bend in March 1814. Long a thorn in the side of American settlers, and so often the willing accomplices of the Spanish, the Creeks were met by Jackson in the Mississippi Territory near present-day Dadeville, Alabama. While the Creeks, specifically the Red Stick Creeks, were vastly outnumbered, Jackson was impressed by their tactical savvy and their military organization. "It is impossible to conceive," he wrote, "a situation more eligible for defense than the one they had chosen and the skill which they manifested in their breastwork was really astonishing." To Jackson's skilled eye, the Creeks lay "in perfect security." Even so, the American artillery barrage, bayonet charge, and numerical superiority told, and more than eight hundred of a thousand Creek warriors were killed at Horseshoe Bend. The resultant

Treaty of Fort Jackson, signed in August 1814, ended the power of the Creek Nation, no matter the friendliness or hostility of the individual factions within it to the United States. The Creeks played no further part in the war, and the United States gained control of what is now central Alabama and southern Georgia.[17]

The major British operation in the South was amphibious. Its target was New Orleans, the vital port on the Mississippi River, and its ultimate objective was the seizure of the Louisiana Territory, which the British aimed to rule by proxy through Spain or as part of the British Empire. This was enormously ambitious. Low-lying New Orleans would have been virtually impossible to defend in perpetuity and at best the city would have become another, more expensive Gibraltar. Initial conquest, however, was not out of the question, not least because of racial tension: white American settlers were terrified that their slaves would rally to the British, who had hundreds of black troops in their army and who, through the naval commander Alexander Cochrane, had offered freedom to runaways. In contrast, the American governor of the new state of Louisiana, William Claiborne, had replaced his mixed-race militia with a whites-only force.

The British and the Americans fought at New Orleans between January 8 and January 18, 1815, before they could receive news of the peace treaty signed in Ghent in faraway Europe on Christmas Eve 1814. The numerical odds had been stacked mightily against the American commander, Andrew Jackson. His force of forty-five hundred comprised some regulars, some militiamen, French and Spanish aristocrats from New Orleans, Choctaw tribesmen, and the piratical crew of Jean Lafitte, the smuggler who was based in nearby Barataria Bay. The British fielded eight thousand regulars, many of them hardened veterans of the Napoleonic Wars, and they were commanded by Cochrane and Edward Pakenham, a hero of the Peninsular War and the brother-in-law of the Duke of Wellington.§ The Americans, however, held two advantages. The first was a series of strong defensive positions on riverbanks and makeshift parapets improvised in part out of bales of cotton. As Wellington later reflected, "The Americans were prepared, with an army, in a fortified position." The second was an inspired and inspirational leader driven by an inveterate hatred of the British. Jackson had been a British prisoner during the Revolutionary War and many of his family had died at British hands: "I owe to Britain a debt of retaliatory

---

§Pakenham was killed at New Orleans. Delivering the eulogy to his brother-in-law, Wellington lay responsibility for the British defeat at the feet of Cochrane. "The expedition to New Orleans . . . still would have been carried," said the Duke, "if the duties of others, that is of the Admiral, had been as well performed as that of whom we now lament."

174 · AN INDEPENDENT EMPIRE

vengeance," he told his beloved wife Rachel, and "should our forces meet I trust I shall pay the debt." His victory at New Orleans, where the Americans inflicted thirty times more causalities than they suffered, was fitting retribution.[18]

Indeed, the Battle of New Orleans was arguably the most-one sided of the war. In December, skirmishes at Lake Borgne and on the eastern banks of the Mississippi had drawn the lines and then, on the morning of January 8, Pakenham sent two forces into pitched battle. The first, under Colonel William Thornton, was ordered to take out American artillery positions on the western bank of the river; the second, the major part of the army, was directed against Jackson's earthworks. Almost every part of the British plan met with calamity. Canals dug for British boats collapsed; ladders brought for crossing American canals and climbing walls were forgotten; the morning fog lifted too soon, exposing the British positions; Pakenham and his second-in-command were struck and killed by grapeshot. Even if Thornton's detachment performed heroic feats, embarrassing the Americans on the riverbanks, the Battle of New Orleans was overall a rout. The United States repelled and destroyed the British army and in only twenty-five minutes more than twenty-five hundred redcoats were lost. The campaign technically continued until January 18 as the Royal Navy attempted to break past Fort St. Philip on the Mississippi River, but the Americans and their privateer allies resisted proudly before the British gave up entirely. This was not just the momentous defeat of the enemy: Jackson and his motley crew had also secured the gateway to the American continental empire.

The Peace

Overtures to peace had begun soon after the declaration of war. In September 1812, Tsar Alexander of Russia, who feared the war would compromise his recent treaties with the British, had offered to act as a mediator. It took months for his offer to reach Washington, but in March 1813 James Madison accepted the proposal and dispatched Albert Gallatin and Delaware's James A. Bayard to St. Petersburg. The British, however, refused mediation, so representatives of both belligerents were sent first to Gothenburg, Sweden, and then to Ghent in present-day Belgium, where negotiations finally began in August 1814. The American commissioners Gallatin, John Quincy Adams, and Henry Clay—in addition to Bayard and Jonathan Russell—formed a formidable team. Yet so confident were the British of victory in the field that they began talks by presenting four demands.

First, all Indian lands should be set aside as a buffer state under British supervision; second, the American navy and army should be excluded from the Great Lakes region; third, the Americans should forfeit their rights to the North Atlantic fisheries; and fourth, part of Maine should be ceded to strengthen Canada. Besides these demands, the British proceeded on the principle of *uti possidetis*, meaning that each side should keep what it held. As a bargaining tactic, the American representatives were instructed to ask for all of Canada.

The Native American "barrier state" proved the major bone of contention, for on that point the United States would not equivocate. The Americans insisted, disingenuously, that "the differences which unhappily subsisted between Great Britain and the United States, and which ultimately led to the present war," were wholly of a maritime nature. The "boundary of the Indian territory," they protested, had "never been a subject of difference. . . . Nor could the American Government have foreseen that Great Britain, in order to obtain peace for the Indians residing within the dominions of the United States, whom she had induced to take part with her in the war, would demand that they should be made parties to the treaty between the two nations." British interference in Indian affairs had long been suffered by the Americans, and there was no chance it would now be permitted. "No maxim of public law has hitherto been more universally established," the Americans told their British counterparts, "than that of suffering no interposition of a foreign Power in the relations between the acknowledged sovereign of the territory and the Indians situated upon it. . . . Whatever may be the relations of Indians to the nation in whose territory they are thus acknowledged to reside, they cannot be considered as an independent Power by the nation which has made such an acknowledgment." The Americans maintained that the proposed barrier state was "utterly unnecessary for the purpose of obtaining a pacification for the Indians." Consequently, British proposals for an independent Indian state would "only be a fit subject of deliberation when it becomes necessary to decide upon the expediency of an absolute surrender of [American] national independence." American hostility to the proposal was profoundly shocking to the British. Writing to the Earl of Bathurst, the secretary of state for war and the colonies, the negotiator Henry Goulburn expressed astonishment at "the fixed determination which prevails in the breast of every American to extirpate the Indians and appropriate their territory," and by the Americans' reluctance to abandon "what they are pleased to call their natural right to do so."[19]

The American negotiators did not develop any great fondness for their

British adversaries. "The tone of all the British notes," complained Adams, "is arrogant, overbearing, and offensive." They were further frustrated by the slow pace of the talks, the British having little authority and referring almost every point to London. The Americans bickered among themselves too. "In discussing with them," Adams confessed, "I cannot always restrain the irritability of my temper." Despite this, conditions in late 1814 were propitious for peace. The United States had learned that it could not expel the British from Canada. Correspondingly, the abdication of Napoleon meant the British had ceased the impressment of American sailors and the seizure of American ships, the two maritime practices that had provoked war in the first place. With both sides desiring settlement, and with neither holding a significant advantage, the Treaty of Ghent restored the status quo ante bellum, except in the West, where the British abandoned the Native Americans for good. Articles 4 to 8 of the Treaty of Ghent meanwhile established new definitions and created joint commissions to resolve the boundary issues left over from the Treaty of Paris and the Jay Treaty. The hero of the piece and of the peace was Gallatin, to whom the Duke of Wellington wrote, "Your moderation and sense of justice, together with your good common sense, places you above all the other delegates, not excepting ours." Pushed through by Gallatin, the Treaty of Ghent was signed on Christmas Eve 1814. It was ratified immediately upon its receipt in Washington in February. The British, however, did not decide finally whether they would adhere to the treaty, keep New Orleans for themselves or hand it over to their Spanish allies, until after they heard of their defeat by Jackson at New Orleans.[20]

The Consequences of War

The Treaty of Ghent might have changed little on the map, but the effects of the war were wide-ranging and long-lasting. In domestic American politics, the War of 1812 was the death knell of the Federalist Party. Having lost the presidency and control of Congress in 1800, the Federalists were long a party on the wane. Recognizing this, and holding beliefs and sympathies inimical to the western and southern Republicans who would come to dominate the United States, extreme Federalists in New England had been considering secession since Jefferson's first term. As Daniel Webster noted, "This design had been formed in the winter of 1803–4, immediately after, and as a consequence of, the acquisition of Louisiana." John Quincy Adams even suggested that Aaron Burr's duel with—and killing of—Alexander Hamilton in July 1804 was a ploy to deny the High Federalists a capable national leader. They were careful not to play their hand too soon. In December 1808, Harrison Gray Otis, the president of the Massachusetts state senate, warned Congressman Josiah Quincy of the dangers of precipitance: "It would be a great misfortune for [Massachusetts] to justify the obloquy of wishing to promote a separation of the States, and of being solitary in that pursuit." Still, the secessionist candle was burning, and Timothy Pickering, the former secretary of state, was keeping it alight.[21]

Timothy Pickering

Timothy Pickering was born in Salem, Massachusetts, in 1763. His early years were markedly similar to those of any number of northern American leaders. First, there was study at Harvard, then the practice of law, followed by service in the Continental Army. His was a colorful military career. Militiamen under Pickering's command at Salem could have fired the "shot heard around the world" were it not for Reverend Thomas Barnard convincing the British to retreat from the town's North Bridge. As adjutant general, Pickering oversaw the forging of Tadeusz Kosciuszko's Great Chain, which prevented the Royal Navy from sailing past West Point on the Hudson River. After the war, having risen as high as quartermaster general, Pickering moved to Pennsylvania, where he represented Luzerne County in the state convention that ratified the 1787 Constitution. By the 1790s, Pickering had become one of the nation's leading political figures, almost an ever-present in the administrations of Washington and Adams. His first major appointment came in 1790 as a commissioner to the Iroquois, with whom he negotiated the 1794 Treaty of Canandaigua that affirmed immense territorial concessions to the United States. In 1791, he became postmaster general and supervised the rapid extension of the postal network. Pickering also served briefly as secretary of war before assuming the office for which he is remembered, secretary of state.

His ascent was not without controversy. When in 1795 the illicit correspondence of Edward Randolph was turned over to Washington's administration, it was Pickering who translated the letters from French into English. It was Pickering, therefore, who depicted Randolph not just as a malcontent but as a traitor. Initially a pro tem replacement for Randolph, Pickering's appointment was made permanent when five other statesmen, including Patrick Henry, turned down the role. Under his stewardship the United States signed the Treaty of San Lorenzo in 1795, enacted the Jay Treaty, suffered the XYZ Affair, and fought the Quasi-War with France. Yet more than the range and rank of the offices that he held, Pickering's

Figure 10.3. *Timothy Pickering* by T. B. Welch after Gilbert Stuart. Library of Congress.

political career was defined by his Anglophilia and by the pro-British policies he advocated. His opposition to Randolph, for instance, was more than personal, it was principled: Pickering wanted to avoid war with Great Britain, so he supported the Jay Treaty that Randolph damned. Likewise, he was a vocal opponent of President Adams's attempts in the late 1790s to make peace with France, whom Pickering wanted to fight alongside Great Britain. Such were the frequency and bitterness of Pickering's disagreements with Adams that he was dismissed from office in 1800.

Far from chastened, Pickering was even more ardent in his Anglomania when he returned to the Capitol as a senator from Massachusetts. Promulgating the idea that New England should secede from the Republican-dominated Union, he conspired to that effect with the British envoy Sir George Henry Rose and denounced the embargo as destructive to Anglo-American relations. In a speech to the Senate in November 1808, Pickering *defended* the British orders in council that had authorized attacks on American shipping and even the practice of impressment. As war with the British grew ever more likely, Pickering remained steadfastly opposed to open conflict from triple motives of love for the former motherland, implacable hatred of Napoleon, and contempt for Republicans. In the oft-repeated phrase, Pickering described the United Kingdom as "The World's last hope—Britain's Fast-anchored Isle."[22]

The Death of Federalism

The War of 1812 catalyzed New England exceptionalism into an explicit desire to secede. Not only were the High Federalists sympathetic to Great Britain because of their cultural Anglophilia, they also feared the westward expansion that victory would inevitably bring: better security in the West meant more western states, and that meant more electoral votes for the Republicans. It was even hoped, by Pickering at least, that British victory at New Orleans would give ballast to the Federalist demands: "From the moment that the British possess New Orleans," he wrote, "the Union is severed." When the unpopularity of the war with New Englanders became clear, secessionist machinations gained greater traction. Many Yankees continued to trade with the British enemy, and though the United States Army was often short of supplies, cattle were sold to the redcoats instead. The Massachusetts state government did little to resist either the occupation of Eastport or the British blockade of its coastline, and when the state militia was eventually called out in 1814 they were not placed at the disposal of the president. Further undermining the idea of national unity, the state's governor, Caleb Strong, sent an agent to the British commander at Halifax to seek a separate peace, while Boston financiers would refuse to purchase federal loans but continue to buy bonds from the British government. Wealthy Bostonians, explained the *Columbian Centinel*, "lend no money to the ruling [Republican] faction, for the same reason they would not lend swords to the tenants of a lunatic hospital."[23]

In February 1814, Pickering stepped up his campaign, urging Samuel Putnam, a justice of the Supreme Court of Massachusetts, to "recollect the times that are past, when circular letters were first sent from the House of Representatives of Massachusetts, the cradle of American liberty." It was in Massachusetts, Pickering reminisced, "whence ensued our organized opposition to mediated oppression, the harbinger of tyranny, but which, as compared with the actual oppression, the tyranny of our own government, would now appear insignificant." Writing to Gouverneur Morris, Pickering outlined his explicit preference for secession. "In adverting to the ruinous system of our government for many years past," he told Morris, "I have even gone so far as to say that a separation of the Northern section of States would be ultimately advantageous, because it would be temporary; and because in the interval the just rights of the states would be recovered and secured; that the Southern States would earnestly seek a reunion, when the rights of both would be defined and established on a more equal and therefore more durable basis."

At Hartford, Connecticut, in December 1814, the discontented Federalists convened. Meeting for three weeks to discuss their grievances with the Republican administrations of Jefferson and Madison, the convention did not represent the will of *all* New England: New Hampshire sent only two delegates and Vermont only one. Moreover, given that many of the most radical voices, including Pickering, were excluded from attendance, the Convention declined to demand the secession of the northern states. Rather, the report of the Convention was intended as a High Federalist articulation of states' rights comparable to the Virginia and Kentucky Resolutions of 1798 and as a strident protest against the supposedly unconstitutional conduct of the federal government. More specifically, the Convention demanded five amendments to the Constitution of 1787: the prohibition of any embargo lasting more than two months; the requirement of a two-thirds majority in Congress for any declaration of war or the admission of a new state; the removal of the three-fifths clause, which counted slaves toward the electoral population of a state, thus inflating the electoral heft of the South; the limitation of presidencies to one term; and, striking at the dominance of Virginia Republicans, the prohibition of successive presidents coming from the same state.[24]

Perhaps, in another context, at another time, the Convention's demands might have been given a respectful hearing. Yet as the Federalist emissaries arrived in Washington in February 1815, the news came first from Ghent that peace had been agreed and then from New Orleans that Jackson was victorious. In the nationalistic euphoria that followed, thinly veiled threats of secession and the Federalist excoriation of the federal government were treated as narrow-minded and even treasonous. For many, the demands of the Hartford Convention were indicative of the petty jealousy, sectionalist myopia, and disloyal Anglomania of New England Federalists who, by demanding exceptional treatment, had repudiated the growth and recent glory of the United States. The word "Federalist" now implied a form of politics that was incompatible with the passionate nationalism that animated the South and the West. The Federalist Party, as a national force, was broken.

In terms of national security, the War of 1812 put an end to British interference in the West. Great Britain no longer gave thought to creating a barrier state and was content finally to abandon its Indian allies. The War of 1812 also vindicated belief in the American experiment itself. Writing in

1816, Albert Gallatin suggested that the war had "renewed and reinstated the national feelings and character which the Revolution had given, and which were daily lessened." The American people were now "more American." They now felt and acted "more as a nation," and so Gallatin hoped that "the permanency of the Union [was] thereby better secured." Prewar indignation about British intrigue with Native Americans had produced a wave of fervent nationalism, the champions of which were William Henry Harrison and Henry Clay; the war itself produced more national heroes such as Andrew Jackson.[25]

The War of 1812 also justified the expansion of the federal government that had been erected to conduct the nation's affairs. Since the establishment of the Continental Army and Navy in 1775, American statesmen had sought to build a modern military force without the sinister connotations of tyranny that belonged to standing armies. The War of 1812 was the great test of those forces, and the test was passed. Of course, there were still persistent administrative problems. Recruitment into the federal forces, for example, was personal, but the Department for War treated recruits as if they were willing to serve under any officer, in any regiment. The victories at the Thames and New Orleans, however, had dispelled prewar pessimism and stoked a newfound sense of pride and purpose in the American military. On the Atlantic, although the Royal Navy eventually reasserted its primacy, the Americans had won the respect of British sailors, something that few could have imagined prior to 1812. Victories on Lake Erie and Lake Champlain even suggested that, as Paine had foreseen in 1776, the United States could in time achieve maritime preeminence and that continued British superiority at sea might depend on not provoking the Americans into becoming serious rivals of the Royal Navy.

The greatest boon of the War of 1812, however, was the time, space, and peace that the United States needed to resolve its outstanding imperial issues. The British in Canada and the Indians in the West were no longer major threats to the integrity and safety of the Union; in France, Napoleon had been defeated for good. American attention could now turn to "internal improvements" and to the Spanish in the South.

CHAPTER 11

American Progress at Spanish Expense, 1815–1819

The East and the West Indies being met in the crown of Spain, it is come to pass that, as one saith in a brave kind of expression, the sun never sets in the Spanish dominions, but ever shines upon one part or other of them: which, to say truly, is a beam of glory . . . wherein the crown of Spain surpasseth all the former monarchies.[1]

—Francis Bacon, *An Advertisement Touching An Holy War* (1623)

In 1783, when the great powers of Europe recognized the independence of the United States, the Spanish Empire covered most of the habitable Americas. In North America, Spanish Louisiana stretched from the Gulf Coast to Canada, and from the Appalachians to the Rockies; within it were the Mississippi and New Orleans, from where Spanish officials maintained excellent relations with the Creeks, the most powerful tribe to the south of the Ohio River. The Spanish then regained the Floridas from the British, while the domain of New Spain spanned even to California settlements on the Pacific. In the Caribbean, the Spanish held the sugar island of Cuba, the eastern half of Hispaniola (Santo Domingo), and Puerto Rico. The whole of mainland Central America from Mexico to Panama, except for what would become British Honduras (today's Belize), was also subject to Spanish rule. South America bore like witness to Spanish dominance: the Viceroyalty of New Granada (today's Colombia, Ecuador, and Venezuela), the Viceroyalty of Peru (including Bolivia), the Captaincy General of Chile, and the Viceroyalty of the Rio de la Plata (Uruguay and Argentina) covered most of the continent. Only Portuguese Brazil, Dutch Guiana, and

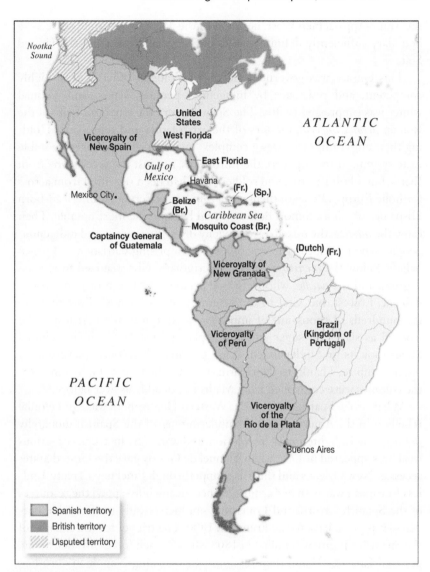

Figure 11.1: Spanish America in 1783

French Guiana stood apart. The Spanish had no intention of loosening their grip on this empire. After 1783, they sought to restrict the United States to the east of the Appalachians, scheming both against and *with*—in the case of James Wilkinson—American citizens. Count Floridablanca, the chief minister of Charles III, was so confident of the future of this Spanish Empire that, notwithstanding the potential for American domination of the Trans-Appalachian West, he believed the Mississippi would serve as "a boundary sufficiently definite and visible" between Spain and the United States.[2]

This empire was governed effectively. Colonial officials were highly competent, and resistance by indigenous peoples, slaves, and colonial whites was suppressed swiftly. The Spanish were the trueborn heirs of the Roman *arcana imperia*, masters of the arts of rule and repression. Holding their empire in place was a complex, racialized, but remarkably stable caste system. At the top were the Europeans, not just the *peninsulares* from Iberia, but administrators and soldiers who had been recruited from across Catholic Europe. Beneath them was a thin layer of creoles, American-born Hispanics of whom Simón Bolívar would become the most notable. Then came the *mestizo*, the mixed-race progeny of the Europeans and indigenous peoples who practiced syncretic religions comprising Christian and pagan beliefs. Below the *mestizo* were the Amerindians, Christianized to varying degrees, and the *pardos*, who were free persons of African or part-African descent. Lowest, but vital to the economy of the Spanish Empire, were the hundreds of thousands of imported or American-born Africans who labored as slaves on sugar and coffee plantations. As the infant United States took its first independent steps, the Spanish colonies constituted a mighty empire. Thanks to the reforms initiated by José de Gálvez in 1765, the colonies were controlled from Madrid as steadily as ever before.[3]

What broke Spanish rule in the Western Hemisphere was not colonial rebellion in the Americas, but the undermining of the Spanish monarchy *in Europe* by Enlightenment, revolution, and war.[4] The first signs of serious weakness appeared in 1795 when Manuel de Godoy gave the United States access to New Orleans and the Mississippi through Pinckney's Treaty. Endless European war with *and* against France meanwhile sapped the resources of the Spanish Crown, and Louisiana—an increasingly unaffordable burden— was given back to the French in 1800. The trigger for the collapse of the Spanish Empire was pulled in 1808 when French forces invaded Spain, deposed Charles IV and then his son before making Napoleon's brother, Joseph, king of Spain and the Indies. For many in Spanish America, the Bonapartist usurpation broke the chain of authority between Madrid and the colonies: Charles's and Ferdinand's American subjects simply did not recognize the legitimacy of Joseph's rule. Spanish Americans who had watched developments in the United States and France with interest, and who had so far resisted revolutionary urges, quickly interpreted the deposition of Ferdinand as the termination of Madrid's authority in the Americas. Spanish control of the colonies was made even more tenuous when Napoleon and Joseph sent emissaries to the New World to proclaim the liberty of the "enslaved" subjects of Spanish America. This was compounded in 1809, when Napoleon promised to recognize the independence of whichever Spanish colonies promised not to establish friendly relations with the British. By 1810, these circumstances had prompted a series of revolts and seizures of power. In Buenos Aires in May, in Bogota in July, and in Santiago in September, juntas claimed power in the name of Ferdinand VII. A new liberal constitution, which granted representation to the colonies in the Cortes, the Spanish parliament, failed to stem the revolutionary tide. The empire on which Francis Bacon's "beam of glory" had once shone was crumbling, and the United States was now in a position to capitalize.

The Lone Star Republic of West Florida

After the Spanish regained the Floridas from Britain, they had maintained the British organization of the territories. Lying to the east of the Apalachicola River, East Florida included St. Augustine and the entire Florida Panhandle, but most of that land was swamp, uninhabited by settlers. West Florida was more important. Lying to the west of the Apalachicola, it included the key settlements of Mobile, Pensacola, and Baton Rouge. It also incorporated portions of the eastern shore of the Mississippi that were vital to maintaining control of the river, which had been Jefferson's primary objective in sending Livingston to negotiate with the French in 1802. Yet while Livingston and Monroe procured New Orleans and Louisiana from France, and while the Americans argued that the two Floridas came along with Louisiana, the French had refused to support this claim. As much as Jefferson, Madison, and the Americans at New Orleans connived at cross-border banditry and intriguing for annexation, Spanish governance of the Floridas endured.

Yet just as Spanish colonists pursued independence across the New World, Madrid's control of the Floridas weakened too. After 1783, American loyalists had poured into West Florida, many of them pledging allegiance to the Spanish Crown in return for the title to their land, light taxation, and freedom to worship as Protestants.[5] The Spanish king was thus the wellspring of order in West Florida and, when Charles IV and his son Ferdinand were deposed by Napoleon, Spanish authority among the Floridians was shaken. If a parent country will not or cannot maintain its authority in the colony adjacent to us," said then Senator Henry Clay in 1810, "and there exists in it a state of misrule and disorder menacing our peace; and if, moreover, such colony, by passing into the hands of any other

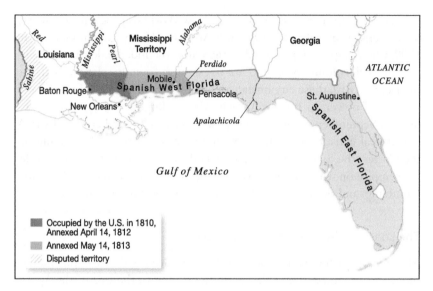

Figure 11.2: East and West Florida

power, would become dangerous to the integrity of the Union, and manifestly tend to the subversion of our laws," the consequence was clear: "We have a right, upon eternal principles of self-preservation, to lay hold of it." For Clay, "this principle alone, independent of any title, would warrant our occupation of West Florida."[6]

By 1810, the settlers of West Florida had banded together in juntas, although in distinction from other Spanish American agitators they preferred the good English name, steeped in revolutionary history, of "conventions." At first, they aimed only to reform the government of West Florida in the name of the king of Spain, but tensions with the Bonapartist monarchy soon pushed the settlers into open revolt. On September 23, 1810, the settlers seized the fort at Baton Rouge; three days later, the independence of the Republic of West Florida was proclaimed. The flag raised by the rebels was a sea of blue adorned by a lone white star.

This would-be republic was not extensive, confined to the district of Baton Rouge, but the revolutionaries set about making and enlarging their new state. They tried but failed to seize Mobile from Spain; they elected a bicameral legislature; and they chose a former American diplomat, Fulwar Skipwith, as their chief executive. This was not to prove a successful experiment in independence. In 1811, William Claiborne annexed the district on the orders of President Madison, and the next year the erstwhile Republic of West Florida joined the Union as part of the new state of Louisiana. Another piece of the Floridas, then, had been yielded to the United States. In Mobile, the Spanish clung on for a short while longer, but this key port was captured by Wilkinson in 1812 and formally annexed by an act of Congress in 1813. Pensacola was then captured by Jackson in November 1814, and even though the Spanish returned briefly when he abandoned it to defend New Orleans from the British, the growing weakness of Spanish rule in the remainder of the Floridas was an invitation to their annexation by the United States.

"The Era of Good Feelings"

With the War of 1812, the United States began to emerge as a great power. Its immediate borders to the north and the west had been rendered secure. At sea, the U.S. Navy had won rare respect from the British, while victories at Baltimore, Plattsburgh, the Thames, and New Orleans had established the United States Army as a major military force. American success in the War of 1812 had also validated the system of national government, with the federal departments of state, the treasury, war, and the navy each having proven their efficacy in convincing fashion. The postwar period witnessed the accelerated expansion and consolidation of the American empire. In the two decades between 1796 and 1816 only Ohio and Louisiana had joined the Union; yet in the six years after the Peace of Ghent, an American territory gained statehood every year: Indiana (1816), Mississippi (1817), Illinois (1818), Alabama (1819), Maine (1820), and Missouri (1821). These last two states were born of the growing crisis over slavery. Southern slaveholders were anxious to extend their "peculiar institution" into the West; northerners were opposed to this on moral grounds and because the Constitution's three-fifths clause gave greater electoral weight to whites in the slave states. For John Quincy Adams, the resolution of the slavery question was essential to the survival of the United States: "The greatest danger of this union," he wrote in April 1820, "was in the overgrown extent of its territory, combining with the slavery question." An attempted solution, the Compromise of 1820, was devised by Henry Clay. Slavery would be permitted in Missouri, but not in any future state north of the parallel 36°30'. At the same time, Maine was detached from Massachusetts and admitted to the Union, balancing the admission of slaveholding Missouri by adding two more senators to the free states' rolls.[7]

The United States also used these years to resolve several lingering issues with the British. The Treaty of Ghent would prove to be the last peace treaty between the nations, but it had not addressed the problem of a potential arms race on the northern lakes and so James Monroe, while secretary of state, had pursued disarmament with the British minister Charles Bagot. As a result of talks at Washington, both parties agreed to limit themselves to two ships on the Upper Lakes—one on Ontario and one on Champlain—with no single ship to exceed one hundred tons displacement, a significant limit given that Perry's flagships at the Battle of Lake Erie, the *Lawrence* and the *Niagara*, were 493 tonners. Finalized by correspondence in April 1817, the pact is known as the Rush-Bagot Treaty after Richard Rush, the Philadelphia lawyer who at the time was both attorney general and pro tempore secretary of state.

It remained to firm up commercial relations with Great Britain, too, since a convention signed in London in July 1815 was merely a stopgap solution that failed to address American trade with the British West Indies or fishing rights in the northeastern Atlantic. The latter of these was an especially important point for New Englanders. Under the terms of the Treaty of Paris, Americans had been allowed to fish on the Grand Banks and to dry their catch on uninhabited shores, but upon the outbreak of war in 1812 the British had declared such rights to be void. The Americans accepted that naval conflict might have suspended these rights, yet when the British sought to keep those fisheries for themselves after 1815, Yankee fishermen were too determined, aggressive, numerous, and well armed to submit meekly to British designs.[8]

Other differences turned on more than fish. The Treaty of Ghent had called in its first article—and, it transpired, in vain—for the return of American slaves who had been "confiscated" by the British, while the old sore of impressment, which the British had never renounced, still festered. There was a further issue concerning the border between the United States and British Canada because the Treaty of Ghent had redefined and as far as possible restored the boundary of 1783 as far west as the Lake of the Woods but no farther. The vast remainder of the continent had long been left to the enjoyment and quarrels of Indians, Métis trappers, the Hudson's Bay Company—the aged trading behemoth that reveled in the nickname "Here Before Christ"—and its upstart Montreal rival the North West Company, but with the Americans having established a trading factory at the mouth of the Columbia River, disputes loomed on the western horizon. Where once these arguments might have been settled by sailors, fur-buyers, and frontiersmen, the relations between the two empires that stretched *a mari usque ad mare* ("from sea to sea") now became the business of diplomats.

Perhaps fortunately for the United States, the years after 1815 had witnessed the ascent of a new generation of British leaders who, rather than trusting in traditional interests, had begun to follow the liberal economics of Adam Smith and David Ricardo, which held that peaceful relations and undisrupted trade with the United States were vital to the national exchequer. Moreover, the development of new enmities with the reactionary autocrats of the Holy Alliance meant the British were loath to find fresh cause to fight with the United States. Thus, when it threatened to let the 1815 convention expire, the Monroe administration found itself in a position to exact concessions on the fisheries *and* the Far West.

The British government moved negotiations to London, where a deal could be worked out with only limited interference from the ever-prickly Secretary of State John Quincy Adams. The deal that emerged, the Convention of 1818, drew a boundary along the forty-ninth parallel west to the "Stony Mountains," now known as the Rockies. The land to the west of the mountains that was "claimed by both countries," and which became known as Oregon, was opened "to the Vessels, Citizens, and Subjects of both powers" for trade, occupation, and settlement. The commercial provisions of the convention of 1815 were renewed for ten more years and the matter of restitution—or, realistically, compensation—for slaves taken by the British was referred to the arbitration of "a Friendly Sovereign or State." Eventually, Tsar Alexander I was chosen as the arbitrator, and he would find in 1823 that the Americans were entitled to "just indemnification for slaves and other private property," the sum of which the British and the Americans agreed, after much haggling, to be $1.2 million. Once again, nothing was said or done about impressment, but with the British never victimizing American sailors again, that injury to national pride and freedom would be healed by time.

With many of their "imperial" issues thus being resolved, American statesmen turned their attention to the domestic condition of the United States. The cause of "internal improvements," the contemporary phrase that described programs of public works, was first propounded in Madison's 1815 Annual Message to Congress. Here, the president had laid out the main policies of what later nationalizers called the "Madisonian Platform." Tariffs would be left on imported goods to protect American manufacturers and to raise revenue for the federal government. A new Bank of the United States would be created to replace the First Bank, whose charter had been allowed to expire in 1811; the new bank would promote the circulation of a single currency to facilitate trade. The federal government would also release funds for the improvement of the armed forces and a series of public works. The most significant "internal improvements" would focus on communication and transportation, vital spheres of development on a continent of mountains, valleys, rivers, and forests. Indeed, a Senate report of 1816 had found that nine dollars could pay for the shipment of one ton of goods from England to the Eastern Seaboard, but those same nine dollars could move those same goods only thirty miles into the American interior. The construction of the National "Cumberland Road," running westward from Maryland, sought to address that issue. Even though Madison vetoed the "Bonus Bill" that would have funded many of these improvements, development continued apace. Where the federal government declined to act, the work was often taken up by individual states. In 1817, New York began the Erie Canal, which connected the East Coast with the Great Lakes via the Hudson River. "Internal improvements" later became a signature aspect of Henry Clay's "American System" and they were vital to the growth of the United States: in the same way that the Post Office had bound the extremities of the Union into a coherent political entity by distributing subsidized newspapers along subsidized post roads, public works united the expanding American empire by practical, physical means.

This growing sense of unity and improvement extended to domestic politics, where the rapid demise of the Federalists, crippled by the narrow-minded sectionalism of the Hartford Convention, left the field clear for Republican hegemony. Having beaten William H. Crawford for the Republican nomination in 1816, James Monroe swept to the presidency, winning 68.2 percent of the popular vote against the Federalist candidate, Rufus King. In the elections to Congress, Republican victories were similarly emphatic: in the House, they gained twenty-six seats to hold an overwhelming majority of 145 to forty; in the Senate, the Republicans held twenty-five seats to the Federalists' thirteen. Following these landslides, Monroe strove to coax the disaffected back into the fold; like Washington in his first term, he embarked on a "Goodwill Tour" of the United States. Known as "The Last Cocked Hat" for his antiquated choice of headwear, Monroe sought to prove—as candidates are wont to promise—that he was the president of all Americans, not just those who voted for him. His most notable venture was into New England, the last bastion of Federalism, where the president was received warmly. It was in fact a Federalist Boston newspaper, the *Columbian Centinel*, which coined the phrase "Era of Good Feelings" to describe the conciliatory mood that prevailed. The Republicans' electoral dominance was then confirmed in 1820. Bereft of energy and organization, the Federalists failed even to nominate a presidential candidate, allowing Monroe and his running mate Daniel Tompkins to take all but one vote in the electoral college. The anomalous ballot was cast by the New Hampshire elector William Plumer, who despised Monroe. He voted instead for the secretary of state, John Quincy Adams.[9]

John Quincy Adams

The politics and character of John Quincy Adams—the second child of the second president and the redoubtable Abigail—were forged in the twin fires of Revolution and Enlightenment. A noted diarist from the age of twelve, Adams spent many of his teenage years in Europe, whether accompanying his father on diplomatic missions to Versailles and The Hague, or traveling with Francis Dana to Russia in pursuit of Catherine the Great's recognition of the United States. Educated at the great Dutch university of Leiden and at Harvard, Adams possessed an intellect that few American statesmen have matched. Fluent in French, German, Dutch, Latin, and Greek, he was a prolific scholar who, besides practicing law, obtained chairs in logic at Brown and rhetoric at Harvard. Adams's later advocacy of a national university and astronomical observatories was testament to the influence of education upon his life. Yet for all his academic brilliance, or perhaps because of it, Adams was a difficult, haughty, and unsympathetic character. Contemptuous of rivals who were inferior to him in education or knowledge, he too frequently acted as if he considered self-explanation and persuasion as optional aspects of politics. The son of the father, Adams also interpreted disagreement as incorrigible hostility, seeing—and in some cases creating—enemies where none had existed.

Despite this lifelong disdain for ceremony, formality, and personal interaction, Adams enjoyed one of the most extensive and important diplomatic careers in American history. His first major appointment came in 1794, at the age of twenty-seven, when he was made the American minister to the Netherlands. Adams served at The Hague for three years before moving to Prussia, where he led the first United States legation as the minister in Berlin. Returning to North America in 1801, Adams served for a brief period in the Massachusetts legislature, then as a Federalist senator for the state, but his support of the embargo caused the legislature to appoint his successor before his term was up, in June 1808. Adams refused to serve as a lame duck, "without exercising the most perfect freedom of agency," and he resigned forthwith. He quickly reentered the diplomatic service. Nominated by Madison as the American minister to Russia, Adams served at St. Petersburg during a momentous period of European history:

Figure 11.3: *John Quincy Adams* (c. 1843) by Albert Southworth and Josiah Hawes. Metropolitan Museum of Art, New York.

he witnessed Tsar Alexander ride off to defeat Napoleon's invasion, having first vowed to his officers to drive Napoleon from Russia or die. The Russian mission was perhaps Adams's favorite, for he declined an appointment to the Supreme Court to remain in St. Petersburg. Yet even here he despaired of the events and entertainments, the essential activities of diplomatic life, which tore him from his books. "The formalities of these court presentations," he wrote in his diary, "are so trifling and insignificant in themselves, and so important in the eyes of princes and courtiers, that they are much more embarrassing to an American than business of greater importance. It is not . . . practicable for a person of rational understanding to value them."[10]

From Russia, Adams traveled to Ghent to negotiate with the British. He made the trip from St Petersburg to the Netherlands without his wife, Louisa Catherine, who was forced to make the same forty-day journey across Napoleonic Europe in the dead of winter, by herself. Upon securing peace, Adams was transferred once more, this time to London. Although he despaired of the lunatic dotage of George III and the idiocy of the Prince Regent, and despite his own deep-rooted Anglophobia, Adams yet managed to pave the way for smoother Anglo-American relations. Having served as the American minister to four major European powers, Adams then became the United States' leading diplomat when James Monroe appointed him as secretary of state in 1817. It was in this role, more than as president, that Adams did most to shape the course of the American empire.

Florida Dreams

After 1811, direct Spanish authority was increasingly confined to the ports of Pensacola, St. Augustine, and Mobile, although the last of these was occupied by an American force led by James Wilkinson in 1813. Beyond these ports, the Spanish held-Floridas were inhabited by Seminole Indians and fugitive slaves who were influenced as much by the British, who traded with them, as by the Spanish who purported to rule them. The Seminoles had long needed European trade and the British had been the major commercial power in Florida since the Seven Years' War, but British interaction with the Indians was not limited to the commercial. To forestall further British interference, Congress passed the first "No Transfer Resolution" in January 1811, advising the president "under certain contingencies" to occupy any part of the Floridas should anyone but Spain attempt to appropriate them.[11] Yet, shortly after the Treaty of Ghent was concluded, a British officer by the name of Nicolls made a defensive *and* offensive treaty with the Seminoles. Once more, then, British intrigue with Native Americans was causing a headache for the United States, and John Quincy Adams was not far wrong in writing that "all the Indian wars with which we have been afflicted have been distinctly traceable to the influence of English traders or agents." In early 1816, the British foreign minister, Lord Castlereagh, had advised the United States not to be hasty in Florida: "Military positions may have been taken by us during the war," Castlereagh warned, "in places which you had taken from Spain, but we never intended to keep them." He implored Adams to "only observe the same moderation," adding that "If we should find you hereafter pursuing a system of encroachment upon your neighbors, what we might do defensively is another consideration."[12]

There had even been attempts to establish an independent Native American state within the Floridas. The Maryland-born loyalist William Augustus Bowles, known as "Estajoca," had been received by George III as "Chief of the Embassy for Creek and Cherokee Nations" and in 1795 he proclaimed himself the "Director General" of the short-lived State of Muskogee. In 1800, Bowles declared war on Spain, but he was captured and shipped to Madrid. Unswayed by the ministers of Carlos IV, Bowles escaped and returned to North America, where in 1803 he declared himself to be "Chief of all Indians." Betrayed and handed over to the Spanish once again, he starved himself to death in captivity in Cuba. Despite the ignominious failure of Bowles's project, the Seminoles and Maroons maintained their resistance to both white settlement and the extension of slavery from Spanish-held territories. This opposition to slavery and indeed the very existence of a free black community was of serious concern to the leaders of the southern United States.[13]

For the Americans, the demise of Spanish authority in East Florida was manifest. The Spanish were too weak to govern the territory effectively, too weak to prevent the Seminoles from harassing American settlers, and too weak to prevent Florida from being used as a base for third-party attacks on the United States. On that last point, Amelia Island, part of the Sea Islands archipelago running from Florida to South Carolina, was playing host to pirates who claimed the protection of letters of marque issued by newly rebellious Hispanic states. The rivers of Florida were meanwhile seen as poorly guarded backdoors into the United States, with Andrew Jackson advising Adams that "while the mouths of the Florida rivers should be accessible to a foreign force, there would be no security for the southern part of the United States."[14]

The American leader most enthusiastic about the annexation of the remains of Spanish Florida was Andrew Jackson. In January 1818, while fighting the First Seminole War, Jackson suggested to President Monroe that the conquest of East Florida could "be done without implicating the government." He suggested it could be "signified . . . through any channel, that the possession of the Floridas would be desirable to the United States, and in sixty days it will be accomplished." He exaggerated only slightly. By 1818, the balance of power between the Spanish and the Americans had swung so dramatically that the United States was more than capable of settling the "Florida Question" on almost exclusively American terms. Nonetheless, Monroe instructed Jackson *not* "to attack any post occupied by Spanish troops." The secretary of war, John C. Calhoun, failed to relay those orders, however, and Jackson, interpreting this unintentional silence as implied consent, marched into East Florida on the pretense of ending British manipulation of the Indians and Maroons.[15]

The invasion was swift and successful; it was also brutal. The most infamous atrocity occurred in April 1818 when Jackson court-martialed and hanged two British citizens, Alexander Arbuthnot and Robert Ambrister, who were accused of conspiring with the Indians. Most of Monroe's cabinet members, appalled by Jackson's impetuosity and his disregard for the chain of command, were ready to repudiate their general. Perhaps surprisingly, Secretary of State Adams stood by Jackson: "I am his official defender against Spain and England," he recorded in his diary.

In November 1818, Adams brought matters to a head. He wrote to George William Erving, the American minister in Madrid, that "Spain must immediately make her election, either to place a Force in Florida, adequate at once to the protection of her Territory, and to the fulfilment of her engagements [Pinckney's Treaty], or cede to the United States a Province of which she retains nothing but the nominal possession." Florida in Spanish hands, Adams wrote, was "derelict, open to the occupancy of every enemy, civilized or savage, of the United States, and serving no earthly purpose than as a post of annoyance to them." Moreover, Adams affected to care little whether the situation in Florida stemmed from luck or design: "The United States," wrote the secretary of state, "can as little compound with impotence as with perfidy."[16]

This defiant letter, which Adams also published in Washington for the edification of the capital's British, Spanish, and French diplomats, persuaded the British to drop the matter. By the summer of 1818, then, the United States had not only launched an invasion of Spanish Florida but had also steadfastly defended the questionable conduct of their general. Yet rather than press home their military advantage, the Americans chose to negotiate for the permanent transfer of the Floridas.[17]

The Adams-Onís Treaty

Given Spain's weakness after 1815, and given that Jackson's army was already in occupation of much of Florida, it may be thought curious that the Americans chose to negotiate, but there were two good reasons for doing so. First, there was more at stake than Florida. There was not yet a definite border between New Spain and the southwestern United States, while both nations held competing claims to the Oregon Country in the far northwest of the continent. Those issues would not be resolved by reinforcing Jackson or expelling the Spanish from Florida. Second, Spanish weakness placed the Americans in a position of enviable but temporary strength at the negotiating table. By 1819, Spain was too weak to restore obedience in her revolted American colonies, and even loyal areas were threatening rebellion. The Spanish Empire was crumbling, and both Spain and the United States knew it. Yet waiting for the implosion of Spanish America would not necessarily benefit the United States. The logic ran that if the Americans entered urgent negotiations with a weak Spain, they might gain something that an independent, buoyant Mexico would never concede; to wit, Spain might give up what it could not retain, but independent Latin American states would not relinquish what they had only just acquired. Naturally, the Spanish were less than thrilled to sign away vast parcels of their ancient American possessions, but when the Monroe administration stood foursquare behind Jackson's incursions into Florida, Luis de Onís y Gonzalez-Vera, the Spanish minister in Washington, was empowered to negotiate even a transcontinental boundary between the two empires. Onís's counterpart in the negotiations would be John Quincy Adams.

Spain wanted two things from any deal: an agreed border between New Spain and the United States, and to delay American recognition of the former Spanish colonies for as long as possible. The United States wanted the legal title to the Floridas and Spanish recognition of American claims in the West, since Madrid had never withdrawn its protest against the Louisiana Purchase. This latter point was deemed essential for fear of exiled Bonapartists trying to establish independent states under Joseph's never-renounced title of king of the Indies. The talks in Washington did not proceed smoothly, not least because of Adams's suspicions of his adversary. In a memorable rant, he described Onís as "bold and overbearing to the utmost extent to which it is tolerated, careless of what he asserts or how grossly it proves to be unfounded, [and] his morality appears to be that of the Jesuits as exposed by Pascal." Relations between the negotiators were so poor that Adams was forced to correspond through an interlocutor, the French minister at Washington, Hyde de Neuville. Happily, the emissary of the restored Bourbon monarchy was a willing proxy, through whom Adams played on Spanish fears that all would be lost eventually, whether to the United States or to rebellious colonists: "We knew we should obtain more by delay than we now offered to accept," he wrote, "and that we might quietly wait for the operation of time."[18]

The Adams-Onís Treaty, also known as the Transcontinental Treaty, was signed at last in February 1819 with terms that focused mainly on territory and borders. The Spanish formally ceded West Florida, part of which had been annexed in 1810, and part in 1813; they also gave up East Florida, which had been occupied by Jackson. The Americans did not pay for the Floridas; they merely had to compensate their own citizens for outstanding claims against the Spanish government. Adams and Onís also agreed on a boundary between Mexico and the United States, making Spanish Texas, which lay to the west of the Sabine River, part of Mexico. Spain further relinquished its claims to the Oregon Country in the northwest. The new boundary between the Spanish and American empires zigzagged north and west, north and west, from the Gulf of Mexico to the Pacific Ocean. From the coast it followed the Sabine River northwest to the thirty-second parallel, then north to the Red River; it then went west along the Red River to the 100th meridian, and north again to the Arkansas River; the next stage followed the Arkansas west to its source, and thence due north to the forty-second parallel; the last "step" of the boundary was drawn due west to the Pacific. Yet despite the tortuous definition of the new border, it was unclear—as with the Treaty of Paris, as with the Louisiana Purchase—what the Americans had gained. For one thing, the headwaters of the Arkansas had not yet been charted, and they would not even be discovered until John C. Fremont's expedition in 1840. This lack of precision troubled the Americans, especially Adams, who knew that "the boundary for us will not only be with Spain, but with her successors." The Spanish, Adams thought, should have cared little for the details because it was futile to dispute them. "Having yielded the point of admitting us to the South Sea," Adams asserted, "it was impossible that [Spain] should have any interest in chaffering for four or five degrees of wilderness, which never will or can be of any value to her." American notions of futility and interest, however, were not shared by a Spanish Empire that would launch a final, vainglorious attempt at the *reconquista* of Mexico in 1829 and defer recognition of Mexican independence until 1836.[19]

The Transcontinental Treaty was not ratified quickly. Upon its receipt, King Ferdinand spitefully granted tracts of Floridian land to his court favorites, an act of twisted generosity that not only created procedural headaches, but threatened American plans to sell the same land: that potential windfall had been earmarked for paying the claims against Spain that the Americans had assumed, and for governing Florida itself. Naturally, this was a delaying tactic on Madrid's part, for it remained in Spanish inter-

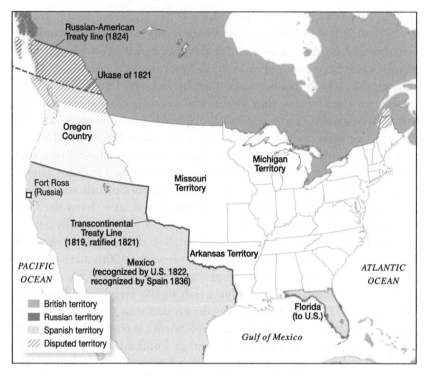

Figure 11.4. Transcontinental treaty line with Russian and British claims

est to prolong ratification, and thereby to delay American recognition of Spain's former colonies. Monroe met this prevarication with fury: in both August and November 1819, he threatened to annex Florida militarily if the treaty was not ratified by the start of the next session of Congress. The president would not, however, follow through on his threat, fearing that any provocation would result in those royal land grants being confirmed and not rescinded. Instead, Monroe threatened anew the annexation of Spanish territory to the west of the Sabine River. In both cases, the president was unsure of his footing, while Adams confessed that he prepared for both invading East Florida *and* recognizing Spain's former colonies: "I was convinced that we should be ultimately obliged to take possession of Florida, and with it, I thought the recognition of the republic of Colombia ought to be simultaneous." Eventually, the land grants *were* rescinded and Monroe rejected Henry Clay's advice to recognize the former Spanish colonies before the Treaty was ratified. It was preferable, Adams told Monroe, to keep the peace and "to avoid anything of which Spain might make a handle."[20]

The Treaty gave Adams most of what he claimed to want from Spain. He could have obtained Texas, too, but as a gesture of goodwill he did not press for it; in fact, Monroe and Adams later celebrated *not* acquiring Texas, territory that would have inflamed sectional tension over slavery. In Adams's mind the Transcontinental Treaty outweighed everything he had accomplished in his diplomatic career, surpassing even the Treaty of Ghent. "My transactions with [Onís]," he wrote in his diary, "have been . . . more important, indeed, than any others in which I have engaged." Perhaps he had a point. Thanks to the diplomatic resolution of a potential crisis in Florida, the United States not only controlled the eastern half of North America, it had cleared the path for westward expansion to the Pacific Coast.[21]

CHAPTER 12

Monsters and the American System

Until Europe shall find it a settled geographical element that the United States and North America are identical, any effort on our part to reason the world out of a belief that we are ambitious will have no other effect than to convince them that we add to our ambition, hypocrisy. . . . If the world do not hold us for Romans they will take us for Jews, and of the two vices I would rather be charged with that which has greatness mingled in its composition.[1]

—John Quincy Adams, November 1819

Even as the transfer of the Floridas and a new Spanish border consolidated the territory of the United States, American statesmen were confronted with new challenges both foreign and domestic. At home, the Panic of 1819 was the first peacetime financial crisis experienced by the United States. The postwar depression that engulfed Europe had encouraged the United Kingdom to "dump" cheap goods into the American market, under-cutting domestic manufacturers whose factories were forced into closure. The widely circulated statement of the British statesman Henry Brougham encouraged the viewpoint that, while the War of 1812 was over, the Americans and the British remained engaged in economic warfare. "It is well worthwhile to incur a loss upon the first exportation," Brougham recommended to the Commons, "in order by the glut, to stifle in the cradle, those rising manufactures, in the United States, which the war had *forced* into existence, contrary to the natural order of things." Besides this problem of dumping, reckless land speculation and overgenerous loan policies had led to widespread foreclosures on mortgaged farms and businesses, especially in the West. These phenomena led to the effective collapse of the American economy, to the vigorous criticism of federal economic policy, and—in some quarters—to the end of the "Era of Good Feelings."[2]

In the realms of foreign policy and security, the reactionary and absolutist powers of continental Europe presented new dangers to the United States. Although the French Revolution "proper" ended with the coup of November 1799, and though Napoleon was now exiled to St. Helena, the republican ideology unleashed by the Revolution and spread by the Revolutionary Wars remained a potent force. Fully aware that democracy and secularism were strengthening across the continent, three of the great powers of Europe united in 1815 to defend their shared beliefs in the primacy of religion and monarchical rule by divine right, in the ideology of "Throne and Altar." At the behest of Tsar Alexander I, the Russian Empire joined with Frederick William III's Kingdom of Prussia and Francis I's Austrian Empire to form the Holy Alliance. These rulers might have belonged to different branches of Christianity—Prussia was Lutheran, Austria was Catholic, and Russia was Orthodox—but the commitment of the Holy Allies to religious absolutism soon created a formal ideological divide across Europe. In this context, and at the western and eastern extremes of the European continent, revolutions broke out against the monarchical autocracy that the Holy Alliance sought to perpetuate. Paying close attention, Americans debated: How should the United States react to these revolutions? Should military or financial support be offered to fellow republicans struggling against tyranny? Or would such policy contravene the early doctrines of American foreign relations that, as regards the affairs of Europe, "permanent" and "entangling" alliances should be avoided? This was a welcome and momentous problem. For the first time, Americans were not debating how best to shield the Union from foreign forces; now, Americans were debating what the United States could or should *do* on the global stage.

Republicanism in Europe

The first of these European revolutions occurred in Spain. In 1820, a coterie of liberal army officers rebelled in Cádiz, where an expeditionary force was preparing for the reconquest of Spanish America. Led by the general Rafael del Riego, the soldiers roused garrisons and civilians, first in Andalucía and then across Spain, and demanded the restoration of the liberal constitution of 1812. To avoid being deposed, Ferdinand VII, who had been restored by the British in 1814, swore to abide by the constitution and so appointed a new liberal government. There followed three years of liberal rule, the Triento Liberali, under the Progresista government, but the new ministry could neither improve the Spanish economy nor reclaim Spain's colonies. Its anticlericalism meanwhile made enemies of the Catholic Church and the Holy Alliance. In 1822, France was authorized by the Congress of Verona to intervene in Spain and Louis XVIII sent the "Hundred Thousand Sons of Saint Louis" across the Pyrenees to end the Spanish dalliance with liberalism.

The second major revolution occurred in Greece, where revolutionaries sought freedom from the Ottoman caliphate. Most of the Hellenic lands had been ruled by the Ottomans from the mid-fifteenth century, even before the fall of Constantinople in 1453, and a series of rebellions over the centuries had met with failure. In 1814, a revolutionary brotherhood, the Filiki Eteria, was founded to launch another campaign for independence. Their first revolt was staged in the Danubian Principalities in March 1821. Although swiftly put down, it proved inspirational to patriots in central Greece, the Peloponnese, Crete, and Macedonia. Greek independence soon became the rage among European elites. Lord Byron, the British poet, lost his life while marshaling an assault on the Ottoman-held fortress at Lepanto near Corinth.

For some Americans, the liberals in Spain and the revolutionaries in Greece belonged to a global republican fraternity that the United States was duty-bound not just to endorse but to support. Discussion of the Spanish situation was relatively muted: while the United States had accredited diplomatic agents at the last liberal bastion of Cádiz, which fell to French forces in September 1823, explicit intervention on behalf of the Spanish liberals was never considered seriously. The Greek War of Independence provoked more substantial debate as certain members of Monroe's cabinet were enchanted by the Greek cause. John Quincy Adams noted that "Mr. Crawford and Mr. Calhoun inclined to countenance this project . . . , taking no heed of Turkey whatever." Albert Gallatin, now the American minister in Paris, pushed for intervention too. Adams, however, scoffed at the idea, and mocked how Gallatin had written, in "one of his last dispatches, as if he was serious, that we should assist the Greeks with our naval force in the Mediterranean—one frigate, one corvette, and one schooner." American resources in the region were indeed minimal, and given that major European powers were already prepared to intervene, American involvement would likely have been inconsequential.[3]

Even so, the cause of Greek independence was taken up widely. "The mention of Greece," reflected James Monroe in his Sixth Annual Message, "fills the mind with the most exalted sentiments and arouses in our bosoms the best feelings of which our nature is capable." The remaining Federalists of New England argued passionately for intervention. In December 1823, Daniel Webster was again a congressman, now representing Massachusetts. He wrote to Edward Everett, the editor of the seminal *North American Review*, about "a meeting of the members of the administration . . . at which, inter alia, they talked of Greece." Webster reported that the discussion was sadly unproductive and noted that Monroe had taken the "pretty high ground," being "afraid of the appearance of interfering in the concerns of [Europe]." But Webster was not deterred, and he promised that "if nothing should occur to alter my present purpose, I shall bring forward a motion [in Congress] on the subject on Monday, and shall propose to let it lie on the table for a fortnight." Webster then urged Everett to find a "tolerable map of modern Greece" that he might share with John Calhoun, the secretary of war, who was "as friendly to the Greeks as yourself." An avowed philhellene who led the Greek Revival movement, Everett afterward made a major speech in favor of Greek independence, and his continued demonstration of support made him an adopted national hero in Greece: his portrait now hangs in the National Gallery in Athens.[4]

The American debate over intervention in Greece weighed more than the merits of the case; it was in fact a debate over the general direction of American foreign policy. Should the United States become an interventionist force in global affairs, defending and advocating the ideals by which its own politics was informed? Or should Americans abide by the warnings of Washington and Jefferson, and focus on building their North American empire while maintaining principled isolation from the quarrels of the Old World? The leading advocate for the interventionist position was Henry Clay.

Henry Clay

The seventh child of a Baptist preacher and a cousin of the abolitionist for whom the boxer Cassius Clay (later Muhammad Ali) was first named, Henry Clay was born in 1777 in Hanover County, Virginia. In Clay's own words he was "rocked in the cradle of the Revolution," for at the age of four he watched the British cavalry ransack his home and desecrate the recently dug graves of his father and grandfather. These traumatic events instilled in Clay a lifelong hatred of the British: "The circumstance of that visit," he declared, "is vividly remembered, and it will be to the last moment of my life." Clay was apt to describe his upbringing in Virginia as unremittingly harsh. He claimed to have inherited only "infancy, ignorance, and indi-

Figure 12.1. *Henry Clay* (1843) by Theodore Sidney Moise. Metropolitan Museum of Art, New York; Gift of Grace H. Dodge, 1909.

gence." He professed to be "an orphan who had never recognized a father's smile . . . poor, penniless . . . , [and] with an imperfect and inadequate education." Clay even coined the phrase "self-made man" to describe his eventual ascent. Much of this was nonsense, for Clay's father had left his mother an estate of five hundred acres, but it was a politically useful story.[5]

Having studied law at Richmond, Clay moved in November 1797 to Kentucky, the western state with which he became indelibly linked. Settling in the frontier town of Lexington, he quickly gained a statewide reputation for his rhetoric and intelligence, but also for his swearing, drinking, and gambling. As a later colleague put it, Clay was and always remained "essentially a gamester." By 1806, Clay was so renowned that the Kentucky legislature appointed him to serve out the term in the United States Senate of John Adair, who had been forced to resign over alleged involvement in the Burr Conspiracy. He had not reached the constitutionally required age of thirty, but Clay spent two months in the Senate. In 1810, having recovered from a leg wound suffered in a duel with John Marshall's cousin, Clay secured another pro tem appointment to the Senate when Buckner Thruston resigned to serve on the federal judiciary. With ferocious, eloquent speeches against the First Bank of the United States (an institution "amenable only to a few stockholders, and they chiefly foreigners") and the crumbling Spanish Empire ("I have no commiseration for princes"), Clay made a lasting mark on national politics. Although confident that he could win election to the Senate in his own right, Clay chose instead to run for the House of Representatives. He cantered to victory in Kentucky's Fifth District. Upon taking his seat in March 1811, Clay was elected Speaker of the House on his first day as a representative, an honor not since repeated.[6]

As tension with Great Britain grew over impressment and interference in the American West, Clay became the most notorious of the "war hawks," the congressmen who clamored for war against the British. With his desire for revenge sated by the declaration of war in 1812, Clay was then sent to Europe as one of the peace commissioners. Upon his return to the United States, Clay resumed his duties as Speaker of the House and became one of the dominant figures of American politics, but his ambitions went well beyond Congress. Yet among major-party candidates to actually secure the nomination, only William Jennings Bryan has lost more presidential elections than Clay. First, there was the debacle of 1824 (see chapter 14). Clay ran again in 1832 as the candidate of the National Republicans, but he was defeated by the incumbent, Andrew Jackson. Having played a leading role in the foundation of the Whig Party, Clay lost the party's presidential nomination in 1840 to William Henry Harrison and then the contentious election of 1844 to the Democrat, James K. Polk. The last defeat devastated Clay: "I will not disguise," he wrote, "that I felt the severity of that blow. . . . My own heart bled and still bleeds."[7]

In spite of these setbacks, Clay's career was punctuated by major achievements, and he became known as "the Great Compromiser" for his role in defusing a series of national crises. In 1820, he brokered the Missouri Compromise between free and slave states; in 1833, he supervised the Compromise Tariff, which brought South Carolina back from the brink of secession; and he was central to the Compromise of 1850, a series of federal laws that tried to stave off the coming conflict between North and South, between free and slave. Though he represented the slave state of Kentucky, and though he owned ninety-five slaves himself, Clay was noted for occasionally ambiguous positions on slavery. He regretted that "there are so many among us of a different caste, of a different physical, if not moral, constitution, who never can amalgamate with the great body of our population," but nonetheless lambasted the South's "peculiar institution." Clay was also a cofounder of the American Colonization Society, which established the West African colony of Liberia—its capital named Monrovia for the president—as a home for "repatriated" blacks. His later years were spent in the Senate, where he, Daniel Webster, and John C. Calhoun formed the "Great Triumvirate" that dominated congressional politics in the 1830s and 1840s.[8]

Henry Clay's ideas on Europe were best articulated in a speech given in his hometown of Lexington, Kentucky, in May 1821. For Clay, the situation in the Old World was the inevitable consequence of Napoleon's defeat. "It was evident," he declared, after the overthrow of Bonaparte, "that the [Holy] [A]lliance . . . would push the principle of legitimacy, a softer and covered name for despotism, to the uttermost extent." The result of legitimism, Clay explained, was the sight of "Congress after Congress assembling in Europe to decide, without ceremony, upon the destiny and affairs of foreign independent states." The United States, which Clay described glowingly as "the greatest offender of all against the principle of legitimacy," was privileged not to have been "brought under their jurisdiction, and subjected to their parental care," good fortune that was derived from "our distance from Europe, and . . . the known bravery of our countrymen."[9]

Distance and bravery, however, were not sufficient to guarantee American liberty in perpetuity. Clay therefore argued that "a sort of counterpoise to the Holy Alliance should be formed in the two Americas in favor of national independence and liberty, to operate by the force of example, and by moral influence; that here a rallying point and an asylum should exist for freemen and freedom." Clay then cited the case of the Kingdom of Naples, where liberal reform had been condemned by the Alliance and crushed by an Austrian invasion, as evidence that liberalism in Europe required protection from the forces of absolutism:

> In the recent lawless attack upon the independence of unoffending Naples, that alliance had thrown off the mask of religion, and peace, and hypocrisy, and fully exposed the naked atrocity of its designs. — A reform, in the government of Naples, had become necessary from the greatest abuses. The reform took place peaceably, without bloodshed, and with the unanimous and enthusiastic concurrence of the whole nation, prince and people. This is the crime of Naples; and for this crime, three individuals, who if they have reached the height of human power, are displaying what is too often its attendant, the height of human presumption, are threatening to pour their countless hordes into her bosom and to devastate her land.

For Clay, the "crime of Naples" was proof that Americans should act as a force for good against the reactionary malevolence of the Holy Allies, those champions of tyranny and hypocrisy. The Alliance professed no objection to revolution, but denounced revolutionaries as nothing more than "jacobins, disorganizers, [and] the foes of order." If military force were involved in such revolution, the influence of the military was "pernicious," so the Allies would put it down. Moreover, while the "Allies graciously allow independent nations to meliorate their institutions and the social conditions," they would not tolerate the instruments that could make those changes. For the absolutist Alliance, the only good change was change driven by monarchy, whereby "the mass of abuse and corruption, and putrefaction, which may have been accumulating for ages, [could] voluntarily . . . purify itself!"[10]

Clay grieved to watch the suffering of Spain, Greece, and Naples. As late as 1824, he would denounce the Ottoman oppression under which the Greeks strained. "The Turk," Clay roared, "in all the elevation of his despotic throne," was but human, "made as we are, of flesh, of muscle, of bones, and sinews." The Turk therefore knew of "the uncalculating valor of American freemen," and so if the Turk should be compelled to understand "that this nation, that our entire political fabric, base, column and entablature, rulers and people, with heart, soul, mind, and strength, are all on the side of the nation he is crushing, he will be more likely to restrain, than to increase his atrocities upon suffering and bleeding Greece." Clay would be more cautious in later years, not least when speaking to the Hungarian rebel Lajos Kossuth, but in the 1810s and '20s he believed that intervention in European affairs was the principled obligation of the United States.[11]

In Search of Monsters

The contradictory position on American foreign policy was put forward by John Quincy Adams. In the spring of 1821, the secretary of state was determined to make "a reply to both Edinburgh and Lexington," meaning Clay and the *Edinburgh Review*, the British periodical that had called for American intervention in Europe. Adams therefore arranged to give the principal oration at Washington's July 4th celebrations; for the first time since leaving his chair in rhetoric at Harvard, he wore his professorial robes, speaking for himself and not as secretary of state. Thus gowned, Adams delivered perhaps the most famous American foreign-policy speech of the nineteenth century. Urging the example of the American Revolution upon the peoples of the world, Adams invoked "that Spirit, which dictated the Declaration" to exhort "every individual among the sceptered lords of mankind, 'Go thou and do likewise!'" Yet, crucially, Adams argued for the international expression of republican sympathy while maintaining physical distance. "Whenever the standard of freedom and independence has been or shall be unfurled there will her heart, her benedictions, and her prayers be. But she goes not abroad in search of monsters to destroy. She is the well-wisher to the freedom and independence of all. She is the champion and vindicator only of her own. She will recommend the general cause, by the countenance of her voice, and the benignant sympathy of her examples."

In the twenty-first-century context of seemingly endless wars in Afghanistan and Iraq, this passage acquires poignant relevance, but in 1821 Adams's speech was not well received. The Philadelphia *Aurora* suggested sarcastically that "it might well be made a standing rule that the annual oration be delivered by the secretary of state, so that the policy of the administration may be in that way apologized for." The *Aurora* even reprimanded Adams for a perceived betrayal of American Revolutionary principles, complaining that "the anniversary which derived so much éclat from the enthusiasm and admiration of all European nations, may be made use of to discourage all future rebellions, and to inculcate this doctrine, that man, as soon as he has no need for the sympathy or generosity of others, shall be told, 'let every man be left to paddle his own canoe.'" The division between interventionism and isolationism was marked, and it permeated more than debates on Europe.[12]

Spanish America and the American System

The second major issue of the early 1820s involved the independence of Spain's former New World colonies. The issue was presented to American statesmen in terms of a series of interconnected questions. Should the United States recognize their independence? If so, under what conditions and when? Once recognition had been declared, how far, if at all, should the United States defend that independence? Once more, Clay and Adams found themselves on opposite sides of the debate. Here, Clay's conception of an "American System" took on a bold, international dimension. In short, Clay argued for the establishment of formal alliances among the republics of the Western Hemisphere, and therefore with the former Spanish colonies whose recognition he urged. He was not the first American to envision such a league. Writing in 1813 to the Prussian geographer Alexander von Humboldt, Thomas Jefferson had suggested that "in whatever governments they end [the rebellious Spanish colonies] will be American Governments, no longer to be involved in the never ceasing broils of Europe." In 1817, Jefferson reaffirmed his belief that a native, American system of government would soon extend across the Western Hemisphere, expressing his hope "that twenty years more will place the *American hemisphere under a system of its own*, essentially peaceable and industrious, and not needing to extract its *comforts* out of the eternal fires raging in the old world."[13]

It was Clay, though, who put forward the most developed idea of a hemispheric American System. An 1818 House speech on the Argentine Provinces of the Rio de la Plata was among his first articulations of the concept. "There could not be a doubt," he told the assembled congressmen, "that Spanish America, once independent, whatever might be the form of the governments established in its several parts . . . would be animated by an American feeling, and guided by an American policy." These new states "would obey the laws of the system of the New World, of which they would compose a part, in contradistinction to that of Europe." In 1820, Clay presented a more defined vision of his American System: "It is in our power," he told the House, "to create a system of which we shall be the center, and in which all South America will act with us. . . . We shall be the center of a system which would constitute the rallying point of human freedom against all the despotism of the old world." With a memorable turn of phrase, Clay beseeched his colleagues to take the lead of this political league. "Let us no longer watch the nod of any European politician—Let us become real and true Americans, and place ourselves at the head of the American System."[14]

The economics of Clay's American System were comparably international. Federal banking and internal improvements might have been domestic policies, but the imposition of prohibitive tariffs was also an act of foreign policy, a means of retaliating against the British Corn Laws that had laid extensive duties upon American agricultural exports. In Clay's worldview, domestic economic policy and foreign policy were inextricably intertwined: "The home market," he declared, "can only be created and cherished by the PROTECTION of our own legislation against the inevitable prostration of our industry, which must ensue from the action of FOREIGN policy and legislation." Clay also understood the vast economic potential of the former Spanish colonies and argued that the United States should trade with South America. "The precious metals are in South America," he told the House, "and they will command the articles wanted in South America, which will purchase them." Beyond the trade in metals, the benefits of hemispheric commerce were manifold. American navigation would benefit by carrying cargo, and the profits of American merchants would soar. The volume of trade to the West Indies and Spanish America was already "respectable," but it could be "constantly augment[ed]." Trading with South America would only assist the United States "in its march to true greatness." Here, "millions and millions will be added to our population, and the increased productive industry will furnish an infinite variety of fabrics for foreign consumption in order to supply our own wants."[15]

In this way, Clay argued that if the territorial destiny of the American empire was dominion over the North American continent, its commercial destiny was hegemony in the Western Hemisphere. "From the character of our population," Clay explained, the United States was obliged to "take the lead in the prosecution of commerce and manufactures." He implored his listeners to imagine "the value of the intercourse" between forty million Americans and seventy million South Americans, and to conceive of the United States as the mercantile heavyweights of the West. "In relation to South America," he declared, "the people of the United States will occupy the same position as the people of New England do to the rest of the United States." American dominance would be inevitable too: "Our enterprize, industry, and habits of economy, will give us the advantage in any competition which South America may sustain with us." More importantly, an American System would counterbalance the absolutist predations of the Holy Alliance, and it would consolidate the independence of the United States by finally separating the New World from the Old. "Our institutions now make us free," Clay confirmed, but "how long shall we continue so, if we mold our opinions on those of Europe?"[16]

The eradication of European influence by means of a political and economic accord was a recurrent theme of Clay's rhetoric. He believed the United States should "develop and improve in the most advantageous manner practicable, the internal resources of our country, and to circumscribe yet further, if not eradicate, the influence of Europe upon America." He demanded that American leaders should "strengthen our union, lay broad foundations of a genuine American policy, and . . . limit more and more that moral and commercial control which [Europe] has too often perniciously exercised over the New World." It followed inevitably that Clay desired "the recognition of the independent governments of South America . . . prior to the close of his public career." He knew that the House had already expressed its support for "the patriot cause," and he hoped that the president would before long "conform to the known sentiments of the whole union." Clay further recommended the adoption of "all means short of actual war . . . [to] give additional tone, and hope, and confidence to the friends of Liberty throughout the world."[17]

Conversely, John Quincy Adams asserted that, "as to an American system, we have it; we constitute the whole of it; there is no community of interests or of principles between North and South America." As early as March 1819, Adams had argued that a simple American policy of detached neutrality was perfectly calculated to support Spanish American independence. "We had been promoting the cause of their independence," he wrote, "far more than we could have done by a formal acknowledgment of their independence." Adams resisted every means of entangling the United States in Spanish America's quest for independence, and he decried those American citizens who wished to involve the nation in such chimerical pursuits. The Irish-born journalist Baptist Irvine, for instance, had been sent by Adams to Venezuela to report on Simón Bolívar, and Adams wrote only scathingly of Irvine's subsequent enthusiasm for South American independence: "He is by birth an Irishman and has no native American feelings. He, therefore, like all the European republicans whom I have known, habitually thinks of liberty as a blessing to be acquired, and never as a blessing to be enjoyed." President Monroe was closer in thinking to Adams than to Clay. Writing to Gallatin in May 1820, he stated that "with respect to the [Spanish] Colonies, the object has been to throw to their side, in a moral sense, the weight of the United States, without so deep a commitment as to make us a party to the contest." What Monroe meant by this "weight" were statements of support and the enactment of neutrality laws that were carefully crafted to favor the former colonies in their disputes with Spain.[18]

Recognition

Recognizing the independence of Spain's colonies came soon after the Adams-Onís Treaty was ratified, soon after the acquisition of the Floridas. In March 1822, in a special message to Congress, President Monroe declared that Colombia, Peru, Chile, Mexico, and the Rio de la Plata were now "in the full enjoyment of their independence" and that the governments of those new republics held "a claim to recognition by other Powers, which ought not to be resisted." The Spanish protested vigorously and denounced "the perfidy and the effrontery" of the United States, but the president and Adams were of a decided mind. In May, Monroe signed a bill that appropriated $100,000 to cover the costs of diplomatic missions to the "independent nations on the American continent." The first formal act of recognition occurred in June, when Manuel Torres—the invalid, dying representative of Colombia—was received in Washington. Given Torres's health, it was an emotional occasion. Adams noted that the Colombian had "scarcely life in him to walk alone," and that, when Monroe sat with Torres "and spoke to him with kindness, he was moved even to tears."[19]

Still, Monroe did not want an active role in Latin American geopolitics. In his Annual Message to Congress in December 1822, the president communicated his hope that time alone would solve the problems of Spanish American independence *without* requiring the intervention of the United States. Expressing regret that peace had not yet "been concluded between Spain and the independent governments south of the United States," Monroe recognized "the competency of these governments to maintain the independence which they had declared." The president was concerned that realities that had so influenced American opinion did not yet have "equal weight with other powers," and he wished "that Spain herself . . . would have terminated on that basis a controversy so unavailing and at the same time so destructive." Monroe nonetheless "cherished the hope that this result will not be long postponed." Nine days later, though, recognition of the Mexican empire was almost forced upon the United States when the Mexican minister José Manuel Zozaya arrived in Washington. Recognition of Chile and the United Provinces at Buenos Aires followed in January 1823 with the appointment of ministers to those places.*[20]

Of course, this was not the end of the United States' interaction with the crumbling Spanish Empire. In fact, much of American foreign policy over the next decade would be formulated with Spanish America in mind.

---

*The appointment of a minister to Peru was delayed until 1826.

American imperialists even spied opportunities to exploit the ongoing collapse of Spanish rule, for Central and South America appeared as fertile fields for revolution and annexation. The sugar island of Cuba, still held by Spain, was an especially alluring target, considered by some as a ripening fruit soon to fall into the basket of the United States. Writing in 1823 to Hugh Nelson, the new American minister to Spain, Adams suggested that "The annexation of Cuba to our federal republic will be indispensable to the continuance and integrity of the Union itself." For Adams, American possession of Cuba was inevitable: "There are laws of political as well as physical gravitation; and if an apple severed by the tempest from its native tree cannot but fall to the ground, Cuba, forcibly disjoined from its unnatural connection with Spain, and incapable of self-support, can gravitate only towards the North American Union." Slaveholders such as John C. Calhoun were even more enthusiastic about acquiring Cuba, a slave island that would buttress the American commitment to slavery while acting as a bulwark against insurrection elsewhere in the Caribbean.[21]

The Spanish American revolutions did more than awaken the cupidity of the United States. Rebellion against the Spanish Crown had also stirred an American desire to see revolutionary republicanism spread and flourish. The formulation of a foreign policy that balanced such republican fraternity with American expansionism *and* isolationism became the focus of the 1820s. Yet while Adams and Monroe might have followed a supportive but detached policy toward Spanish America, the renewed fervor of European imperialism would in 1823 force the United States to adopt a more strident position.

CHAPTER 13

The Monroe Doctrine

These United States of America, which we have seen arise and
grow, and which during their . . . youth [have] already mediated
projects which they dared then avow, have suddenly left a sphere
too narrow for their ambition, and have astonished Europe by
a new act of revolt, unprovoked, fully as audacious, and no less
dangerous than the former. They have distinctly and clearly
announced their intention to set not only power against power, but,
to express it more exactly, altar against altar.[1]

—Prince Klemens von Metternich, January 1824

For many of the crowned heads and statesmen of the Old World, the possession and prosperity of colonies—whether in America, Africa, or Asia—
were integral to the strength and survival of the motherland. Colonies were
sources of precious raw materials, lucrative export markets for domestic
manufactures, strategic military and naval bases, and symbols of prestige
and power. Colonies, their defense, and their acquisition therefore had
been driving factors in many of the global wars of the long eighteenth century, not least in the American Revolutionary War. Moreover, the chains
of authority that bound the colony to the motherland were thought to
reinforce the strength of domestic governments. Such beliefs were never
more evident than in European attitudes toward the crumbling Spanish
Empire: the replacement of subservient colonies by independent republics,
from which Europe would not benefit directly, was a terrifying prospect.
As the French philosopher and statesman François Réné de Chateaubriand
wrote in May 1822, "If the new world ever becomes entirely republican,
the monarchies of the old world will perish."[2]

The reverse was also true. If constitutional liberalism ever triumphed in Spain, complete independence in Spanish America would surely follow. The only surprise, at least for the French, was that Madrid did not realize this. The French diplomat Edmond de Boislecomte wrote that "We are astonished at the error, committed by so many Spaniards, of believing that they could induce the American insurgents to obey, by suffering to share with them the liberty which the revolution had brought to the motherland." The Spanish remained blind to the fact that, "as the sovereignty of the people was the basis of the Spanish constitution, this principle would give to the Spanish Americas the same right to free themselves from Spain as that which the Spaniards had invoked to liberate themselves from absolute power." Consequently, almost as soon as Spanish American independence became reality, the colonial powers of Europe scrambled to *re*colonize Spanish America. These schemes of reconquest would prove intolerable to the United States.[3]

European Eyes on Spanish America

Of all the European powers, the hungriest for colonial expansion were the French, whose plan to seize control of the newly independent states involved the installation of puppet Bourbon princes at the head of monarchical governments. Some factions in the Americas were occasionally amenable to these plans. In November 1819, the Congress at Buenos Aires voted to install the Prince of Lucca as king of the United Provinces of the Rio de la Plata. It was not until the early 1820s, however, that Louis XVIII's ultra-royalist prime minister, Joseph de Villèle, planned systematically for the recolonization of Spanish America. Mexico was the primary target. At first, the French proposed naval and financial aid for Mexican conservatives, to which Villèle added a Spanish princeling who would serve as the figurative head of a new Mexican state. Villèle reasoned that the Mexicans, desirous of stability, recognition, and independence, would accept the offer eagerly. The threat of French intervention loomed again in the summer of 1823. Instructions sent to the Marquis de Talaru, the French ambassador at Madrid, noted that Mexico was "yet imperfectly separated from Spain." Talaru was reminded of the opportunity presented to France, since "by the exercise of care, reason, and skill it would perhaps be possible to establish in America great monarchies governed by princes of the house of Bourbon." In this way, the French hoped "to combat the waxing systems of republics, while Spain would retain the sovereign power as well as immense advantages in these fine colonies, which are about to escape from her control."[4]

In July 1823, the French stepped up their campaign when Villèle wrote to the eldest son of Charles X, the Duc d'Angoulème, who had commanded the Hundred Thousand Sons of Saint Louis and stayed at Madrid thereafter. "Latin princes," suggested Villèle, should be "placed at the head of hereditary appanages in the Spanish Indies." The French would "furnish to Spain the maritime force necessary for the transportation . . . to the colonies of the Infantes as well as a few soldiers and funds sufficient to guarantee the success of the operations." Villèle believed his plan would be supported across Europe, that it was "very proper that these operations should be favored by the different cabinets of Europe in order to reestablish peace and order in the New World, to honor by a useful conclusion . . . our intervention in Spain, and to make more tolerable to France, by this consideration and by the new markets furnished to our products, the extraordinary expense which we have incurred and which we should have to incur for Spain." Three days later, long before the previous missive could have arrived at Madrid, Villèle wrote again, reaffirming the practicality of installing Bourbon princes across Spanish America. "In all those countries," he declared, "armed parties exist which favor the motherland. If the Infantes should not find in Spanish America submissive realms, they would at least find realms which could easily be subjugated by the aid of our navy and our credit. Their use for this purpose would be approved by France because of her anticipation of the commercial advantages which those sacrifices would assure her in the future." The French offered similar aid to the Portuguese respecting Brazil. "Our ambassador who goes to Lisbon," avowed Villèle, "will favor with all his influence a similar arrangement between Portugal and Brazil."[5]

These French plans would come to naught. For one thing, Ferdinand VII refused to countenance any partition of his nominal empire, regardless of his prospects for reconquering it. There was also another, insuperable obstacle to French ambitions in Spanish America: the British. Striving to maintain a favorable balance of power in Europe, London had expressed its opposition to any kind of recolonization in the Americas. This was sufficient to stop the French in their tracks, simply because the Royal Navy's command of the Atlantic could not be challenged by any or all of the European powers. Even from the beginning of their intrigue, the French understood this handicap. As early as December 1822, Villèle had sounded out the Duke of Wellington during the Congress of Verona. Writing to George Canning, the British foreign minister, Wellington reported the

French view that "If the Spanish Government wished to send an Infante to Mexico or Peru, or to any part of the Spanish America, attended by troops, with a view to make an endeavor to renew the connection between those Colonies and Spain, the expedition now fitting in the ports of France should be at the orders of the Spanish Government to carry the Infante and the troops wherever they pleased." The scenario was anathema to the British, who had planned to cultivate *exclusive* commercial relations with the new republics. They would not support the French in either acquiring the former colonies for themselves *or* restoring them to Spain. The French were therefore compelled to subscribe to the "Polignac Memorandum," a document of October 9, 1823 prepared by George Canning following a meeting with Jules de Polignac, the French ambassador to the United Kingdom. The memorandum stated that the British would not help Spain to recover its American colonies, and that the French agreed to the same.[6]

Some historians have alleged that, given British opposition, the menace of French intervention was "imaginary," but French commitment to their plan was in fact sincere. Even after the Polignac Memorandum was publicized, even when the British had publicly declared their disapproval, French plotting abounded. In November, Villèle directed Polignac to ask the British about settling the Spanish colonies on the Brazilian model, where the colonies would enjoy practical independence but remain subordinate to Spanish princes. The inquiry was dismissed, but still the French persisted. Polignac tried to "bury" the Memorandum and prevent its further distribution, and in December he urged a proposal to the rest of Catholic Europe of "an association with Spain" in order "to reconquer her overseas possessions." The same month, Chateaubriand instructed a French naval agent who was en route to the Americas to propose the scenario of "real independence" to the Mexicans, who would govern their own affairs but swear loyalty to a European prince.[7]

The French were not the only Europeans with eyes on the Americas. In the preceding decades, the Russians had moved steadily southward along the Pacific Coast, founding Fort Ross in 1812 in what is now Sonoma County, California, where they remained in occupation until 1841. A decree of Alexander I dated September 16, 1821 then closed the coast above forty-five degrees north to foreign traders and vessels. The most ominous sign came in October 1823 when the Russian minister at Washington told John Quincy Adams that St. Petersburg would not receive diplomatic agents from the former Spanish colonies: Madrid had hinted to the czar that, if they adopted a pro-Spanish position, Spain might yield the Russians territory on the Pacific Coast. Adams was therefore anxious to check Russian as much as French aggression. His distaste for Russian imperialism had certainly been long-standing. Writing in December 1817 to Alexander Hill Everett, the American chargé d'affaires in the Netherlands, Adams decried that "Alexander of the Neva is not so near nor so dangerous a neighbor to us as Philip was to the Athenians, but I am afraid his love of peace is of the same character as was that of Philip of Macedon. Absolute princes who can dispose of large masses of human force must naturally in applying them be aided by all the pacific dispositions that they can find or make among those whom they visit with the exercise of their power. In the intercourse between power and weakness, peace in the language of the former means the submission of the latter to its will." Adams was irked especially by the correspondence that Noah Worcester, a Unitarian minister, had begun with the Russians through the Massachusetts Peace Society. The secretary of state observed that while niceties were being exchanged, "the venerable founder of the Holy League is sending five or six ships of the line, and several thousand promoters of peace armed with bayonets to Cadiz, and thence to propagate goodwill elsewhere." Adams cautioned that if such peace societies should "fall into the fashion of corresponding upon the objects of their institutions with foreign Emperors and Kings, they may at some future day find themselves under the necessity with corresponding with attorney generals and petit juries."[8]

The British, too, were interested in the collapse of the Spanish Empire. They, like the French and Spanish, were disconcerted by the spread of republicanism. For fear of encouraging the Irish, British recognition of the former Spanish colonies was delayed until all hope of reestablishing monarchical government in the Americas was forsaken. The British were more concerned, though, with the commercial implications of Spanish American independence: George Canning was not alone at Westminster in concocting plans for exclusive commercial treaties with the former Spanish colonies and for exploitation of their mines of precious metals. Yet, above all, the British were anxious to preserve the balance of power in Europe, and this meant checking the imperialism of both the Russians and the French. What the British feared most, therefore, was precisely the French plan to create puppet states that could be controlled from Paris or Madrid. For that reason, even if the British preferred to exclude the United States from the burgeoning trade of the new republics, they were keen to recruit Monroe and Adams to their plan of preventing European recolonization of the Western Hemisphere.

John Quincy Adams had already considered the possibility of Anglo-American cooperation, writing in his diary in June 1823 that the two governments should "compare their ideas and purposes together, with a view to the accommodation of the great interests upon which they have hitherto differed." Canning, however, took the formal lead when he suggested to Richard Rush, the American minister in London, that the two nations should issue a joint declaration disparaging European intervention in the Spanish colonial conflict. In his letter to Rush, the British foreign minister outlined five "opinions and feelings" on the affairs of the Western Hemisphere:

(1) We conceive the recovery of the Colonies by Spain to be hopeless.

(2) We conceive the Question of the Recognition of them, as Independent States, to be one of time and circumstance.

(3) We are, however, by no means disposed to throw any impediment in the way of an arrangement between them and the mother country by amicable negotiations.

(4) We aim not at the possession of any portion of them ourselves.

(5) We could not see any portion of them transferred to any other Power with indifference.

Assuming the Americans concurred in these "opinions," Canning asked: "Why should we hesitate mutually to confide them with each other; and to declare them in the face of the world?" Of course, it was impossible for the United States to accept all five proposals. The fourth, which stipulated the self-denial of territorial acquisition, was inimical to American imperialism. Consequently, there was no joint declaration by the nations that Canning described as "the two chief commercial and maritime states of both [old and new] worlds." Yet with the exception of Canning's fourth "opinion," what followed in Monroe's Seventh Annual Address to Congress in December 1823 would not depart dramatically from the blueprint proposed by the British foreign minister.[9]

George Canning

In the first few decades of the nineteenth century, the European system of international politics was dominated by balance-of-power thinking and by the imperial states of France, Russia, Austria, and the United Kingdom. Ever since the Declaration of Independence, the United States had striven to extricate itself from this system. This was also the era of "Great Men," of European statesmen who determined the course of world events;

Figure 13.1: *George Canning* (1825) by Sir Thomas Lawrence. National Portrait Gallery, London.

the American diplomats who sought to establish the United States as an independent empire were therefore obliged to deal directly with these Great Men of Europe. With respect to France, this meant Talleyrand; with respect to Austria, Metternich; with respect to the United Kingdom in the 1820s, this meant George Canning.

The son of an actress and a failed entrepreneur—a parentage that his rivals always held against him—Canning had been a brilliant scholar at Oxford and had trained as a lawyer, but his obsession was politics. Although first attached to the opposition Whigs of the 1780s, Canning's breakthrough came with his violent denunciation of the French Revolution and the patronage of the Pittite "Tories" of the 1790s. Entering the Commons as MP for an Isle of Wight constituency, Canning developed a reputation for stunning oratory, biting invective, and cruel wit. Moreover, as the editor of the *Anti-Jacobin Review*, he became a leading, acerbic voice of British conservatism. In tribute to Pitt's leadership during the French Revolution, Canning penned the song that gave Pitt his soubriquet, "The Pilot That Weathered the Storm."

Changing constituencies at will under the unreformed electoral system, Canning began his ascent to the summit of British politics. In 1804, he was made treasurer of the navy under Pitt, and by 1807 he was secretary of state for foreign affairs under Portland. This initial spell as foreign minister was defined by three events. The first was the bombardment of Copenhagen in September 1807 to ensure the Danish fleet was not appropriated by Napoleonic France. The second, in the same year, was the supervision of the Portuguese royal family's flight to Brazil. The third began with a dispute over the deployment of troops by Lord Castlereagh, who at the time was secretary for war. Castlereagh wished to send the troops to the Netherlands; Canning wanted them in Portugal. Canning therefore maneuvered the poorly Portland into dismissing his rival but, when Castlereagh discovered the plot, he challenged Canning to the most famous duel in British history. It was a laughable mismatch: Canning had never fired a gun before, while Castlereagh was one of the finest shots in the country. Canning missed by a distance; Castlereagh hit Canning in the leg.

Following the duel, Canning was excluded from office until 1816, when he was made president of the Board of Control, a cabinet-level office responsible for governing East Indian affairs. Then, in 1822, tragedy returned him to the front bench of national politics. Since 1812, Castlereagh had been foreign minister, managing the coalitions that defeated Napoleon and then orchestrating the Congress of Vienna and the Quadruple Alliance. Yet by 1822 Castlereagh's "Congress system" of international politics had disintegrated, and the foreign minister had become the target of intense public criticism. Castlereagh had also begun to exhibit the symptoms of a mental breakdown. In August 1822, finding only a pen-knife since his wife had confiscated his razors, he slit his own throat. Upon the sorry death of his nemesis, Canning was the natural successor to the Foreign Office. Opposing Castlereagh's program of Continental alliances, he returned under the banner "Every nation for itself and God for us all." Canning's second term was dominated by the issue of slave emancipation in the British West Indies, by the demise of Spanish America, and by check-ing the colonial ambitions of the restored French monarchy. Of these latter issues, he famously told the House of Commons that "I resolved that if France had Spain, it should not be Spain 'with the Indies.' I called the New World into existence, to redress the balance of the Old."[10] Canning at last ascended to the British premiership in 1827 when Lord Liverpool, prime minister since 1812, was incapacitated by a stroke. Within four months of taking office, however, Canning was dead at the age of fifty-seven. Perhaps the greatest British statesman of his time, he became one of the world's "lost leaders."

The Monroe Doctrine

European plans for recolonizing the Americas horrified American states-men in practice and in principle. Under Monroe as under Washington, they wished to reject balance-of-power chicanery and to expel European influence—whether political, military, commercial, or ideological—from the New World. This required foreign policy to be conducted on Ameri-can terms, not in league with European allies. "It would be more candid," stated John Quincy Adams, "as well as more dignified, to avow our prin-ciples explicitly to Russia and France, than to come in as a cockle-boat in the wake of the British man-of-war." Following extensive discussion with his cabinet, James Monroe decided to proclaim this position to the world; in his Annual Message to Congress in December 1823, he articulated a long-term vision for American foreign policy.[11]

Corresponding to the factors informing his policy, the president expounded three major principles that became known as the Monroe Doc-trine. First, the United States would not intervene in Europe, neither on behalf of the Greeks nor the Spanish. "In the wars of the European powers relating to themselves," the president declared, "we have never taken any part, nor does it comport with our policy to do so." Second, the United States would oppose new European colonial ventures in the Americas.

"The American continents," stated Monroe, "by the free and independent condition which they have assumed and maintain, are henceforth not to be considered as subjects for future colonization by any European powers." This "noncolonization principle" prompted Chateaubriand to ask the British minister at Paris about the possibility of a joint remonstrance. Third, the United States would oppose European interference in the newly independent states of Latin America:

> We should consider any attempt on their part to extend their system to any portion of this hemisphere as dangerous to our peace and safety. With the existing colonies or dependencies of any European power we have not interfered and shall not interfere. But with the Governments who have declared their independence and maintained it, and whose independence we have, on great consideration and on just principles acknowledged, we could not view any interposition for the purpose of oppressing them, or controlling in any other manner their destiny, by any European power in any other light than as the manifestation of an unfriendly disposition toward the United States.

Although not specified in Monroe's Address, the United States also adopted the "no-transfer principle," details of which were communicated separately to Russia and London. Henceforth, the Americans would oppose the transfer of any former Spanish colonies from Spain to another European power. Earlier in his tenure as secretary of state, John Quincy Adams had written to Henry Middleton, the American minister to Russia, that "for the repose of Europe, as well of America, the European and American political systems should be kept as separate and distinct from each other as possible." The Monroe Doctrine now sought to turn that ideal into reality.[12]

In the courts of the Holy Allies, Monroe's Address provoked an explosive response. Prince Klemens von Metternich, the reactionary Austrian diplomat, raged to the Russian foreign minister, Count Nesselrode, that the United States had, in this "indecent" declaration, "cast blame and scorn on the institutions of Europe [that were] most worthy of respect, on the principles of its greatest sovereigns, [and] on the whole of these measures which a sacred duty no less than an evident necessity has forced our governments to adopt." By making "these unprovoked attacks, in fostering revolutions . . . , [and] in extending a helping hand to those which seem to prosper," Metternich argued the Americans had lent "new strength to the apostles of the sedition, and reanimate[d] the courage of every conspirator." For the Austrian minister, the Monroe Doctrine posed mortal danger to European interests. "If this flood of evil doctrine and pernicious examples should extend over the whole of America," he asked, "what would become of our religious and political institutions, of the moral force of our governments, and of that conservative system which has saved Europe from complete dissolution?" Nesselrode agreed with Metternich. He wrote in turn to Baron Tuyll, the Russian minister at Washington, that the Doctrine "enunciates views and pretensions so exaggerated, it establishes principles so contrary to the rights of European powers, that it merits only the most profound contempt."[13]

The British were much less concerned; after all, George Canning had effectively proposed the Monroe Doctrine to the Americans. Canning planned to use the United States as a balancing weight against the colonial pretensions of the Russians and the French. Writing to the British minister to Russia, he claimed that "the effect of the ultra-liberalism of our Yankee co-operators, on the ultra-despotism of our Aix-la-Chapelle allies, gives me just the balance that I wanted." The British parliamentary opposition was even more enthusiastic in its support of Monroe's Address, and it placed sufficient pressure on Liverpool's ministry that His Majesty's government soon declared its support of Latin American independence. Even so, Monroe's strident tone and the guardianship of the Western Hemisphere that the United States pretended to assume were not to Canning's liking. Writing in 1826 to Benjamin Vaughan, a British radical who had emigrated to Boston, Canning complained that "the avowed pretension of the United States to put themselves at the head of the confederacy of all the Americas and to sway that Confederacy against Europe is *not* a pretension identified with our interests or one that we can countenance or tolerate." The British had wanted the United States to act as second fiddle in their version of the world order; instead, they found their former colony aspiring to exclude all European influence, even British influence, from the Western Hemisphere.[14]

In the former Spanish colonies, Monroe's Address was interpreted giddily as American commitment to their struggle against Spain and the Holy Allies. José María Salazar, the Colombian minister to the United States, wrote to Adams that his government had received the Address with "the greatest pleasure." Salazar now wanted to know what steps the United States would take to turn this Doctrine into policy. Colombia expected the Americans "to resist any interference of the Holy Alliance for the purpose of subjugating the new republics or of interfering with their form of government." Salazar continued:

Colombia desires to know if the United States will enter into a treaty of alliance with her to save America from the calamities of a despotic system. . . . Colombia desires to know if the government of Washington interprets foreign intervention to mean the employment of Spanish forces against America at a juncture when Spain is occupied by a French army, and when the government of Spain is under the influence of France and her Allies. . . . It appears that affairs are already in the condition depicted in the declaration of President Monroe.

He therefore requested from Adams "those explanations which may serve Colombia for guidance in her policy and in her system of defense." Yet Salazar and his peers were to be disappointed. While they expected the practical assistance that they discerned in Monroe's Address, Monroe's administration would do nothing without British cooperation and congressional approval. It was not until the Roosevelt Corollary of 1904 that the Monroe Doctrine was reformulated to justify direct intervention in Latin America by the United States.[15]

Moreover, the Doctrine did *not* prevent the French from concocting further plans. In the spring of 1825, Charles X's foreign minister gave a hearing to Gregor MacGregor, a Scottish adventurer, who proposed to conquer Mexico with five thousand men and an infante. In December 1828, he raised the same scheme with the British ambassador, Viscount Granville. As late as 1829, the French still conspired with South American monarchists. That September, the Colombian foreign minister suggested that a French prince could succeed Bolívar as the Colombian head of state. Then, in November, the French consul-general in Santiago reported that Chilean elites had offered "the aid and influence of their respective parties in order to receive as [the] liberator of Chile, a prince who would be sent them from Europe." Throughout the 1820s, then, the French under Louis XVIII and Charles X pined for New World colonies that would bring them untold wealth while counteracting the republican influence of the United States. They even conceived of Mexico as a buffer state, much as the British had once looked upon the Indian lands of the American Northwest. Yet after 1823, European plans to recolonize Spanish America were only plans, so long as Britain opposed them, and so long as the United States played its self-written role as the watchman of the Western Hemisphere.[16]

The Monroe Doctrine was the clearest and most significant articulation of American foreign policy since George Washington's Farewell Address, and, in a way, the Doctrine reiterated the critical aspect of the Address:

that the United States wished to shield itself from European quarrels. The Doctrine also began a bold new chapter in the international relations of the Union, for it avowed an American commitment to the independence and isolation of the whole Western Hemisphere. In practical effect, the Doctrine would lead to war only if it was adopted by Congress as guiding policy. As it was read, Monroe's Address was merely a statement of the president's intentions; it required affirmative support from Congress to make permanent changes to American foreign policy. The articulation of the Monroe Doctrine nonetheless marked the emergence of the United States as a great power in global politics. Only nine years since Washington, DC, was burned and since payments were stopped by the Treasury Department, the wishes and the interests of the United States had been solicited even by the British. The Union was now secure, so much so that a young lawyer from Illinois would declare in 1837 that "all the armies of Europe, Asia, and Africa combined . . . could not by force take a drink from the Ohio, or make a track on the Blue Ridge, in a trial of a thousand years."[17]

CHAPTER 14

The Congress of Panama

My notions of the Moral influence of the people of the U.S. are
lofty and extensive, I confess; But at least, I would Sadly Regret if
it were not fully exercised at the Congress of panama, and in Every
Concern of South America. It would Be in My Opinion leaving the
field to the intrigues of European Monarchy and Aristocracy.[1]

—Marquis de Lafayette to Henry Clay, February 1826

If Hernán Cortés, Vasco Núñez de Balboa, and Francisco Pizarro and his
brothers personify the founding of the Spanish Empire, the fall of the same
will be forever linked with one man, Simón Bolívar. Born in 1783 into a
wealthy Venezuelan family, the man who became known as El Libertador
was at first, even though his father was a closet revolutionary, a typical
creole aristocrat of the Spanish New World. Raised by the slave Hipólita
and educated in military science at Madrid, Bolívar spent the most part
of eight years in Europe from 1799. Surrounded by the chaos, the brilliance, and the example of Napoleonic rule, in August 1805 the young
Bolívar and two of his friends would climb the Palatine Hill in Rome. On
that auspicious summit, where the grandees of the Roman Republic had
built their palaces, Bolívar and his companions "knelt down, embraced,
and swore that we would liberate our country or die trying." Returning to
Venezuela, he became involved in the high politics of independence when
the Supreme Junta of Caracas, which had been established in the wake
of Joseph Bonaparte's accession as king of the Indies, appointed him to a
diplomatic delegation to the United Kingdom. Nothing came of the mission, but Bolívar soon became central to the cause of Venezuelan and South
American independence.[2]

227

The path toward independence was not straightforward; in fact, it was violent, difficult, and erratic. The First Republic of Venezuela went unrecognized and survived for no more than a year until its capitulation at San Mateo. Bolívar then led the Admirable Campaign of 1813 to establish the Second Republic of Venezuela, but it fell the next year to Spanish reconquest. When Bolívar penned his "Letter from Jamaica," a plea to the British and to liberal Europe for intervention in South America, he was in peripatetic exile. It was only with the assistance of the free blacks of Haiti, and with the establishment in 1819 of the Third Republic, that the independence of Venezuela became likely. The Congress of Angostura then merged Venezuela with New Granada to form Gran Colombia, but Bolívar's mission of liberation was continental. His wars continued across South America and, by 1825, he was president of the independent states of Gran Colombia, Peru, *and* Bolivia.

Despite his veneration of the French and American Revolutions, and though he told the American sailor Hiram Paulding that "Washington awoke in me a desire to be just like him," Bolívar was far from a republican ideologue. He certainly did not look to the United States as the model for South America. For Bolívar, the federal, egalitarian system constructed by Madison and the Federalists was completely unsuitable for the Hispanic republics. Such *federales*, he wrote, "believe that Colombia is filled with simpletons who sit around the firesides of Bogota, Tunja, and Pamplona." Advocates of federal republicanism had failed to notice that the new states of Latin America were instead populated by "the Caribs of the Orinoco, the cowboys of the Apure, the seamen of Maracaibo, the boatmen of the Magdalena, the bandits of Patia, the indestructible citizens of Pasto, the Guajibos of Casanare, and all the savage hordes from Africa and America who roam untamed as wild deer in the Wilderness of Colombia." Such men could not be governed, Bolívar thought, by a decentralized, federal system. Over time, Bolívar became even less sanguine of the republican potential of Venezuelans. "We are the vile offspring," he wrote, "of the predatory Spaniards who came to America to bleed her white and to breed with the victims. Later the illegitimate offspring of these unions joined with the offspring of slaves . . . from Africa. With such racial mixture and such a moral record, can we afford to place laws above leaders and principles above men?"[3]

Speaking at the inauguration of the Second National Congress of Venezuela in 1819, Bolívar elaborated upon the differences between the North and South American systems. Declaring that he could not seriously compare "the position and character of two states as dissimilar as the English-

Figure 14.1: *Simon Bolivar* (1827) by Charles Turner. National Portrait Gallery, London.

American and the Spanish-American," Bolívar expressed amazement that the American Union had survived and flourished. "Although the people of North America are a singular model of political virtue and moral rectitude; although that nation was cradled in liberty, reared on freedom, and maintained by liberty alone; and . . . although those people . . . are unique in the history of mankind," he marveled "that so weak and complicated a government as the federal system has managed to govern them in the difficult and trying circumstances of their past." Bolívar went on to cite Montesquieu, not Madison: "Does not *L'Esprit des lois* state that laws should be suited to the people for whom they are made; that it would be a major coincidence if those of one nation could be adapted to another?" Laws, he continued, "should be in keeping with . . . the inhabitants, their inclinations, resources, number, commerce, habits, and customs. This is the code we must consult, not the code of Washington!" Bolívar even advised the study of the British, not the American, constitution, "for that body of laws appears destined to bring the greatest possible good for the peoples that adopt it." Not without reason, American statesmen looked upon Bolívar with only guarded favor.[4]

The Congress of Panama

In a letter of December 7, 1824, Bolívar wrote to the governments of Columbia, Mexico, Rio de la Plata, Chile, and Central America. He asked them to join Peru in sending ministers to a conference he planned to hold in Panama in 1826. "The day our plenipotentiaries make the exchange of their powers," he wrote to the Colombian foreign minister, "will stamp in the diplomatic history of the world an immortal epoch." This kind of conference, which the former British foreign minister Lord Castlereagh had made a staple of European diplomacy, was a long-standing dream of Bolívar's. Indeed, in his 1815 "Letter from Jamaica," he had already conceived of Panama as the hub of continental cooperation, where "an august assembly of representatives of republics, kingdoms, and empires" might "deliberate upon the high interests of peace and war. . . . How beautiful it would be," he wrote, "if the Isthmus of Panama could be for us what the Isthmus of Corinth was for the Greeks!" Bolívar did not invite the isolationist Paraguay, nor the former Portuguese colony of Brazil. Nor indeed did he invite the United States, for he wished only for a conference of former Spanish colonies, a congress of Hispanic republics. However, Francisco de Paula Santander, the vice-president of Gran Colombia, instructed the Colombian minister in Washington to invite the United States, an act that created a deep, personal rift between him and Bolívar.[5]

The invitation was received in Washington by a new administration. Having served as president since 1817, James Monroe announced that he would not seek election to a third term in office. Four potential successors emerged: the soldier and senator from Tennessee, Andrew Jackson; the secretary of state, John Quincy Adams; the Speaker of the House, Henry Clay; and the secretary of the treasury from Georgia, William H. Crawford. Each of the candidates enjoyed a regional advantage. Jackson was a hero of the South; Adams was a son of New England; Clay was the leading western statesman; and Crawford commanded significant support in east-

Figure 14.2. Central and South American republics in 1826 and the Congress of Panama

232 · AN INDEPENDENT EMPIRE

ern states such as Virginia. When the results were announced in December 1824, none of the candidates had achieved a majority in the electoral college. Jackson won the plurality, taking ninety-nine electors and 41 percent of the popular vote, beating Adams, who was in second place. Crawford came third, with forty-one electoral votes, despite having been incapacitated by a stroke. In accordance with the Twelfth Amendment, the election was turned over to the House of Representatives. Clay, finishing outside the top three in the electoral college, was not on the House ballot, and he fumed at Jackson's success: "I cannot believe that killing 2,500 Englishmen at New Orleans qualifies [a man] for the various, difficult, and complicated duties of the Chief Magistracy." Clay's role in the election, however, was far from over. As Speaker of the House, he threw his weight behind Adams, for despite their differences on foreign affairs, Adams's policies on economic protection and internal improvements were not dissimilar to the domestic aspects of Clay's American System. Adams promptly won the House vote on the first ballot and Clay was named secretary of state in the new administration. While Adams celebrated his elevation to "the summit of laudable, or at least blameless, worldly ambition," the Jacksonians denounced a "corrupt bargain" and labeled Clay "the Judas of the West." Jackson never forgave Clay.* When asked near death if he had any regrets, Jackson is said to have replied, "Yes, I didn't shoot Henry Clay."[6]

During eight years as secretary of state, Adams had advocated the cautious but detached support of international republicanism. He had also been the primary author of the foreign-policy doctrine that protested European interference in the Western Hemisphere. Conversely, Henry Clay, the new secretary of state, had argued for the practical support of revolutionary republicanism and the active alliance of the republics of the Americas. During four years as the twin architects of American foreign policy, Clay and Adams would face several notable challenges. One such was the potential for revolution in Cuba and Puerto Rico and the attractiveness of those still-loyal Spanish colonies to other European powers. Another was the need to negotiate commercial treaties with the British, especially on trade with the West Indies. Clay and Adams would enjoy some success. Conducting the diplomacy of the United States in line with the American System, Clay concluded twelve commercial treaties, more than during any previous presidential term; the British were even persuaded to pay indemnity to slaveholders whose "property" had been freed during the War of

---

*Nor would Jackson forgive Clay for inciting deeply personal attacks on his wife, Rachel, during the bitter general election of 1828. Jackson would defeat John Quincy Adams, but he always blamed the attacks on Rachel for his wife's untimely death in December that year.

1812. Nothing, however, would test them more than Bolívar's call for pan-Americanism.

Although a later document listed seventeen points of business—including, spectacularly, "the consummat[ion] of the union of the new states and the British Empire"—the agenda of the Congress of Panama was boiled down to four main items: first, continued and coordinated resistance to the European colonization of the Americas; second, the potential for military action to liberate Cuba and Puerto Rico; third, the establishment of diplomatic and commercial relations with Haiti; and fourth, the creation of maritime laws for the Western Hemisphere. In Clay's opinion, the United States should have accepted its invitation immediately: the Congress of Panama represented more than a chance to promote the concept of the American System, since the very occurrence of the Congress would make the System real. Clay therefore spent months working on Adams, urging the participation of the United States. When the president was eventually persuaded, American attendance was announced in Adams's first Annual Message to Congress in December 1825. The cabinet assumed that popular and congressional approval for the mission would follow swiftly, but they were mistaken. In fact, the next four months witnessed a ferocious debate over American participation at Panama and the direction of American foreign policy. It some quarters, the debate was even perceived as a struggle over the very soul of the Union itself.[7]

Support for U.S. Participation

Following the Annual Message, the president, his secretary of state, and their supporters mounted a campaign to promote—and to gain senatorial approval for—American participation at Panama. The commonest line of argument concerned the furtherance of the Monroe Doctrine, which by 1825 was not yet regarded as an integral, let alone inviolable, aspect of American foreign policy. For Adams, subtle direction of the Congress of Panama could extend the operation of the Doctrine across the entire hemisphere. "It may be so developed," he argued, "to the new Southern Nations that they will all feel it as an essential appendage to their independence." Specifically, the president conceived of the Congress as a means of buttressing the noncolonization principle first articulated by Monroe. Addressing both Houses on December 26, Adams declared that "an agreement between all the parties represented at the meeting, that each will guard, by its own means, against the establishment of any future European Colony within its borders, may be found advisable."[8]

In parts of the United States, most often in northern and eastern states, politicians and publishers were supportive of Adams's plans. The *North American Review*, the foremost New England periodical of the nineteenth century, was already enamored of Bolívar's Congress. In January 1826, the *Review* described "the alliance about to be established between the new American republics, by the delegates assembled at the Isthmus of Panama" as ranking "among the most remarkable events of political history." The *Review*'s readers were reminded of the feats of the ancient Greek leagues of Amphictyon and Achaea. They were also referred to the more recent alliances of the smaller European states, but told that "none of them has existed under circumstances so imposing, or been instituted on principles so broad and just in their political bearings, or been calculated to affect so deeply and widely the destiny of future generations, as that about to be formed by the Congress of Panama." Bolívar's summons, the *Review* went on, was a clarion call to liberty in "a hemisphere of the globe [which] has become freed from the yoke of bondage, by hard struggles and by an energy, which only the spirit of freedom could inspire." The United States could not ignore the Congress, for "although our own government is at present widely separated from the sphere of its action, yet it must necessarily, at a future day, participate largely of the influence of its measures."[9]

In his 1825 Message to Congress, Adams promised that American attendance at Panama would neither compromise the nation's neutrality nor commit the United States to military action. Participation was "compatible with that neutrality from which it is neither our intention nor the desire of the American States that we should depart." Several northern papers took the president at his word, expressing relief that the Union would not be bound to decisions taken in Panama. New York's *Albion* agreed that "the objects of the Congress will be *deliberative* and not *legislative*, and that the United States will concur in no measures that may impart hostility to European states." In the House, Daniel Webster was the administration's strongest ally. He too emphasized the detached nature of American participation: the Congress of Panama was "a diplomatic meeting" like the European conferences of Westphalia and Utrecht. The United States would not join a government or a league, and "no nation [at Panama would be] a party to anything done in such assemblies, to which it does not expressly make itself a party."[10]

Others supported the Congress in the hope of establishing the United States as the undisputed leader of the Western Hemisphere. To that end, the *Boston Repertory* and the *Saturday Evening Post* reprinted the thoughts of the French minister Chateaubriand:

The most important feature in the foreign policy of the Anglo-Americans, is the sending of an ambassador to the Congress of Panama, a resolution which, followed by a prudent choice of the person to be sent, may consolidate the liberty of a whole hemisphere. . . . The noble post of being at the head of a new world is certainly well worth the sacrifice of a few dollars in duties and a few bales of cotton.

The *Democratic Press* of Philadelphia meanwhile urged politicians who opposed the Congress to temper their language, for fear that Latin American trade deals would be offered to the British instead of the United States. "Great Britain has made treaties with these governments," stated the *Press*, "acknowledging their independence." The British, moreover, had "loaned them nearly a hundred millions of dollars; given them immense credits for goods; and, on all occasions, and in various ways, sought to win their good opinions and secure their commerce." The *Press* also warned that "other European nations manifest similar dispositions, and thus impose upon us, if we desire their friendship or their commerce, the duty of showing that we are not less friendly disposed than other, and more distant nations." Successful participation in the Congress promised untold riches for the United States. Senator Josiah Johnston of Louisiana therefore argued that "the establishment of principles of a liberal commercial intercourse" required "deliberation and consultation with the Spanish American states."[11]

Supporters of the Panama mission also endowed it with a higher, moral purpose. The president argued that an American presence would encourage and promote religious liberty throughout the hemisphere, since "some of the southern nations [were] . . . so far under the dominion of prejudice that they have incorporated with their political constitutions an exclusive church without toleration of any other than the dominant sect." In the House in April 1826, Daniel Webster underscored the didactic dimension of the American mission. The United States had been "the great Northern Light" that had illuminated the path toward Spanish American independence, and so the Union now had a duty of care toward its southern pupils. The moral imperative of the Panama mission transcended party lines too. Edward Livingston was a Jacksonian from Louisiana and the son of Robert, who had sworn in George Washington as president and negotiated the Louisiana Purchase. He despised the Holy Alliance and celebrated the "counteraction of the Congress of Panama." Livingston believed that the work of the Congress would proceed "not from physical, but from moral force; not by alliances or coalitions, or by bayonets . . . but by the force of truth." The very calling of the Congress, he continued, constituted a victory over the Holy Allies:

> Can it be doubted that the spectacle of an assembly of free Republics, which have just entered into political existence, meeting for the purpose of discussing those principles of liberty and equality of rights on which they are all founded, and debating in what manner, and by what means, those rights can be best preserved . . . pursuing, in short, the very reverse, in all things, of the retrograde march of the monarchs of Europe: can it be doubted, I say, that this spectacle must have an important effect in counteracting the policy of the Holy Alliance? And what is there to alarm us in this?

Livingston stated that American support of the Congress was essential. There would be no qualms and no misgivings at Panama, only the prosecution of justice: "Who will regret that we have assisted to throw this counterpoise to the degradation and slavery of man into the scale? . . . No member in this House: no man in this country."[12]

Opposition to U.S. Participation

Support for the Panama mission, however, was far from universal, and opposition rallied behind the resolution of the Senate Committee on Foreign Relations that "it is not expedient at this time for the United States to send any ministers to the Congress of American nations assembled at Panama." The congressman and future president James Polk even compared the Panama controversy to the Revolutionary Crisis when he warned that "Every Patriot should be at his post." The lines of opposition were manifold. Senator Hugh White of Tennessee believed that the independent republics were simply not worth American protection from European predators. "If these new States set so little value upon independence," said White, so "as to require such an agreement to stimulate them to exert their means to prevent colonies from being planted within their limits, then I shall conclude they are unfit for self-government, and that no agreement with them, upon any subject, can be of much utility to us." If American superintendence was necessary to the development of the Western Hemisphere, it followed for White that the Western Hemisphere was not worthy of superintendence.[13]

Others believed that the Congress at Panama, in contradiction of President Adams's protests, would involve the United States in lengthy and costly military action. James Buchanan, then a congressman from Pennsylvania, dismissed the president's apologies. "The task of the Panama Congress," Buchanan told the House, "is to establish a strict and intimate alliance and union between all and each of the seven Republics who have freed themselves of Spain." Buchanan would "look upon the day of [the Congress's] consummation as the darkest which this country will ever have beheld." Rather than send ministers to *support* the Congress, Buchanan recommended that American representatives should seek to "break up this Congress." Levi Woodbury, a senator from New Hampshire, likewise decried the credulity of anyone believing that attendance at Panama would not bind the United States into military alliance. "I have been utterly astonished," he told the Senate, "that any gentleman could read these documents, and still contend that this was not a belligerent Congress."[14]

There was also an ideological objection to Panama. Senator Robert Hayne of South Carolina ironically used Clay's concept of the American System to define his opposition by deriding what "some of our statesmen . . . are pleased to call 'An America System.'" For Hayne, such a term implied "restriction and Monopoly, and when applied to our foreign policy, 'entangling alliances.'" Such things were "the fruit of that prurient spirit which will not suffer the nation to advance gradually in the development of its great resources . . . but would accelerate its march by the most unnatural and destructive stimulants." Andrew Jackson, writing to Buchanan, even renounced the Panama mission as the potential betrayal of Washington's ideal of isolation:

> I cannot see, for my part, how it follows that the primary interests of the United States will be safer in the hands of others, than in her own; or in other words, that it can ever become necessary to form entangling alliances, or any connection with the governments of South America which may infringe upon that principle of equality among nations which is the basis of their independence, as well as all their international rules.

For Jackson, "the doctrine of Washington [was] as applicable to the present as to the then primary interests of Europe." He therefore believed, "so far as our own peace and happiness are concerned," that the United States had little proper business in South America. Buchanan concurred, declaring in the House that "we have ourselves grown great by standing alone and pursuing an independent policy." That path alone had led the

United States "to national happiness and national glory," and the Congress of Panama threatened this progress.[15]

Opposition to Panama was also personal, since American participation had become a signature policy of Adams and Clay, both of whom were wildly unpopular in certain circles. The Jacksonians, for example, had never forgiven the president and the secretary of state for the "corrupt bargain" of 1824. One of their more implacable enemies was Senator John Randolph, who believed it was a duty "to leave nothing undone that I may lawfully do, to pull down this administration." He despised Adams, and was no less contemptuous of his supporters: "They who, from indifference, or with their eyes open, persist in hugging the traitor to their bosom, deserve to be insulted . . . deserve to be slaves, with no other music to soothe them but the clank of the chains which they have put on themselves have given to their offspring." With vicious reference to Clay, Randolph told the Senate that the Congress of Panama was but a "Kentucky cuckoo's egg, laid in a Spanish-American nest." The pair of Clay and Adams were even mocked as "the coalition of Blifil and Black George," the Puritan and the gamekeeper from Henry Fielding's *Tom Jones*. For the personal insult, the secretary of state demanded personal satisfaction from the senator, and so they fought a duel in the forest across the river from Georgetown. Randolph refused to shoot, while Clay but singed Randolph's coat.[16]

The issue of slavery cast further shadows over the Panama debates. The *anti*slavery sympathies of Bolívar and the *libertadores* were well known, and southern slaveholders feared that the Congress would agitate for slave insurrections in Cuba and Puerto Rico akin to those in Saint Domingue (the 1790s), Barbados (1816), and Demerara (1823). For John Macpherson Berrien of Georgia, this was a direct threat to "the safety of the Southern States." He asked his fellow senators, "Can you suffer these Islands to pass into the hands of buccaneers, drunk with their new-born liberty?" Of course, it was a rhetorical question: "Cuba and Puerto Rico," Berrien insisted, "*must remain as they are.*" In this, Berrien was supported even by senators from northern, "free" states. John Holmes of Maine warned that if it became known "that the rights of the slaves of Cuba are to be discussed," then "every philanthropist and fanatic in Europe will be on the alert . . . , the blacks will take fire, and the scenes of St. Domingo will be re-acted at home." It had also been mooted that the South American states would recognize the independence of Haiti. For Thomas Hart Benton of Missouri, such diplomatic recognition would do more than provide symbolic hope to the slaves of the southern states. "The peace of eleven states in the Union," he declared, "will not permit black Consuls and Ambassadors to establish themselves in our cities, and to parade through our country, and give their fellow blacks in the United States proof in hand of the honors which await them, for a like successful effort on their part."[17]

Anticipating the states' rights arguments of the antebellum period, representatives of the slave states avowed that slavery was a domestic, internal issue and that diplomatic, international discussion of the matter was inappropriate. James Buchanan was willing only "to consider slavery as a question entirely domestic, and leave it to those States in which it exists." Robert Hayne likewise insisted that "The question of slavery . . . must be considered and treated entirely as a DOMESTIC QUESTION." Indeed, the only way that many southerners would support the Panama mission was if the American delegation went to *oppose* antislavery agitation. Thomas Reed, a senator from Mississippi, was unconvinced by the Congress and especially skeptical of its focus on slavery. If the Congress of Panama had "the power of giving Hayti equal rank with communities of men composed of the descendants of the Saxons, the Franks, and ancient Germans," then Reed was "prepared to deprecate a mission charged with such deleterious powers." Yet Reed confessed that if "one of the objects of the mission is to *prevent* this disastrous recognition," then he was ready "to see in it objects greatly salutary to the interests of the Southern People bordering upon the Gulf of Mexico." Robert Hayne echoed the call for "our Ministers to South America and Mexico to *protest* against the independence of Hayti."[18]

This opposition was hugely significant for domestic partisan politics. The First Party System of Federalism and Republicanism had died, but the Congress of Panama quickly became the issue around which nebulous elements of the Jacksonian Democrats, and therefore the Second Party System, began to coalesce. Martin van Buren was a senator from New York. In 1824, he had supported William Crawford for the presidency, not Jackson, but he quickly became the founding operative and theorist of the nascent Democratic Party. Van Buren recognized the Congress of Panama as a vital spur to the formation of his party: it was "the first tangible point for the opposition which had been anticipated and could not have been avoided without an abandonment of cherished principles, and which there was in truth no disposition to avoid." Adams, too, appreciated that Panama was a rallying point for his enemies. "This is the first subject," he noted, "upon which a great effort has been made in both Houses to combine the discordant elements of the Crawford and Jackson and Calhoun men into a united opposition against the Administration."[19]

The American Mission

Despite the partisan slings and arrows, Adams had become convinced of the universal mission of republicanism. He believed it was essential for the United States to participate in Bolívar's conference, and he continued to lobby an intransigent Congress for approval and the necessary funds. Addressing the House in April 1826, he spoke of how the former Spanish colonies "have now been transformed into eight independent nations, extending to our very borders." Moreover, "seven of them [were] Republics like ourselves," and Adams insisted that they "have already important political connections; with reference to whom our situation is neither distant nor detached; whose political principles and systems of government, congenial with our own, must and will have an action and counteraction upon us and ours to which we cannot be indifferent if we would." The president had nominated two American delegates to be sent to Panama. The first was Richard C. Anderson, a Republican from Kentucky who had served in the House from 1817 to 1821. In January 1823, Anderson had been appointed as the American minister to Colombia, in which capacity he signed the Anderson-Gaul Treaty of 1824. Already in South America, he was a natural choice. He was to be joined by John Sergeant of Pennsylvania, another former congressman and a passionate advocate of Clay's American System. Anderson and Sergeant would be accompanied and supervised by William B. Rochester of New York, yet another former representative who was narrowly defeated by DeWitt Clinton in his state's gubernatorial election of 1826. Clay and Adams had hoped to send this party to Panama by January 1826, but it was not until March that the Senate—where Randolph and Calhoun had been as obstructive as possible—confirmed the appointments of Sergeant and Anderson. It took another month for the House to raise $40,000 to pay for the mission. Clay, however, had long been preparing the ministers' instructions and the resulting document, which ran to more than eighteen thousand words, articulated what the secretary described as "a policy of good neighborhood."[20]

To Bolívar's chagrin, the opening of the Congress had been delayed repeatedly to accommodate the tardiness of the United States. When it opened at last on June 22, 1826, still without the Americans, the Congress's president declared:

> This day may be called the day of America. From this day, the people enjoy freely their political liberty, and each individual conforms to his social compacts. A strict and eternal bond united the four Repub-

lics of Colombia, Guatemala, Mexico, and Peru. All engage mutually to assist each other against their foreign oppressors, and against
those who may attempt to infringe the rights they have recovered.

The ministers in attendance agreed to serve as "a council in times of great
conflict" and "as a point of contact in common dangers." The Congress had
been "charged with the formation of our new body of international law . . .
[and] organized and invested with all the powers competent to attain the
important and dignified end for which it is convoked." One delegate even
proclaimed the Congress to be "the last attempt to ascertain whether Mankind can be happy," deeming that Bolívar's efforts made him "superior to
Hercules and Theseus." The early days of the Congress were thus defined
by optimism.

There was also a foreign presence at the Congress, for the British and
the Dutch had sent observers to Panama. The European envoys were
greeted warmly, their presence interpreted as explicit support for Bolívar's
project. This was not necessarily the case: George Canning had sent the
British representatives not to assist pan-Americanism but to develop commercial relations. He instructed the British representative Edward Dawkins
to remind the new republics "of the benefits which they have derived and
continue to derive from a friendly intercourse with Great Britain."[21]

The British also had full opportunity to pursue deals with the new
republics, for the United States in fact played no part in the Congress of
Panama. Sergeant had refused to travel during high summer, which he
described as the "sickly season," while Anderson was making slow progress from Colombia. Then, after only twenty-three days, the Congress was
forced into adjournment by the oppressive Panamanian summer: yellow
fever was rampant, claiming the lives of two Britons and two Colombians.
Nine days later, the diseases of the tropical lowlands claimed another victim
when Richard Anderson, still en route from Colombia, died at Cartagena
without ever making it to Panama. Bolívar's and Clay's plans for hemispheric alliance were descending rapidly into farce. There was still hope for
the Congress itself, for the ministers agreed to reconvene by March 1827
in cleaner air and at higher altitude at Tacubaya outside of Mexico City. In
November 1826, therefore, Sergeant finally left the United States for his
new destination of Mexico, while Joel Poinsett—the incumbent American minister to Mexico—was chosen to replace Anderson. American plans,
however, were thwarted once more: domestic upheaval across South and
Central America meant that only Colombia sent ministers to Tacubaya,
and the Congress of Panama never reconvened. Even worse, the business

of the Congress itself—all that could be accomplished in the twenty-three days in session—came to nothing, for whatever measures had been passed by the delegates went unratified by their domestic governments.

John Quincy Adams had from the beginning seen the Congress of Panama was an aspirational, rather than practical, undertaking. It was, he acknowledged, "a measure speculative and experimental." It was always possible that "accident unforeseen and mischance not to be anticipated may baffle all [the Congress's] high purposes and disappoint its fairest expectations." Bolívar too admitted the failure of the Congress. Writing to a friend in August 1826, he confessed that the Congress, "an institution that would have been admirable had it proved more effective, must inevitably be compared to the foolish Greek who, from a rock, thought he could direct a fleet at sea." The influence of the Congress amounted to "nothing more than a shadow," and its decrees were "mere recommendations." For Bolívar, Clay, and Adams, the Congress of Panama and the American were reduced to pipe dreams and embarrassments. In Clay's later correspondence with Bolívar he wrote wistfully of "the course which the government of the United States took on that memorable occasion" and "the interest which was inspired in this country by the arduous struggles of South America." Not until Woodrow Wilson and the League of Nations would Americans again express such enthusiasm for international political alliance.[22]

Conclusion

Is it not well then, when we have trodden the highway of
independent nations for half a century, to pause on the ascent we
have gained, and look back on the course we have pursued; to
compare for a few moments our conditions at the commencement
of our career and at this stage of it?[1]

—George Benedict, *An Oration . . . on the Fourth of July 1826*

On December 5, 1826, in the year of the fiftieth anniversary of the Declaration of Independence, the representatives and senators of the United
States met in Washington for President John Quincy Adams's Annual Message to Congress. They gathered in the Capitol, burned by the British in
1814 but now reconstructed and once more the home of the American
legislature. The Message to Congress would not be read by Adams himself.
In 1801, Thomas Jefferson had deemed its personal delivery too monarchical, too much like the British "Speech from the Throne," and the practice
had been discontinued. Rather, the congressmen sat beneath the copper-
covered dome of the Capitol and listened to the Clerk of the House, who
relayed a Message in which Adams depicted the United States as the scene
of limitless prosperity. "In the survey of our extensive country," wrote the
president, "we have generally to observe abodes of health and regions of
plenty. . . . We are, as a people, increasing with unabated rapidity in population, wealth, and national resources." While Americans might have differed
on "how to turn the beneficence of heaven to the improvement of our
own condition," the transformation witnessed over the past half century
was scarcely credible in its magnificence: "how resplendent and sublime is
the transition from gloom to glory!" Nor would the American people rest

243

on these laurels. "There is a spirit animating us all," wrote Adams, "which will not suffer the bounties of Providence to be showered upon us in vain, but will receive them with grateful hearts, and apply them with unwearied hands to the advancement of the general good."[2]

The American ascent was clearly reflected in the foreign affairs of the nation. Despite some "collisions of interest and . . . unsatisfied claims of justice," Adams reported that the United States had "the happiness of enjoying peace and a general good understanding" in its "intercourse with the other nations of the earth." Beginning with Russia, the president mourned the death of the Emperor Alexander, but reassured Congress that "the sentiments of the reigning Emperor [Nicholas] toward the United States [were] altogether conformable to those" of his predecessor. Adams therefore hoped for the continuance of "that harmony and good understanding between the two nations which, founded in congenial interests, cannot but result in the advancement of the welfare and prosperity of both." With reference to France, ruled since 1815 by the restored Bourbon monarchy, Adams reported that American "relations of commerce and navigation . . . [were] in a state of gradual and progressive improvement." Friendly "dispositions have been on both sides encouraged and promoted" and would "continue to be cherished and cultivated on the part of the United States."[3]

Adams then reminded Congress that "treaties of amity, navigation, and commerce [had been] negotiated and signed . . . with the Government of Denmark . . . and with the Federation of Central America." The president drew attention to American relations with Spain, Portugal, and the German kingdom of Prussia. Although such relations had "not materially varied since the last session of Congress," Adams could yet declare that "friendly intercourse" existed between those nations and the United States. Adams even adverted to the "successful maintenance of our relations of peace and protection with the Indian tribes." There were only two disappointments in foreign affairs. The first was the failure to participate in the Congress of Panama, which "deprived the United States of the opportunity of possessing precise and authentic information of the treaties which were concluded." The second was the United Kingdom's refusal to open its West Indian ports to American shipping, although Adams declared that "our own dispositions and purposes towards Great Britain are all friendly and conciliatory."[4]

Even if the foreign relations of the United States were to sour and if the failure of diplomacy led to war, the American republic was now in an unprecedented position of security and military strength. Of the United States Army, the president declared that "every branch of the service is marked with order, regularity, and discipline" and that "the moral character of the Army is in a state of continual improvement." The United States Navy was likewise a formidable force. American warships, frigates, and sloops presented "a line of floating fortifications along the whole range of our coast, ready to meet any invader who might attempt to set foot upon our shores." Combined with coastal fortifications, the navy placed in the republic's possession "the most effective sinews of war." Beyond American waters, the navy "afforded protection to our commerce" and "contributed to make our country advantageously known to foreign nations," while doing much to eradicate piracy in the Caribbean and even the western Mediterranean.[5]

In some respects, the Message to Congress was hubristic, best understood in the context of Adams's presidency. He was beleaguered, suffering the repeated humiliations of the Panama debacle. In the recent elections to Congress, the Jacksonians had strengthened their hold over the House, seizing twelve seats in New York alone. The weakness of Adams's position was soon borne out in the 1828 presidential election, where Jackson would beat him by "twelve points." The 1826 Message was therefore the defense of Adams's record as much as an honest assessment of American progress. Indeed, given the rapacious ambition of the American Empire, the talk of "relations of peace and protection" with Native American tribes was more risible than accurate. Nonetheless, there were several elemental truths in what the president related to Congress: by 1826, the United States had emerged as one of the world's great powers, the predominant empire on the North American continent, worthy of the name of the American Empire, and a serious geopolitical rival to the empires of the Old World.

This view was held by American and European observers alike. In the German states, the United States was regarded as not only the exemplary federal union but the exemplary empire, its westward expansion the perfect model for imperial conquest. Alexander von Humboldt, the Prussian geographer, noted how Native Americans "usually withdrew when the whites approached," while the traveler Gottfried Duden was so beguiled by the Missouri River Valley that he propounded widespread emigration from Germany into the American West. The French intellectual Alexis de Tocqueville—sent to the United States to investigate the American penal system—soon reported on the remarkable progress of the American Empire. In *Democracy in America*, Tocqueville observed that "Within the frontiers of the Union the profoundest peace prevails, as within the heart of some great empire; abroad, it ranks with the most powerful nations of the earth." The United States, he wrote, "possesses the keys of the globe, its flag is respected in the most remote seas. The Union is as happy and as free as a small people, and as glorious and as strong as a great nation."[6]

It was in the United Kingdom, however, that the American Empire was most feared and respected. In May 1826, debate raged in the House of Commons about the British Navigation Laws. It had been proposed that restrictions on the United States should be lifted, or at least eased. William Huskisson, the president of the Board of Trade, refused even to countenance the idea* He declared that "In Commerce, in navigation, in naval power, and maritime pretensions, the United States are our most formidable rival." Huskisson understood that American ambition was limitless. He knew that "there exists, towards us, a spirit of rivalry in the United States." He therefore doubted the wisdom of "any measure tending to encourage the growth" of the American marine. Such measures were suited only to "states less jealous of our maritime ascendancy in time of war," states that confined "their views upon the ocean to the industrious employment of their sea-faring people, without looking to the ulterior object of one day disputing with us the dominion of that ocean." The United States, Huskisson warned, was "a new and formidable power."[7]

Indeed, such was the prevailing fear of American growth that the British West Indian colonies were thought vulnerable to the United States. Since 1823, the British Anti-Slavery Society had been campaigning for the emancipation of slaves in the British West Indies. As part of a countercampaign, slaveholders and their allies had warned that, by testing the loyalty of the West Indian colonies, Parliament invited their annexation by the United States. The historian Archibald Alison wrote of how "that ambitious state . . . the master of the Gulf of Mexico . . . is not an inattentive observer of the fair prey which is thus falling into its hands." West Indian merchants in London were told that "the Cabinet of Washington . . . is watching the progress of events in Jamaica; its emissaries are in the island." A British pamphleteer suggested that, in "aiming to be mistress of the new world," the United States was "ever awake to our mistaken policy of undervaluing our colonies, and ready to receive them. Wary and watchful, soaring on eagle wings, she is ready to embrace the happy moment when she may pounce on her prey, and . . . snatch from the crown of England one of its brightest gems, and triumphantly display the star-spangled banner of the Union on the walls where the flag of England was wont to wave with so much glory to herself." The American

---

*Huskisson was one of the intellectual powerhouses of Lord Liverpool's government in the 1820s, but he is best remembered for his death. In September 1830, he was run over by George Stephenson's Rocket and so became the first railway passenger casualty.

Empire, in the panicked minds of British imperialists, was ready to seize upon any sign of British weakness.[8]

Of course, much of this British rhetoric was deluded. The American presidents of the 1820s had not developed plans for the exploitation of Britain's emancipation crisis, nor for the annexation of the British West Indies. After the Missouri Compromise of 1820, which regulated the extension of slavery into future states of the Union, most politicians outside of the South and many within it, such as Henry Clay and James Monroe, opposed any scheme to acquire new "slave states."[9] Nonetheless, the British colonists of the Caribbean, imperialists in the motherland, and even the "Great Men" of Parliament recognized that the United States, far from a struggling nation almost stillborn in its independence, had become one of the great powers of the world. It was now readily perceived as the imperious and imperial guardian of the Western Hemisphere.

The year 1826 also marked a watershed in the history of American foreign relations. Since 1776, the statesmen and diplomats of the United States had been driven by the need to expand and secure the frontiers of the American Empire, to isolate the Union from the balance-of-power politics of the Old World, and to develop federal institutions that could bind the extremities of the Union into a coherent political and economic entity. By 1826, American leaders had achieved their main ambitions. The existing territory of the American Empire was no longer considered prey by the Old World, whose empires had either collapsed (the Spanish), diminished (the French), or found another quarry (the British and the Orient). The Monroe Doctrine had declared the ultimate separation of the United States from Europe and proclaimed American guardianship of the Western Hemisphere, positions that even the mighty British respected. The United States' attempted participation in the Congress of Panama was the major foreign-policy venture of the administration of John Quincy Adams, who was arguably the last president with an intimate connection to the founders of the nation. In 1828, Adams would lose the presidential election to Andrew Jackson in a landslide. Together with the Democratic Party's control of both chambers of Congress, there began an era of new politics and new priorities.

Of course, the recurrent themes of the first five decades of the United States did not disappear completely. The continuous westward expansion of the American Empire, for example, would bring the Union into repeated conflict with Native Americans and other powers. Jackson's administration began the formal eviction of the "Five Civilized Tribes"—the Chickasaw, Choctaw, Creek, Seminole, and Cherokee—from east of the Mississippi to west of the great river. The Oregon boundary dispute with the United Kingdom became a major political and diplomatic issue in the 1840s and a key part of James K. Polk's election platform in 1844. The Union's 1845 annexation of Texas then provoked the Mexican-American War of 1846–48, and the resultant Treaty of Guadalupe Hidalgo transferred the land of the present-day states of California, Arizona, and New Mexico to the United States. The institutions of the federal government would likewise remain a source of controversy, and the extension of their power into the frontier lands of the American West became a defining challenge of the mid- and late nineteenth century. Controversy over federal power and westward expansion would also, of course, combine fatally as eventual causes of the American Civil War. Yet in the decades after 1826, the themes of independence and security from foreign threats were no longer the principal agenda and daily concern of American leaders.

The United States would not have survived to experience new challenges beyond 1826 without the implementation of successful foreign policies, the intelligent prosecution of diplomacy, and judicious deployment of military force in the first five decades of independence. The American Union could not have thrived within the European system of international politics, nor could participation in such a system have given the United States the time and space necessary for its political consolidation and territorial growth: the foreign policy of the early United States was therefore defined by the avoidance of "entangling alliances" and enshrined by the Monroe Doctrine in 1823. In terms of diplomacy, debilitating issues in the American West could not have been resolved without Pinckney's Treaty, nor could festering problems with the British have been solved without John Jay's Treaty, while the territorial integrity of the Union was secured only in 1819 by John Quincy Adams's negotiations with Spain. Even the primal problem of support during the American Revolution might not have been resolved but for the diplomatic brilliance of Benjamin Franklin. Lastly, the Americans would never have secured independence from Europe but for the United States Navy, which won the Quasi-War with France, or the United States Army, which defeated the British at New Orleans. The United States was born of abstract ideals, but its survival and its story were rooted in these realities of diplomacy and war.

Notes

Introduction

1. "The King's Speech on Opening the Session," October 26, 1775, *The Parliamentary History of England, from the Earliest Period to the Year 1803*, ed. William Cobbett (36 vols., London: T.C. Hansard, 1806–20), 18:696.

2. "Journal of the Western Expedition. Part I: From St. Louis to the Conejos. Diary of An Expedition made under the Orders of the War Department, by Captain Z.M. Pike, in the Years 1806 and 1807, to Explore the Internal Parts of Louisiana," in *The Journals of Zebulon Montgomery Pike with Letters and Related Documents*, ed. Donald Jackson (2 vols., Norman: University of Oklahoma Press, 1966), 1:379, 383; Zebulon Pike to James Monroe, June 11, 1812, in *Journals of Pike*, 1:viii, ix.

3. James Wilkinson to Zebulon Pike, June 24, 1806, in *Journals of Pike*, 1:286.

4. James Wilkinson to Zebulon Pike, June 24, 1806, in *Journals of Pike*, 1:286.

5. "Journal of the Western Expedition," 374, 376, 379.

6. "Journal of the Western Expedition," 379–80, 382, 383.

7. "Journal of the Western Expedition," 383–84.

8. *Diary and Autobiography of John Adams*, ed. L. H. Butterfield (4 vols., Cambridge, MA: Belknap Press of Harvard University Press, 1961), 2:97.

9. Caleb Wallace to James Madison, November 12, 1787, *The Papers of James Madison*, Congressional Series, ed. William T. Hutchinson et al. (17 vols., Chicago: University of Chicago Press, 1962–91), 10:249–51.

Chapter 1

1. Adam Smith, *An Inquiry into the Nature and Causes of the Wealth of Nations* (Edinburgh: Thomas Nelson, [1776] 1834), 404.

2. Thomas Babington Macaulay, *The History of England from the Accession of James the Second* [1848] (4 vols., London: J.M. Dent & Sons, 1906), 2:379, 374, 378.

3. *Memoirs of John, Duke of Marlborough; with his Original Correspondence: Col-*

lected from the Family Records at Blenheim, and Other Authentic Sources, ed. William Coxe (3 vols., London: Longman, Hurst, Rees, Orme, and Brown, 1818–19), 1:315.

4. The most engaging portrayal of the Georgian kings is still J. H. Plumb, *The First Four Georges* (London: B.T. Batsford, 1956).

5. [John Wilkes], *The North Briton*, 45 (April 1763), 318.

6. Financial figures taken from Edmund S. Morgan and Helen M. Morgan, *The Stamp Act Crisis: Prologue to Revolution* (Chapel Hill: University of North Carolina Press, [1953] 1995), 21–22; Amherst quoted in Francis Parkman, *The Conspiracy of Pontiac: And the Indian War after the Conquest of Canada* [1851] (Boston: Little, Brown 1870), 2:36; Amherst on smallpox quoted in Howard H. Peckham, *Pontiac and the Indian Uprising* (Detroit: Wayne State University Press, [1947] 1994), 226.

7. Thomas Whateley, *The Regulations Lately Made Concerning the Colonies and the Taxes Imposed upon Them, Considered* (London: J. Wilkie, 1765), 101.

8. Townshend quoted in Edmund S. Morgan, ed., *Prologue to Revolution: Sources and Documents on the Stamp Act Crisis, 1764–1766* (Chapel Hill: University of North Carolina Press, 1959), 32; Hinshelwood quoted in *The Boisterous Sea of Liberty: A Documentary History of America from Discovery through the Civil War*, ed. David Brion Davis and Steven Mintz (Oxford: Oxford University Press, 1998), 148.

9. *Diary and Autobiography of John Adams*, 1:265.

10. James Otis, "Considerations on Behalf of the Colonists. In a Letter to a Noble Lord," in *Collected Political Writings of James Otis*, ed. Richard Samuelson (Indianapolis: Liberty Fund, 2015), 254.

11. ". . . shocking dog . . ." quoted in Shearer West, "Wilkes's Squint: Synecdochic Physiognomy and Political Identity in Eighteenth-Century Print Culture," *Eighteenth Century Studies* 33, no. 1 (1999): 65; Sandwich and Wilkes quoted in Andrew Jackson O'Shaughnessy, *The Men Who Lost America: British Command during the Revolutionary War and the Preservation of Empire* (London: Oneworld, 2014), 320.

12. "An Act for the better securing the Dependency of His Majesty's Dominions in America upon the Crown and Parliament of Great Britain," 6 Geo. 3 c. 12.

13. "An act for granting certain duties in the British colonies and plantations in America; for allowing a drawback of the duties of customs upon the exportation, from this kingdom, of coffee and cocoa nuts of the produce of the said colonies or plantations; for discontinuing the drawbacks payable on china earthen ware exported to America; and for more effectually preventing the clandestine running of goods in the colonies and plantations," 7 Geo. 3 c. 46; Townshend quoted in Robert J. Chaffin, "The Townshend Acts of 1767," *William and Mary Quarterly* 27, no. 1 (1970): 115.

14. "John Hancock and Four Other Boston Selectmen, September 14, 1768, to the Selectmen of Medway," quoted in Davis and Mintz, *Boisterous Sea of Liberty*, 152.

15. Smith, "Notes for Mr. Hamilton on the American Dispute" (November 1775); quoted in Daniel J. Hulsebosch, *Constituting Empire: New York and the Transformation of Constitutionalism in the Atlantic World, 1664–1830* (Chapel Hill: University of North Carolina Press, 2005), 94.

16. *London Chronicle*, January 23, 1766, and January 28, 1766; Benjamin Franklin to Lord Kames, February 25, 1767, in *The Papers of Benjamin Franklin, Volume XIV: January 1, 1767, through December 31, 1767*, ed. Leonard W. Labaree, Helen C.

Boatfield, and James H. Huston (New Haven: Yale University Press, 1970), 62–71; Burke, April 19, 1774, *Parliamentary History of England*, 17:1265.

17. Jack P. Greene, "Bridge to Revolution: The Wilkes Fund Controversy in South Carolina, 1769–1775," *Journal of Southern History* 29, no. 1 (1963): 21–22; on the interaction between the Wilkes and the American taxation controversies, see also Eliga Gould, *The Persistence of Empire: British Political Culture in the Age of the American Revolution* (Chapel Hill: University of North Carolina Press, 2000), 136–38.

18. Hillsborough quoted in Richard Archer, *As if an Enemy's Country: The British Occupation of Boston and the Origins of Revolution* (Oxford: Oxford University Press, 2010), 90, 191; John Adams to Matthew Robinson, March 2, 1786, *The Works of John Adams, with a Life of the Author by C.F. Adams. Volume VIII: Letters and State Papers, 1782–1799*, ed. Charles Francis Adams (Boston: Little, Brown and Company, 1853), 384.

19. John Adams to James Warren, December 17, 1773, *Papers of John Adams*, 2:1–2.

20. George III quoted in Peter David Garner Thomas, *Tea Party to Independence: The Third Phase of the American Revolution, 1773–1776* (Oxford: Oxford University Press, 1991), 29, 40; "An act to discontinue, in such manner, and for such time as are therein mentioned, the landing and discharging, shipping of goods, wares, and merchandise, at the town, and within the harbour, of Boston, in the province of Massachusetts Bay, in North America," 14 Geo. III. c. 19.

21. Houghton quoted in John Bartlet Brebner, *The Neutral Yankees of Nova Scotia: A Marginal Colony during the Revolutionary Years* (New York: Columbia University Press, 1937), 341.

22. See Alan Taylor, *American Revolutions: A Continental History, 1750–1804* (New York: W. W. Norton, 2016), 83.

23. Peter Wraxall quoted in Daniel K. Richter, *Before the Revolution: America's Ancient Pasts* (Cambridge: Belknap Press of Harvard University Press, 2011), 371–73.

24. Edwin Wolf, "The Authorship of the 1774 Address to the King Restudied," *The William and Mary Quarterly* 22, no. 2 (1965), 211; Benjamin Franklin to Charles Thomson, February 5, 1775, in *Papers of Franklin*, 21:476.

25. "Concord Hymn" in *The Complete Works of Ralph Waldo Emerson*, ed. Edward Waldo Emerson (12 vols., New York: Houghton Mifflin, 1903–4), 9:158.

26. Ethan Allan, *A Narrative of Col. Ethan Allen's Captivity, from the Time of His Being Taken by the British, near Montreal, on the 25th day of September, in the Year 1775, to the Time of his Exchange, on the 6th Day of May, 1778* (3rd ed., Burlington, VT: H. Johnson & Co., [1779] 1838), 17; Thomas, *Tea Party to Independence*, 113–16; P. J. Marshall, *The Making and Unmaking of Empires: Britain, India, and America c. 1750–1783* (Oxford: Oxford University Press, 2005), 196, 342.

27. Clinton quoted in O'Shaughnessy, *Men Who Lost America*, 86; George Edward Ellis, ed., *Sketches of Bunker Hill, Battle and Monument: With Illustrative Documents* (3rd ed., Charlestown, MA: N.p., 1843), 116.

28. "Thoughts on Defensive War," *The Pennsylvania Magazine, or, American Monthly Museum, Volume I* (Philadelphia, PA: R. Aitken, 1775), 313.

29. Felix Gilbert, *To the Farewell Address: Ideas of Early American Foreign Policy*

(Princeton: Princeton University Press, [1961] 1970), 43; Thomas Paine, "Common Sense," in *The Writings of Thomas Paine: Volume I, 1774–1779*, ed. Moncure Daniel Conway (New York: AMS Press, 1967), 92.

30. Paine, "Common Sense," 102, 92, 95, 88.

31. Thomas Paine, "The American Crisis," in *Writings of Thomas Paine*, 170.

32. *Journals of the Continental Congress, 1774–1789*, ed. Worthington Chauncey Ford et al. (34 vols., Washington, DC: Government Printing Office, 1904–37), 5:507.

33. *Journals of the Continental Congress*, 3:392; John Marshall, *The Life of George Washington*, ed. Robert Faulkner and Paul Carrese (Indianapolis: Liberty Fund, [1838] 2000), 48.

Chapter 2

1. [John Dickinson], *A Declaration by the Representatives of the United Colonies of North-America, Now Met in General Congress at Philadelphia, Setting Forth the Causes and Necessity of Their Taking Up Arms* (Philadelphia, 1775).

2. Howe's secretary, Ambrose Serle, quoted in Joseph J. Ellis, *Revolutionary Summer: The Birth of American Independence* (New York: Alfred A. Knopf, 2013), 133; Paine, "The American Crisis," in *Writings of Thomas Paine*, 170.

3. John Adams to John Winthrop, June 23, 1776 in *Papers of John Adams*, 4:331–33.

4. Jonathan R. Dull, *The French Navy and the Seven Years' War* (Lincoln: University of Nebraska Press, 2005), 236.

5. Choiseul quoted in Robert Tombs and Isabelle Tombs, *That Sweet Enemy: The British and the French from the Sun King to the Present* (London: Pimlico, 2007), 154.

6. For d'Eon, see Simon Burrows, *Blackmail, Scandal, and Revolution: London's French Libellistes, 1758–92* (Manchester: Manchester University Press, 2006), 41–43; for Beaumarchais, see Frank W. Brecher, *Securing American Independence: John Jay and the French Alliance* (Westport, CT: Praeger, 2003), 63.

7. Beaumarchais quoted in Bradford Perkins, *The Cambridge History of American Foreign Relations, Volume I: The Creation of a Republican Empire, 1776–1865* (Cambridge: Cambridge University Press, 1995), 27–28.

8. *The Last Journals of Horace Walpole during the Reign of George III from 1771–1783*, ed. A. Francis Steuart (2 vols., London: John Lane, 1910), 2:42.

9. "Extracts from the Congress Accounts of the Northern Expeditions," *The Gentleman's Magazine and Historical Chronicle*, 48 (February 1778), 67.

10. Stark's words remain popular. They were quoted by Senator Bob Smith in a March 2000 debate on a constitutional amendment respecting flag desecration: *Congressional Record*, 146:3:3609; Burgoyne quoted in O'Shaughnessy, *Men Who Lost America*, 154.

11. O'Shaughnessy, *Men Who Lost America*, 123.

12. George Washington to Horatio Gates, March 6, 1779, in Glenn F. Williams, *Year of the Hangman: George Washington's Campaign against the Iroquois* (Yardley, PA: Garsington, 2005), 200, 194; George Washington to Lafayette, July 4, 1779, in *The Papers of George Washington*, Revolutionary War Series, ed. Philander D. Chase et al.

(22 vols., Charlottesville: University of Virginia Press, 1985–2013), 21:349–51; Max M. Mintz, *Seeds of Empire: The American Revolutionary Conquest of the Iroquois* (New York: New York University Press, 1999), 98, 196.

13. Cabinet of Versailles to Otto, August 30, 1787, in George Bancroft, *History of the Formation of the Constitution of the Constitution of the United States* (2 vols., New York: D. Appleton, 1882), 2:438.

14. [Comte de Vergennes], "Paper Submitted to the King and marked '*approuvé*' in Answer to the Decision of the Spanish Court of the 23rd December, 1777," January 7, 1778, in *B.F. Stevens's Facsimiles of Manuscripts in European Archives Relating to America, 1773-1783, with Descriptions, Editorial Notes, Collations, References, and Translations* (25 vols., London: N.p., 1889–95), 21:1824.

15. For the British in Philadelphia, see O'Shaughnessy, *Men Who Lost America*, 110; Jared Sparks, *The Life of Gouverneur Morris, with Selections from His Correspondence and Miscellaneous Papers; Detailing Events in the American Revolution, the French Revolution, and in the Political History of the United States* (3 vols., Boston: Gray & Bowen, 1832), 1:154; Livingston and McKean quoted in William C. Stinchcombe, *The American Revolution and the French Alliance* (Syracuse, NY: Syracuse University Press, 1969), 15; John Murray, *Nehemiah, or The Struggle for Liberty Never in Vain, When Managed with Virtue and Perseverance. A Discourse Delivered at the Presbyterian Church in Newbury-Port, Nov. 4th, 1779* (Newbury, MA: John Mycall, 1779), 50.

16. Lord Carlisle to Lady Carlisle, New York, July 21, 1778, quoted in Frank Paul Mann, "The British Occupation of Southern New York during the American Revolution and the Failure to Restore Civilian Government," PhD diss., Syracuse University (2013), 222.

17. George Washington to Samuel Washington, August 31, 1780, *Founders Online*, http://founders.archives.gov/documents/Washington/99-01-02-03134, accessed October 28, 2016.

18. For Kościuszko, see Reneé Critcher Lyons, *Foreign-Born American Patriots: Sixteen Volunteer Leaders in the Revolutionary War* (Jefferson, NC: McFarland and Company, 2014), 114–15; for Kovats, see Lyons, *Foreign-Born American Patriots*, 133–40; for von Steuben, see Paul Lockhart, *The Drillmaster of Valley Forge: The Baron de Steuben and the Making of the American Army* (New York: Smithsonian Books, 2008); for Swedish participation in the Revolutionary War, see H. A. Barton, "Sweden and the War of American Independence," *William and Mary Quarterly* 23, no. 3 (1966): 408–30.

19. Brecher, *Securing American Independence*, 51.

20. Andrew Jackson O'Shaughnessy, *An Empire Divided: The American Revolution and the British Caribbean* (Philadelphia: University of Pennsylvania Press, 2000), 189, and O'Shaughnessy, *Men Who Lost America*, 185.

21. Phillip Callbeck to Molyneux Shuldham, January 10, 1776, in *Naval Documents of the American Revolution*, ed. William Bell Clark et al. (11 vols., Washington, DC: U.S. Government Printing Office, 1964–2005), 3:710; Rodney quoted in O'Shaughnessy, *Men Who Lost America*, 299.

22. For a general overview of the role of the Dutch in the Revolutionary War, to which this section owes much, see Jan Willem Schulte Nordholt, *The Dutch Republic and American Independence*, trans. Herbert H. Rowen (Chapel Hill: University of North Carolina Press, 1982).

23. Joseph Plumb Martin, *A Narrative of Some of the Adventures, Dangers, and Sufferings of a Revolutionary Soldier; interspersed with Anecdotes of Incidents that Occurred within his own Observation* (Hallowell, Maine: Glazier, Masters & Co., 1830), 174.

24. North and Germain in *The Historical and Posthumous Memoirs of Sir Nathaniel William Wraxall, 1772-1784*, ed. Henry B. Wheatley (5 vols., London: Bickers & Son, 1884), 2:138–39; House of Commons, February 28, 1782, *Parliamentary History of England*, 22:1089.

25. John Adams to Benjamin Franklin, April 16, 1781, *Papers of John Adams*, 11:261. For a magisterial account of how diplomatic isolation from Europe eventually led to British defeat, see Brendan Simms, *Three Victories and a Defeat: The Rise and Fall of the First British Empire, 1714–1783* (London: Allen Lane, 2007).

Chapter 3

1. Benjamin Franklin to Josiah Quincy Sr., September 11, 1783, *Papers of Franklin*, 40:611–13.

2. "A Letter from Phocion to the Considerate Citizens of New York [January 1–27 1784]," *The Papers of Alexander Hamilton*, ed. Harold C. Syrett (27 vols., New York: Columbia University Press, 1961–87), 3:483–97.

3. Vergennes to Franklin, December 1782, translated in *Letters from France: The Private Diplomatic Correspondence of Benjamin Franklin, 1776–1785*, ed. Brett F. Woods (New York: Algora, 2007), 180; Samuel Flagg Bemis, *The Diplomacy of the American Revolution* (Bloomington: Indiana University Press, [1935] 1957), 86.

4. George Washington to Benjamin Franklin, October 18, 1782, *Founders Online*, http://founders.archives.gov/documents/Washington/99-01-02-09754, accessed October 20, 2016; September 14, 1782, *Diary and Autobiography of John Adams*, 3:5–10.

5. For the most extensive firsthand account of the Siege of Gibraltar, see John Drinkwater, *A History of the Siege of Gibraltar, 1779-1783. With a Description and Account of That Garrison from the Earliest Periods* (London: John Murray, [1785] 1861); Edward S. Corwin, *French Policy and the American Alliance of 1778* (Hamden, CT: Archon Books, [1916] 1962), 356.

6. *John Jay: The Winning of the Peace: Unpublished Papers, 1780-1784*, ed. Richard B. Morris (2 vols., New York: Harper and Row, 1980), 2:134; "Report on Cornwallis-Laurens Exchange," September 25, 1782, *Papers of James Madison*, Congressional Series, 5:163–65.

7. John Adams, June 23, 1779, *Diary and Autobiography*, 2:379–96; Benjamin Franklin, "An Account of the New Invented Pennsylvanian Fire-Places," November 15, 1744, *Papers of Franklin*, 2:419–46.

8. Vergennes quoted in Stacy Schiff, *Benjamin Franklin and the Birth of America: Franklin's French Adventure, 1776–85* (London: Bloomsbury, 2006), 287; John Adams, May 10, 1779, *Diary and Autobiography*, 2:366–67; Thomas Jefferson to Robert Walsh, December 4, 1818, *Memoirs, Correspondence, and Private Papers of Thomas Jefferson, Late President of the United States*, ed. Thomas Jefferson Randolph (London: Henry Colburn and Richard Bentley, 1829), 3:319.

9. Benjamin Franklin to Juliana Ritchie, January 19, 1777, *Papers of Franklin*,

23:211–12; John Adams to Benjamin Franklin, September 13, 1783, *Papers of Franklin*, 40:626–28.

10. This and all subsequent quotations from the Treaty are taken from The Definitive Treaty of Peace, Paris, 3 September 1783, https://www.ourdocuments. gov/doc.php?doc=6&page=transcript, accessed October 20, 2016.

11. William Heath, *William Wells and the Struggle for the Old Northwest* (Norman: University of Oklahoma Press, 2015), p. 64.

12. John Adams, November 29, 1782, *Diary and Autobiography*, 3:40–85; John Adams to Elbridge Gerry, December 14, 1782, *Papers of John Adams*, 14:124–25.

13. Vergennes to Rayneval, December 4, 1782, in *The Revolutionary Diplomatic Correspondence of the United States*, ed. Francis Wharton (6 vols., Washington, D.C.: U.S. Government Printing Office, 1889), 6:107; Rayneval quoted in James Cable, *The Political Influence of Naval Force in History* (Basingstoke: Macmillan, 1998), 51; Henry Strachey to Evan Nepean, November 29, 1782, in *The Emerging Nation: A Documentary History of the Foreign Relations of the United States under the Articles of Confederation, 1780-1789*, ed. Mary A. Giunta (3 vols., Washington, DC: National Historical Publications and Records Commission, 1996), 1:690; *The Journal and Correspondence of William Lord Auckland*, ed. G. Hogge (2 vols., London: Bentley, 1861–62), 1:40; Richard B. Morris, *The Peacemakers: The Great Powers and American Independence* (New York: Harper and Row, 1965); David McCullough, *John Adams* (New York: Simon and Schuster, 2001), 285.

14. Bemis, *Diplomacy of the American Revolution*, 256; Thomas Jefferson to John Jay, April 23, 1786, *The Papers of Thomas Jefferson*, Original Series, ed. Julian P. Boyd et al. (41 vols., Princeton: Princeton University Press, 1950–2014), 9:402–3.

15. For a full treatment of Northeast border diplomacy through the Webster-Ashburton Treaty of 1842, which fixed the paper definition of the border to the present day, see Francis Carroll, *A Good and Wise Measure: The Search for the Canadian-American Boundary, 1783–1842* (Toronto: University of Toronto Press, 2001).

16. "Jay's Account of Conferences with Gardoqui and Del Camp," September 3–15, 1780, *The Correspondence and Public Papers of John Jay*, ed. Henry P. Johnston (4 vols., New York: G.P. Putnam, 1890), 1:395; *Knoxville Gazette*, October 6–10, 1792, quoted in *Papers of Hamilton*, 13:27–29 n2.

17. Henry Laurens to Edward Bridgen, August 10, 1782, *The Papers of Henry Laurens*, ed. David R. Chesnutt et al. (16 vols., Columbia: University of South Carolina Press, 1968–2002), 15:555; "An Act for Granting a More Effectual Relief in Cases of Certain Trespasses," March 17, 1783, *Laws of the State of New-York, Comprising the Constitution and the Acts of the Legislature, since the Revolution, from the First to the Fifteenth Session, Inclusive* (2 vols., New York: Thomas Greenleaf, 1792), 1:62.

18. Rev. Andrew Kippis, *Considerations on the Provisional Treaty with America, and the Preliminary Articles of Peace with France and Spain* (London: T. Cadell, 1783), 53.

Chapter 4

1. Alexander Hamilton, *Federalist*, 23, "The necessity of a government at least equally energetic with the one proposed," in Alexander Hamilton, James Madison,

and John Jay, *The Federalist Papers*, ed. Lawrence Goldman (Oxford: Oxford University Press, [1787–88] 2008), 114.

2. George Washington to George Clinton, September 11, 1783, *Founders Online*, National Archives, http://founders.archives.gov/documents/Washington/99-01-02-11810, accessed October 21, 2016.

3. Charles Cotesworth Pinckney, "Observations on the Plan of Government Submitted to the Federal Convention, in Philadelphia, on the 28th of May, 1787," in *The Records of the Federal Convention of 1787*, ed. Max Farrand (3 vols., New Haven: Yale University Press, 1911), 3:106–7.

4. Jay quoted in Norman A. Graebner, Richard Dean Burns, and Joseph M. Siracusa, *Foreign Affairs and the Founding Fathers: from Confederation to Constitution, 1776–1787* (New York: Praeger, 2011), 16.

5. John Baker Holroyd, Earl of Sheffield, *Observations on the Commerce of the American States* (6th ed., London: J. Debrett, 1784), 246; John Adams to John Jay, February 14, 1788, *Founders Online*, http://founders.archives.gov/documents/Adams/99-02-02-0344, accessed October 21, 2016.

6. "Jefferson's Reply to the Representations of Affairs in America by British Newspapers," published in the *Leiden Gazette*, November 1784, quoted in Gould, *Among the Powers of the Earth*, 125–26; Hamilton, *Federalist Papers*, 15:74.

7. Hamilton, *Federalist Papers*, 15:73; James Madison, "Reply to the New Jersey Plan," June 19, 1787, in *The Papers of Madison*, Congressional Series, 10:55–63; "Mr. Charles Cotesworth Pinckney's Speech, in Answer to Mr. Jay, Secretary for Foreign Affairs, on the Question of a Treaty with Spain, delivered in Congress, August 16, 1786," in *Journals of the Continental Congress*, 31:947; George Washington, "Undelivered First Inaugural Address: Fragments, April 30, 1789," in *The Papers of George Washington*, Presidential Series, ed. Dorothy Twohig et al. (17 vols., Charlottesville: University of Virginia Press, 1987–2013), 2:158–73.

8. Hamilton, *Federalist*, 15:74; John Jay, "An Address to the People of the State of New-York on the Subject of the Constitution, Agreed upon at Philadelphia, the 17th of September, 1787," in *Correspondence and Public Papers of John Jay*, 3:300; John Adams to Thomas Jefferson, September 4, 1785, *Papers of John Adams*, 17:390–91; John Adams to John Jay, August 10, 1785, *Papers of John Adams*, 17:321–23; John Adams to John Jay, February 14, 1788, *Founders Online*, http://founders.archives.gov/documents/Adams/99-02-02-0344, accessed October 21, 2016.

9. Mark David Hall, *Roger Sherman and the Creation of the American Republic* (Oxford: Oxford University Press, 2013), 2; *Records of the Federal Convention*, 1:347; Hamilton, *Federalist*, 15:74; Hamilton, *Federalist*, 12:64.

10. Jay, "Address to the People of the State of New York"; on the pirate threat and its jihadi pretext see the conversation of Adams and Jefferson with the envoy of Tunis in American Commissioners to John Jay, March 28, 1786, *Founders Online*, https://founders.archives.gov/documents/Adams/06-18-02-0115, accessed July 1, 2019; discussed below p. 142.

11. John Adams to John Jay, June 10, 1785, *Papers of John Adams*, 17:175–78.

12. Hamilton, *Federalist*, 15:73.

13. George Washington to George Plater, October 25, 1784, *The Papers of George Washington*, Confederation Series, ed. W. W. Abbot (6 vols., Charlottesville: University of Virginia Press, 1992–97), 2:106–10.

14. Walter Stahr, *John Jay: Founding Father* (London: Bloomsbury, 2005), 213; Richard Henry Lee to George Washington, July 15, 1787, *Papers of Washington*, Confederation Series, 5:258–60; James Monroe to Patrick Henry, August 12, 1786, *Letters of Members of the Continental Congress*, ed. Edmund Cody Burnett (8 vols., Washington, DC: Carnegie Institute of Washington, 1921–36), 8:422; "Mr. Charles Pinckney's Speech," in *Journals of the Continental Congress*, 943.

15. George Washington to Henry Lee Jr., July 26, 1786, *Papers of Washington*, Confederation, 4:170–71.

16. Jay, "Address to New York," 300; Hamilton, *Federalist*, 15:73; John Dickerson Sergeant quoted in Robert L. Brunhouse, *The Counter-Revolution in Pennsylvania, 1776–1790* (Harrisburg: Pennsylvania Historical Commission, 1942), 175; Randolph, *Records of the Federal Convention*, 1:26; James Madison, "Vices of the Political System of the United States," April 1787, *Papers of Madison*, Congressional Series, 9:345–58.

17. Hamilton, "Letter from Phocion to the Considerate Citizens of New York," January 1–27, 1784, *Papers of Hamilton*, 3:483–97; Edmund Randolph, "Letter on the Federal Constitution, October 16, 1787," in *Pamphlets on the Constitution of the United States, Published during Its Discussion by the People, 1787–1788*, ed. Paul Leicester Ford (New York: N.p., 1888), 261; Jay, "Address to New York," 299; John Jay to Thomas Jefferson, July 14, 1786, *Papers of Jefferson*, Original Series, 10:134–36; *Records of the Federal Convention*, 1:467.

18. "Letters from the Federal Farmer. I. October 8, 1787," in *The Complete Anti-Federalist*, ed. Herbert J. Storing (7 vols., Chicago: University of Chicago Press, 1981), 1:225; Melancton Smith in *The Debates in the Several State Conventions, on the Adoption of the Federal Constitution, as Recommended by the General Convention at Philadelphia, in 1787*, ed. Jonathan Elliot (4 vols., Washington, DC: N.p., 1836–45), 2:223; William Grayson to James Monroe, March 22, 1786, in *The Writings of James Madison, Comprising his Public Papers and His Private Correspondence, Including Numerous Letters and Documents Now for the First Time Printed*, ed. Gaillard Hunt (9 vols., New York: Putnam, 1901–10), 2:403–404n; Mason, *Complete Anti-Federalist*, 1:257.

19. "Candidus" [Benjamin Austin], originally published in *Independent Chronicle*, Boston, December 20, 1787, in *Birth of the Bill of Rights: Encyclopedia of the Anti-Federalists*, ed. Jon L. Wakelyn (2 vols., Westport, CT: Greenwood Press, 2004), 2:108; "A Columbian Patriot" [Mercy Otis Warren, wrongly attributed to Elbridge Gerry], "Observations on the New Constitution, and on the Federal and State Conventions," in *Pamphlets on the Constitution*, 19; *Secret Proceedings and Debates of the Convention Assembled at Philadelphia, in the Year 1787*, ed. Luther Martin (Louisville, KY: Alston Mygatt, 1844), 215.

20. Pierce Butler to Weedon Butler, October 8, 1787, *Records of the Federal Convention*, 3:103.

21. Madison, *Federalist*, 14:67–68, 45:232.

22. Hamilton, *Federalist*, 70:344; Madison, *Federalist*, 40:193; "Medium," *Hampshire Chronicle*, December 25, 1787.

23. *Debates in the State Conventions*, 4:149–50; 3:160.

24. However, the term "Anti-Federalist" made its first appearance in 1786 in the dispute over a congressional impost; Hulsebosch, *Constituting Empire*, 191, 372n81.

25. On the roots of Shays' Rebellion, namely fiscal mismanagement and excessive zeal for rapid repayment by *opponents* of a permanent debt, see Edwin J. Perkins, "Massachusetts and Shays' Rebellion," in *American Public Finance and Financial Services* (Columbus: Ohio State University Press, 1994), 173–86.

26. Madison, *Federalist*, 45:228; James Madison to Edmund Pendleton, February 24, 1787, *Papers of Madison*, Congressional Series, 9:294–96; John Hector St. John to William Short, June 10, 1788, *The Documentary History of the Ratification of the Constitution*, ed. Merrill Jensen (27 vols., Madison: State Historical Society of Wisconsin, 1976–), 18:174.

27. *Debates in the Several State Conventions*, 5:258; Hamilton, *Federalist*, 59:295; William Smith to John Jay, September 4, 1786, in *The Diplomatic Correspondence of the United States of America, from the Signing of the Definitive Treaty of Peace, September 10, 1783, to the Adoption of the Constitution, March 4, 1789* (7 vols., Washington, DC: Blair & Rives, 1837), 5:431–2; Jay, *Federalist*, 5:28; Madison, *Federalist*, 41:202.

28. Hamilton, *Federalist*, 8:43; William Pierce to George Turner, May 19, 1787, *Supplement to the Records of the Federal Convention of 1787*, ed. James H. Huston (New Haven: Yale University Press, 1987), 10; Madison, *Federalist*, 85:429; Madison, *Federalist*, 44:228; James Madison to George Nicholas, April 8, 1788, *Papers of Madison*, Congressional Series, 11:11–15; Hamilton, *Federalist*, 84:417.

29. "Candidus," December 20, 1787, in *Complete Anti-Federalist*, 4:130–37; "Federal Farmer," in *Complete Anti-Federalist*, 1:229; "Federal Farmer" quoted in *Empire and Nation*, ed. Forrest McDonald (Indianapolis: Liberty Fund, 1962), 96, 109.

30. "Federal Farmer," *Empire and Nation*, 91; Henry, *Debates in the State Conventions*, 3:139; [Melancton Smith], "An Address to the People of the State of New-York, Showing the Necessity of Making Amendments to the Constitution, proposed for the United States, previous to its Adoption, by a Plebeian," *Pamphlets on the Constitution*, 94; "Centinel," "The Hobgoblins of Anarchy and Dissension Among the States," *Independent Gazetteer*, January 16, 1788.

Chapter 5

1. Marquis de Condorcet, *Outlines of an Historical View of the Progress of the Human Mind: Being a Posthumous Work of the Late M. de Condorcet. Translated from the French* (London: J. Johnson, 1795), 266–67.

2. Hamilton, *Federalist*, 85:432.

3. The classic single-volume account of the French Revolution, to which the present work owes much, remains Simon Schama, *Citizens: A Chronicle of the French Revolution* (New York: Vintage Books, 1989).

4. Tennis Court Oath quoted in Schama, *Citizens*, 359.

5. Louis XVI quoted in Schama, *Citizens*, 362; Mirabeau quoted in Schama, *Citizens*, 363; Desmoulins quoted in Schama, *Citizens*, 382.

6. Launay quoted in Schama, *Citizens*, 404–5.

7. Declaration of the Rights of Man and the Citizen, August 26, 1789, preamble.

8. Marquis de Lafayette to George Washington, March 17, 1790, in *The Papers of George Washington*, Presidential Series, ed. Dorothy Twohig et al. (17 vols.,

Charlottesville: University of Virginia Press, 1987–2013), 5:243; Thomas Paine to Washington, May 1, 1790, *Papers of Washington*, Presidential Series, 5:369.

9. Thomas Jefferson to William Short, August 10, 1790, in *Papers of Jefferson*, Original Series, 17:121–25. In that letter Jefferson does not mention French Indian diplomacy in the North-East, in which Moustier acted. In October 1784, the secretary of the French legation, François de Barbé-Marbois, accompanied the Marquis de Lafayette to the Federal Indian council at Fort Stanwix. Lafayette addressed the council at the behest of the Oneidas, whom Barbé-Marbois had previously visited, and in private meeting told the Indians that the king of France would soon resume Indian diplomacy. Moustier himself also appeared at the Fort Schuyler council of September 1788; Alan Taylor, *The Divided Ground: Indians, Settlers, and the Northern Borderland of the American Revolution* (New York: Random House, 2006), 205–6, 216.

10. For the size of the early United States army, see James R. Jacobs, *The Beginnings of the U.S. Army, 1783–1812* (Princeton: Princeton University Press, 1947), 50.

11. Talleyrand quoted in David O. Stewart, *The Summer of 1787: The Men Who Invented the Constitution* (New York: Simon and Schuster, 2007), 94.

12. The most detailed academic study of the Whiskey Rebellion remains Thomas P. Slaughter, *The Whiskey Rebellion: Frontier Epilogue to the American Revolution* (Oxford: Oxford University Press, 1986).

13. Lyndon B. Johnson, "Commencement Address in New London at the United States Coast Guard Academy," June 3, 1964, in *Public Papers of the Presidents of the United States: Lyndon B. Johnson. Volume 1, 1963–64: November 22, 1963 to June 30, 1964* (Washington, DC: United States Government Printing Office, 1965), 741. Johnson was in fact referring to the foundation of the Coast Guard, not to the Whiskey Rebellion, but the operative sentiment is the same.

14. Thomas Jefferson to Edward Carrington, March 31, 1781, in *Papers of Jefferson*, Original Series, 11:48–50.

15. "George Washington to the United States Senate and House of Representatives," December 3, 1793, in Papers of Washington, Presidential Series, 14:462–69; "To George Washington from the United States House of Representatives," November 10, 1792, in Papers of Washington, Presidential Series, 11:366–68. For further on the imperial and nationalizing role of the post office and postal subsidies for newspapers see Michael S. Kochin, "Empire and Communications: Washington's Farewell Address," *American Political Thought* 8 (Summer 2019): 347–64.

16. Louis XVI quoted in Schama, *Citizens*, 669.

17. Thomas Jefferson to William Short, January 3, 1793, in *Papers of Jefferson*, Original Series, 25:14–17; [Alexander Hamilton], "Americanus No. II," [February 7, 1794], in *Papers of Hamilton*, 16:2–19.

18. Marshall, *Life of Washington*, 5:401; Washington to the Cabinet, April 18, 1793, *Papers of Washington*, Presidential Series, 12:452–54; Washington to Hamilton, May 5, 1793, *Papers of Washington*, Presidential Series, 12:515–16; "To George Washington from A CITIZEN," July 4, 1793, in *Papers of Washington*, Presidential Series, 13:175–78; Marshall, *Life of Washington*, 5:401.

19. Marshall, *Life of Washington*, 5:402; Proclamation of Neutrality, April 22,

1793; [Alexander Hamilton], "Pacificus No. VI," July 17, 1793, in *Hamilton Papers*, 15:100–106.

20. Marshall, *Life of Washington*, 5:410.

21. Notes of Cabinet Meeting and Conversation with Edmond Charles Genet, July 5, 1793, in *Papers of Jefferson*, Original Series, 26:437–39. Jefferson's game is best understood as a corollary of a remark by the historian Peggy Liss that "in the arena of power politics, as the situation warranted, national leaders employed one or another of those men adjudged most disaffected, powerful, and if neglected potentially dangerous to national interests": Peggy K. Liss, *Atlantic Empires: The Network of Trade and Revolution* (Baltimore: Johns Hopkins University Press, 1983), 119.

22. *Vermont Gazette*, March 15, 1793.

23. Matthew Schoenbachler, "Republicanism in the Age of Democratic Revolution: The Democratic-Republican Societies of the 1790s," *Journal of the Early Republic*, no. 18, no. 2 (1998): 245; Washington to Burgess Ball, September 25, 1794, in *Papers of Washington*, Presidential Series, 16:722–24; Washington, Sixth Annual Message, November 19, 1794, *American Presidency Project*, http://www.presidency.ucsb.edu/ws/index.php?pid=29436.

24. Jefferson to James Madison, August 3, 1793, *Papers of Jefferson*, 26:606–7.

25. Proclamation on Expeditions against Spanish Territory, March 24, 1794, in *Papers of Washington*, Presidential Series, 15:446–47; the Neutrality Act of 1794 effectively remains in force as 18 U.S. Code § 960—Expedition against friendly nation.

Chapter 6

1. "Camillus" [Alexander Hamilton], "The Defence No. II," July 25, 1795, in *Papers of Hamilton*, 18:493–501.

2. Montagu, House of Commons, February 21, 1787, in *Parliamentary History of England*, 26:494.

3. The Earl of Carlisle, House of Lords, February 17, 1783, *Parliamentary History of England*, 23:377.

4. Brigadier General Allan Maclean to Arent S. de Peyster, July 8, 1783, quoted in Jerald A. Combs, *The Jay Treaty: Political Battleground of the Founding Fathers* (Berkeley: University of California Press, 1970), 11.

5. The details of Brant's biography are taken from Isabel Thompson Kelsay, *Joseph Brant, 1743–1807: Man of Two Worlds* (Syracuse, NY: Syracuse University Press, 1984), 75, 77, 38.

6. Kelsay, *Brant*, 579.

7. Benjamin Franklin to Thomas Pownall, August 19, 1756, in *Papers of Franklin*, 6:486–88; Brant's last words quoted in Kelsay, *Brant*, 652. On the aspirations of Federalist Indian policies, see the useful summary in Taylor, *Divided Ground*, 234–40.

8. Gouverneur Morris to George Washington, May 29, 1790, in *Papers of Washington*, Presidential Series, 5:430–39; *The Correspondence of Lieut.-Governor John Graves Simcoe, with Allied Documents Relating to His Administration of the Government*

of Upper Canada, ed. E. A. Cruikshank (5 vols., Toronto: Ontario Historical Society, 1923–31), 1:200.

9. Lord Dorchester to the Seven Nations of Lower Canada, February 18, 1794, in *Correspondence of Simcoe*, 2:49–150; Combs, *Jay Treaty*, 121.

10. Washington to Henry Knox, November 19, 1790, in *Papers of Washington*, Presidential Series, 6:668–70.

11. Robert Woolsey to John Edwards, 2 November 1793, in *Correspondence of Simcoe*, 2:96; quoted in Taylor, *Divided Ground*, 279.

12. Henry Knox to Anthony Wayne, March 31, 1794; Knox to Wayne, June 7, 1794, in *Anthony Wayne: A Name in Arms*, ed. Richard C. Knopf (Pittsburgh: University of Pittsburgh Press, 1960), 319, 336–38; Taylor, *Divided Ground*, 284–85.

13. William Clark, "William Clark's Journal of General Wayne's Campaign," ed. R. C. McGrane, *Mississippi Valley Historical Review* 1, no. 3 (1914): 418–44, 430; Heath, *William Wells*, 214.

14. Anthony Wayne to William Campbell, August 22, 1794, and William Campbell to Anthony Wayne, August 22, 1794, quoted in Samuel Jones Burr, *The Life and Times of William Henry Harrison* (8th ed., New York: L.W. Ransom, 1840), 269–70.

15. John Quincy Adams, November 24, 1795, in *Memoirs of John Quincy Adams: Comprising Portions of His Diary from 1795 to 1848*, ed. Charles Francis Adams (12 vols., Philadelphia: J.B. Lippincott, 1874–77), 1:137–38.

16. Jay's words have been widely quoted in secondary sources since the 1950s, beginning with Bradford Perkins, *The First Rapprochement* (1955), but we have not found a primary source that confirms that Jay in fact said this. The words ascribed to Jay bear a suspicious resemblance to those spoken by Stephen Douglas at Springfield on July 17, 1858, during his campaign against Lincoln for the Senate: "I will not recur to the scenes which took place all over the country in 1854 when that Nebraska bill passed. I could then travel from Boston to Chicago by the light of my own effigies." In a document supposedly written in 1870, James Buchanan is quoted as having said to a friend during the 1860 secession crisis that "If I withdraw Anderson from Sumter, I can travel home to Wheatlands by the light of my own burning effigies"; Gaillard Hunt, "Narrative and letter of William Henry Trescot concerning the negotiations between South Carolina and President Buchanan in December, 1860," *American Historical Review* 13, no. 3 (April 1908), 552.

17. "Camillus" [Alexander Hamilton and Rufus King], "The Defence No. 1," July 22, 1795, in *Papers of Hamilton*, 18:479–89.

18. Jefferson to Philip Mazzei, April 24, 1796, in *Papers of Jefferson*, Original Series, 29:81–83.

19. Translation of Mr. Fauchet's Political Dispatch, No. 10, October 31, 1794, in *A Vindication of Mr. Randolph's Resignation* (Philadelphia: Samuel H. Smith, 1795), 45, 46; John Quincy Adams to Abigail Adams, March 20, 1796, in *The Adams Papers*, Family Correspondence, ed. L. H. Butterfield et al. (11 vols., Cambridge: Harvard University Press, 1963–), 11:222–24.

20. Fisher Ames, "On the Treaty with Great Britain," in *Works of Fisher Ames*, ed. and enlarged by William B. Allen, 2 vols. (Indianapolis: Liberty Fund, 1983), 2:1174, 1176.

21. "Camillus," "The Defence No. 1."

22. Andro Linklater, *An Artist in Treason: The Extraordinary Double Life of General James Wilkinson* (New York: Walker, 2009); Theodore Roosevelt, *The Winning of the West, Volume Three: The Founding of the Trans-Alleghany Commonwealths* (Lincoln: University of Nebraska Press, [1894] 1995), 124.

23. The full text of the Farewell Address may be found here: https://www.our-documents.gov/doc.php?doc=15&page=transcript, accessed October 23, 2016.

Chapter 7

1. John Marshall to George Washington, October 24–27, 1797, in *The Papers of George Washington*, Retirement Series, ed. W. W. Abbot (4 vols., Charlottesville: University of Virginia Press, 1998–99), 1:424–27.

2. Corday quoted in Schama, *Citizens*, 739; Gouverneur Morris to Washington, October 18, 1793, in *Papers of Washington*, Presidential Series, 14:229–31.

3. James Franklin, *The Present State of Hayti (Saint Domingo) with Remarks on Its Agriculture, Commerce, Laws, Religion, Finances, and Population, etc., etc.* (London: John Murray, 1828), 271.

4. "Britannicus," *A Reply to Article VII of the Edinburgh Review for October 1823, on T. Clarkson's Treatise on the Improvement and Emancipation of Slaves in the British Colonies* (London: James Ridgway, 1824), 17.

5. *Aurora General Advertiser* quoted in Alfred N. Hunt, *Haiti's Influence on Antebellum America: Slumbering Volcano in the Caribbean* (Baton Rouge: Louisiana State University Press, 1988), 20–21; Chalmers to Pitt, quoted in C. L. R. James, *The Black Jacobins: Toussaint L'Ouverture and the San Domingo Revolution* (2nd ed., New York: Vintage Books, 1963), 132.

6. Marcus Rainsford, *An Historical Account of the Black Empire of Hayti*, ed. Paul Youngquist and Gregory Pierrot (Durham, NC: Duke University Press, [1805] 2013), xix.

7. On the vicissitudes of trade between the United States and revolutionary Saint-Domingue, see Ashli White, *Encountering Revolution: Haiti and the Making of the Early Republic* (Baltimore: Johns Hopkins University Press, 2010), 154–65.

8. James Monroe to James Madison, February 27, 1796, in *Papers of Madison*, Congressional Series, 16:236–37.

9. Pierre Adet to Timothy Pickering, October 27, 1796, in *A Collection of State Papers, Relative to the War Against France, Now Carrying on by Great Britain and the Several Other European Powers* (11 vols., London: J. Debrett, 1794–1802), 5:256; Pickering to Adet, 3 November, 1796, *Collection of State Papers*, 5:260–61; Victor Hugues, "Decree: The Special Agents of the Executive Directory to the Windward Islands," February 1, 1797, in *Message from the President of the United States, Transmitting Copies of the Several Instructions to the Ministers of the U. States to the Government of France, and of the Correspondence with Said Government, Having Reference to the Spoliations Committed by That Power on the Commerce of the United States, Anterior to September 30, 1800* (Washington, DC: Gales & Seaton, 1826), 383.

10. John Adams to John Quincy Adams, March 31, 1797, *Adams Papers, Family Correspondence*, 12:55–56; John Adams, "Special Session—Message, May 16, 1797," *The Addresses and Messages of the Presidents of the United States, together with the Declaration of Independence and Constitution of the United States* (New York: McLean & Taylor, 1839), 71.

11. Adams, "Special Session," 71.

12. Gouverneur Morris to George Washington, March 17, 1792, in Sparks, *Life of Gouverneur Morris*, 166.

13. Carnot quoted in Philip G. Dwyer, *Talleyrand* (London: Longman, 2002), 79.

14. *State Papers and Publick Documents of the United States from the Accession of George Washington to the Presidency, Exhibiting a Complete View of Our Foreign Relations since That Time*, 3rd ed. (12 vols., Boston: T.B. Wait & Sons, 1819), 3:492, 482.

15. *State Papers and Publick Documents of the United States from the Accession of George Washington to the Presidency, Exhibiting a Complete View of Our Foreign Relations since That Time*, 3rd ed., 3, 204.

16. "Titus Manlius" [Alexander Hamilton], "The Stand No. 1," March 30, 1797, in Papers of Hamilton, 21:381–87; Harper and Knox quoted in Stanley Elkins and Eric McKitrick, *The Age of Federalism: The Early American Republic, 1788–1800* (Oxford: Oxford University Press, 1993), 645–46.

17. John Adams to George Washington, June 22, 1798, in *The Writings of George Washington from the Original Manuscript Sources, 1745–1799*, ed. John C. Fitzpatrick (Westport, CT: Greenwood Press, 1970), 36:312n; John Adams to James McHenry, October 22, 1798, quoted in Elkins and McKitrick, *Age of Federalism*, 606; Harper, *American Machiavelli*, 240; Sharp, *American Politics in the Early Republic*, 214–15; Hamilton to Theodore Sedgwick, February 2, 1799, quoted in Ellis, *Founding Brothers*, 194.

18. Lyon quoted in Juhani Rudanko, *Discourses of Freedom of Speech: From the Enactment of the Bill of Rights to the Sedition Act of 1918* (London: Palgrave Macmillan, 2012), 117; Thomas Jefferson to John Taylor, June 4, 1798, *Papers of Jefferson*, Original Series, 30:387–90.

19. Donald R. Hickey, "The Quasi-War: America's First Limited War, 1798–1801," *The Northern Mariner* 18, nos. 3–4 (2008): 75; Christopher Kingston, "Marine Insurance in Philadelphia during the Quasi-War with France, 1795–1801," *Journal of Economic History* 71, no. 1 (2011): 174.

20. Paul Douglas Newman, *Fries's Rebellion: The Enduring Struggle for the American Revolution* (Philadelphia: University of Pennsylvania Press, 2005), 170.

21. George van Santvoord, *Sketches of the Lives and Judicial Services of the Chief-Justices of the Supreme Court of the United States* (New York: Charles Scribner, 1854), 282; Hamilton to Theodore Sedgwick, December 22, 1800, *Hamilton Papers*, 25:269–71.

22. John Adams to James Lloyd, January 28, 1815, *Founders Online*, http://founders.archives.gov/documents/Adams/99-02-02-6401, accessed October 22, 2016; John Adams to Francois Adriaan van der Kemp, December 28, 1800, *Founders Online*, http://founders.archives.gov/documents/Adams/99-02-02-4729, accessed October 22, 2016.

23. Horace Binney, *An Eulogy on the Life and Character of John Marshall, Chief Justice of the Supreme Court of the United States, Delivered at the Request of the Councils of Philadelphia, on the 24th September, 1835* (Philadelphia: J. Crissy and G. Goodman, 1835), 22–23.

24. *William Marbury v. James Madison, Secretary of State of the United States*, 5 U.S. 137 (1803).

25. *James McCulloch v. The State of Maryland, John James*, 17 U.S. 316 (1819); *The Cherokee Nation v. The State of Georgia*, 30 U.S. 1 (1831).

Chapter 8

1. Alexander Hamilton, "Purchase of Louisiana," July 5, 1803, *Papers of Hamilton*, 26:129–36.

2. Thomas Jefferson to Spencer Roane, September 6, 1819, *Founders Online*, http://founders.archives.gov/documents/Jefferson/98-01-02-0734, accessed October 22, 2016; Thomas Jefferson, "First Inaugural Address, March 4, 1801," *Papers of Jefferson*, 33:148–52.

3. Henry Adams, *The History of the United States of America during the Administrations of Thomas Jefferson and James Madison* (9 vols., Cambridge: Cambridge University Press, [1889–91] 2011), 1:340, 357.

4. *The Memoir of General Toussaint Louverture*, trans. and ed. Philippe R. Girard (Oxford: Oxford University Press, 2014), 155.

5. Saint Domingue Constitution of 1801, Title II, Article 3; Adams, *History*, 1:397–98.

6. Rochambeau quoted in James, *Black Jacobins*, 360; Robert Debs Heinl, Nancy Gordon Heinl, and Michael Heinl, *Written in Blood: The Story of the Haitian People* (2nd ed., Lanham, MD: University Press of America, 1996), 108–9.

7. Thomas Jefferson to John Jay, August 14, 1785, *Papers of Jefferson*, Original Series, 8:372–75; Pierre Adet to Charles-François Delacroix, December 21, 1796, in *Correspondence of the French Ministers to the United States, 1791–1797*, ed. Frederick J. Turner (Washington, DC: Government Printing Office, 1904), 983.

8. Thomas Jefferson to Robert R. Livingston, April 18, 1802, *Papers of Jefferson*, Original Series, 37:263–67.

9. Ibid.

10. Rufus King to James Madison, April 2, 1803, *The Papers of James Madison*, Secretary of State Series, ed. Robert J. Brugger et al. (10 vols., Charlottesville: University of Virginia Press, 1986–), 4:474–76.

11. Livingston and Talleyrand quoted in Bruce Cumings, *Dominion from Sea to Sea: Pacific Ascendancy and American Power* (New Haven: Yale University Press, 2009), 57; for Talleyrand and Malta, see George Dangerfield, *Chancellor Robert R. Livingston of New York, 1746–1813* (New York: Harcourt, Brace, 1960), 261–63.

12. Thomas Jefferson to Joseph Priestly, January 29, 1804, in *Memoirs, Correspondence, and Miscellanies, from the Papers of Thomas Jefferson*, ed. Thomas Jefferson Randolph (Charlottesville, VA: F. Carr, 1829), 4:14; Napoleon quoted in E. Wilson Lyon, *Louisiana in French Diplomacy, 1759–1804* (Norman: University of Oklahoma Press, 1934), 206–7; George Cabot to Rufus King, July 1, 1803, in *Life and Letters of George Cabot*, ed. Henry Cabot Lodge (2nd ed., Boston: Little, Brown, 1878), 331.

13. Abraham Ellery to Alexander Hamilton, October 25, 1803, *Papers of Hamilton*, 26:163–67.

14. Adams, *History*, 2:43–44.

15. Bucker F. Melton Jr., *Aaron Burr: Conspiracy to Treason* (New York: John Wiley and Sons, 2002), 66, 156.

16. American Commissioners to John Jay, March 28, 1786, *Founders Online*, https://founders.archives.gov/documents/Adams/06-18-02-0115, accessed July 1, 2019.

17. *State Papers and Publick Documents (2nd ed.)*, 4:381; *An Abridgement of the Laws of the United States: Or, A Complete Digest of All Such Acts of Congress as Concern the United States at Large*, ed. William Graydon (Harrisburg, PA: John Wyeth, 1803), 327.

18. Nelson quoted in Jeremy Black, *The War of 1812 in the Age of Napoleon* (Norman: University of Oklahoma Press, 2009), 125. On the Derna campaign, see A. B. C. Whipple, *To the Shores of Tripoli: The Birth of the U.S. Navy and Marines* (New York: William Morrow, 1991); Richard Zacks, *The Pirate Coast: Thomas Jefferson, The First Marines, and the Secret Expedition of 1805* (New York: Hyperion, 2005).

Chapter 9

1. Thomas Jefferson to United States Congress, January 17, 1806, *Founders Online*, http://founders.archives.gov/documents/Jefferson/99-01-02-3030, accessed October 22, 2016.

2. Thomas Jefferson to Sir John Sinclair, June 30, 1803, *Papers of Jefferson*, Original Series, 40:637–39; James Madison to Jefferson, September 30, 1805, *Papers of Madison*, Secretary of State Series, 10:387–88; Jefferson to Sinclair, June 30, 1803, *Papers of Jefferson*, Original Series, 40:637–39.

3. Daniel J. Ennis, *Enter the Press-Gang: Naval Impressment in Eighteenth-Century British Literature* (Newark: University of Delaware Press, 2002), 140; "Great Britain—Impressed American Seamen. Communicated to the Senate, March 2, 1808," *Documents, Legislative and Executive, of the Congress of the United States, from the First Session of the First to the Third Session of the Thirteenth Congress, Inclusive*, ed. Walter Lowrie and Matthew St. Clair Clarke (38 vols., Washington, DC: Gales and Seaton, 1832–61), 3:36; *Niles's Weekly Register*, October 28, 1815, 9:155.

4. James Madison to James Monroe, January 5, 1804, *Writings of James Madison*, Secretary of State Series, 7:96.

5. Thomas Jefferson to James Monroe, March 21, 1807, *Founders Online*, http://founders.archives.gov/documents/Jefferson/99-01-02-5326, accessed October 22, 2016; Thomas Jefferson to United States Congress, October 27, 1807, *Founders Online*, http://founders.archives.gov/documents/Jefferson/99-01-02-6665, accessed October 22, 2016.

6. Adams, *History*, 2:97–99.

7. James Madison to James Monroe, July 6, 1807, *Founders Online*, http://founders.archives.gov/documents/Madison/99-01-02-1846, accessed October 22, 2016; Albert Gallatin to Joseph H. Nicholson, July 17, 1807, *The Writings of Albert Gallatin*, ed. Henry Adams (3 vols., Philadelphia: J.B. Lippincott & Co., 1879), 1:339; Thomas Jefferson to Pierre Samuel Du Pont de Nemours, July 14, 1807, *Founders Online*, http://founders.archives.gov/documents/Jefferson/99-01-02-5960, accessed October 22, 2016.

8. Randolph quoted in Francis D. Cogliano, *Emperor of Liberty: Thomas Jefferson's Foreign Policy* (New Haven: Yale University Press, 2014), 219.

9. John Page to Thomas Jefferson, July 12, 1807, *Founders Online*, http://founders.archives.gov/documents/Jefferson/99-01-02-5946, accessed October 22, 2016; Gallatin to Jefferson, December 18, 1807, *Writings of Gallatin*, 1:368; Thomas

Jefferson to United States Congress, November 8, 1808, *Founders Online*, http://founders.archives.gov/documents/Jefferson/99-01-02-9054, accessed October 22, 2016; Thomas Jefferson to George Logan, March 21, 1801, *Papers of Jefferson*, Original Series, 33:390–91.

10. Thomas Jefferson, "Special Message, December 18, 1807," *Addresses and Messages*, 132.

11. David Dzurec, "Of Salt Mountains, Prairie Dogs, and Horned Frogs: The Louisiana Purchase and the Evolution of Federalist Satire, 1803–1823," *Journal of the Early Republic* 25, no. 1 (2015): 104–5; J. van Fenstermaker and John E. Filer, "The U.S. Embargo Act of 1807: Its Impact on New England Money, Banking, and Economic Activity," *Economic Inquiry* 28, no. 1 (1990): 165.

12. John Lambert, *Travels through Canada, and the United States of North America, in the Years 1806, 1807, & 1808* (2 vols., London: C. Cradock and W. Joy, 1813), 2:64–65.

13. Samuel Smith, December 19, 1805, quoted in Burton Spivak, *Jefferson's English Crisis: Commerce, Embargo, and the Republican Revolution* (Charlottesville: University Press of Virginia, 1979), 40–41.

14. *Annals of Congress*, Ninth Congress, 1st Session, 668–69.

15. Albert Gallatin to James Madison, September 9, 1808, *Founders Online*, http://founders.archives.gov/documents/Madison/99-01-02-3509, accessed October 22, 2016; John Quincy Adams to Ezekiel Bacon, December 21, 1808, *Writings of John Quincy Adams*, ed. Washington Chauncey Ford (7 vols., New York: Macmillan, 1913–17), 3:279.

16. Gallatin to Badollet, October 22, 1832, in Nicholas Dungan, *Gallatin: America's Swiss Founding Father* (New York: New York University Press, 2010), 156.

Chapter 10

1. Henry Clay, "Speech on the New Army Bill," House of Representatives, January 8, 1813, in *The Life and Speeches of the Hon. Henry Clay*, ed. Daniel Mallory (2 vols., New York: Robert P. Bixby, 1832), 1:257.

2. Heath, *William Wells and the Struggle for the Old Northwest*, 314–15, 354.

3. Harrison quoted in Adam Jortner, *The Gods of Prophetstown: The Battle of Tippecanoe and the Holy War for the American Frontier* (Oxford: Oxford University Press, 2012), 187; Jackson quoted in Robert M. Owens, *Mr. Jefferson's Hammer: William Henry Harrison and the Origins of American Indian Policy* (Norman: University of Oklahoma Press, 2007), 221; Blount quoted in William A. Walker Jr., "Martial Sons: Tennessee Enthusiasm for the War of 1812," *Tennessee Historical Quarterly* 20, no. 1 (1961): 26.

4. John Quincy Adams to William Eustis, October 26, 1811, *Writings of John Quincy Adams*, 4:262; Roach quoted in Jon Latimer, *1812: War with America* (Cambridge: Harvard University Press, 2007), 35; "Representative Daniel Sheffey Opposes the War of 1812," January 3, 1812, in *Landmark Debates in Congress: From the Declaration of Independence to the War in Iraq*, ed. Stephen W. Stathis (Washington, DC: CQ Press, 2009), 59.

5. Thomas Jefferson to James Madison, May 30, 1812, in *The Papers of James*

Madison, Presidential Papers, ed. Robert A. Rutland et al. (7 vols., Charlottesville: University of Virginia Press, 1984–), 4:426.

6. James Madison to Henry Wheaton, February 26, 1827, *The American Founding Era*, http://rotunda.upress.virginia.edu/founders/default.xqy?keys=FGEA-chron-1820-1827-02-26-1, accessed October 23, 2016.

7. *The Papers of Henry Clay*, ed. James F. Hopkins et al. (9 vols., Lexington: University of Kentucky Press, 1959–), 1:451; Jones quoted in Lawrence S. Kaplan, *Entangling Alliances with None: American Foreign Policy in the Age of Jefferson* (Kent, OH: Kent State University Press, 1987), 130.

8. Monroe quoted in Roger H. Brown, *The Republic in Peril: 1812* (New York: W. W. Norton, 1964), 38.

9. Caleb Strong quoted in Robert Mann, *Wartime Dissent in America: A History and Anthology* (Basingstoke: Palgrave Macmillan, 2010), 25; "Desultory Remarks," *Niles's Weekly Register*, 2:363.

10. Dacres quoted in Walter R. Borneman, *1812: The War That Forged a Nation* (New York: Harper Collins, 2004), 87.

11. Boyle's "Proclamation to Blockade" in George Coggeshall, *History of the American Privateers and Letters-of-Marque, during Our War with England* (New York: N.p., 1861), 361–62; *The New Annual Register, or General Repository of History, Politics, and Literature, for the Year 1814* (London: George Stockdale, 1815), 321.

12. "Memoir of Major General Robert Ross," *The United Service Journal and Naval and Military Magazine, Part I* (London: Henry Colburn, 1829), 414–15; Hunter quoted in Latimer, *1812*, 318.

13. James Madison to James Monroe, November 28, 1818, *Letters and Other Writings of James Madison, Fourth President of the United States* (4 vols., Philadelphia: J.B. Lippincott, 1865), 3:113; Henry Clay to Thomas Bodley, December 18, 1813, *Papers of Henry Clay*, 1:841; Thomas Jefferson to William Duane, August 4, 1812, *The Papers of Thomas Jefferson*, Retirement Series, ed. J. Jefferson Looney (11 vols., Princeton: Princeton University Press, 2004–), 5:293–94; "Proclamation to the Inhabitants of Canada," July 12, 1812, in William Hull, *Memoirs of the Campaign of the North Western Army of the United States, A.D. 1812, in a Series of Letters Addressed to the Citizens of the United States* (Boston: True & Greene, 1824), appendix no. II, 18.

14. For this and much more on the American invasion of Canada, see Pierre Berton, *The Invasion of Canada: 1812–1813* (Toronto: Anchor Canada, [1980] 2011), 225.

15. On Tecumseh's death, see Latimer, *1812*, 189.

16. Duke of Wellington quoted in Alexander DeConde, *A History of American Foreign Policy* (3rd ed., 2 vols., New York: Charles Scribner, 1978), 1:104.

17. Jackson to Thomas Pinckney, March 28, 1814, in *The Papers of Andrew Jackson*, ed. Sam B. Smith, Harriet Chappell Owsley, et al. (10 vols., Knoxville: University of Tennessee Press, 1980–), 3:52.

18. Duke of Wellington quoted in Richard Holmes, *Wellington: The Iron Duke* (London: Harper Collins, 2003), 206; Andrew Jackson quoted in Robert V. Remini, *Andrew Jackson: A Biography* (New York: Palgrave Macmillan, 2008), 76.

19. "The Ministers Plenipotentiary and Extraordinary of the United States to

the Plenipotentiaries of His Britannick Majesty," August 24, 1814, *State Papers and Publick Documents of the United States* (2nd ed., 10 vols., Boston: T.B. Wait, 1817), 9:377–83; Goulburn quoted in *Writings of John Quincy Adams*, 5:182–83n.

20. *Memoirs of John Quincy Adams*, October 12, 1814, 3:51, 37; Wellington quoted in *Writings of John Quincy Adams*, 5:235n. On what-ifs concerning the Battle of New Orleans see Daniel Walker Howe, *What Hath God Wrought: The Transformation of America, 1815-1848* (Oxford: Oxford University Press, 2007), 17.

21. Daniel Webster, *A Discourse, Delivered at Plymouth, December 22, 1820, in Commemoration of the First Settlement of New-England* (Boston: Wells and Lilly, 1821), 25; Otis to Quincy, December 15, 1808, quoted in Adams, *History*, 4:403.

22. Pickering quoted in Bradford Perkins, *Prologue to War: England and the United States, 1805–1812* (Berkeley: University of California Press, 1970), 57.

23. Pickering quoted in Kaplan, *Entangling Alliances*, 65; *Centinel* quoted in Perkins, *Prologue*, 389.

24. Timothy Pickering to Samuel Putnam, December 8, 1814, in *Documents Relating to New-England Federalism, 1800–1815*, ed. Henry Adams (Boston: Little, Brown, 1877), 393; Pickering to Gouverneur Morris, October 21, 1814, *Documents Relating to Federalism*, 400–401.

25. Albert Gallatin to Matthew Lyon, May 7, 1816, *Writings of Gallatin*, 1:700.

Chapter 11

1. Francis Bacon, "An Advertisement Touching An Holy War. To the Right Reverend Father in God, Lancelot Andrews, Lord Bishop of Winchester, And Counsellor of Estate to His Majesty" in *The Works of Francis Bacon, Baron of Verulam, Viscount St. Albans, and Lord High Chancellor of England* (10 vols., London: W. Baynes and Son, 1824), 3:476.

2. Floridablanca quoted in Corwin, *French Policy*, 240.

3. For a brief account of the Gálvez reforms and their consequences, see Liss, *Atlantic Empires*, 65–74.

4. As Jeremy Adelman argues, in Spanish America "anticolonialism and nationalism were the effects, not the causes, of imperial collapse": Jeremy Adelman, *Sovereignty and Revolution in the Iberian Atlantic* (Princeton: Princeton University Press, 2009), 177.

5. Andrew McMichael, *Atlantic Loyalties: Americans in Spanish West Florida, 17851810* (Athens: University of Georgia Press, 2008).

6. "On the Line of the Perdido" (1810), in Speeches of the Hon. Henry Clay of the Congress of the United States, ed. Richard Chambers (Cincinnati: Shepherd and Stearns, 1842), p. 22.

7. *Memoirs of John Quincy Adams*, 5:58.

8. See Charles B. Elliott, *The United States and the Northeast Fisheries: A History of the Fishery Question* (Minneapolis: University of Minnesota Press, 1887); still unsurpassed.

9. *Columbian Centinel*, July 12, 1817.

10. John Quincy Adams to William Branch Giles, November 15, 1808, *Writings of John Quincy Adams*, 3:243; *Memoirs of John Quincy Adams*, November 4, 1809, 2:50.

11. *Statutes at Large, Acts of the 11th Congress,* 666; Liss, *Atlantic Empires,* 111.

12. John Quincy Adams to George W. Erving, November 28, 1818, in *Message from the President of the United States,* 25; *Memoirs of John Quincy Adams,* January 25, 1816, 3:290.

13. For Bowles, see J. Leitch Wright Jr., *William Augustus Bowles: Director General of the Creek Nation* (Athens: University of Georgia Press, 1967).

14. *Memoirs of John Quincy Adams,* February 3, 1819, 4:239.

15. Andrew Jackson to James Monroe, January 6, 1818, *Papers of Andrew Jackson,* 4:167, 165.

16. Adams, *Message from the President,* 19; Adams to George William Irving, November 28, 1818, *Writings of John Quincy Adams* 6:474-511.

17. *Memoirs of John Quincy Adams,* December 30, 1818, 4:201.

18. *Memoirs of John Quincy Adams,* March 8, 1819, 4:206; November 4, 1818, 4:61.

19. *Memoirs of John Quincy Adams,* January 30, 1819, 4:237.

20. *Memoirs of John Quincy Adams,* September 21, 1820, 5:180; December 3, 1819, 4:461.

21. *Memoirs of John Quincy Adams,* April 11, 1819, 4:329.

Chapter 12

1. *Memoirs of John Quincy Adams,* November 16, 1819, 4:439.

2. "Speech on the Distressed State of Agriculture, Delivered in the House of Commons, April 9, 1816," in *Speeches of Henry, Lord Brougham, upon Questions Relating to Public Rights, Duties, and Interests; with Historical Introductions* (2 vols., Philadelphia: Lea and Blanchard, 1841), 1:274.

3. *Memoirs of John Quincy Adams,* August 15, 1823, 6:173.

4. James Monroe, "Sixth Annual Message," December 3, 1822; Daniel Webster to Edward Everett, December 6, 1823, in *The Private Correspondence of Daniel Webster,* ed. Fletcher Webster (2 vols., Boston: Little, Brown, 1857), 1:332–33.

5. For an elegant profile of Clay, see Robert V. Remini, *Henry Clay: Statesman for the Union* (New York: Norton, 1991), 2, 4–5.

6. "On Renewing the Charter of the First Bank of the United States," United States Senate, 1811, *Speeches of Henry Clay,* 1:220; "On the Line of the Perdido," Senate, December 25, 1810, *Speeches of Henry Clay,* 1:201.

7. Clay quoted in Remini, *Henry Clay,* 666.

8. "On African Colonization," House of Representatives, January 20, 1827, in *Life and Speeches of Clay,* 1:519.

9. "Toast and Response at Public Dinner," May 19, 1821, in *Papers of Henry Clay,* 3:80.

10. "Toast and Response at Public Dinner," May 19, 1821, in *Papers of Henry Clay,* 3:80–81.

11. "Speech on Mission to Greece," January 23, 1824, *Papers of Henry Clay,* 3:606.

12. John Quincy Adams to Robert Walsh Jr., July 10, 1821, in *Writings of John Quincy Adams,* 7:117; Adams quoted in Samuel Flagg Bemis, *John Quincy Adams and the Union* (New York: Knopf, 1956), 357; *Aurora,* July 18, 1821, quoted in Arthur

Preston Whitaker, *The United States and the Independence of Latin America: 1800–1830* (Baltimore: Johns Hopkins University Press, 1941), 366.

13. Thomas Jefferson to Alexander von Humboldt, December 6, 1813, *Papers of Jefferson*, Retirement Series, 7:29–32; Jefferson to Dominick Lynch, June 26, 1817, *Papers of Jefferson*, Retirement Series, 11:478.

14. "On the Emancipation of South America," House of Representatives, March 24, 1818, *Life and Speeches of Clay*, 1:329; "Mission to South America," House of Representatives, May 10, 1820, *Life and Speeches of Clay*, 1:429–30.

15. "On American Industry," House of Representatives, March 30, 31, 1824, *Life and Speeches of Clay*, 1:450; "On the Emancipation of South America," 1:332.

16. "Mission to South America," 1:429–30.

17. Clay quoted in James E. Lewis Jr., *The American Union and the Problem of Neighborhood: The United States and the Collapse of the Spanish Empire, 1783–1829* (Durham, NC: University of North Carolina Press, 1998), 158; *Papers of Henry Clay*, 3:80.

18. *Memoirs of John Quincy Adams*, September 19, 1820, 5:176; March 16, 1819, 4:300; November 22, 1819, 4:444–45; James Monroe to Albert Gallatin, May 26, 1820, quoted in Harry Ammon, *James Monroe: The Quest for National Identity* (Charlottesville: University Press of Virginia, 1971), 412.

19. James Monroe, "Political Condition of the Spanish Provinces of South America, Communicated to Congress, March 8, 1822," *Documents, Legislative and Executive*, 4:819; William Spence Robertson, "The United States and Spain in 1822," *American Historical Review* 4, no. 4 (1915): 784; *Memoirs of John Quincy Adams*, June 19, 1822, 6:23.

20. James Monroe, "Sixth Annual Message," December 3, 1822.

21. John Quincy Adams to Hugh Nelson, April 28, 1823, *Writings of John Quincy Adams*, 7:372–73.

Chapter 13

1. Prince Metternich to the Russian foreign minister, Count Karl Nesselrode, January 19, 1824, quoted in Dexter Perkins, *The Monroe Doctrine, 1823–26* (Cambridge: Harvard University Press, 1927), 167.

2. Chateaubriand to Montmorency, May 28, 1822, quoted in W. P. Cresson, "Chateaubriand and the Monroe Doctrine," *North American Review* 217, no. 809 (1923): 481.

3. Boiselcomte quoted in William Spence Robertson, *France and Latin-American Independence* (New York: Octagon Books, 1967), 246–47.

4. Robertson, *France*, 261.

5. Robertson, *France*, 261–63.

6. Duke of Wellington to George Canning, December 10, 1822, in *Despatches, Correspondence, and Memoranda of Field Marshal Arthur, Duke of Wellington, K.G.*, ed. the Duke of Wellington [his son] (London: John Murray, 1867), 1:639.

7. Polignac to Chateaubriand, December 12, 1823, quoted in Harold Temperley, "French Designs on Spanish America in 1820–5," *English Historical Review* 40, no. 157 (1925): 52; Robertson, *France*, 313.

8. John Quincy Adams to Alexander Hill Everett, December 29, 1817, *Writings of John Quincy Adams*, 6:280–81.

9. *Memoirs of John Quincy Adams*, June 19, 1823, 6:152; the five "opinions" and the American reaction to each of them are found in *The Writings of James Monroe*, ed. Stanislaus Murray Hamilton (7 vols., New York: G.P. Putnam's Sons, 1898–1903), 6:406–7; Canning quoted in Martin Sicker, *The Geopolitics of Security in the Americas: Hemispheric Denial from Monroe to Clinton* (Westport, CT: Praeger, 2002), 19; *Writings of Monroe*, 6:379.

10. Canning, *Hansard*, House of Commons, December 12, 1826, vol. 16, cc 397–98.

11. *Memoirs of John Quincy Adams*, November 7, 1823, 6:179.

12. James Monroe, "Seventh Message to Congress," December 2, 1823, https://ourdocuments.gov/doc.php?doc=23&page=transcript, accessed October 23, 2016; John Quincy Adams to Henry Midleton, July 5, 1820, *Writings of John Quincy Adams*, 7:50–51.

13. Metternich and Nesslrode quoted in Perkins, *Monroe Doctrine*, 167–68.

14. Canning to Bagot, January 22, 1824, quoted in Bradford Perkins, *Castlereagh and Adams: England and the United States, 1812–1823* (Berkeley: University of California Press, 1964), 342; Canning to Vaughan, February 18, 1826, quoted in Harold Temperley, *The Foreign Policy of Canning, 1822–1827: England, the Neo-Holy Alliance, and the New World* (London: G. Bell and Sons, 1925), 158.

15. Salazar quoted in William Spence Robertson, "South America and the Monroe Doctrine, 1824–1828," *Political Science Quarterly* 30, no. 1 (1915): 89–90.

16. Robertson, *France*, 517.

17. Abraham Lincoln, "The Perpetuation of Our Political Institutions: Address Before the Young Men's Lyceum of Springfield, Illinois," January 27, 1838.

Chapter 14

1. Lafayette to Clay, February 28, 1826 in Papers of Clay, 5:137.

2. Hiram Paulding, *Un Rasgo de Bolívar en Campaña*, trans. "L.M." (New York: Imprenta de Don Juan de la Granja, 1835), 72.

3. Paulding, 71; "Colombia is filled . . ." quoted in John Lynch, *Simón Bolívar: A Life* (New Haven: Yale University Press, 2006), 144; "We are the vile offspring . . ." quoted in Lynch, Simón Bolívar, 217.

4. "The Angostura Discourse" in *The Political Thought of Bolívar: Selected Writings*, ed. Gerald E. Fitzgerald (The Hague: Martinus Nijhoff, 1971), 51, 51–52, 56.

5. "Circular Letter of Invitation to the Congress of Panama" in *Political Thought of Bolívar*, 76; "The Jamaica Letter" in *Political Thought of Bolívar*, 41.

6. Henry Clay to Francis Preston Blair, January 29, 1825, in *Papers of Henry Clay*, 4:47; *Memoirs of John Quincy Adams*, 7:98; Jackson quoted in Remini, *Henry Clay*, 1, 1n.

7. Seventeen points of business are listed in a draft of February 1826, *Political Thought of Bolívar*, 77–78.

8. *The Executive Proceedings of the Senate of the United States, on the Subject of*

the Mission to the Congress at Panama, Together with the Messages and Documents Relating Thereto (Washington, DC: Senate of the United States, 1826), 4

9. "Alliance of the Southern Republics," *The North American Review* 22, no. 50 (1826), 162, 164.

10. John Quincy Adams, "First Annual Message," December 6, 1825; The *Albion or British, Colonial, and Foreign Weekly Gazette*, March 25, 1826, quoted in Frances L. Reinhold, "New Research on the First Pan-American Congress Held at Panama in 1826," *Hispanic American Historical Review* 18, no. 3 (1938): 347; *Gales's & Seaton's Register of Debates*, April 14, 1826, 2264.

11. Quoted in Reinhold, "New Research on the First Pan-American Congress," 349; *Democratic Press* quoted in Reinhold, "New Research," 349; Johnston quoted in Andrew R. L. Clayton, "The Debate over the Panama Congress and the Origins of the Second American Party System," *Historian* 47, no. 2 (1985): 224.

12. Adams, "Message of the President of the United States to the Senate, Relative to the Panama Mission," December 26, 1825, *Register of Debates*, 19th Congress, 1st Session, Appendix, 43; *Speech of Mr. Webster, of Mass. in the House of Representatives, on the Panama Mission, Delivered on the 14th April, 1826* (Washington, DC: Davis & Force, 1826), 60; Livingston, *Register of Debates*, February 1, 1826, 1227–28.

13. Senate Resolution, *Register of Debates*, 19th Congress, 1st Session, Appendix, 100; Polk, April 21, 1826, *Register of Debates*, 2478; White, Senate, *Register of Debates*, March 1826, 206.

14. Buchanan, House, April 11, 126, *Register of Debates*, 2174; Woodbury, Senate, Register of Debates, March 1826, 187.

15. Hayne, Senate, March 1826, *Register of Debates*, 166–67; Andrew Jackson to James Buchanan, April 8, 1826, *Papers of Jackson*, 6:163; Buchanan, House, April 11, 1826, *Register of Debates*, 2182.

16. Randolph, Senate, March 30, 1826, *Register of Debates*, 397, 403–4.

17. Berrien, in French Ensor Chadwick, *The Relations of the United States and Spain: Diplomacy* (New York: Charles Scribner, 1909), 212; Holmes, Senate, March 2016, *Register of Debates*, 274; Benton, Senate, March 2016, *Register of Debates*, 330.

18. Buchanan, House, April 11, 1826, *Register of Debates*, 2180; *The Speech of Mr. Hayne, Delivered in the Senate of the United States, on the Mission to Panama, March 1826* (Washington, DC: Gales & Seaton, 1826), 19; Reed, Senate, March 1826, *Register of Debates*, 342; Hayne, Speech, 1821.

19. *The Autobiography of Martin van Buren*, ed. John C. Fitzpatrick (Washington, DC: Government Printing Office, 1920), 199; *Memoirs of John Quincy Adams*, January 31, 1826, 7:111.

20. John Quincy Adams, "Special Message," March 15, 1826, http://www.presidency.ucsb.edu/ws/?pid=66632, accessed October 23, 2016.

21. International American Conference. *Reports of Committees and Discussions Thereon. Volume IV. Historical Appendix. The Congress of 1826 at Panama and Subsequent Movements toward a Conference of American Nations* (Washington, DC: Government Printing Office, 1890), 101, 187, 104; H. W. V. Temperley, "The Later American Policy of George Canning," *American Historical Review* 11, no. 4 (1906): 787.

22. "On the Panama Mission," appendix, *Register of Debates*, 19th Congress, 1st Session, 73; Bolívar quoted in Stefano Spoltore, "The Panama Congress: A Failed Attempt at Latin American Union," *Federalist* 45, no. 1 (2003): 57; Henry Clay to Simon Bolívar, October 27, 1828, *Papers of Henry Clay*, 7:517.

Conclusion

1. George Benedict, *An Oration, Delivered at Burlington, Vt., on the Fourth of July 1826. Being the Fiftieth Anniversary of American Independence* (Burlington, VT: E. & T. Mills, 1826), 4.

2. John Quincy Adams, "Second Annual Message," December 5, 1826, *American Presidency Project*, http://www.presidency.ucsb.edu/ws/?pid=29468, accessed October 22, 2016.

3. John Quincy Adams, "Second Annual Message".

4. John Quincy Adams, "Second Annual Message".

5. John Quincy Adams, "Second Annual Message".

6. Jens-Uwe Guettel, *German Expansionism, Imperial Liberalism, and the United States, 1776–1845* (Cambridge: Cambridge University Press, 2012), 59–60, 58; Alexis de Tocqueville, *Democracy in America*, trans. Henry Reeve (4th ed., 2 vols., New York: Henry G. Langley, 1845), 1:175.

7. *Hansard*, Commons, May 12, 1826, vol. 15, cc 1168, 1182.

8. Archibald Alison, "The West India Question," *Blackwood's Edinburgh Magazine* 31, no. 190 (1832), 413; *The Speeches of Mr Barrett and of Mr Burge, at a General Meeting of Planters, Merchants, and Others Interested in the West-India Colonies; Assembled at the Thatched-House Tavern, on the 18th May, 1833* (London: A.J. Valpy, 1833), 7; James Franklin, *A Short View of the West India Question; With Remarks on the Right Hon. Wm. Huskisson's Letter to Sir John Keane, K.C.B., Lieut.-Governor of Jamaica* (London: N.p., 1828), 105.

9. On the vicissitudes of expansionist faith in the aftermath of the Missouri crisis, see Lyon Rathbun, "The Debate over Annexing Texas and the Emergence of Manifest Destiny," *Rhetoric and Public Affairs* 4, no. 3 (2001): 459–93.

Bibliography

Printed Primary Sources

An Abridgement of the Laws of the United States: Or, A Complete Digest of All Such Acts of Congress as Concern the United States at Large. Edited by William Graydon. Harrisburg, PA: John Wyeth, 1803.

The Adams Papers, Family Correspondence. Edited by L. H. Butterfield et al. 11 vols. Cambridge: Harvard University Press, 1963–.

The Addresses and Messages of the Presidents of the United States, together with the Declaration of Independence and Constitution of the United States. New York: McLean & Taylor, 1839.

Alison, Archibald. "The West India Question." *Blackwood's Edinburgh Magazine* 31, no. 190 (1832), 412–23.

Allan, Ethan. *A Narrative of Col. Ethan Allen's Captivity, from the Time of His Being Taken by the British, near Montreal, on the 25th day of September, in the Year 1775, to the Time of his Exchange, on the 6th Day of May, 1778.* 3rd ed. Burlington, VT: H. Johnson & Co., [1779] 1838.

The Autobiography of Martin van Buren. Edited by John C. Fitzpatrick. Washington, DC: Government Printing Office, 1920.

B.F. Stevens's Facsimiles of Manuscripts in European Archives Relating to America, 1773–1783, with Descriptions, Editorial Notes, Collations, References, and Translations. 25 vols. London: N.p., 1889–95.

Benedict, George, *An Oration, Delivered at Burlington, Vt., on the Fourth of July 1826, Being the Fiftieth Anniversary of American Independence.* Burlington, VT: E. & T. Mills, 1826.

Binney, Horace. *An Eulogy on the Life and Character of John Marshall, Chief Justice of the Supreme Court of the United States, Delivered at the Request of the Councils of Philadelphia, on the 24th September, 1835.* Philadelphia: J. Crissy and G. Goodman, 1835.

"Britannicus." *A Reply to Article VII of the Edinburgh Review for October 1823, on T. Clarkson's Treatise on the Improvement and Emancipation of Slaves in the British Colonies.* London: James Ridgway, 1824.

Collected Political Writings of James Otis. Edited by Richard Samuelson. Indianapolis: Liberty Fund, 2015.

A Collection of State Papers, Relative to the War Against France, Now Carrying on by Great Britain and the Several Other European Powers. 11 vols. London: J. Debrett, 1794–1802.

The Complete Anti-Federalist. Edited by Herbert J. Storing. 7 vols. Chicago: University of Chicago Press, 1981.

The Complete Works of Ralph Waldo Emerson. Edited by Edward Waldo Emerson. 12 vols. New York: Houghton Mifflin, 1903–4.

Condorcet, Marquis de. *Outlines of an Historical View of the Progress of the Human Mind: Being a Posthumous Work of the Late M. de Condorcet. Translated from the French.* London: J. Johnson, 1795.

The Correspondence and Public Papers of John Jay. Edited by Henry P. Johnston. 4 vols. New York: G.P. Putnam, 1890.

Correspondence of Lieut.-Governor John Graves Simcoe, with Allied Documents Relating to His Administration of the Government of Upper Canada. Edited by E.A. Cruikshank. 5 vols. Toronto: Ontario Historical Society, 1923–31.

Correspondence of the French Ministers to the United States, 1791–1797. Edited by Frederick J. Turner. Washington, DC: Government Printing Office, 1904.

The Debates in the Several State Conventions, on the Adoption of the Federal Constitution, as Recommended by the General Convention at Philadelphia, in 1787. Edited by Jonathan Elliot. 4 vols. Washington, DC: N.p., 1836–45.

Despatches, Correspondence, and Memoranda of Field Marshal Arthur, Duke of Wellington, K.G. Edited by the Duke of Wellington [his son]. London: John Murray, 1867.

Diary and Autobiography of John Adams. Edited by L. H. Butterfield. 4 vols. Cambridge: Belknap Press of Harvard University Press, 1962.

[Dickinson, John]. *A Declaration by the Representatives of the United Colonies of North-America, Now Met in General Congress at Philadelphia, Setting Forth the Causes and Necessity of Their Taking Up Arms.* Philadelphia, 1775.

The Diplomatic Correspondence of the United States of America, from the Signing of the Definitive Treaty of Peace, September 10, 1783, to the Adoption of the Constitution, March 4, 1789. 7 vols. Washington, DC: Blair & Rives, 1837.

Documents, Legislative and Executive, of the Congress of the United States, from the First Session of the First to the Third Session of the Thirteenth Congress, Inclusive. Edited by Walter Lowrie and Matthew St. Clair Clarke. 38 vols. Washington, DC: Gales and Seaton, 1832–61.

Documents Relating to New England Federalism, 1800–1815. Edited by Henry Adams. Boston: Little, Brown, 1877.

The Documentary History of the Ratification of the Constitution. Edited by Merrill Jensen. 27 vols. Madison: State Historical Society of Wisconsin, 1976–.

Drinkwater, John. *A History of the Siege of Gibraltar, 1779–1783. With a Description and Account of That Garrison from the Earliest Periods.* London: John Murray, [1785] 1861.

The Executive Proceedings of the Senate of the United States, on the Subject of the Mission to the Congress at Panama, Together with the Messages and Documents Relating Thereto. Washington, DC: Senate of the United States, 1826.

Franklin, James. *The Present State of Hayti (Saint Domingo) with Remarks on Its Agriculture, Commerce, Laws, Religion, Finances, and Population, etc., etc.* London: John Murray, 1828.

Franklin, James. *A Short View of the West India Question; With Remarks on the Right Hon. Wm. Huskisson's Letter to Sir John Keane, K.C.B., Lieut.-Governor of Jamaica.* London: N.p., 1828.

Giunta, Mary A., ed. *The Emerging Nation: A Documentary History of the Foreign Relations of the United States under the Articles of Confederation, 1780–1789.* 3 vols. Washington, DC: National Historical Publications and Records Commission, 1996.

Hamilton, Alexander, James Madison, and John Jay. *The Federalist Papers.* Edited by Lawrence Goldman. Oxford: Oxford University Press, [1787–88] 2008.

The Historical and Posthumous Memoirs of Sir Nathaniel William Wraxall, 1772–1784. Edited by Henry B. Wheatley. 5 vols. London: Bickers & Son, 1884.

Holroyd, John Baker, Earl of Sheffield. *Observations on the Commerce of the American States.* 6th ed. London: J. Debrett, 1784.

Hull, William. *Memoirs of the Campaign of the North Western Army of the United States, A.D. 1812, in a Series of Letters Addressed to the Citizens of the United States.* Boston: True & Greene, 1824.

International American Conference. Reports of Committees and Discussions Thereon. Volume IV. Historical Appendix. The Congress of 1826 at Panama and Subsequent Movements toward a Conference of American Nations. Washington, D.C.: Government Printing Office, 1890.

John Jay: The Winning of the Peace: Unpublished Papers, 1780–1784. Edited by Richard B. Morris. 2 vols. New York: Harper & Row, 1980.

The Journal and Correspondence of William Lord Auckland. Edited by G. Hogge. 2 vols. London: Bentley, 1861–62.

Journals of the Continental Congress, 1774–1789. Edited by Worthington Chauncey Ford et al. 34 vols. Washington, DC: Government Printing Office, 1904–37.

The Journals of Zebulon Montgomery Pike with Letters and Related Documents. Edited by Donald Jackson. 2 vols. Norman: University of Oklahoma Press, 1966.

Kippis, Andrew. *Considerations on the Provisional Treaty with America, and the Preliminary Articles of Peace with France and Spain.* London: T. Cadell, 1783.

Lambert, John, *Travels through Canada, and the United States of North America, in the Years 1806, 1807, & 1808.* 2 vols. London: C. Cradock and W. Joy, 1813.

The Last Journals of Horace Walpole during the Reign of George III from 1771–1783. Edited by A. Francis Steuart. 2 vols. London: John Lane, 1910.

Laws of the State of New-York, Comprising the Constitution and the Acts of the Legislature, since the Revolution, from the First to the Fifteenth Session, Inclusive. 2 vols. New York: Thomas Greenleaf, 1792.

Letters and Other Writings of James Madison, Fourth President of the United States. 4 vols. Philadelphia: J.B. Lippincott, 1865.

Letters from France: The Private Diplomatic Correspondence of Benjamin Franklin, 1776–1785. Edited by Brett F. Woods. New York: Algora, 2007.

Letters of Members of the Continental Congress. Edited by Edmund Cody Burnett. 8 vols. Washington, DC: Carnegie Institute of Washington, 1921–36.

Life and Letters of George Cabot. Edited by Henry Cabot Lodge. 2nd ed. Boston: Little, Brown, 1878.

The Life and Speeches of the Hon. Henry Clay. Edited by Daniel Mallory. 2 vols. New York: Robert P. Bixby, 1832.

Marshall, John. *The Life of George Washington*. Edited by Robert Faulkner and Paul Carrese. Indianapolis: Liberty Fund, [1838] 2000.

The Memoir of General Toussaint Louverture. Translated and edited by Philippe R. Girard. Oxford: Oxford University Press, 2014.

Memoirs, Correspondence, and Miscellanies, from the Papers of Thomas Jefferson. Edited by Thomas Jefferson Randolph. Charlottesville: F. Carr, 1829.

Memoirs, Correspondence, and Private Papers of Thomas Jefferson, Late President of the United States. Edited by Thomas Jefferson Randolph. London: Henry Colburn and Richard Bentley, 1829.

Memoirs of John, Duke of Marlborough; with his Original Correspondence: Collected from the Family Records at Blenheim, and Other Authentic Sources. Edited by William Coxe. 3 vols. London: Longman, Hurst, Rees, Orme, and Brown, 1818–19.

Memoirs of John Quincy Adams: Comprising Portions of His Diary from 1795 to 1848. Edited by Charles Francis Adams. 12 vols. Philadelphia: J.B. Lippincott, 1874–77.

Message from the President of the United States, Transmitting Copies of the Several Instructions to the Ministers of the U. States to the Government of France, and of the Correspondence with Said Government, Having Reference to the Spoliations Committed by That Power on the Commerce of the United States, Anterior to September 30, 1800. Washington, DC: Gales & Seaton, 1826.

Message from the President of the United States, Transmitting, in Pursuance of a Resolution of the House of Representatives, Such Further Information, in Relation to Our Affairs with Spain, as in His Opinion, Is Not Inconsistent with the Public Interest to Divulge. Washington, DC: E. de Krafet, 1819.

Murray, John. *Nehemiah, or The Struggle for Liberty Never in Vain, When Managed with Virtue and Perseverance. A Discourse Delivered at the Presbyterian Church in Newbury-Port, Nov. 4th, 1779*. Newbury, MA: John Mycall, 1779.

Naval Documents of the American Revolution. Edited by William Bell Clark et al. 11 vols. Washington, DC: U.S. Government Printing Office, 1964–2005.

The New Annual Register, or General Repository of History, Politics, and Literature, for the Year 1814. London: George Stockdale, 1815.

Pamphlets on the Constitution of the United States, Published during Its Discussion by the People, 1787–1788. Edited by Paul Leicester Ford. New York: N.p., 1888.

The Papers of Alexander Hamilton. Edited by Harold C. Syrett. 27 vols. New York: Columbia University Press, 1961–87.

The Papers of Andrew Jackson. Edited by Sam B. Smith, Harriet Chappell Owsley, et al. 10 vols. Knoxville: University of Tennessee Press, 1980–.

The Papers of Benjamin Franklin. Edited by Leonard W. Labaree et al. 41 vols. New Haven: Yale University Press, 1959–2014.

The Papers of George Washington. Revolutionary War Series, edited by Philander D. Chase et al. 22 vols. Charlottesville: University of Virginia Press, 1985–2013.

The Papers of George Washington. Presidential Series, edited by Dorothy Twohig et al. 17 vols. Charlottesville: University of Virginia Press, 1987–2013.

The Papers of George Washington. Confederation Series, edited by W.W. Abbot et al. Charlottesville: University of Virginia Press, 1992–1997.

The Papers of George Washington. Retirement Series, edited by W. W. Abbot. 4 vols. Charlottesville: University of Virginia Press, 1998–99.

The Papers of Henry Clay. Edited by James F. Hopkins et al. 9 vols. Lexington: University of Kentucky Press, 1959–.

The Papers of Henry Laurens. Edited by David R. Chesnutt et al. 16 vols. Columbia: University of South Carolina Press, 1968–2002.

The Papers of James Madison. Congressional Series, edited by William T. Hutchinson et al. 17 vols. Chicago: University of Chicago Press, 1962–91.

The Papers of James Madison. Secretary of State Series, edited by Robert J. Brugger et al. 10 vols. Charlottesville: University of Virginia Press, 1986–.

The Papers of James Madison. Presidential Papers, edited by Robert A. Rutland et al. 7 vols. Charlottesville: University of Virginia Press, 1984–.

The Papers of John Adams. Edited by Robert J. Taylor et al. 18 vols. Cambridge: Belknap Press of Harvard University Press, 2003–.

The Papers of Thomas Jefferson. Original Series, edited by Julian P. Boyd et al. 41 vols. Princeton: Princeton University Press, 1950–2014.

The Papers of Thomas Jefferson. Retirement Series, edited by J. Jefferson Looney. 11 vols. Princeton: Princeton University Press, 2004–.

The Parliamentary History of England, from the Earliest Period to the Year 1803. Edited by William Cobbett. 36 vols. London: T.C. Hansard, 1806–20.

Paulding, Hiram. *Un Rasgo de Bolívar en Campaña.* Translated by "L.M." New York: Imprenta de Don Juan de la Granja, 1835.

The Pennsylvania Magazine, or, American Monthly Museum, Volume I. Philadelphia: R. Aitken, 1775.

The Political Thought of Bolívar: Selected Writings. Edited by Gerald E. Fitzgerald. The Hague: Martinus Nijhoff, 1971.

The Private Correspondence of Daniel Webster. Edited by Fletcher Webster. 2 vols. Boston: Little, Brown, 1857.

The Records of the Federal Convention of 1787. Edited by Max Farrand. 3 vols. New Haven: Yale University Press, 1911.

The Revolutionary Diplomatic Correspondence of the United States. Edited by Francis Wharton. 6 vols. Washington, DC: U.S. Government Printing Office, 1889.

Secret Proceedings and Debates of the Convention Assembled at Philadelphia, in the Year 1787. Edited by Luther Martin. Louisville, KY: Alston Mygatt, 1844.

Smith, Adam. *An Inquiry into the Nature and Causes of the Wealth of Nations.* Edinburgh: Thomas Nelson, [1776] 1834.

Sparks, Jared. *The Life of Gouverneur Morris, with Selections from His Correspondence and Miscellaneous Papers; Detailing Events in the American Revolution, the French Revolution, and in the Political History of the United States.* 3 vols. Boston: Gray & Bowen, 1832.

The Speech of Mr. Hayne, Delivered in the Senate of the United States, on the Mission to Panama, March 1826. Washington, DC: Gales & Seaton, 1826.

Speech of Mr. Webster, of Mass. in the House of Representatives, on the Panama Mission, Delivered on the 14ᵗʰ April, 1826. Washington, DC: Davis & Force, 1826.

Speeches of Henry, Lord Brougham, upon Questions Relating to Public Rights, Duties, and Interests; with Historical Introductions. 2 vols. Philadelphia: Lea and Blanchard, 1841.

The Speeches of Mr Barrett and of Mr Burge, at a General Meeting of Planters, Merchants, and Others Interested in the West-India Colonies; Assembled at the Thatched-House Tavern, on the 18th May, 1833. London: A.J. Valpy, 1833.

State Papers and Publick Documents of the United States from the Accession of George Washington to the Presidency, Exhibiting a Complete View of Our Foreign Relations since that Time. 2nd ed. 10 vols. Boston: T.B. Wait, 1817.

State Papers and Publick Documents of the United States from the Accession of George Washington to the Presidency, Exhibiting a Complete View of Our Foreign Relations since That Time. 3rd ed. 12 vols. Boston: T.B. Wait & Sons, 1819.

Supplement to the Records of the Federal Convention of 1787. Edited by James H. Huston. New Haven: Yale University Press, 1987.

Tocqueville, Alexis de. *Democracy in America.* Translated by Henry Reeve. 4th ed. 2 vols. New York: Henry G. Langley, 1845.

A Vindication of Mr. Randolph's Resignation. Philadelphia: Samuel H. Smith, 1795.

Webster, Daniel, *A Discourse, Delivered at Plymouth, December 22, 1820, in Commemoration of the First Settlement of New-England.* Boston: Wells and Lilly, 1821.

Whateley, Thomas. *The Regulations Lately Made Concerning the Colonies and the Taxes Imposed upon Them, Considered.* London: J. Wilkie, 1765.

Works of Fisher Ames, Compiled by a Number of His Friends, to Which Are Prefixed Notices of His Life and Character. Boston: T.B. Wait & Co., 1809.

The Works of Francis Bacon, Baron of Verulam, Viscount St. Albans, and Lord High Chancellor of England. 10 vols. London: W. Baynes and Son, 1824.

The Works of John Adams, with a Life of the Author by C.F. Adams. Edited by Charles Francis Adams. 10 vols. Boston: Little, Brown and Company, 1850–56.

The Writings of Albert Gallatin. Edited by Henry Adams. 3 vols. Philadelphia: J.B. Lippincott & Co., 1879.

The Writings of George Washington from the Original Manuscript Sources, 1745–1799. Edited by John C. Fitzpatrick. Westport, CT: Greenwood Press, 1970.

The Writings of James Madison, Comprising his Public Papers and His Private Correspondence, Including Numerous Letters and Documents Now for the First Time Printed. Edited by Gaillard Hunt. 9 vols. New York: Putnam, 1901–10.

The Writings of James Monroe. Edited by Stanislaus Murray Hamilton. 7 vols. New York: G.P. Putnam's Sons, 1898–1903.

Writings of John Quincy Adams. Edited by Washington Chauncey Ford. 7 vols. New York: Macmillan, 1913–17.

The Writings of Thomas Paine: Volume I, 1774–1779. Edited by Moncure Daniel Conway. New York: AMS Press, 1967.

Newspapers and Journals

The Albion or British, Colonial, and Foreign Weekly Gazette
Annals of Congress
Columbian Centinel
Congressional Record
Gales's & Seaton's Register of Debates in Congress
The Gentleman's Magazine and Historical Chronicle
Hampshire Chronicle

Hansard
Independent Gazetteer
The London Chronicle.
Niles's Weekly Register
The North American Review
The North Briton
The United Service Journal and Naval and Military Magazine
Vermont Gazette
The West Indian Reporter

Laws and Legal Cases

"An Act for the better securing the Dependency of His Majesty's Dominions in
America upon the Crown and Parliament of Great Britain," 6 Geo. 3 c. 12.
"An act for granting certain duties in the British colonies and plantations in America; for allowing a drawback of the duties of customs upon the exportation,
from this kingdom, of coffee and cocoa nuts of the produce of the said colonies
or plantations; for discontinuing the drawbacks payable on china earthen ware
exported to America; and for more effectually preventing the clandestine running of goods in the colonies and plantations," 7 Geo. 3 c. 46.
The Cherokee Nation v. The State of Georgia, 30 U.S. 1 (1831).
James McCulloch v. The State of Maryland, John James, 17 U.S. 316 (1819).
Public Papers of the Presidents of the United States: Lyndon B. Johnson. Volume 1, 1963–
64: November 22, 1963 to June 30, 1964. Washington, DC: United States Government Printing Office, 1965.
William Marbury v. James Madison, Secretary of State of the United States, 5 U.S. 137
(1803).

Secondary Sources

Adams, Henry. The History of the United States of America during the Administrations of
Thomas Jefferson and James Madison. 9 vols. Cambridge: Cambridge University
Press, [1889–91] 2011.
Adelman, Jeremy. Sovereignty and Revolution in the Iberian Atlantic. Princeton:
Princeton University Press, 2009.
Ammon, Harry. James Monroe: The Quest for National Identity. Charlottesville: Uni
versity Press of Virginia, 1971.
Archer, Richard. As If an Enemy's Country: The British Occupation of Boston and the
Origins of Revolution. Oxford: Oxford University Press, 2010.
Bancroft, George. History of the Formation of the Constitution of the United States. 2
vols. New York: D. Appleton, 1882.
Barton, H. A. "Sweden and the War of American Independence." William and Mary
Quarterly 23, no. 3 (1966): 408–30.
Bemis, Samuel Flagg. The Diplomacy of the American Revolution. Bloomington: Indi-
ana University Press, [1935] 1957.
Bemis, Samuel Flagg. John Quincy Adams and the Union. New York: Knopf,
1956.

Berton, Pierre. *The Invasion of Canada: 1812–1813.* Toronto: Anchor Canada, [1980] 2011.

Black, Jeremy. *The War of 1812 in the Age of Napoleon.* Norman: University of Oklahoma Press, 2009.

Borneman, Walter R. *1812: The War That Forged a Nation.* New York: Harper Collins, 2004.

Brebner, John Barlet. *The Neutral Yankees of Nova Scotia: A Marginal Colony during the Revolutionary Years.* New York: Columbia University Press, 1937.

Brecher, Frank W. *Securing American Independence: John Jay and the French Alliance.* Westport, CT: Praeger, 2003.

Brown, Roger H. *The Republic in Peril: 1812.* New York: W. W. Norton, 1964.

Brunhouse, Robert L. *The Counter-Revolution in Pennsylvania, 1776–1790.* Harrisburg: Pennsylvania Historical Commission, 1942.

Burr, Samuel Jones. *The Life and Times of William Henry Harrison.* 8th ed. New York: L.W. Ransom, 1840.

Burrows, Simon. *Blackmail, Scandal, and Revolution: London's French Libellistes, 1758–92.* Manchester: Manchester University Press, 2006.

Cable, James. *The Political Influence of Naval Force in History.* Basingstoke: Macmillan, 1998.

Chadwick, French Ensor. *The Relations of the United States and Spain. Diplomacy.* New York: Charles Scribner, 1909.

Chaffin, Robert J. "The Townshend Acts of 1767." *William and Mary Quarterly* 27, no. 1 (1970).

Clayton, Andrew R. L. "The Debate over the Panama Congress and the Origins of the Second American Party System." *Historian* 47, no. 2 (1985): 219–38.

Coggeshall, George. *History of the American Privateers and Letters-of-Marque, during Our War with England.* New York: N.p., 1861.

Cogliano, Francis D. *Emperor of Liberty: Thomas Jefferson's Foreign Policy.* New Haven: Yale University Press, 2014.

Combs, Jerald A. *The Jay Treaty: Political Battleground of the Founding Fathers.* Berkeley: University of California Press, 1970.

Corwin, Edward S. *French Policy and the American Alliance of 1778.* Hamden, CT: Archon Books, [1916] 1962.

Cresson, W. P. "Chateaubriand and the Monroe Doctrine." *North American Review* 217, no. 809 (1923): 475–87.

Critcher Lyons, Reneé. *Foreign-Born American Patriots: Sixteen Volunteer Leaders in the Revolutionary War.* Jefferson, NC: McFarland and Company, 2014.

Cumings, Bruce. *Dominion from Sea to Sea: Pacific Ascendancy and American Power.* New Haven: Yale University Press, 2009.

Cunningham, Noble E., Jr. "Who Were the Quids?" *Mississippi Valley Historical Review* 50, no. 2 (1963): 252–63.

Dangerfield, George. *Chancellor Robert R. Livingston of New York, 1746–1813.* New York: Harcourt, Brace, 1960.

Davis, David Brion, and Steven Mintz, eds. *The Boisterous Sea of Liberty: A Documentary History of America from Discovery through the Civil War.* Oxford: Oxford University Press, 1998.

DeConde, Alexander. *A History of American Foreign Policy.* 3rd ed. 2 vols. New York: Charles Scribner, 1978.

Dull, Jonathan R. *The French Navy and the Seven Years' War*. Lincoln: University of Nebraska Press, 2005.

Dungan, Nicholas. *Gallatin: America's Swiss Founding Father*. New York: New York University Press, 2010.

Dwyer, Philip G. *Talleyrand*. London: Longman, 2002.

Dzurec, David. "Of Salt Mountains, Prairie Dogs, and Horned Frogs: The Louisiana Purchase and the Evolution of Federalist Satire, 1803–1823." *Journal of the Early Republic* 25, no. 1 (2015): 79–108.

Elkins, Stanley, and Eric McKitrick. *The Age of Federalism: The Early American Republic, 1788–1800*. Oxford: Oxford University Press, 1993.

Elliott, Charles B. *The United States and the Northeast Fisheries: A History of the Fishery Question*. Minneapolis: University of Minnesota Press, 1887.

Ellis, George Edward, ed. *Sketches of Bunker Hill, Battle and Monument: With Illustrative Documents*. 3rd ed. Charlestown, MA: N.p., 1843.

Ellis, Joseph J. *Founding Brothers: The Revolutionary Generation*. New York: Vintage, 2003.

Ellis, Joseph J. *Revolutionary Summer: The Birth of American Independence*. New York: Alfred A. Knopf, 2013.

Ennis, Daniel J. *Enter the Press-Gang: Naval Impressment in Eighteenth-Century British Literature*. Newark: University of Delaware Press, 2002.

Fenstermaker, J. van, and John E. Filer. "The U.S. Embargo Act of 1807: Its Impact on New England Money, Banking, and Economic Activity." *Economic Inquiry* 28, no. 1 (1990): 163–84.

Gilbert, Felix. *To the Farewell Address: Ideas of Early American Foreign Policy*. Princeton: Princeton University Press, [1961] 1970.

Gould, Eliga H. *Among the Powers of the Earth: The American Revolution and the Making of a New World Empire*. Cambridge: Harvard University Press, 2012.

Graebner, Norman A., Richard Dean Burns, and Joseph M. Siracusa. *Foreign Affairs and the Founding Fathers: From Confederation to Constitution, 1776–1787*. New York: Praeger, 2011.

Greene, Jack P. "Bridge to Revolution: The Wilkes Fund Controversy in South Carolina, 1769–1775." *Journal of Southern History* 29, no. 1 (1963).

Guettel, Jens-Uwe. *German Expansionism, Imperial Liberalism, and the United States, 1776–1945*. Cambridge: Cambridge University Press, 2012.

Hall, Mark David. *Roger Sherman and the Creation of the American Republic*. Oxford: Oxford University Press, 2013.

Harper, John Lamberton. *American Machiavelli: Alexander Hamilton and the Origins of U.S. Foreign Policy*. Cambridge: Cambridge University Press, 2007.

Heath, William. *William Wells and the Struggle for the Old Northwest*. Norman: University of Oklahoma Press, 2015.

Heinl, Robert Debs, Nancy Gordon Heinl, and Michael Heinl. *Written in Blood: The Story of the Haitian People*. 2nd ed. Lanham, MD: University Press of America, 1996.

Hickey, Donald R. "The Quasi-War: America's First Limited War, 1798–1801." *Northern Mariner* 18, nos. 3–4 (2008): 67–77.

Holmes, Richard. *Wellington: The Iron Duke*. London: Harper Collins, 2003.

Hulsebosch, Daniel J. *Constituting Empire: New York and the Transformation of Constitutionalism in the Atlantic World, 1664–1830*. Chapel Hill: University of North Carolina Press, 2005.

Howe, Daniel Walker. *What Hath God Wrought: The Transformation of America, 1815-1848*. Oxford: Oxford University Press, 2007.

Hunt, Alfred N. *Haiti's Influence on Antebellum America: Slumbering Volcano in the Caribbean*. Baton Rouge: Louisiana State University Press, 1988.

Jacobs, James R. *The Beginnings of the U.S. Army, 1783–1812*. Princeton: Princeton University Press, 1947.

James, C. L. R. *The Black Jacobins: Toussaint L'Ouverture and the San Domingo Revolution*. 2nd ed. New York: Vintage Books, 1963.

Jortner, Adam. *The Gods of Prophetstown: The Battle of Tippecanoe and the Holy War for the American Frontier*. Oxford: Oxford University Press, 2012.

Kaplan, Lawrence S. *Entangling Alliances with None: American Foreign Policy in the Age of Jefferson*. Kent, OH: Kent State University Press, 1987.

Kelsay, Isabel Thompson, *Joseph Brant, 1743–1807: Man of Two Worlds*. Syracuse, NY: Syracuse University Press, 1984.

Kingston, Christopher. "Marine Insurance in Philadelphia during the Quasi-War with France, 1795–1801." *Journal of Economic History* 71, no. 1 (2011): 162–84.

Knopf, Richard C., ed. *Anthony Wayne: A Name in Arms*. Pittsburgh: University of Pittsburgh Press, 1960.

Kochin, Michael S. "Empire and Communications: Washington's Farewell Address." *American Political Thought* 8 (Summer 2019):347-364.

Latimer, Jon. *1812: War with America*. Cambridge: Harvard University Press, 2007.

Lewis, James E., Jr. *The American Union and the Problem of Neighborhood: The United States and the Collapse of the Spanish Empire, 1783–1829*. Durham: University of North Carolina Press, 1998.

Linklater, Andro. *An Artist in Treason: The Extraordinary Double Life of General James Wilkinson*. New York: Walker, 2009.

Liss, Peggy K. *Atlantic Empires: The Network of Trade and Revolution*. Baltimore: Johns Hopkins University Press, 1983.

Lockhart, Paul. *The Drillmaster of Valley Forge: The Baron de Steuben and the Making of the American Army*. New York: Smithsonian Books, 2008.

Lynch, John. *Simón Bolívar: A Life*. New Haven: Yale University Press, 2006.

Lyon, E. Wilson. *Louisiana in French Diplomacy, 1759–1804*. Norman: University of Oklahoma Press, 1934.

Maier, Pauline. *Ratification: The People Debate the Constitution, 1787–1788*. New York: Simon and Schuster, 2010.

Mann, Frank Paul. "The British Occupation of Southern New York during the American Revolution and the Failure to Restore Civilian Government." PhD diss., Syracuse University, 2013.

Mann, Robert. *Wartime Dissent in America: A History and Anthology*. Basingstoke: Palgrave Macmillan, 2010.

McCullough, David. *John Adams*. New York: Simon and Schuster, 2001.

McDonald, Forrest, ed. *Empire and Nation*. Indianapolis: Liberty Fund, 1962.

McMichael, Andrew. *Atlantic Loyalties: Americans in Spanish West Florida, 1785–1810*. Athens: University of Georgia Press, 2008.

Melton, Bucker F., Jr. *Aaron Burr: Conspiracy to Treason*. New York: John Wiley and Sons, 2002.

Mintz, Max M. *Seeds of Empire: The American Revolutionary Conquest of the Iroquois.* New York: New York University Press, 1999.

Morgan, Edmund S., ed. *Prologue to Revolution: Sources and Documents on the Stamp Act Crisis, 1764–1766.* Chapel Hill: University of North Carolina Press, 1959.

Morgan, Edmund S., and Helen M. Morgan. *The Stamp Act Crisis: Prologue to Revolution.* Chapel Hill: University of North Carolina Press, [1953] 1995.

Morris, Richard B. *The Peacemakers: The Great Powers and American Independence.* New York: Harper and Row, 1965.

Newman, Paul Douglas. *Fries's Rebellion: The Enduring Struggle for the American Revolution.* Philadelphia: University of Pennsylvania Press, 2005.

Nordholt, Jan William Schulte. *The Dutch Republic and American Independence.* Translated by Herbert H. Rowen. Chapel Hill: University of North Carolina Press, 1982.

O'Shaughnessy, Andrew Jackson. *An Empire Divided: The American Revolution and the British Caribbean.* Philadelphia: University of Pennsylvania Press, 2000.

O'Shaughnessy, Andrew Jackson. *The Men Who Lost America: British Command during the Revolutionary War and the Preservation of Empire.* London: Oneworld, 2014.

Owens, Robert M. *Mr. Jefferson's Hammer: William Henry Harrison and the Origins of American Indian Policy.* Norman: University of Oklahoma Press, 2007.

Parkman, Francis. *The Conspiracy of Pontiac: And the Indian War after the Conquest of Canada.* Boston: Little, Brown [1851] 1870.

Peckham, Howard H. *Pontiac and the Indian Uprising.* Detroit: Wayne State University Press, [1947] 1994.

Perkins, Bradford. *The Creation of a Republican Empire, 1776–1865.* Vol. 1 of *The Cambridge History of American Foreign Relations.* Cambridge: Cambridge University Press, 1995.

Perkins, Bradford. *Castlereagh and Adams: England and the United States, 1812–1823.* Berkeley: University of California Press, 1964.

Perkins, Bradford. *Prologue to War: England and the United States, 1805–1812.* Berkeley: University of California Press, 1970.

Perkins, Dexter. *The Monroe Doctrine, 1823–26.* Cambridge: Harvard University Press, 1927.

Perkins, Edwin J. "Massachusetts and Shays' Rebellion." In Perkins's *American Public Finance and Financial Services,* 173–86. Columbus: Ohio State University Press, 1994.

Rainsford, Marcus. *An Historical Account of the Black Empire of Hayti.* Edited by Paul Youngquist and Gregory Pierrot. Durham, NC: Duke University Press, [1805] 2013.

Rathbun, Lyon. "The Debate over Annexing Texas and the Emergence of Manifest Destiny." *Rhetoric and Public Affairs* 4, no. 3 (2001): 459–93.

Reinhold, Francis L. "New Research on the First Pan-American Congress Held at Panama in 1826." *Hispanic American Historical Review* 18, no. 3 (1938): 342–63.

Remini, Robert V. *Andrew Jackson: A Biography.* New York: Palgrave Macmillan, 2008.

Remini, Robert V. *Henry Clay: Statesman for the Union.* New York: W. W. Norton, 1991.

Richter, Daniel K. *Before the Revolution: America's Ancient Pasts.* Cambridge: Belknap Press of Harvard University Press, 2011.

Robertson, William Spence. *France and Latin-American Independence.* New York: Octagon Books, 1967.

Robertson, William Spence. "South America and the Monroe Doctrine, 1824–1828." *Political Science Quarterly* 30, no. 1 (1915): 82–105.

Robertson, William Spence. "The United States and Spain in 1822." *American Historical Review* 4, no. 4 (1915): 781–800.

Roosevelt, Theodore. *The Founding of the Trans-Alleghany Commonwealths.* Vol. 3 of *The Winning of the West.* Lincoln: University of Nebraska Press, [1894] 1995.

Rudanko, Juhani. *Discourses of Freedom of Speech: From the Enactment of the Bill of Rights to the Sedition Act of 1918.* London: Palgrave Macmillan, 2012.

Santvoord, George van. *Sketches of the Lives and Judicial Services of the Chief-Justices of the Supreme Court of the United States.* New York: Charles Scribner, 1854.

Schama, Simon. *Citizens: A Chronicle of the French Revolution.* New York: Vintage Books, 1989.

Schiff, Stacy. *Benjamin Franklin and the Birth of America: Franklin's French Adventure, 1776–85.* London: Bloomsbury, 2006.

Schoenbachler, Matthew. "Republicanism in the Age of Democratic Revolution: The Democratic-Republican Societies of the 1790s." *Journal of the Early Republic* 18, no. 2 (1998): 237–61.

Sharp, James Roger. *American Politics in the New Republic.* New Haven: Yale University Press, 1993.

Sicker, Martin. *The Geopolitics of Security in the Americas: Hemispheric Denial from Monroe to Clinton.* Westport, CT: Praeger, 2002.

Simms, Brendan. *Three Victories and a Defeat: The Rise and Fall of the First British Empire, 1714–1783.* London: Allen Lane, 2007.

Slaughter, Thomas P. *The Whiskey Rebellion: Frontier Epilogue to the American Revolution.* Oxford: Oxford University Press, 1986.

Spivak, Burton. *Jefferson's English Crisis: Commerce, Embargo, and the Republican Revolution.* Charlottesville: University Press of Virginia, 1979.

Spoltore, Stefano. "The Panama Congress: A Failed Attempt at Latin American Union." *Federalist* 45, no. 1 (2003): 52–58.

Stahr, Walter. *John Jay: Founding Father.* London: Bloomsbury, 2005.

Stathis, Stephen W., ed. *Landmark Debates in Congress: From the Declaration of Independence to the War in Iraq.* Washington, DC: CQ Press, 2009.

Stewart, David O. *The Summer of 1787: The Men Who Invented the Constitution.* New York: Simon and Schuster, 2007.

Stinchcombe, William C. *The American Revolution and the French Alliance.* Syracuse, NY: Syracuse University Press, 1969.

Taylor, Alan. *American Revolutions: A Continental History, 1750–1804.* New York: W. W. Norton, 2016.

Taylor, Alan. *The Divided Ground: Indians, Settlers, and the Northern Borderland of the American Revolution.* New York: Random House, 2006.

Temperley, Harold. *The Foreign Policy of Canning, 1822–1827: England, the Neo-Holy Alliance, and the New World.* London: G. Bell and Sons, 1925.

Temperley, Harold. "French Designs on Spanish America in 1820–5." *English Historical Review* 40, no. 157 (1925): 34–53.

Temperley, Harold. "The Later American Policy of George Canning." *American Historical Review* 11, no. 4 (1906): 779–97.

Thomas, Peter David Garner. *Tea Party to Independence: The Third Phase of the American Revolution, 1773–1776*. Oxford: Oxford University Press, 1991.

Tombs, Robert, and Isabelle Tombs. *That Sweet Enemy: The British and the French from the Sun King to the Present*. London: Pimlico, 2007.

Wakelyn, Jon L., ed. *Birth of the Bill of Rights: Encyclopaedia of the Anti-Federalists*. 2 vols. Westport, CT: Greenwood Press, 2004.

Walker, William A., Jr. "Martial Sons: Tennessee Enthusiasm for the War of 1812." *Tennessee Historical Quarterly* 20, no. 1 (1961): 21–37.

West, Shearer. "Wilkes's Squint: Synecdochic Physiognomy and Political Identity in Eighteenth-Century Print Culture." *Eighteenth Century Studies* 33, no. 1 (1999).

Whipple, A. B. C. *To the Shores of Tripoli: The Birth of the U.S. Navy and Marines*. New York: William Morrow, 1991.

Whitaker, Arthur Preston. *The United States and the Independence of Latin America: 1800–1830*. Baltimore: Johns Hopkins University Press, 1941.

Williams, Glenn F. *Year of the Hangman: George Washington's Campaign against the Iroquois*. Yardley, PA: Garsington, 2005.

Wolf, Edwin, "The Authorship of the 1774 Address to the King Restudied." *William and Mary Quarterly* 22, no. 2 (1965).

Wright, J. Leitch, Jr. *William Augustus Bowles: Director General of the Creek Nation*. Athens: University of Georgia Press, 1967.

Zacks, Richard. *The Pirate Coast: Thomas Jefferson, the First Marines, and the Secret Expedition of 1805*. New York: Hyperion, 2005.

Online Sources

The American Founding Era. http://rotunda.upress.virginia.edu/founders/FGEA.html

The American Presidency Project. http://www.presidency.ucsb.edu/index.php

"The Definitive Treaty of Peace, Paris, 3 September 1783." https://www.ourdocuments.gov/doc.php?doc=6&page=transcript

Founders Online. http://founders.archives.gov.

"George Washington's Farewell Address." https://www.ourdocuments.gov/doc.php?flash=true&doc=15&page=transcript

Jay, John. "An Address to the People of the State of New-York On the Subject of the Constitution, Agreed upon at Philadelphia, The 17th of September, 1787." https://oll.libertyfund.org/pages/1787-jay-address-to-the-people-of-n-y-pamphlet

Index

Adams, Henry, 133

Adams, John: and resistance to Stamp Act, 12; defends British soldiers after Boston massacre, 16; in Congress (1774, 1775–78), 26; on Dutch contribution to American Revolutionary War, 42; negotiator of Treaty of Paris (1783), 46–51; Minister to Britain (1785–88), 51, 60, 61–62; Vice President (1789–97), 117; President (1797–1801), 111, 117–18, 125, 127–28; and XYZ Affair, 122–23; on navigation acts as cradle of naval power, 63; and trade policy, 61–62; quoted, 5, 17, 27, 41. *See also* Quasi-War with France

Adams, John Quincy: life, 191–93, 247; portrait, 192; on Edmund Randolph affair, 106; Minister to the Netherlands (1794–97), 191; Minister to Prussia (1797–1801), 191; Senator from Massachusetts (1803–8), 156; supports Jefferson's Embargo, 156; and impressment, 162; Minister to Russia (1809–14), 191–92; on New England Federalists and secession, 176–77; plenipotentiary at Ghent (1814), 174–77, 193; Secretary of State (1817–1825), 189; negotiates Adams-Onís Treaty (1819), 195–99; opposes intervention in Greece, 202; opposes intervention in Spanish America, 211; and Monroe Doctrine, 218–19,

222–23; and election of 1824, 230–32; President (1825–29), 1826 annual message, 243–45; and Congress of Panama, 233–34, 242, 244–45; and election of 1828, 245, 247; on British relations with Indians, 193; on intervention, 208; on Russian expansionism in North America, 217–18; on Holy Alliance, 218; on annexation of Cuba, 213; on slavery and expansion, 187, 199; quoted, 200

Adams-Onís Treaty (1819, ratified 1821), 195–99, 248; map, 198

Addington, Henry (Prime Minister of the United Kingdom, 1801–4), 131, 132; and French control of New Orleans, 138

Adelman, Jeremy, 268 n. 4

Adet, Pierre (French Minister to US, 1795–96), 116–17; on Jefferson, 137

Administration of Justice Act (1774), 17. *See also* Sixth Amendment (1791)

agriculture, 19, 61; protection, 210. *See also* Land Ordinance (1785)

Alexander I (Emperor of Russia, 1801–25), 191–92, 244: offers to mediate between US and Britain (1812), 174; arbitrates regarding slave compensation issue after War of 1812, 189; and Holy Alliance, 201; decree of 1821 closing Pacific coast above 45° N to foreign traders, 217

289

Clinton, Henry (British Commander-in-Chief in America, 1778–82), 32, 44
Clinton, James, 33
Coast Guard, United States, 259 n. 13
Cobbett, William, 125–26
Cochrane, Alexander, 173, 173n
Collingwood, Cuthbert, 146
Colombia: and Bolívar, 228; US recognition of independence, 212; and Monroe Doctrine, 224–25; and French imperial ambitions, 225; and Congress of Panama, 230, 240–41
Columbia River, 188. *See also* Oregon
Commerce. *See* trade
Common Sense (Thomas Paine), 22–24
Concord, Battle of (April 19, 1775), 20–21
Concord Hymn (Ralph Waldo Emerson), 20
Congress (prior to 1787 Constitution), 43–44: First Continental Congress, 19–20; weaknesses, 56, 57, 58–66; delays ratifying Treaty of Paris (1783), 59. *See also* Declaration of Independence (1776), Articles of Confederation
Congress (under 1787 Constitution), 68; war powers, 124; and Monroe Doctrine, 226. *See also* Senate, House of Representatives
Congress of Panama (1826), 227, 230–42, 244–45; map, 231; counteraction to Holy Alliance, 235–36; support for US participation, 232–36; opposition to US participation, 236–39; American mission to, 240–41; Britain and, 241; Dutch and, 241; reconvened to Tacubaya, Mexico, 241–42
Connecticut: in Stamp Act Congress, (1765), 12; ratifies 1787 Constitution, 72. *See also* Hartford Convention
Constitution (1787): drafting, 66–69; ratification, 69–74. *See also* Presidency, Congress (under 1787 Constitution); judiciary, Senate, House of Representatives; Sixth Amendment (1791)
Constitutional Convention (1787), 66–69
Constitution, USS (165)
Continental Army, 26, 36; peace establishment of garrisons in West, 59

Continental Congress. *See* Congress (prior to 1787 Constitution).
Continental System, 150, 152–53, 156–57
Convention of Mortefontaine (1800). *See* Mortefontaine, Convention of (1800)
Cornwallis, Charles, 1st Marquess, 40–1
Corps of Discovery. *See* Lewis and Clark Expedition
covert operations, 88. *See also* intelligence, strategy, tactics
Craig, James (Governor-General of Canada, 1807–11), 160, 161
Crawford, William H. (US Minister to France, 1813–14; Secretary of War, 1815–16; Secretary of the Treasury, 1816–25): and election of 1824, 230–32
Creek (Indians), 4: and Spain, 54, 73, 182; and Tecumseh, 161, 161n; in War of 1812, 172–73; and removal, 247–48
Credit. *See* debt
Crèvecœur, J. Hector St. John de: attacks Patrick Henry as disunionist, 70
Croker, John Wilson, 166
Cuba, 182, 213, 232–33, 238

Dalling, John, 37
Davie, William Richardson, 126–27
Dearborn, Henry, 169
Derna, Battle of (1805), 144–45
debt: private debts under Treaty of Paris (1783), 55–56, 57; public debt, 62; and Hamiltonian system, 80–81. *See also* finance
Decatur, Stephen, 143–44, 165–66
Declaration of Independence (1776), 25
Declaratory Act (1766), 13
Delaware (Indians), and Treaty of Greenville (1795), 102–3
Delaware (state): in Stamp Act Congress, (1765), 12; delays ratification of Articles of Confederation, 43; ratifies 1787 Constitution, 72
Democratic-Republican Societies, 89. *See also* Republican Party
Democrats (US political party): coalesce around dispute over US participation in Congress of Panama, 239; and 1828 elections, 247
Desmoulins, Camille, 78

(1781), 38; and Louisiana Purchase, 140; occupied by Andrew Jackson (1814), 187. *See also* Florida; West Florida

Pennsylvania: in Stamp Act Congress, (1765), 12; fails to enforce treaty rights of French subjects, 61; "Congress are our creatures," 65; ratifies 1787 Constitution, 72; and Whiskey Rebellion (1791–94), 81–83; Fries' Rebellion (1799–1800), 125–26

Perceval, Spencer (Prime Minister of the United Kingdom, 1809–12): explains orders in council, 150; assassinated by bankrupt merchant (1812), 164

Perry, Oliver Hazard, 170

Peru: Spanish Viceroyalty, 182; U.S. recognition of independence, 212, 212n; French imperial notions toward, 217; and Congress of Panama, 230, 240–41

Pétion, Alexandre (President of Haiti, 1807–18), 134

Philadelphia: British occupation of (1777–78), 33, 35; Howe abandons (1778), 38

Philadelphia Convention (1787). *See* Constitution (1787), drafting

Philadelphia, USS, 143–44

Pickering, Timothy: life, 177–79; portrait, 178; and Randolph Affair, 177–78; Secretary of State (1795–1800), 116–17, 178; fired by John Adams, 127; defends British blockade of France and French territories, 178–79; as secessionist, 177–80; and Indians, 97, 177

Pike Expedition, 1–4, 109

Pike, Zebulon: life, 1; and Pike Expedition, 1–4; and War of 1812, 169

piracy, 245; of Barbary States, 141–5; under pretext of jihad, 142, 256 n. 10. *See also* privateering; Quasi-War with France; Barbary Wars

Pinckney, Charles Cotesworth: advocate of constitutional reform, 59; and mission to France (1797–98), 119, 121–23; defeated by Madison for Presidency in 1808, 156

Pinckney, Charles: advocate of constitutional reform and 1787 Constitution, 61

Pinckney, Thomas US minister to Britain (1792–96), 107; negotiates Pinckney's Treaty, 107–8 *See also* Pinckney's Treaty

Pinckney's Treaty (1795), 107–8, 184, 195, 248

Pinkney, William (US minister to Britain, 1805–7), 149–50

Pitt, William (the elder), 14

Pitt, William (the younger), 97, 100, 131–32, 221; American Intercourse Bill of (1783), 51, 60; and Jay Treaty, 103; intervention in Saint Domingue, 114–15; praised, 221; quoted, 146

Plattsburgh, Battle of (1814), 171–72

Poinsett, Joel (US Minister to Mexico, 1825–30): chosen to replace Richard C. Anderson as delegate to Congress at Tacubaya, 241

Polignac, Jules de (French ambassador to Britain, 1823–29), 217

Polignac Memorandum, 217

Polverel, Etienne, 114

Pontiac's Rebellion (1763), 9–10, 95.

Poland: Polish volunteers in Revolutionary War, 36, 41

Polk, James: opposed to US participation in Congress of Panama, 236; President (1845–49), 248

Port Dover raid (1814), 166

Portugal, 216, 244. *See also* Brazil

Potwatomi (Indians): and Treaty of Greenville (1795), 102–3

Post Office, United States, 48: and newspaper subsidies, 83–84, 110, 259 n. 15

Presidency: designed by 1787 Constitution with George Washington in mind, 68; President as Commander-in-Chief, 68, 69, 83n

privateering: put under Federal control by 1787 Constitution, 69; privateers commissioned by Genet, 88; French privateers targeting American vessels, 116–17, 125; in War of 1812, 166; commissioned by revolutionary states of Spanish America, 194

President, USS, 160

Prévost, George (Governor General of Canada, 1812–15), 171–72

Procter, Henry, 170–71

Tocqueville, Alexis de, 245–46
Torres, Mauel (envoy of Colombia to the
US, 1822), 212
Toussaint L'Overture, 115, 133–35;
appeals to Napoleon, 134–35
Townshend Acts (1767), 14
Townshend, Charles, 11; and Townshend
Acts, 14.
trade 6, 26–27, 61, 111; protection, 210;
with Britain, 51, 60, 76, 92–93, 188;
with France, 60; with Prussia, 58–59;
with Saint Domingue, 262 n. 7; with
Spain, 64–65; with Spanish America,
210; with British West Indies, 61, 93,
104, 232, 244; inability of Congress
under the articles to protect or promote, 57, 59–62, 65–66; and Barbary
pirates, 141–45; 256 n. 10; British
blockade of France and French possessions in Wars of French Revolution
and Napoleonic Wars, 93–99; 103–5;
150–53, 156–75, 164, 178. *See also* boy-
cotts; Jefferson's Embargo; insurance;
Model Treaty; Jay Treaty; navigation
laws; privateering; smuggling; Tariff
Act (1789); Continental System
Transcontinental Treaty (1819, ratified
1821). *See* Adams-Onís Treaty (1819,
ratified 1821)
Trans-Appalachian West: Congress
makes ordinances for, 58; British posts
in, 63, 94–95; disaffected by Jay's negotiation with Spain (1786), 64–65; and
Whiskey Rebellion, 81–83, 89; French
ambitions in, 136–37; British relations
with Indians after evacuation of posts,
160–62, 180. *See also* Indians, Mississippi (river), navigation by United States;
Northwest Indian Wars; War of 1812
Treasury, Department of (United States),
80
Treaties: ratification under 1787 Constitution, 68. *See also* Senate, House of
Representatives
Treaty of Amity and Commerce with
France (1778), 34. *See also* France
Treaty of Paris (1763), 9
Treaty of Paris (1783), 43–57; borders as
drawn by, 49–50; 51–55; debts issue,

54–55; loyalists betrayed by, 51, 56;
delay in ratification by Congress, 59
Trecothick, Barlow, 13
Trespass Act (1783), 56
Tripoli, 141–5; and Marines' Hymn, 145.
See also Barbary Wars
Tripoli Harbor, Battles of (1804), 143–44
Tunis, 141–5, 256 n. 10
Turgot, Anne Robert Jacques, Baron de
l'Aulne, 30, 76
Turkey. *See* Ottoman Empire

United Kingdom. *See* Britain
United States, USS, 165–66
United States Army, 100, 244–45, 248:
and 1787 Constitution, 69; and Pike
Expedition, 1–4; condition before War
of 1812, 162; in War of 1812, 181. *See
also* Continental Army; Legion of the
United States; Northwest Indian War;
Quasi-War; War of 1812
United States Coast Guard, 259 n. 13
United States Marine Corps: in Barbary
Wars, 143–45
United States Navy, 160, 245, 248: weakness after Revolutionary War, 62–63,
federalized by 1787 Constitution, 69; and
confrontation with France, 118, 124–25;
and Barbary Wars, 143–45; and *Chesapeake* incident, 150–52; in War of 1812,
165–66, 169–72, 181; British demand
exclusion of US Navy from Great Lakes
in Ghent negotiations (1814), 175; limitation on Great Lakes (1817), 187–88
union: as security device, 70–71
Ushant, Battle of (1778), 36

Valmy, Battle of (1792), 85
Van Buren, Martin (President, 1837–
1841): on Panama Congress as spur to
formation of Democratic Party, 239
Van Rensselaer, Stephen, 169
Vans Murray, William, 126–27
Vergennes, Charles Gravier, Comte de
(foreign minister of France, 1774–87),
30, 46, 76; view of United States, 34,
48; on terms of Treaty of Paris (1783),
50–51; and French imperial ambitions
in North America, 132

Printed and bound by CPI Group (UK) Ltd, Croydon, CR0 4YY

09/06/2025

14685647-0005